PLATO'S
THEORY OF KNOWLEDGE

The Library of Liberal Arts

OSKAR PIEST, FOUNDER

PLATO'S
THEORY OF
KNOWLEDGE

(The *Theaetetus* and the *Sophist* of Plato)

Translated, with a running commentary, by
FRANCIS M. CORNFORD

The Library of Liberal Arts
published by
Bobbs-Merrill Educational Publishing
Indianapolis

NOTE ON THE TEXT

The present edition of Francis M. Cornford's *Plato's Theory of Knowledge* is reprinted from the original English edition in the "International Library of Psychology, Philosophy, and Scientific Method" by arrangement with the Humanities Press, New York, and Routledge & Kegan Paul, Ltd., London.

Copyright © 1957 by The Bobbs-Merrill Company, Inc.
Printed in the United States of America
All rights reserved. No part of this book shall be reproduced or transmitted in any form or by any means, electronic or mechanical, including photocopying, recording, or by any information or retrieval system, without written permission from the Publisher:

The Bobbs-Merrill Company, Inc.
4300 West 62nd Street
Indianapolis, Indiana 46268

First Edition
Fifteenth printing—1982
Library of Congress Catalog Card Number: 57-4254
ISBN 0-672-60294-6(pbk.)

PREFACE

WHEN the Editor, some eleven years ago, invited me to contribute to this series, I offered a translation of the *Theaetetus* with a running commentary. I have since added the *Sophist*. Meanwhile the book has been announced under the title, *Plato's Theory of Knowledge*, which may seem to promise more than I have performed. My object was to make accessible to students of philosophy who cannot easily read the Greek text, two masterpieces of Plato's later period, concerned with questions that still hold a living interest. A study of existing translations and editions has encouraged also the hope that scholars already familiar with the dialogues may find a fresh interpretation not unwelcome. A commentary has been added because, in the more difficult places, a bare translation is almost certain, if understood at all, to be misunderstood.

This danger may be illustrated by a quotation from a living philosopher of the first rank :

' It was Plato in his later mood who put forward the suggestion " and I hold that the definition of being is simply power ". This suggestion is the charter of the doctrine of Immanent Law.'[1]

Dr. Whitehead is quoting Jowett's translation. If the reader will refer to the passage (p. 234 below), he will see that the words are rendered : ' I am proposing as a mark to distinguish real things that they are nothing but power.'[2] A mark of real things may not be a ' definition of being '. This mark, moreover, is offered by the Eleatic Stranger to the materialist as an improvement on his own mark of real things, tangibility. The materialist accepts it, ' having for the moment no better suggestion of his own to offer '. The Stranger adds that Theaetetus and he may perhaps change their minds on this matter later on. Plato has certainly not committed himself here to a ' definition of being '. So much could be dis-

---

[1] A. N. Whitehead, *Adventures of Ideas* (1933), p. 165. I am not suggesting that Dr. Whitehead fundamentally misunderstands the master who has deeply influenced his own philosophy, but only pointing out how a profound thinker may be misled by a translation.

[2] This rendering is itself doubtful, the construction of the words, as they stand in the MSS, being obscure and difficult.

covered from an accurate translation ; but the word ' power '
still needs to be explained. It has been rendered by ' potency ',
' force ', ' *Möglichkeit* ', ' *puissance de relation* '. Without some
account of the history of the word *dynamis* in Plato's time and
earlier, the student accustomed to the terms of modern philosophy
may well carry away a false impression.

To meet difficulties such as this, I have interpolated, after each
compact section of the text, a commentary which aims at discovering
what Plato really means and how that part of the argument is
related to the rest. There are objections to dissecting the living
body of a Platonic dialogue. No other writer has approached
Plato's skill in concealing a rigid and intricate structure of reasoning
beneath the flowing lines of a conversation in which the suggestion
of each thought as it arises seems to be followed to an unpre-
meditated conclusion. In these later dialogues, however, the bones
show more clearly through the skin ; and it is likely that Plato
would rather have us penetrate his meaning than stand back with
folded hands to admire his art. An interpolated commentary,
giving the reader the information he needs when and where he
needs it, may be preferred to the usual plan of stowing away such
information in an introduction at the beginning and notes at the
end. It is not clear why we should be forced to read a book in
three places at once. This book, at any rate, is designed to be
read straight through.

The translation follows Burnet's text, except where I have given
reasons for departing from it or proposed corrections of passages
that are probably or certainly corrupt. I have tried to follow
Plato's own practice of keeping to the current language of educated
conversation and refusing to allow any word to harden into a
technical term. The commentary attempts only to interpret
Plato from his own writings and those of his forerunners and
contemporaries, and accordingly avoids, so far as possible, the
misleading jargon of modern philosophy. Terms like ' sub-
jectivism ', ' relativism ', ' sensationalism ', even when defined,
often mask ambiguities of thought that are lost sight of as this
token currency passes from hand to hand.

At the risk of appearing arrogant or ill-informed, I have, for
the most part, ignored interpretations which I cannot accept.
Also I have not loaded the notes with acknowledgments of my
debts to other scholars. Among works which have most helped
me I would mention Campbell's editions ; Apelt's translations
(which contain full bibliographies) ; M. Diès' editions in the *Collection des Universités de France* ; E. Stölzel, *Die Behandlung des
Erkenntnisproblems bei Platon* (Halle, 1908) ; J. Stenzel, *Entwicklung*

PREFACE

der platonischen Dialektik (Breslau, 1917) ; C. Ritter, *Neue Unter-suchungen über Platon* (München, 1910) ; V. Brochard, *Études de philosophie ancienne* (Paris, 1912) ; and the well-known writings of John Burnet and Professor A. E. Taylor.

CAMBRIDGE   F. M. C.

1934

CONTENTS

. . . .

CONTENTS

CONTENTS

xi

CONTENTS

INTRODUCTION

SINCE the commentary aims at furnishing the reader with information as the need arises, it will be enough, by way of introduction,
to indicate the place of the *Theaetetus* and the *Sophist* in the series
of Plato's dialogues, and to define briefly the position from which
the inquiry starts.

Our two dialogues belong to a group consisting of the *Parmenides*,
the *Theaetetus*, the *Sophist*, and the *Statesman*. As M. Diès has
observed,[1] Plato leaves no doubt that the dialogues are meant to
be read in this order. The *Parmenides* describes a meeting imagined
as taking place about 450 B.C. between Socrates, who would then
be about twenty, and the Eleatic philosophers, Parmenides and
Zeno. To suppose that anything remotely resembling the conversation in this dialogue could have occurred at that date would
make nonsense of the whole history of philosophy in the fifth and
fourth centuries ; and I believe, with M. Diès, that the meeting
itself is a literary fiction, not a fact in the biography of Socrates.
No ancient historian of philosophy mistook it for the record of an
actual event, which, had it occurred, would have been a very
important landmark. The *Theaetetus* (183E, p. 101) alludes to this
meeting, and it is once more recalled in the *Sophist* (217C, p. 166)
in terms that can only refer to the *Parmenides*. The *Theaetetus*,
again, ends with an appointment which is kept at the beginning
of the *Sophist* ; and the *Sophist* itself is openly referred to in the
Statesman.

As for the order of composition, no one doubts that the *Sophist*
and the *Statesman*, which contain one continuous conversation,
are later than the *Theaetetus*. In the *Theaetetus* many critics have
noticed that the style changes towards the end in the direction
of Plato's later manner. If that is so, stylometric results based
on the dialogue as a whole will be misleading. The latter part
of the *Theaetetus*, as we have it, may have been finished years
after the beginning, and the *Parmenides* may have been composed
in the interval. On the other hand, we need not suppose any very
long gap between the completion of the *Theaetetus* and the composition of the *Sophist* and the *Statesman*.

---

[1] *Parménide* (1923), p. xii.

I

INTRODUCTION

It is now agreed that this group as a whole is earlier than the *Timaeus*, the *Philebus*, and the *Laws*, and later than the *Meno*, the *Phaedo*, and the *Republic*. The *Republic* is the centre of a group of less technical works, intended, not primarily for students of philosophy, but for the educated public, who would certainly not read the *Parmenides* and would find the *Theaetetus* and the *Sophist* intolerably difficult. These more popular writings would serve the double purpose of attracting students to the Academy and of making known to the Greek world a doctrine which, in common with most scholars, I hold to be characteristically Platonic. Its two pillars are the immortality and divinity of the rational soul, and the real existence of the objects of its knowledge—a world of intelligible ' Forms ' separate from the things our senses perceive.[1] Neither doctrine clearly appears in any dialogue that can be dated, on grounds of style, as distinctly earlier than the *Meno*. Both are put forward in the *Phaedo* in a manner suggesting that Plato arrived at them simultaneously and thought of them as interdependent.

The *Meno* had already announced the theory of *Anamnesis* : that knowledge is acquired, not through the senses or as information conveyed from one mind to another by teaching, but by recollection in this life of realities and truths seen and known by the soul before its incarnation. Socrates bases this doctrine on an account which he believes to be true,[2] learnt from men and women who are wise in religious matters and from inspired poets. The human soul is immortal (divine) and is purified through a round of incarnations, from which, when completely purified, it may finally escape. ' So the soul is immortal and has been many times reborn ; and since it has seen all things, both in this world and in the other, there is nothing it has not learnt. No wonder, then, that it can recover the memory of what it has formerly known concerning virtue or any other matter. All Nature is akin and the soul has learnt all things ; so there is nothing to prevent one who has recollected—learnt, as we call it—one single thing from discovering all the rest for himself, if he is resolute and unwearying in the search ; for seeking or learning is nothing but recollection '.

---

[1] I agree with Mr. J. D. Mabbott (' Aristotle and the χωρισμός of Plato ', *Classical Quarterly*, xx (1926), 72) that the ' separate ' existence of the Forms, attacked by Aristotle, is not to be explained away.

[2] *Meno* 81A, λόγος ἀληθής, not μῦθος, though the form which contains the true account may be mythical. So at *Gorgias* 523A, he calls the myth of the judgment of the dead a λόγος ἀληθής, though Callicles may think it a μῦθος. I take the Socrates of the *Meno* and the *Phaedo* as stating Plato's beliefs, not those of the historic Socrates.

Socrates goes on to prove this doctrine by experiment. By questioning a slave who has never been taught geometry, he elicits from him, after several wrong attempts, the solution of a not very easy problem of construction. He claims that he has not ' taught ' the slave the true belief he now has, any more than the false beliefs he produced at first. At the outset the slave had not knowledge ; but these beliefs were in him, including the true belief which he did not know. They have been ' stirred up in him, as it were in a dream ', and if he were questioned again and again in various ways, he would end by having knowledge in place of true belief— knowledge which he would have recovered out of his own soul. This knowledge must have been acquired before birth. ' If, then, the truth of things is always in our soul, the soul must be immortal ; hence you may confidently set about seeking for and recovering the memory of what you do not know, that is to say, do not re- member.' Socrates adds that, in some respects, he could not defend the whole account ; but he is convinced of the practical conclusion, that we shall be the better for believing that we can discover truth we do not know. Owing to Plato's dramatic method, we cannot fix the extent of Socrates' reservation. It might mean that the historic Socrates did not hold this theory, or, more probably, that the details of reincarnation, purgatory, and so forth, as described by Pindar and others, are ' mythical ' : as such Plato always represents them elsewhere. But the reservation does not extend to the hypothetical conclusion which Socrates and Meno have both accepted : *If* the truth of things is always in the soul, *then* the soul is immortal.

Some modern critics, wishing perhaps to transform Plato's theory into something that we can accept, reduce the doctrine of *Anamnesis* to a form in which it ceases to have any connection with the pre-existence of the soul. But Plato unquestionably believed in immortality ; and in the *Phaedo*, where Recollection is reaffirmed, it is the one proof of pre-existence which is accepted as satisfactory by all parties to the conversation.

The doctrine of Recollection marks a complete break with current beliefs both about the nature of the soul and about the sources of knowledge. The soul was popularly regarded as a mere shadow or *eidolon*, an unsubstantial wraith, that might well be dissipated when detached from the body. And if common sense could be said to have any view of the common characters called Forms (εἴδη) in the Socratic dialogues, it would be the empiricist view that they are present in sensible things, and that our knowledge of them is conveyed through the senses perhaps by images, like the Atomists *eidola*, thrown off by material bodies. Among the

3

philosophic theories which Socrates, in the *Phaedo*, says he had found unsatisfying is the doctrine ' that it is the brain that gives us perceptions of hearing, sight, and smell, and out of these arise memory and belief, and from these again, when they have settled down into quiescence, comes knowledge '. Plato's break with all theories deriving knowledge by abstraction from sensible objects carried with it an equally firm repudiation of popular notions of the soul as either a flimsy double of the body or a resultant, supervening on the mixture of bodily elements. In other words, the ' separation ' of the Platonic Forms from any dependence on material things went with the separation of the soul which knows them from any dependence on the physical organism. The *Phaedo* is designed to plead for both conclusions concurrently. It is not claimed that either doctrine is proved ; but it is claimed that if the Forms exist and can be known, then the soul is immortal. Plato himself believed both ; and his Socrates, unlike the Socrates of the earlier dialogues, now uses every resource of eloquence to convince his hearers of what he believes but does not know.

In his opening discourse it is assumed from the outset that the soul can exist without the body ; for ' to be dead ' is defined as meaning ' that the body has come to be separate by itself apart from (χωρὶς) the soul, and the soul separate by itself apart from the body '. [1] So much might be said of the wraith or shadow-soul of popular belief ; but the properties which Socrates goes on to ascribe to the separable soul are very different. The contrast is not between mind and matter, or even between soul and body as commonly understood. The psyche here is what was later called by Plato and Aristotle the Reason (νοῦς), or the spirit, in opposition to the flesh. [2] To the flesh belong the senses, and the bodily appetites and pleasures. The spirit's proper function is thought or reflection, which lays hold upon unseen reality and is best carried on when the spirit withdraws from the flesh to think by itself, untroubled by the senses. The pursuit of wisdom is a ' loosing and separation (χωρισμός) of the soul from the body '—a rehearsal of that separation called death (67D).

The effect of this introductory discourse is to establish in the reader's mind, before the argument begins, the idea of a complete detachment of the thinking self from the body and its senses and passions. This idea, though unfamiliar, would be easier for Plato's public to grasp than that detachment of Forms from sensible things

---

[1] 64C. In the *Gorgias* myth (524B), death is already described as the ' severance (διάλυσις) of two things—body and soul—from one another '.

[2] Cf. F. M. Cornford, ' The Division of the Soul ', *Hibbert Journal* (Jan. 1930), p. 206.

which it is his other purpose to announce clearly for the first time. If the reader will forget all that he has learnt about the Forms from later writings and put himself in the situation of Plato's readers who knew only the earlier dialogues, he will find that he is being led, step by step, to recognise the separate existence of the Forms.

The Forms are first mentioned as the objects of the soul's reflection, when withdrawn from the senses. All that is pointed out here (65D) is that those entities which were the familiar topics of Socrates' conversation are perceived by thought, not by the senses. When Socrates and his friends considered, What is Justice?, they were trying to define the Just ' by itself ' ($αὐτό$), and to discover ' what it is ' ($δ \, ἔστι$) or its ' being ' ($οὐσία$). Any reader of the earlier dialogues might agree that Justice, not being a thing that can be seen or touched, will be known by pure thought when the soul is ' set free from eyes and ears and the body as a whole '.

There follows a long and elaborate defence of *Anamnesis*, addressed to the more difficult task of convincing the reader, on the one hand, that the soul has pre-existed, and on the other, that his own vague notions of how we first become acquainted with a thing like ' Justice itself ' are radically wrong. We not only cannot perceive it ; we cannot extract it from any sense-impressions. This might be argued more easily in the case of the moral Forms, which are obviously not sensible ; but Plato is no less concerned with the mathematical Forms. He undertakes to prove that we cannot derive our knowledge of Equality from the perception of equal things. The same two sticks sometimes appear equal to one person and unequal to another ; but no one ever thinks that ' equals ' are unequal or that Equality is Inequality. The sight of nearly equal things causes us to think of Equality, and we judge that they fall short of that ideal standard. It is argued that we must have obtained knowledge of true Equality before we began to use our senses, that is to say, before our birth ; and this carries with it the pre-existence of the soul. Whether the argument seems sound to the modern reader or not, *Anamnesis* is accepted by all parties and later reaffirmed (92A) ; nor is any doubt ever cast upon it in Plato's other works. The upshot is that the Forms have an existence separate from things as surely as the spirit has an existence separate from the body.

The next argument is to urge that the soul not only has pre-existed, but is by nature indestructible. It is not composed or put together out of parts into which it might be dissolved. It is reasonable, we are told, to identify incomposite things with things that never undergo any sort of change. Now the reader who has grasped the distinction between ideal Equality and the nearly equal things of sense, will agree that Forms must always be what they are and can suffer no kind of change. The many things that bear the same names as the Forms are perpetually changing in all respects ; and these are the things we see and touch, whereas the Forms are unseen. It is thus laid down that there are two orders of things : the unseen, exempt from all change, and the seen, which change perpetually. Finally it is argued as probable that the soul, which is unseen, most resembles the divine, immortal, intelligible, simple, and indissoluble ; while the body most resembles the human, mortal, unintelligible, complex, and dissoluble. The separation of the two worlds or orders of being is here very sharply marked. No relation between them is described ; no transition from sense to thought is suggested. Even the fact that sensible experience may be the occasion of Recollection is lost sight of. Socrates recurs to the language of his opening discourse. When the soul uses any of the senses, it is dragged down into the world of change and becomes dizzy and confused. Only when thinking by itself can it escape into that other region of pure, eternal, and unchanging being.

Thus, by a series of steps, the reader acquainted with the earlier dialogues is led to see that the moral terms which Socrates was always discussing belong to a distinct order of realities, and that knowledge of them cannot be extracted from impressions of sense. Throughout, the separation of the Forms is intertwined with and illustrated by the separation of the divine spirit from all dependence on the mortal body. The conclusion is that the two doctrines stand or fall together.[1]

The separate reality of the Forms created a problem which is courageously faced, though not solved, in the later group to which our dialogues belong. How are those separate Forms related to the things we touch and see in this world of becoming ? The *Phaedo* itself (100C–D) had indicated that to speak of a thing as ' partaking of ' a Form is to use a metaphor that leaves it obscure how an eternal and unchanging Form or its character can be ' present in ' or ' shared by ' transient individual things in time and space. In the *Parmenides* Socrates is represented as putting forward the theory of separate Forms to dispose of Zeno's paradoxical antinomies, and as confronted with this very difficulty of participation by Zeno's master, Parmenides. It is significant that the great founder of the Eleatic school should dominate the discussion here, and that a Stranger from Elea should take the lead in the *Sophist*

[1] *Phaedo* 76DE, 92D.

and the *Statesman*. Parmenides had been the first to raise the problem which the theory of Forms was intended to solve. This problem had two aspects. In Parmenides' poem it is presented chiefly as the problem that arises when a world of real being is distinguished from a world of ' seeming ' or appearance, which is somehow false and unreal, or, as Parmenides himself declared, totally false and unreal. This aspect we shall encounter, as the problem of *eidola*, stated, but not solved, in the *Sophist*. Parmenides had also drawn the corresponding distinction between the senses, which profess to reveal appearances, and rational thought apprehending true reality. The *Theaetetus* will formulate and examine the claim of the senses to yield knowledge. The discussion moves in the world of appearance and proves that, if we try to leave out of account the world of true being, we cannot extract knowledge from sensible experience.

The theory of Forms, as stated in the *Phaedo*, was meant to deal with both aspects of the problem bequeathed by Parmenides. The eternal and intelligible Forms were to provide rational thought with objects of knowledge. The transient existence or ' becoming ' of sensible things in the world of appearance was to be grounded in the world of true being by some kind of participation ; they were thus to be endowed with an ambiguous half-reality, not left, as in Parmenides' uncompromising system, totally unsupported. But our series of dialogues opens with a trenchant criticism of Plato's own theory as giving no intelligible account of the derivation of appearances from reality. The discussion starts from Zeno's counter-attack on the critics of Parmenides. Zeno had put forward a series of arguments, reducing (as he thought) to absurdity their defence of the common-sense belief in the existence of a plurality of real things. His first argument is quoted : ' If there are many things, then they must be both like and unlike.' From both horns of the dilemma Zeno deduced what he regarded as impossible consequences. Socrates replies that no impossibilities result, if you recognise ' a Form, Likeness, just by itself ', and another contrary Form, Unlikeness. That things which are simply ' alike ' and nothing else should be ' unlike ' is no doubt impossible ; but there is no difficulty in supposing that individual concrete things should partake of both Forms at once and so come to be both like and unlike. One thing can have many names, partake of many Forms, some of which may be contrary to others. The difficulties disappear ' if you distinguish the Forms apart by themselves ' and realise that individual things partake of them.

Parmenides' criticisms are directed against this ' separation ' (χωρισμός) of the Forms, on which the *Phaedo* had laid so much stress,[1] and the consequent difficulty of conceiving clearly the ' participation ' which is to bridge the gulf. Socrates is confronted with two questions, which he finds it difficult to answer.

The first is the extent of the world of Forms. Several classes of terms are mentioned, and Socrates is asked if he recognises separate Forms for each class. (1) First come the terms which had figured in Zeno's dilemmas : Likeness, Unlikeness ; Unity, Plurality ; Motion, Rest, etc.[2] To these are added (2) the moral Forms, ' Just, Beautiful, Good, etc.'. About these two classes Socrates has no doubts. (3) The next class contains (a) Forms such as ' Man ', ' separate from ourselves and all other men ', and (b) Fire and Water. (These terms correspond to the products of divine workmanship described in the *Sophist* 266B (p. 326) : ' ourselves and all other living creatures and the elements of natural things —fire, water, and their kindred '. Living organisms and the four elements of which all bodies are composed are the two classes of things in the physical world with the best claim to represent Forms —the models after which the divine creator of the *Timaeus* works.) Socrates says he has often felt some uncertainty about these. (Probably they were not contemplated in the early stages of the theory, which started with mathematical and moral Forms. But they are contemplated in the *Timaeus*.[3]) Last come (4) Hair, Clay, Dirt, and other undignified things. (Hair, an organic part of a living creature, was one of Anaxagoras' homœomerous substances ; and here it may stand for all organic compounds of the elementary bodies. ' Clay ', as Socrates remarks at *Theaetetus* 147C (p. 22), is ' earth mixed with moisture '. Clay and Dirt, as casual mixtures of the elements, have the least claim to Forms.) Socrates at first replies that he thinks there are no Forms for these undignified things ; but he has been troubled with doubts ' whether it may not be the same with everything '. Then, fearing to fall into an abyss of absurdity, he has returned to the study of Forms of the first two classes. Parmenides remarks that when he is older he

[1] *Parm.* 129D (Socrates), ἐάν τις διαιρῆται χωρὶς αὐτὰ καθ' αὑτὰ τὰ εἴδη. 130B (Parmenides), αὐτὸς σὺ οὕτω διῄρησαι ὡς λέγεις, χωρὶς μὲν εἴδη αὐτὰ ἄττα, χωρὶς δὲ τὰ τούτων αὖ μετέχοντα ; καί τί σοι δοκεῖ εἶναι αὐτὴ ὁμοιότης χωρὶς ἧς ἡμεῖς ὁμοιότητος ἔχομεν. Here ' the likeness we have ' is distinguished from the Form, Likeness itself, as in the *Phaedo*, ' the tallness in us ' is distinguished from Tallness itself. The separate Form is conceived as somehow communicating its character (ἰδέα, μορφή) to the individual thing. But how ?

[2] Motion and Rest are included at 129E (cf. *Phaedrus* 261D). These terms (and the moral Forms) will reappear among the ' common terms ' of *Theaetetus* 185C ff. (p. 104), where ' unity and number in general ', ' odd ' and ' even ', etc., are added. The mathematical Forms belong to this class.

[3] *Timaeus* 51C (on Forms of the elements) practically quotes *Parm.* 130D.

will be more philosophical and pay less regard to vulgar esteem. Here this question is dropped. No mention has been made of Forms for artificial objects or for sensible qualities like Hot and Cold, although ' Hot ' and ' Cold ' had figured in the ideal theory of the *Phaedo*, and the *Republic* had appeared to recognise a divinely created Form of Bedstead.

What is the extent of the world of Forms ? Plato never answers this question.[1] The difficulty arises from the double origin of the theory. As Aristotle tells us in his account of Platonism,[2] one root was the Socratic inquiry after the definition of ' universals '. Socrates, who was not concerned with any system of Nature, confined himself to the attempt to define moral terms, such as ' Just '. Plato (who was concerned with ontology), accepting the Heracleitean Flux as applied to sensible things, saw that the subject of a Socratic definition could not be any sensible thing, since such things are in perpetual change and cannot be known ; so he said that it must be a separate entity, to which he gave the name ' Form ', and that the group of sensible things bearing the same name partake of that Form. The underlying assumption here is that every common name must have a fixed meaning, which we think of when we hear the name spoken : speaker and hearer thus have the same object before their minds. Only so can they understand one another and any discourse be possible. On this showing, however, all common names have the same right to have a Form for their meaning ; and so we arrive at the statement (*Rep.* 596A) : ' we are accustomed to assume a single form (*or* character, εἶδος) for every set of things to which we apply the same name.' We can say : ' This is hot ', ' This is dirty ', ' This is human ', ' This is just ', and so on. If all such statements are on the same footing, we ought to recognise a common character or Form for every existing common name, and moreover for every entity that might be distinguished by a separate name. The world of Forms ought to be indefinitely more numerous than the vocabulary of any language.

But how does this theory look if we start from the other root of Platonism—the Pythagorean doctrine of Numbers as the real being of all things ? According to Aristotle, Plato conceived the relation of things to Forms in the same way as the Pythagoreans conceived the relation of things to Numbers : when he said that things ' partake of ' Forms he was only making a verbal change in their

---

[1] If *Epistle* VII, 342A ff. be accepted as genuine, Plato recognised, at the end of his life, Forms of mathematical objects, moral terms, every natural and artificial body, the four elements, every species of living creature, every moral quality, all actions and affections (342D).

[2] *Metaph.* A, 6.

9

statement that things ' represent ' (*or* embody) Numbers. The Form now becomes something more than the meaning of a common name —an entity whose metaphysical status Socrates, probably, had never inquired into. Socrates had ' no system of Nature ' ; but Plato endows the Forms with a ' separate ' existence in an intelligible world of true being, where they replace the Pythagorean Numbers as the reality which appearances are somehow to represent. There is no trouble about the mathematical Forms, which are certainly distinct from visible and tangible bodies and constitute a realm of eternal truth. The moral Forms, again, may stand as ideals, never perfectly embodied in human action and character. Forms of both these classes can be maintained as eternal things which the soul can know (as the *Phaedo* asserts) without any recourse to the bodily senses. Further, when we come to physics, we can accommodate the fixed types of natural species and of the four elements. But what is to be said of the legion of other common names—nouns, adjectives, verbs—which also have fixed meanings ? ' Clay ' is a common name ; but can physics or metaphysics recognise an eternal exemplar of clay and of every distinguishable variety of clay ? And what of sensible qualities, like hot and cold ? Is Heat or Cold or Redness the sort of object that can be known, independently of all sense experience, by a disembodied soul ? Is Redness or Hotness an eternally real Form accounting for the ' becoming ' of red or hot things in the physical world ? Do bodies ' partake ' of Redness when no one is seeing them, or of Hotness when no one feels their heat ? Such may have been the questions which embarrassed Plato with the uncertainty confessed by Socrates in the *Parmenides*. The most formidable consequence of recognising a Form for every common name would be that no limit could then be set to the world of Forms. The unlimited cannot be known, and if the Forms are unknowable, their *raison d'être* is gone. But Plato leaves this question without an answer.

Parmenides then turns to his second line of criticism : How are the separate Forms related to the things that ' partake of ' them ?

(1) If we press one natural meaning of ' partake ' or ' share ', are we to suppose that the Form as a whole is in each of the things, or that each thing contains a part of it ? Either supposition is absurd. This dilemma can, indeed, be taken as merely an objection to certain misleading associations of the word ' partake '.[1] Many things can ' share ' in one Form in the sense that they all have the same relation to it. But the question, what that relation can be, remains unanswered.

(2) The suggestion that the Form might be only a ' thought ' in

[1] Cf. G. C. Field in *Mind*, xxxvi, pp. 87 ff.

our minds is decisively rejected. The Form is not a mental existent ; it must be an object of thought, of which any number of minds may, or may not, think.

(3) Finally it is suggested that, while the Form has its separate reality, what is present here is not the Form, but a copy or image of it. One original can have many copies. The relation will then be ' likeness '. But this will lead to an infinite regress. If the original and the copy are alike, they have a common character, but then there will be just as much reason to posit another Form for original and copy to partake of as there was to posit the original Form for all the copies to partake of. The conclusion is that the relation ' partaking ' cannot be reduced to ' likeness ', but we must look for some other account of it. The point might be argued thus : it may be true that the copy is, at least in some degree, like the original ; but that cannot be all that is meant. Likeness subsists between any two copies, but we do not say that one copy ' partakes of ' another.

The upshot of all this criticism is that no intelligible account has yet been given of the relation between Forms and things ; the metaphors will not bear serious scrutiny. Parmenides ends with a picture of the ideal world as withdrawn beyond the reach of human knowledge. A god might know the Forms, but can we know any-thing beyond the things in our world ? On the other hand, Par-menides himself acknowledges that the Forms are a necessity of thought ; without them philosophic discourse, or indeed discourse of any kind, is impossible. This conclusion can only mean that the difficulties cannot be insuperable. Plato's intention may be to show that he is as aware as any of his critics that they exist, and to set his pupils to think about them.

There is one further problem, mooted by Socrates himself in the *Parmenides*, which is dealt with in the *Sophist*. This concerns the relations of Forms, not to things, but to one another. Socrates has just made his point that, if separate Forms are recognised, a concrete thing can very well partake both of Likeness and of Unlikeness. ' But,' he then adds, ' if you do separate the Forms apart by themselves—Likeness and Unlikeness, Plurality and Unity, Motion and Rest, and all such things—it would be extraordinarily interesting to me if anyone could then show that these Forms themselves can be combined and separated . . . if one could exhibit this same problem as everywhere involved in the Forms themselves,' as we have seen it to be in visible things.[1] This challenge is not taken up in the early part of the *Parmenides*. The terms ' com-bined ' and ' separated ' we shall find in the *Sophist* used for the

[1] *Parm.* 129E.

relations reflected in affirmative and negative true statements about Forms. This problem is confined to the ideal world ; it would remain if there were no sensible things at all. In such statements as ' Likeness exists ', ' Likeness is different from Unlikeness ', the meaning consists entirely of Forms ; there is no reference to individual things, and the problem of participation does not arise. The question is : How can the unity of the Form, which had been so much emphasised, be reconciled with its ' blending ' with other Forms ? A Form is ' one being '. Does it, like Parmenides' One Being, exclude any sort of plurality, or is a Form both one and many ?

This question is bound up with the methods of Collection and Division, which will be illustrated in the *Sophist* and there identified with the dialectical study of the Forms. The early part of the *Parmenides* points forward to the analysis of the blending of Forms in that context. Meanwhile, some of the arguments in the later part have a positive bearing on this question of their unity. Take the bare Eleatic dilemmas : Either a thing is or it is not ; Either a thing is one (and not many) or it is many (and not one) ; If the One is, the many are not ; if the many are, the One is not. Such reasoning must leave us either with a One Being, or Existent Unity, excluding all plurality (as in Parmenides' own system), or with a plurality having no sort of unity. Now, some of the arguments developed in the second part of the *Parmenides* show that on either hypothesis no knowledge or discourse is possible. A bare unity or a bare plurality cannot exist or be known or even spoken of. These results are deduced by reasoning at least as cogent as Zeno's ; and in the *Sophist* Parmenides' One Being will be criticised on similar lines. The arguments point to a positive conclusion : the unity of the ' beings ' recognised by Platonism—the whole realm of Forms as a ' one being ' and each Form as a ' one being '—must be shown to be consistent with their being also complex and so a plurality. The study of Forms in the *Sophist* will clear up the perplexities and paradoxes based by the Eleatics and their successors on the too rigid Parmenidean conceptions of Unity and Being, Plurality and Not-being.

But before passing to the world of Forms, where the true objects of knowledge are to be found, Plato fixes attention, in the *Theaetetus*, on the world of transient becoming and ambiguous appearance, revealed by the senses. Writing for students acquainted with the great systems of the sixth and fifth centuries, he is now prepared to set his own doctrine beside the two opposed philosophies of Parmenides and Heracleitus, and to define what he will take, and what he will not take, from either. He will also meet the challenge of the first and greatest of the Sophists. Protagoras, in conscious opposition to Parmenides, had flatly denied that ' what seems to men '—what seems real to our senses and true to our judgment—is to be condemned as unreal or false because it disagrees with the properties ascribed by Eleatic reasoning to a One Being which we can never perceive. Man, declares Protagoras, is the measure of all things ; what seems real and true to me is real and true to me ; what seems so to you, is so to you. Your perceptions and judgments may not agree with mine ; but neither of us can have any ground for saying that the other is wrong. Such was the fundamental position of that Sophistry which Plato intends to analyse in the second of our two dialogues. The Sophist is the denizen of the world of appearances ; they are for him the sole reality. Plato himself cannot accept Parmenides' condemnation of appearances as totally unreal and of the senses as totally misleading. Accordingly, the *Theaetetus* examines afresh the claim of this lower world to yield knowledge—a claim that common sense would endorse and that Protagoras himself had pressed to the point of declaring that it yields the only knowledge we can ever have.

THEAETETUS

THE main dialogue is prefaced by an introductory conversation between Eucleides and Terpsion of Megara, friends of Socrates who were present at his death. Plato evidently wished to record his affection for Theaetetus, a member of the Academy credited with important discoveries in mathematics. Eucleides' account of how he came to write the main dialogue is obviously fictitious. No such conversation could have taken place in Socrates' lifetime.

The anonymous commentary on the *Theaetetus*,[1] believed to date from the first or second century of our era, records the existence of a second 'rather frigid' introductory dialogue of about the same number of lines, beginning, 'Boy, are you bringing the dialogue about Theaetetus?' It has been argued that this lost introduction was probably written by Plato—for why should anyone forge such a document?—and that the obvious occasion for substituting the existing one would be the death of Theaetetus. The conclusion would then be that the main dialogue was at least partly written before that event. But it is not likely that the long and flattering description in the main dialogue of Theaetetus as a youth was written in his lifetime; and if it was not, the lost introduction may be assumed to have been merely a rejected draft which happened to be preserved. The whole dialogue—introduction and all —may, then, be dated after the fighting near Corinth in 369 B.C.[2] Theaetetus would then be a little under 50, if he was a lad of 15 or 16 in the year of Socrates' death, the imaginary date of the main dialogue.

EUCLEIDES. TERPSION

142. EUCLEIDES. Have you only just come to town, Terpsion?
TERPSION. No, some time ago. What is more, I was looking for you in the market-place and surprised that I could not find you.
EUCL. I was not in the city.

[1] Ed. Diels-Schubart, Berl. Klassikertexte, 1905.
[2] The case for this date is fully argued by Eva Sachs, *De Theaeteto* (Berlin, 1914), pp. 22 ff.

142.   TERPS. Where were you, then?

EUCL. On my way down to the harbour I met them carrying Theaetetus to Athens from the camp at Corinth.

TERPS. Alive or dead?

B.   EUCL. Only just alive. He is suffering from severe wounds, and still more from having caught the sickness that has broken out in the army.

TERPS. The dysentery?

EUCL. Yes.

TERPS. How sad that such a man should be so near death!

EUCL. An admirable man, Terpsion, and a brave one. Indeed, only just now I was hearing warm praise of his conduct in the battle.

TERPS. There is nothing strange in that; it would have been much more surprising if he had behaved otherwise.

C.   But why did he not stay here at Megara?

EUCL. He was eager to get home. I begged him to stay, but he would not listen to my advice. I went some way with him, and then, as I was coming back, I recalled what Socrates had said about him, and was filled with wonder at this signal instance of his prophetic insight. Socrates must have met him shortly before his own death, when Theaetetus was little more than a boy. They had some talk together, and Socrates was delighted with the promise he showed. When I visited Athens he repeated to me their conversation,

D.   which was well worth the hearing; and he added that Theaetetus could not fail to become a remarkable man if he lived.

TERPS. And apparently he was right. But what was this conversation? Could you repeat it?

EUCL. Certainly not, just from memory. But I made

143.   some notes at the time, as soon as I got home, and later on I wrote out what I could recall at my leisure. Then, every time I went to Athens, I questioned Socrates upon any point where my memory had failed and made corrections on my return. In this way I have pretty well the whole conversation written down.

TERPS. True; I have heard you mention it before, and indeed I have always meant to ask you to show it to me; only I have let the matter slip till this moment. Why should we not go through it now? In any case I am in need of a rest after my walk to town.

B.   EUCL. For that matter, I should be glad of a rest myself; for I went as far as Erineon with Theaetetus. Let us go

16

143B. indoors, and, while we are resting, my servant shall read to us.

TERPS. Very well.

EUCL. This is the book, Terpsion. You see how I wrote the conversation—not in narrative form, as I heard it from Socrates, but as a dialogue between him and the other persons he told me had taken part. These were Theodorus the geometer and Theaetetus. I wanted to avoid in the

c. written account the tiresome effect of bits of narrative interrupting the dialogue, such as ' and I said ' or ' and I remarked ' wherever Socrates was speaking of himself, and ' he assented ' or ' he did not agree ', where he reported the answer. So I left out everything of that sort, and wrote it as a direct conversation between the actual speakers.[1]

TERPS. That was quite a good notion, Eucleides.

EUCL. Well, boy, take the book and read.

THE MAIN DIALOGUE

The main dialogue is an imaginary conversation, supposed to have taken place shortly before the trial and death of Socrates, a date at which Theaetetus would be just old enough to take part. He is introduced to Socrates by Theodorus of Cyrene, a distinguished mathematician who has been lecturing on geometry at Athens.

143D–151D. *Introductory Conversation*

The opening section characterises the speakers and introduces the subject of discussion : the definition of knowledge. For the rest, it is concerned with method. Socrates, as in several earlier dialogues, dwells on the distinction (which must, it seems, have been difficult for the ordinary reader to grasp) between giving a number of instances of knowledge and defining the meaning of the name ' knowledge ' which applies to them all. He ends by describing his own technique. Like the midwife who is past childbearing, Socrates' function is not to produce his own ideas and impart them to others, but to deliver their minds of thoughts with which they are in labour, and then to test whether these thoughts are genuine children or mere phantoms.

---

[1] Since the *Parmenides* is composed in the narrative form here rejected as tiresome and never again used by Plato, it may be inferred that this introductory dialogue was written after the *Parmenides*.

17

143D. SOCRATES. If I took more interest in the affairs of Cyrene, Theodorus, I should ask you for the news from those parts and whether any of the young men there are devoting themselves to geometry or to any other sort of liberal study. But really I care more for our young men here and I am anxious rather to know which of them are thought likely to distinguish themselves. That is what I am always on the look-out for myself, to the best of my powers, and I make inquiries of anyone whose society I see the young men ready to seek. Now you attract a large following, as you

E. deserve for your skill in geometry, not to mention your other merits. So, if you have met with anyone worthy of mention, I should be glad to hear of it.

THEODORUS. Yes, Socrates, I have met with a youth of this city who certainly deserves mention, and you will find it worth while to hear me describe him. If he were handsome, I should be afraid to use strong terms, lest I should be suspected of being in love with him. However, he is not handsome, but—forgive my saying so—he resembles you in being snub-nosed and having prominent eyes, though

144. these features are less marked in him. So I can speak without fear. I assure you that, among all the young men I have met with—and I have had to do with a good many— I have never found such admirable gifts. The combination of a rare quickness of intelligence with exceptional gentleness and of an incomparably virile spirit with both, is a thing that I should hardly have believed could exist, and I have never seen it before. In general, people who have such keen and ready wits and such good memories as he, are also quick-tempered and passionate ; they dart about

B. like ships without ballast, and their temperament is rather enthusiastic than strong ; whereas the steadier sort are somewhat dull when they come to face study, and they forget everything. But his approach to learning and inquiry, with the perfect quietness of its smooth and sure progress, is like the noiseless flow of a stream of oil. It is wonderful how he achieves all this at his age.

SOCR. That is good news. Who is his father ?

THEOD. I have heard the name, but I do not remember it. However, there he is, the middle one of those three

C. who are coming towards us. He and these friends of his have been rubbing themselves with oil in the portico outside,

144C. and, now they have finished, they seem to be coming this way. See if you recognise him.

SOCR. Yes, I do ; his father was Euphronius of Sunium, just such another as his son is by your account. He was a man of good standing, and I believe he left a considerable fortune. But I don't know the lad's name.

D. THEOD. His name is Theaetetus, Socrates ; but I fancy the property has been squandered by trustees. None the less, liberality with his money is another of his admirable traits.

SOCR. You give him a noble character. Please ask him to come and sit down with us.

THEOD. I will. Theaetetus, come this way and sit by Socrates.

SOCR. Yes, do, Theaetetus, so that I may study the char-
E. acter of my own countenance ; for Theodorus tells me it is like yours. Now, suppose we each had a lyre, and Theodorus said they were both tuned to the same pitch, should we take his word at once, or should we try to find out whether he was a musician ?

THEAET. We should try to find that out.

SOCR. And believe him, if we discovered that he was musical, but not otherwise ?

THEAET. True.

SOCR. And now, if this alleged likeness of our faces is a matter of any interest to us, we must ask whether it is a
145. skilled draughtsman who informs us of it.

THEAET. I agree.

SOCR. Well, is Theodorus a painter ?

THEAET. Not so far as I know.

SOCR. Nor an expert in geometry either ?

THEAET. Of course he is, Socrates ; very much so.

SOCR. And also in astronomy and calculation and music and in all the liberal arts ?

THEAET. I am sure he is.

SOCR. Then, if, in the way of compliment or otherwise, he tells us of some physical likeness between us, there is no special reason why we should attend to him.

THEAET. Possibly not.

B. SOCR. But suppose he should praise the mind of either of us for its virtue and intelligence. Would there not be good reason why the one who heard the other praised should be eager to examine him, and he should be equally eager to show his quality ?

145B. THEAET. Certainly, Socrates.

SOCR. Now is the time, then, my dear Theaetetus, for you to show your qualities and for me to examine them. I can assure you that, often as Theodorus has spoken to me in praise of citizen or stranger, he has never praised anyone as he was praising you just now.

THEAET. That is good hearing, Socrates. But perhaps he
C. was not speaking seriously.

SOCR. No, that would not be like Theodorus. Do not try to slip out of your bargain on the pretext that he was not serious. We don't want him to have to give evidence on oath. In any case no one is going to indict him for perjury ; so do not be afraid to abide by your agreement.[1]

THEAET. Well, so it shall be, if you wish it.

SOCR. Tell me, then : you are learning some geometry from Theodorus ?

THEAET. Yes.

D. SOCR. And astronomy and harmonics and arithmetic ?

THEAET. I certainly do my best to learn.

SOCR. So do I, from him and from anyone else who seems to understand these things. I do moderately well in general ; but all the same I am puzzled about one small matter which you and our friends must help me to think out. Tell me : is it not true that learning about something means becoming wiser in that matter ?

THEAET. Of course.

SOCR. And what makes people wise is wisdom, I suppose.

THEAET. Yes.

E. SOCR. And is that in any way different from knowledge ?

THEAET. Is what different ?

SOCR. Wisdom. Are not people wise in the things of which they have knowledge ?

THEAET. Certainly.

SOCR. Then knowledge and wisdom are the same thing ?

THEAET. Yes.

SOCR. Well, that is precisely what I am puzzled about : I cannot make out to my own satisfaction what knowledge is.

146. Can we answer that question ? What do you all say ? Which of us will speak first ? Everyone who misses shall ' sit down and be donkey ', as children say when

---

[1] I question Burnet's punctuation here. The last sentence seems to mean : ' Even if he were on oath, there is no one to indict him for perjury, but you can keep your agreement without fear of getting him into trouble by not coming up to his estimate.'

146. they are playing at ball ; anyone who gets through without missing shall be king and have the right to make us answer any question he likes. Why are you all silent ? I hope, Theodorus, that my passion for argument is not making me ill-mannered, in my eagerness to start a conversation and set us all at ease with one another like friends ?

B. THEOD. Not at all, Socrates ; there is nothing ill-mannered in that. But please ask one of these young people to answer your questions ; I am not at home in an abstract discussion of this sort, nor likely to become so at my age. But it is just the thing for them, and they have a far better prospect of improvement ; youth, indeed, is capable of improving at anything. So do not let Theaetetus off ; go on putting your questions to him.

SOCR. You hear what Theodorus says, Theaetetus. I do

C. not think you will want to disobey him ; and it would be wrong for you not to do what an older and wiser man bids you. So tell me, in a generous spirit, what you think knowledge is.

THEAET. Well, Socrates, I cannot refuse, since you and Theodorus ask me. Anyhow, if I do make a mistake, you will set me right.

SOCR. By all means, if we can.

THEAET. Then I think the things one can learn from Theodorus are knowledge—geometry and all the sciences you mentioned just now ; and then there are the crafts of

D. the cobbler and other workmen. Each and all of these are knowledge and nothing else.

SOCR. You are generous indeed, my dear Theaetetus— so open-handed that, when you are asked for one simple thing, you offer a whole variety.

THEAET. What do you mean, Socrates ?

SOCR. There may be nothing in it, but I will explain what my notion is. When you speak of cobbling, you mean by that word precisely a knowledge of shoe-making ?

THEAET. Precisely.

E. SOCR. And when you speak of carpentry, you mean just a knowledge of how to make wooden furniture ?

THEAET. Yes.

SOCR. In both cases, then, you are defining what the craft is a knowledge of ?

THEAET. Yes.

SOCR. But the question you were asked, Theaetetus, was not, what are the objects of knowledge, nor yet how many

146E. sorts of knowledge there are. We did not want to count
them, but to find out what the thing itself—knowledge—is.
Is there nothing in that?

THEAET. No, you are quite right.

147. SOCR. Take another example. Suppose we were asked
about some obvious common thing, for instance, what clay
is ; it would be absurd to answer : potters' clay, and oven-
makers' clay, and brick-makers' clay.

THEAET. No doubt.

SOCR. To begin with, it is absurd to imagine that our
answer conveys any meaning to the questioner, when we use
the word ' clay ', no matter whose clay we call it—the doll-
B. maker's or any other craftsman's. You do not suppose a
man can understand the name of a thing, when he does not
know what the thing is?

THEAET. Certainly not.

SOCR. Then, if he has no idea of knowledge, ' knowledge
about shoes ' conveys nothing to him?

THEAET. No.

SOCR. ' Cobblery ', in fact, or the name of any other art has
no meaning for anyone who has no conception of knowledge.

THEAET. That is so.

SOCR. Then, when we are asked what knowledge is, it is
absurd to reply by giving the name of some art. The answer
is : ' knowledge of so-and-so ' ; but that was not what the
C. question called for.

THEAET. So it seems.

SOCR. And besides, we are going an interminable way
round, when our answer might be quite short and simple.
In this question about clay, for instance, the simple and
ordinary thing to say is that clay is earth mixed with
moisture, never mind whose clay it may be.

THEAET. It appears easy now, Socrates, when you put it
like that. The meaning of your question seems to be the
same sort of thing as a point that came up when your
D. namesake, Socrates here, and I were talking not long ago.[1]

SOCR. What was that, Theaetetus?

THEAET. Theodorus here was proving to us something
about square roots, namely, that the sides (or roots) of
squares representing three square feet and five square feet

---

[1] The following passage is discussed and interpreted by Sir Thomas Heath,
Greek Mathematics, i, 155, and *The Thirteen Books of Euclid's Elements*, ii, 288.
Theaetetus' friend, the young Socrates, takes his place as respondent in the
Statesman.

147D.   are not commensurable in length with the line representing
one foot ; and he went on in this way, taking all the separate
cases up to the root of seventeen square feet: There for
some reason he stopped. The idea occurred to us, seeing
that these square roots were evidently infinite in number,
to try to arrive at a single collective term by which we
E.   could designate all these roots.

Socr. And did you find one ?

Theaet. I think so ; but I should like your opinion.

Socr. Go on.

Theaet. We divided number in general into two classes.
Any number which is the product of a number multiplied
by itself we likened to the square figure, and we called such
a number ' square ' or ' equilateral '.

Socr. Well done !

Theaet. Any intermediate number, such as 3 or 5 or any
148.   number that cannot be obtained by multiplying a number
by itself, but has one factor either greater or less than the
other, so that the sides containing the corresponding figure
are always unequal, we likened to the oblong figure, and we
called it an oblong number.

Socr. Excellent ; and what next ?

Theaet. All the lines which form the four equal sides of
the plane figure representing the equilateral number we
defined as *length*, while those which form the sides of squares
B.   equal in area to the oblongs we called ' *roots* '(surds), as not
being commensurable with the others in length, but only in
the plane areas to which their squares are equal. And there
is another distinction of the same sort in the case of solids.

Socr. Nothing could be better, my young friends ; I am
sure there will be no prosecuting Theodorus for false witness.

Theaet. But, Socrates, I cannot answer your question
about knowledge as we answered the question about the
length and the root. And yet you seem to want something of that kind ; so, on the contrary, it does appear
that Theodorus was not speaking the truth.

C.   Socr. Why, if he had praised your powers of running
and declared that he had never met with a young man
who was so good a runner, and then you had been beaten
in a race by the greatest of runners at the height of his
powers, do you think that his praise would have been any
the less truthful ?

Theaet. No, I don't.

Socr. Well, as I said just now, do you fancy it is a small

23

148C. matter to discover the nature of knowledge ? Is it not one of the hardest questions ?

THEAET. One of the very hardest, I should say.

SOCR. You may be reassured, then, about Theodorus'
D. account of you, and set your mind on finding a definition of knowledge, as of anything else, with all the zeal at your command.

THEAET. If it depends on my zeal, Socrates, the truth will come to light.

SOCR. Forward, then, on the way you have just shown so well. Take as a model your answer about the roots : just as you found a single character to embrace all that multitude, so now try to find a single formula that applies to the many kinds of knowledge.

E. THEAET. But I assure you, Socrates, I have often set myself to study that problem, when I heard reports of the questions you ask. But I cannot persuade myself that I can give any satisfactory solution or that anyone has ever stated in my hearing the sort of answer you require. And yet I cannot get the question out of my mind.

SOCR. My dear Theaetetus, that is because your mind is not empty or barren. You are suffering the pains of travail.

THEAET. I don't know about that, Socrates. I am only telling you how I feel.

149. SOCR. How absurd of you, never to have heard that I am the son of a midwife, a fine buxom woman called Phaenarete !

THEAET. I have heard that.

SOCR. Have you also been told that I practise the same art ?

THEAET. No, never.

SOCR. It is true, though ; only don't give away my secret. It is not known that I possess this skill ; so the ignorant world describes me in other terms as an eccentric person who reduces people to hopeless perplexity. Have you been told that too ?

B. THEAET. I have.

SOCR. Shall I tell you the reason ?

THEAET. Please do.

SOCR. Consider, then, how it is with all midwives ; that will help you to understand what I mean. I dare say you know that they never attend other women in childbirth so long as they themselves can conceive and bear children, but only when they are too old for that.

24

149B.   THEAET.   Of course.

SOCR.   They say that is because Artemis, the patroness of childbirth, is herself childless; and so, while she did not allow barren women to be midwives, because it is

c.   beyond the power of human nature to achieve skill without any experience, she assigned the privilege to women who were past child-bearing, out of respect to their likeness to herself.

THEAET.   That sounds likely.

SOCR.   And it is more than likely, is it not, that no one can tell so well as a midwife whether women are pregnant or not?

THEAET.   Assuredly.

SOCR.   Moreover, with the drugs and incantations they

d.   administer, midwives can either bring on the pains of travail or allay them at their will, make a difficult labour easy, and at an early stage cause a miscarriage if they so decide.

THEAET.   True.

SOCR.   Have you also observed that they are the cleverest match-makers, having an unerring skill in selecting a pair whose marriage will produce the best children?

THEAET.   I was not aware of that.

SOCR.   Well, you may be sure they pride themselves on

e.   that more than on cutting the umbilical cord. Consider the knowledge of the sort of plant or seed that should be sown in any given soil; does not that go together with skill in tending and harvesting the fruits of the earth? They are not two different arts?

THEAET.   No, the same.

SOCR.   And so with a woman; skill in the sowing is not to be separated from skill in the harvesting?

THEAET.   Probably not.

150.   SOCR.   No; only, because there is that wrong and ignorant way of bringing together man and woman which they call pandering, midwives, out of self-respect, are shy even of matchmaking, for fear of falling under the accusation of pandering. Yet the genuine midwife is the only successful matchmaker.

THEAET.   That is clear.

SOCR.   All this, then, lies within the midwife's province; but her performance falls short of mine. It is not the way of women sometimes to bring forth real children,

b.   sometimes mere phantoms, such that it is hard to tell the

25

150B. one from the other. If it were so, the highest and noblest task of the midwife would be to discern the real from the unreal, would it not?

THEAET. I agree.

SOCR. My art of midwifery is in general like theirs; the only difference is that my patients are men, not women, and my concern is not with the body but with the soul that is in travail of birth. And the highest point of my

C. art is the power to prove by every test whether the offspring of a young man's thought is a false phantom or instinct with life and truth. I am so far like the midwife, that I cannot myself give birth to wisdom; and the common reproach is true, that, though I question others, I can myself bring nothing to light because there is no wisdom in me. The reason is this: heaven constrains me to serve as a midwife, but has debarred me from giving birth.

D. So of myself I have no sort of wisdom, nor has any discovery ever been born to me as the child of my soul. Those who frequent my company at first appear, some of them, quite unintelligent; but, as we go further with our discussions, all who are favoured by heaven make progress at a rate that seems surprising to others as well as to themselves, although it is clear that they have never learnt anything from me; the many admirable truths they bring to birth have been discovered by themselves from within. But the delivery is heaven's work and mine.

E. The proof of this is that many who have not been conscious of my assistance but have made light of me, thinking it was all their own doing, have left me sooner than they should, whether under others' influence or of their own motion, and thenceforward suffered miscarriage of their thoughts through falling into bad company; and they have lost the children of whom I had delivered them by bringing them up badly, caring more for false phantoms than for the true; and so at last their lack of understanding

151. has become apparent to themselves and to everyone else. Such a one was Aristides, son of Lysimachus, and there have been many more. When they come back and beg for a renewal of our intercourse with extravagant protestations, sometimes the divine warning that comes to me forbids it; with others it is permitted, and these begin again to make progress. In yet another way, those who seek my company have the same experience as a woman with child: they suffer the pains of labour and, by night

151. and day, are full of distress far greater than a woman's ;
B. and my art has power to bring on these pangs or to allay
them. So it fares with these ; but there are some, Theaetetus, whose minds, as I judge, have never conceived at
all. I see that they have no need of me and with all good-
will I seek a match for them. Without boasting unduly,
I can guess pretty well whose society will profit them. I
have arranged many of these matches with Prodicus, and
with other men of inspired sagacity.

And now for the upshot of this long discourse of mine.
I suspect that, as you yourself believe, your mind is in labour
with some thought it has conceived. Accept, then, the
C. ministration of a midwife's son who himself practises his
mother's art, and do the best you can to answer the questions I ask. Perhaps when I examine your statements I
may judge one or another of them to be an unreal phantom.
If I then take the abortion from you and cast it away,
do not be savage with me like a woman robbed of her
first child. People have often felt like that towards me
and been positively ready to bite me for taking away
some foolish notion they have conceived. They do not see
that I am doing them a kindness. They have not learnt
D. that no divinity is ever ill-disposed towards man, nor is
such action on my part due to unkindness ; it is only that
I am not permitted to acquiesce in falsehood and suppress
the truth.

So, Theaetetus, start again and try to explain what
knowledge is. Never say it is beyond your power ; it will
not be so, if heaven wills and you take courage.

Midwifery and Anamnesis.—It is significant that this introductory conversation runs closely parallel with the first part of an
earlier dialogue, the *Meno.* When asked to define Virtue, Meno
made the same mistake as Theaetetus, offering a list of virtues
instead of a definition of the ' single form ' common to them all.
Socrates' illustration of a correct definition (' Figure ' means ' the
boundary of a solid ') was drawn, as here, from mathematics.
Meno's complaint that Socrates does nothing but reduce others to
perplexity is here quoted by Socrates himself.[1] At this point there
follows in the *Theaetetus* the description of the art of midwifery,
in the *Meno* the theory of *Anamnesis*—that all learning is the

[1] *Meno* 79E, ἤκουον . . . ὅτι σὺ οὐδὲν ἄλλο ἢ αὐτός τε ἀπορεῖς καὶ τοὺς ἄλλους
ποιεῖς ἀπορεῖν. *Theaet.* 149A, λέγουσι . . . ὅτι . . . ἀτοπώτατός (ἀπορώτατος
conj. Stallb.) εἰμι καὶ ποιῶ τοὺς ἀνθρώπους ἀπορεῖν.

recovery of latent knowledge always possessed by the immortal soul.[1] One of the few valuable remarks of the Anonymous Commentator is upon the equivalence of these two conceptions: ' Socrates calls himself a midwife because his method of teaching was of that kind . . . for he prepared his pupils themselves to make statements about the subject by unfolding their natural ideas and articulating them, in accordance with the doctrine that what is called learning is really recollection, and that every human soul has had a vision of reality, and needs, not to have knowledge put into it, but to recollect ' (on 149A). There is some evidence that the historic Socrates professed the art of a spiritual midwife [2] ; but Anamnesis appears first in the middle group of dialogues and provides the link between two Platonic doctrines : the eternal nature of the human soul and the ' separate ' existence of Forms, the proper objects of knowledge. The probable inference is that Anamnesis was a theory which squared the profession and practice of Socrates with Plato's discovery of the separately existing Forms and his conversion from Socratic agnosticism to a belief in immortality.

Now the *Theaetetus* will later have much to say about memory. Why is there no mention of that peculiar impersonal memory of knowledge possessed before birth ? There is no ground for supposing that Plato ever abandoned the theory of Anamnesis. It cannot be mentioned in the *Theaetetus*, because it presupposes that we know the answer to the question here to be raised afresh : What is the nature of knowledge and of its objects ? For the same reason all mention of the Forms is, so far as possible, excluded. The dialogue is concerned only with the lower kinds of cognition, our awareness of the sense-world and judgments involving the perception of sensible objects. Common sense might maintain that, if this is not all the ' knowledge ' we possess, whatever else can be called knowledge is somehow extracted from such experience. The purpose of the dialogue is to examine and reject this claim of the sense-world to furnish anything that Plato will call ' knowledge '. The Forms are excluded in order that we may see how we can get on without them ; and the negative conclusion of the whole discussion means that, as Plato had taught ever since the discovery of the Forms, without them there is no knowledge at all.

The Marks of Knowledge.—The Greek word for ' knowledge ', like the English, can mean either the faculty of knowing or that which is known. The problem here is to define the faculty or function of knowing, though it cannot be defined without reference

---

[1] On *Anamnesis*, see Introd., p. 2.   [2] Aristophanes, *Clouds* 137.

to its objects. If we are to decide whether sensation or perception or belief is to be called knowledge or not, we must assume certain marks that any candidate for the title must possess. As Plato argues elsewhere,[1] it is a question partly of the inherent qualities of our state of mind, partly of the nature of the objects, and from differences in the state of mind differences in the objects can be inferred. In *Republic* V this is applied to the contrast between Knowledge (γνῶσις) and Opinion (δόξα), in the wide sense which covers all acquaintance with sensible things and judgments about them. The states of mind differ in that knowledge is *infallible*, whereas opinion may be true or false. It is inferred that the objects of knowledge must be completely *real* and unchanging, while the objects of opinion are not wholly *real* and are mutable.

So here, these two marks of knowledge are assumed at the outset. Socrates will point out that Theaetetus' identification of perception with knowledge means that perception is *infallible* and has the *real* for its object (152C). Hence what the dialogue proves is that neither sense-perception nor judgment (δόξα) of the types considered possesses both these marks. We shall find that perception, although with due qualifications it may be called infallible, has not the real for its object.

The discussion falls into three main parts, in which the claims of (I) Perception, (II) True Opinion or Belief, (III) True Belief accompanied by an 'account' or explanation of some kind, are examined and rejected.

I. THE CLAIM OF PERCEPTION TO BE KNOWLEDGE

151D–E. *Theaetetus identifies knowledge with perception*

Plato naturally starts with the position of common sense, that knowledge comes to us from the external world through the senses. In his own view this is the lowest type of cognition ; he works upwards from beneath towards the world of intelligible objects, so as to see whether we can find knowledge at these lower levels without having to cross the boundary between the sensible and the intelligible.

151D. THEAET. Well, Socrates, with such encouragement from a person like you, it would be a shame not to do one's best to say what one can. It seems to me that one who

E. knows something is perceiving the thing he knows, and, so far as I can see at present, knowledge is nothing but perception.

SOCR. Good ; that is the right spirit in which to express

[1] *Rep.* V, 477 ff.

151E.   one's opinion. But now suppose we examine your offspring together, and see whether it is a mere wind-egg or has some life in it. Perception, you say, is knowledge ?
THEAET. Yes.

The Meaning of ' Perception '.—In ordinary usage *aesthesis*, translated ' perception ', has a wide range of meanings, including sensation, our awareness of outer objects or of facts,[1] feelings, emotions, etc. At 156B the term is said to cover perceptions (sight, hearing, smell), sensations of heat and cold, pleasures and pains, and even emotions of desire and fear. All these are seated in the sentient part of the soul, inseparably associated with the body.[2] Theaetetus' words, ' one who knows *something* is perceiving the thing he knows ', suggest that he is chiefly thinking of perception of external objects, and the criticism which follows narrows down the word to that sense or at least treats sense-perception of external objects as typical of all *aesthesis*. The only case analysed is vision.

151E–152C. *Dialectical combination of Theaetetus' position with Protagoras' doctrine*

Socrates at once starts upon the dialectical treatment of Theaetetus' suggestion. ' Dialectical ' has some implications which may escape the modern reader. He will readily understand that dialectic means a co-operative inquiry carried on in conversation between two or more minds that are equally bent, not on getting the better of the argument, but on arriving at the truth. A tentative suggestion (' *hypothesis* ') put forward by one speaker is corrected and improved until the full meaning is clearly stated. The criticism that follows may end in complete rejection or lead on to another suggestion which (if the examination has been skilfully conducted) ought to approach nearer to the truth.[3] In the present instance three successive suggestions will be made, and all will be rejected.

A less familiar feature of dialectic is the treatment of current

----

[1] Aristotle, *Politics* 1276A, 29 : Babylon was so huge that when the city fell, it was three days before some of the inhabitants *became aware* of the event (αἰσθέσθαι). At *de anima*, 427A, 19, Aristotle remarks that thinking and the exercise of intelligence are commonly regarded as ' a sort of perception ', for in both the soul discerns and becomes acquainted with something that exists.

[2] *Timaeus* 42A.

[3] Cf. *Theaet*. 187B, where Socrates, after Theaetetus' first definition of knowledge has been rejected, says : ' Blot out all we have been saying and see if you can get a clearer view from the position you have now reached. Tell us once more what knowledge is.'

views, whether popular or philosophic. Aristotle regularly begins his treatises with a review of received opinions, proceeding on the avowed assumption that any belief accepted by common sense or put forward by wise men is likely to contain some measure of truth, however faultily expressed. It is the business of dialectic, by sympathetic comparison and criticism, to elicit these contributions and to make the best that can be made of them. It is here that a modern reader is likely to be misled. He will expect a philosopher who criticises another philosopher to feel himself bound by the historical question, what that other philosopher actually meant. But neither Plato nor Aristotle is writing the history of philosophy ; rather they are philosophising and concerned only to obtain what light they can from any quarter. We can never assume, as a matter of course, that the construction they put upon the doctrines of other philosophers is faithful to historic fact.

Plato's procedure here is a classic example of dialectical method. The first object is to bring to light the full meaning of the bare statement that perception is knowledge. This is accomplished in the first section of the argument ending (160E) with the remark that Theaetetus' child has now been brought to birth. Socrates also says that, in the course of elucidation, Theaetetus' identification of perception with knowledge ' has turned out to coincide ' with the Heracleitean doctrine that all things are in motion and the Protagorean dictum that man is the measure of all things. What has really happened is that Plato has given an account of the nature of perception which involves elements taken from Protagoras and Heracleitus—elements that Plato himself accepts as true when they are guarded and limited with the necessary qualifications. Protagoras and Heracleitus, in fact, are handled as if they were parties to the discussion who could be laid under contribution.[1] Having adopted these elements of truth, Plato will be free, in the subsequent criticism, to point out what he will not accept from Protagoras and the extreme Heracleiteans.

151E. SOCR. The account you give of the nature of knowledge
152. is not, by any means, to be despised. It is the same that was given by Protagoras, though he stated it in a somewhat different way. He says, you will remember, that ' man is the measure of all things—alike of the being of things that are and of the not-being of things that are not '. No doubt you have read that.

[1] Compare Socrates' proposal to ' follow up ' the meaning of Protagoras' saying ($\dot{\epsilon}\pi\alpha\kappa o\lambda o\upsilon\theta\dot{\eta}\sigma\omega\mu\epsilon\nu$ $\alpha\dot{\upsilon}\tau\tilde{\omega}$ 152B) with Aristotle, *Met.* 985A, 4 : ' If we were to follow out ($\dot{\alpha}\kappa o\lambda o\upsilon\theta o\acute{\iota}\eta$) Empedocles' view and interpret it according to its meaning and not to its lisping expression, we should find . . .

152.   THEAET. Yes, often.

SOCR. He puts it [1] in this sort of way, doesn't he ?—that
any given thing ' is to me such as it appears to me, and is
to you such as it appears to you,' you and I being men.

THEAET. Yes, that is how he puts it.

B.   SOCR. Well, what a wise man says is not likely to be nonsense. So let us follow up his meaning. Sometimes, when
the same wind is blowing, one of us feels chilly, the other
does not ; or one may feel slightly chilly, the other quite
cold.

THEAET. Certainly.

SOCR. Well, in that case are we to say that the wind in
itself is cold or not cold ? Or shall we agree with Protagoras
that it is cold to the one who feels chilly, and not to the
other ?

THEAET. That seems reasonable.

SOCR. And further that it so ' appears ' to each of us ?

THEAET. Yes.

SOCR. And ' appears ' means that he ' perceives ' it so ? [2]

THEAET. True.

C.   SOCR. ' Appearing ',[3] then, is the same thing as ' perceiving ',
in the case of what is hot or anything of that kind. They
are to each man such as he *perceives* them.

THEAET. So it seems.

SOCR. Perception, then, is always of something that *is*,
and, as being knowledge, it is infallible.

THEAET. That is clear.

The main point here is stated in Socrates' last speech. ' Perception is knowledge ' means that perception is an *infallible* apprehension of what *is*, or is *real*. These are the two marks of knowledge,
which any candidate to the title must possess.

Theaetetus' statement, so interpreted, certainly does not exhaust
the meaning of Protagoras' saying. Protagoras' word ' appears '
was not confined to what appears *real* to me in sense-perception ;
it included, as we shall see later, what appears *true* to me, what I

---

[1] λέγει can mean ' say ' or ' mean '. Since *Crat.* 386A repeats the formula
in almost the same words, it may well be a quotation.

[2] Ast's conjecture ' αἰσθάνεται ' for αἰσθάνεσθαι is confirmed by the Berlin
papyrus (Diels, *Vors.*⁴ ii, 228). Cf. 164B, τὸ δέ γε ' οὐχ ὁρᾷ ' ' οὐκ ἐπίσταταί '
ἐστιν.

[3] φαντασία is simply the substantive corresponding to the verb φαίνεσθαι, as
at *Soph.* 264A (p. 319). We can substitute Theaetetus' word αἰσθάνεται for
Protagoras' word φαίνεται without change of meaning.

think or judge to be true.[1] On that point Plato will part company with Protagoras ; but here, as the qualification ' in the case of what is hot or anything of that kind ' indicates, we are taking only the relevant application of the doctrine to the immediate perception of sensible qualities.

So far as the infallibility of such perception is concerned, we shall see that Theaetetus, Protagoras, and Plato are in agreement. The second claim—that what appears to me in perception ' is ', or exists, or is real—is at present ambiguous and obscure. Protagoras is represented as asserting that when the wind appears cold to me, then it is cold *to me*, however it may appear and be *to you*. Neither of us has any ground for saying that the other is wrong. Each is the sole measure or criterion or judge [2] of the existence or reality *for him* of what he perceives. What remains obscure is the meaning of the addition ' *to me* ' or ' *for me* '. It is probable that Protagoras actually meant something different from the construction put upon the phrase by Plato for his own purpose.

Socrates, in his illustration from the wind, introduces a distinction between what may be called the sense-object and the physical object. There are two different sense-objects, the coolness that appears to me and the warmth that appears to you. There is one physical object, ' the same wind ' that is blowing. How are the two sense-objects related to the single physical object ? Socrates asks whether the wind in itself is cold or not. Did Protagoras think that the cold and the warmth were qualities (or perhaps rather ' things ') both residing in a neutral or public physical object, the wind in itself ? The answer suggested by Socrates as Protagorean is that the wind is cold *to him who feels chilly*, but not to the other. This is open to several interpretations. The ambiguity may be intentional. It would be entirely in accordance with dialectical procedure that Plato should ignore what Protagoras actually meant and adopt such a construction of his words as would contribute to his own analysis of sense-perception.[3] Two possible interpretations are as follows.

(1) *The wind in itself is both warm and cold*. ' Warm ' and ' Cold ' are two properties which can co-exist in the same physical object. I perceive the one, you perceive the other. ' The wind is cold *to me* ' means that the cold is the property that appears to me or

---

[1] Diog. L. ix, 15 : ' Protagoras held that the mind consists solely of the senses.' This is probably a false inference from our passage, to which Diogenes refers.

[2] At 178B Plato uses the word κριτήριον, and at 160C κρίτης.

[3] So the Anonymous Commentator : ' Plato himself knew that Protagoras' opinion about knowledge was not the same as Theaetetus'. Hence the words Κινδυνεύεις . . . τὰ αὐτὰ ταῦτα ' (151E).

affects me, though it is not the property that appears to or affects you. To say simply that ' the wind is cold ' would naturally be taken to imply that it was not warm. But in fact it is both ; so we add ' to me ', meaning that I am aware of that property, though you are aware of the other.

(2) *The wind in itself is neither warm nor cold*. It has neither of the properties we severally perceive and is not itself perceptible ; it is something that exists outside us and originates my feeling of cold and yours of warmth. Our sense-objects, the warm and the cold, do not exist independently in the public physical object, but only come into existence when the act of perceiving them takes place. ' The wind is cold *to me* ' means that it is not cold in itself apart from me, but only gives me the feeling of cold. This cold which ' appears ' to me exists *for me* as a private object of perception of which I alone can be aware. The fact that your private object is different does not justify you in discrediting my perception as false or denying that its object exists, or is real.[1]

It is probable that Protagoras held the first and simpler of these two views [2]—that the wind is both warm and cold. The second view is an essential feature in the theory of perception presently to be advanced as a ' secret doctrine '—a phrase which implies that it was not to be found in Protagoras' book. The first view has not broken with the naïve realism of common sense, which does not doubt that objects have the qualities we perceive. It agrees with the doctrine of Protagoras' contemporary Anaxagoras, who taught that opposite qualities (or things) such as ' the hot ' and ' the cold ' co-exist inseparably in things outside us, and that perception is by contraries. ' What is just as warm or just as cold (as the sentient organ) neither warms nor cools on its approach ; we do not become

---

[1] Professor Taylor (*Plato, the Man and his Work*, 1926, p. 326) thinks that the view Plato ascribes to Protagoras ' denies that there is a *common* real world which can be known by two percipients. Reality itself is individual in the sense that I live in a private world known only to me, you in another private world known only to you. Thus if I say the wind is unpleasantly hot and you that it is disagreeably chilly, we both speak the truth, for each of us is speaking of a " real " wind, but of a " real " wind which belongs to that private world to which he, and only he, has access. No two of these private worlds have a single constituent in common, and that is precisely why it can be held that each of us is infallible about his own private world. Protagoras . . . denies the reality of the " common environment " presupposed by " intra-subjective intercourse ".'

This interpretation seems to me much too advanced for Protagoras' date, and it contradicts the language of our passage, for it asserts that there are two real winds, both private and totally unconnected, whereas Socrates says ' when the *same wind* is blowing ' and asks if ' *the* wind in itself ' is cold or not.

[2] Cf. Brochard, *Études de Philosophie* (Paris, 1926), Protagoras et Démocrite.

aware of the sweet or the sour by means of those qualities themselves ; rather we become aware of the cold by means of the hot,
of the sweet by means of the sour, according to the deficiency (in us)
of any given quality ; for he says they are all present in us.' [1]
If Protagoras accounted for the same wind feeling cold to me and
warm to you by the obvious explanation (suggested below at
158E ff.) that I am already hot, you are cold, the agreement with
Anaxagoras is clear. Both, again, are at one with Heracleitus, on
the point that opposites co-exist inseparably.[2] In the main fifth-
century controversy, the Eastern or Ionian tradition maintained
that the senses were to be trusted and that things were mixtures of
the opposites apprehended by sense. The Western tradition included the Eleatics, who denied the evidence of the senses and the
reality of the opposites. They influenced the Atomists, who said
that the sensible opposites were ' conventional ' (subjective), not
properties of the ' real ' atoms. Protagoras' doctrine must have
been a reply to the Eleatic denial of appearances. It is probable
that he would maintain that ' hot ' and ' cold ' could co-exist in the
same real thing without any contradiction. Finally, this view is
supported by Sextus [3] : ' Protagoras says that matter contains
the underlying grounds of all appearances, so that matter considered as independent can be all the things that appear to all.
Men apprehend different things at different times according to
variations in their conditions. One in a normal state apprehends
those things in matter which can appear to a normal person ; a
man in an abnormal state apprehends what can appear to the
abnormal. The same applies to different times of life, to the states
of sleeping or waking, and to every sort of condition. So man
proves, according to him, to be the criterion of what exists : everything that appears to man also exists ; what appears to no man does
not exist.' If Protagoras held this view, his doctrine was not
' subjectivist ', and even the term ' relativism ' is dangerously misleading. For him both the sense-objects exist independently of any
percipient. The hot and the cold, together with any other properties we can perceive in the wind, would constitute ' the wind in
itself '. Since at this date such properties were regarded as ' things ',
not as qualities needing some other ' thing ' to possess and support
them, Protagoras would deny that the wind was anything more

---

[1] Theophrastus, *de Sensu* 28 (on Anaxagoras).

[2] Sextus, *Pyrrh. Hyp.* ii, 63 : ' Because honey seems bitter to some, sweet
to others, Democritus said it is neither sweet nor sour, Heracleitus that it was
both.'

[3] *Pyrrh. Hyp.* i, 218. Sextus was no doubt influenced by the *Theaetetus*,
but appears to have had independent sources also.

than the sum of these properties, which alone appear to us. ' What appears to no man does not exist.'

The conclusion is that the second view, presently to be formulated —the wind in itself is neither warm nor cold till it meets with a percipient—is a construction put by Plato himself on Protagoras' ambiguous statement. By a legitimate extension of the historic doctrine, Plato adapts it to the theory he intends to attribute to the ' more refined ' thinkers.

152c–153d. *Dialectical combination with the Heracleitean doctrine of Flux*

Plato next introduces another element required for his theory of sense-perception. It is drawn from Heracleitus : ' All things are in motion.' The suggestion that Protagoras taught this as a ' secret doctrine ' to his ' pupils ' would deceive no one. Protagoras had no school ; anyone could attend his lectures and read his books. Plato is hinting that the doctrine of universal flux is really drawn from another quarter, and he goes on to attribute it to Homer and all philosophers except Parmenides. There is no more ground here for inferring that Protagoras was a Heracleitean than for inferring that Homer was one. Plato's intention is to accept from Heracleitus the doctrine that all sensible objects are perpetually changing—a fundamental principle of his own philosophy. But to Plato sensible objects are not ' all things '. He will later point out that the un-restricted assertion, ' All things are always changing ', makes know-ledge impossible.

152c. Socr. Can it be, then, that Protagoras was a very ingenious person who threw out this dark saying for the benefit of the common herd like ourselves, and reserved the truth as a secret doctrine to be revealed to his disciples ? [1]

D. Theaet. What do you mean by that, Socrates ?

Socr. I will tell you ; and indeed the doctrine is a remark-able one. It declares that nothing is *one* thing just by itself, nor can you rightly call it by some definite name, nor even say it is of any definite sort. On the contrary, if you call it ' large ', it will be found to be also small ; if ' heavy ', to be also light ; and so on all through, because nothing is *one* thing or *some* thing or of any definite sort. All the things we are pleased to say ' are ', really are in process of becoming, as a result of movement and change and of blending one

---

[1] *Truth* was the title of Protagoras' book which opened with the famous saying. At 160a Socrates again suggests, ironically, that this *Truth* may have been speaking in cryptic oracles.

152E. with another.[1] We are wrong to speak of them as ' being ', for none of them ever is ; they are always becoming. In this matter let us take it that, with the exception of Parmenides, the whole series of philosophers agree—Protagoras, Heracleitus, Empedocles—and among the poets the greatest masters in both kinds, Epicharmus [2] in comedy, Homer in tragedy. When Homer speaks of ' Oceanus, source of the gods, and mother Tethys ',[3] he means that all things are the offspring of a flowing stream of change. Don't you understand him so ?

THEAET. Certainly.

153. SOCR. Who, then, could challenge so great an array, with Homer for its captain, and not make himself a laughing-stock ?

THEAET. That would be no light undertaking, Socrates.

SOCR. It would not, Theaetetus. Their doctrine that ' being ' (so-called) and ' becoming ' are produced by motion, ' not-being ' and perishing by rest, is well supported by such proofs as these [4] : the hot or fire, which generates and controls all other things, is itself generated by movement and friction—both forms of change. These are ways of producing fire, aren't they ?

B. THEAET. Yes.

SOCR. And further, all living things are born by the same processes ? [5]

THEAET. Assuredly.

SOCR. Again, the healthy condition of the body is undermined by inactivity and indolence, and to a great extent preserved by exercise and motion, isn't it ?

THEAET. Yes.

SOCR. And so with the condition of the soul. The soul acquires knowledge and is kept going and improved by learning and practice, which are of the nature of movements. By

---

[1] The Ionian doctrine that things are mixtures of opposites, considered as things that can be blended in various proportions. This figures in Empedocles as the composition of complex substances by the juxtaposition of opposed elements. Hence Empedocles is included below, though he did not hold the Flux doctrine.

[2] Epicharmus, *frag.* 2 (Diels), ἐν μεταλλαγᾷ δὲ πάντες ἐντὶ πάντα τὸν χρόνον, κτλ.

[3] Quoted *Crat.* 402B, with Orphic verses and Hesiod.

[4] The proofs may be borrowed from the later Heracleitean literature, and partly, perhaps, from medical writers under Heracleitean influence. Cf. [Hippocrates] *de victu* I.

[5] Was Plato's source acquainted with the primitive analogy, frequently noted by anthropologists, between the sexual act and the use of the fire-drill ?

153B.   inactivity, dullness, and neglect of exercise, it learns nothing
  c.   and forgets what it has learnt.

  THEAET.   True.

  SOCR.   So, of the two, motion is a good thing for both soul
  and body, and immobility is bad.

  THEAET.   So it appears.

  SOCR.   Need I speak further of such things as stagnation in
  air or water, where stillness causes corruption and decay,
  when motion would keep things fresh ; or, to complete the
  argument, press into its service that ' golden rope ' in
  D.   Homer,[1] proving that he means by it nothing more nor less
  than the sun, and signifies that so long as the heavens and
  the sun continue to move round, all things in heaven and
  earth are kept going ; whereas if they were bound down and
  brought to a stand, all things would be destroyed and the
  world, as they say, turned upside down ?

  THEAET.   I agree with your interpretation, Socrates.

In this Heracleitean doctrine two propositions may be distinguished.

(1) The first is essential to the Heracleitean harmony of opposites :
No contrary can exist apart from its own contrary.   This is the meaning here given to the statement that ' nothing is one thing just by
itself '.   You cannot give it the name of any contrary, such as
' large ' or ' heavy ', without also calling it ' small ' or ' light '.
Plato makes this ' blending of opposites ' characteristic of the particular things of sense.   Thus at *Rep.* 479A ff. against the lover of
appearances who believes only in the many beautiful things, not in
Beauty itself, it is urged that there is no one beautiful thing that
will not also appear ugly, and that large or heavy things have no
better claim to be so called than to be called small or light.   This
inseparability of opposites was, as we saw, held also by Protagoras,
if it is true that he regarded the wind in itself as both hot and cold.
Here is the real point of contact between Protagoras, Heracleitus,
and Plato.

(2) The second proposition is :   All the things we speak of as
having ' being ', never really ' *are* ', but are always in process of
becoming, as the result of motion.   There is no obvious reason why
Protagoras should hold this, any more than Anaxagoras did.[2]   But

---

[1] Socrates, in the vein of sophistic interpretation of the poets, misuses the
passage where Zeus challenges the gods to see if they can drag him down by
a golden rope.   If he chose to pull his hardest, he could drag them all up with
earth and sea as well.   *Iliad* viii, 18 ff.

[2] Sextus indeed (*Pyrrh. Hyp.* i, 217 = *Vors.* 74A, 14) says Protagoras held
that ' matter is in flux ' (τὴν ὕλην ῥευστὴν εἶναι), and as it flows waste is

as applied to sensible things, Plato accepted the Heracleitean thesis.[1] The real being of intelligible objects is always the same, never admitting any kind of modification ; but the many things perceived by sense never remain in the same condition in any respect.[2] This principle Plato now builds into his doctrine of sense-perception. The effect is to modify Protagoras' statement, ' I am the measure of what *is* ; what appears to me *is* to me '. For this ' *is* ' we now substitute ' becomes '. In the sphere of perception I am the measure of what becomes, but never is ; and the Protagorean claim (152c) that ' perception is always of what *is* ' gives place to the Platonic doctrine : Perception is always of what is in process of becoming.

153D–154B. *Preliminary account of the nature of sense-objects and percipients*

The next step is to give a precise meaning to the words ' for me ' or ' to me ' in the Protagorean formula, ' What appears to me is *for me* or *to me* ', and the Platonic formula, ' What I perceive becomes *for me* or *to me* '. The interpretation now to be given is : The quality I perceive (my sense-object) becomes or arises at the moment when it is perceived and only *for* a single percipient ; it has no enduring independent existence in the physical object at other times. Here again, if we are right, Plato is going beyond Protagoras.

153D.   SOCR. Think of it, then, in this way. First, to take the case of the eyes, you must conceive that what you call white colour has no being as a distinct thing outside your eyes nor yet inside them, nor must you assign it any fixed place. Other-

E.   wise, of course, it would have its being in an assigned place and abide there, instead of arising in a process of becoming.
THEAET. Well, but how am I to think of it ?
SOCR. Let us follow out our recent statement and lay it down that there is no single thing that is in and by itself.[3]

repaired by additions and our sensations are modified according to various times of life and bodily conditions. This may mean no more than the constant waste *in our bodies* repaired by nutrition (cf. *Symp.* 207D), an alternation of hunger and repletion which would modify the pleasures of eating. Sextus' source is unknown. He may have been misled by Socrates' dialectical inclusion of Protagoras among the adherents of the Flux doctrine (152E).

[1] Ar., *Met.* A 6,987a, 32 : ' For having in his youth first become familiar with Cratylus and with the Heraclitean doctrines (that all sensible things are ever in a state of flux and there is no knowledge about them), these views he held even in later years ' (Ross trans.).

[2] *Phaedo* 78D.

[3] This rather bare and obscure statement here receives a new meaning. At 152D ἓν μὲν αὐτὸ καθ' αὑτὸ οὐδέν ἐστιν meant that no quality (contrary) exists *without its contrary*. This was compatible with the independent existence of qualities. Now μηδὲν αὐτὸ καθ' αὑτὸ ἕν ὄν means (as again at

153E. On that showing we shall see that black or white or any colour you choose is a thing that has arisen out of the meeting of our eyes with the appropriate motion. What we say ' is '
154. this or that colour will be neither the eye which encounters the motion nor the motion which is encountered, but something which has arisen between the two and is peculiar to each several percipient. Or would you be prepared to maintain that every colour appears to a dog or any other creature just such as it appears to you ?

THEAET. Certainly not.

SOCR. Or to another man ? Does anything you please appear to him such as it appears to you ? Are you quite sure of that ? Are you not much rather sure that it does not even appear the same to yourself, because you never remain in the same condition ?

THEAET. I think that is much nearer the mark.

This preliminary statement, explaining what is meant by ' becomes for me ', will be expanded presently. So far, a number of points have been very briefly stated. On the side of the object, white colour has no permanent being anywhere ; it arises between the sense-organ and the physical object when they encounter. Also, it is peculiar to the individual percipient in two ways : my sense-object is *private* to me in that no one else can see just what I see, and *peculiar* in that no two people, looking at the same thing, will see precisely similar colours ; nor will even the same person at different moments, because the condition of his sense-organ will be always varying.

The above statements refer mainly to the object of perception. It remains to be added that the subject (which at this stage is identified with the sense-organ, not the mind) must equally have no fixed qualities. If it carried permanent qualities of its own, it could not adapt itself to each new object ; those inherent qualities would obstruct the required modification of the organ.

154B. SOCR. So then, if the thing that we measure ourselves against or the thing we touch really were large or white or hot, it would never become different the moment it encountered a different person, supposing it to undergo no change in itself. And again, if the thing which measures itself against the object or touches it were any one of these things (large, white, etc.), then, when a different thing

156E, 8 and 157A, 8) that no thing just by itself (i.e. *apart from a percipient*) has, existing in it, any single quality that we perceive. All such qualities arise between it and the percipient at the moment of perception.

154B. came into contact with it or were somehow modified, it, on its side, if it were not affected in itself, would not become different.

The expression 'measure ourselves against' looks at first sight like a reference to Protagoras' use of the word in 'Man is the *measure* of all things'. 'Measure' suggests a constant standard of reference; a measure which itself perpetually varied would be useless. But in the present case the subject is no more constant than the object, and the common implication of constancy must be ruled out. The sense-organ is undergoing perpetual modification no less than the external object, and its fluidity offers no obstruction to any fresh affection from without. It appears, however, in the next section that the literal measurement of a large thing against a small is intended.

154B–155D. *Some puzzles concerning size and number*

If Socrates now proceeded at once to the fuller statement of the theory of sense perception, there would be no difficulty. But here Plato interpolates some alleged puzzles about what we call 'relations' of size and number, whose relevance to their context is by no means obvious. Nor is it easy for us to understand why anyone should be perplexed by them.

154B. SOCR. (*continues*). For as things are,[1] we are too easily led into making statements which Protagoras and anyone who maintains the same position would call strange and absurd.
THEAET. How so? What statements do you mean?

C. SOCR. Take a simple example, which will make my meaning quite clear. When you compare six dice with four, we say that the six are more than the four or half as many again; while if you compare them with twelve, the six are fewer—only half as many—and one cannot say anything else. Or do you think one can?
THEAET. Certainly not.
SOCR. Well then, suppose Protagoras or somebody else asks you: Can anything become larger or more otherwise than by being increased? What will you answer?
THEAET. I should answer No, if I were to speak my mind

D. with reference to this last question; but having regard to your previous one, I might reply Yes, to guard against contradicting myself.

---

[1] 'As things are' (νῦν) apparently means 'on the current assumption, which has just been denied, that things have permanent qualities'.

154D. SOCR. An excellent answer ; really, you might be inspired. But apparently, if you say Yes, it will be like the situation in Euripides : the tongue will be incontrovertible, but not the heart.

THEAET. True.

SOCR. Now, if you and I were like those clever persons who have canvassed all the thoughts of the heart, we might

E. allow ourselves the luxury of trying one another's strength in a regular sophistical set-to, with a great clashing of arguments. But being only ordinary people, we shall prefer first to study the notions we have in our own minds and find out what they are and whether, when we compare them, they agree or are altogether inconsistent.

THEAET. I should certainly prefer that.

SOCR. So do I ; and, that being so, suppose we look at the question again in a quiet and leisurely spirit, not with

155. any impatience but genuinely examining ourselves to see what we can make of these apparitions that present themselves to our minds. Looking at the first of them, I suppose we shall assert that nothing can become greater or less, either in size or in number, so long as it remains equal to itself. Is it not so ?

THEAET. Yes.

SOCR. And secondly, that a thing to which nothing is added and from which nothing is taken away is neither increased nor diminished, but always remains the same in amount.

THEAET. Undoubtedly.

B. SOCR. And must we not say, thirdly, that a thing which was not at an earlier moment cannot be at a later moment without becoming and being in process of becoming ?

THEAET. It certainly seems so.

SOCR. Now these three admissions, I fancy, fight among themselves in our minds when we make those statements about the dice ; or when we say that I, being of the height you see, without gaining or losing in size, may within a year be taller (as I am now) than a youth like you, and

C. later on be shorter, not because I have lost anything in bulk, but because you have grown. For apparently I am later what I was not before, and yet have not become so ; for without the process of becoming the result is impossible, and I could not be in process of becoming shorter without losing some of my bulk. I could give you countless other examples, if we are to accept these. For I think you

155C. follow me, Theaetetus ; I fancy, at any rate, such puzzles are not altogether strange to you.

THEAET. No ; indeed it is extraordinary how they set me wondering whatever they can mean. Sometimes I get quite dizzy with thinking of them.

D. SOCR. That shows that Theodorus was not wrong in his estimate of your nature. This sense of wonder is the mark of the philosopher. Philosophy indeed has no other origin, and he was a good genealogist who made Iris the daughter of Thaumas.[1]

What is the point of these alleged puzzles ? Though Socrates continues : ' Do you begin to understand why these things are so, according to the doctrine we are attributing to Protagoras ? ' nothing more is said about them in the following context, which analyses the process of sense-perception. Socrates leaves Theaetetus —and us—to think out these puzzles for ourselves.

We have just been told that sensible qualities like ' white ' and ' hot ' have no independent and permanent existence either in objects outside us or in our sense-organs. They arise or ' become ' between object and organ when the two encounter one another. If either object or organ carried about with it permanent qualities, this becoming could not occur. And at 154B ' large ' was grouped with ' white ' and ' hot ', as if it were a quality on the same footing with them ; just as earlier (152D) ' large ' and ' small ', ' heavy and light ', were taken as typical of all contraries.

The puzzle about the dice is this : When we compare six dice with four, we say that the six are *more*. At another moment, when we compare them with twelve, we say they are *less*. Yet the six dice have not increased or diminished in number. Common sense, we are told, holds that nothing can be at one moment what it was not at another, without becoming ; that a thing cannot become greater or less so long as it remains the same in amount ; and that it does remain the same in amount, so long as nothing is added or subtracted. How, then, can the dice, which have remained the same in amount, have become less ?

It is clear that the difficulty here exists only for one who thinks of ' large ' as a quality residing in the thing which is larger than something else, with ' small ' as the answering quality residing in the smaller thing. If that is so, then, when the large thing is

---

[1] The *Cratylus* connects Iris with εἴρειν (408B), and εἴρειν (λέγειν) with dialectic (398D). So Iris (philosophy) is daughter of Thaumas (wonder). Since our passage is unintelligible without the *Cratylus*, the *Theaetetus* must be the later of the two.

compared with something larger instead of something smaller, he will suppose that it has lost its quality 'large' and gained instead the quality 'small'. By suffering this internal change it will have 'become small'. He will then be puzzled when we point out that the thing has not altered in size.

Now when Plato wrote the *Phaedo*, he certainly regarded 'tallness' as an inherent property of the tall person. 'Phaedo is taller than Socrates' was analysed as implying (1) that there are two Forms, Tall and Short, of which Phaedo and Socrates severally partake; (2) that Phaedo contains an instance of Tallness (called 'the tallness *in us*'), and Socrates an instance of Shortness; (3) that neither the Forms, Tall and Short, nor their instances in us can change into their opposites; and consequently (4) that, if Socrates should grow and become taller than Phaedo, the instance of shortness in Socrates must either 'perish' or 'withdraw' to give place to an instance of tallness. This analysis unquestionably means that the person who becomes taller or shorter than another suffers an internal change. The example chosen lends itself to this view because 'tallness' was commonly ranked as a physical excellence, with beauty, health and strength, and as such it is mentioned earlier in the *Phaedo*.[1] Plato himself shares the ordinary view and thinks of tallness as an internal property on the same footing as 'hot' or 'white', not as standing for a *relation between* the taller person and the shorter.

Now in our passage, though he repeats his example of Socrates, who is now taller than Theaetetus, becoming shorter when Theaetetus outgrows him, he remarks that Socrates will not have changed in size. And in the case of the dice it is equally obvious that the six dice do not become more or fewer in the sense of increasing or diminishing in number. Further, he hints that light on the puzzles here is to be drawn from the theory of sense-perception, which tells us that an object can 'become white' *for* a percipient without undergoing any internal change of quality irrespective of a percipient. When we say it 'becomes white for me' we do not mean that it has lost some other colour and gained whiteness

---

[1] At *Phaedo* 65D, Tallness (μέγεθος), Health, Strength, are instanced as Forms, together with Just, Beautiful, Good. That μέγεθος means 'tallness' (not 'absolute magnitude' or 'mathematical magnitude') is evident from *Meno* 72D. Meno has said that excellence (ἀρετή) in a man is one thing, in a woman another. Socrates asks whether this applies to physical excellences: are health, tallness (μέγεθος), or strength different things in men and in women? Tallness and beauty are coupled at 72B, as in Homer's phrase καλός τε μέγας τε. There is no question of the absolute or mathematical magnitude of men and women. At *Phaedo* 65D tallness appears without beauty because καλόν has just before been used in its moral sense.

instead. In itself, apart from a percipient, it is neither white nor of any other colour. The change meant by 'becoming white' (for me) is not an internal exchange of qualities, but a change that occurs 'between' the object and the sense-organ. Neither of the two carries about with it a permanent property, independent of their meeting.

The inference seems to be that Plato, since writing the *Phaedo*, has given up the view that any of these qualities—hot, white, large —is an instance of a Form residing in an individual thing and perishing or withdrawing out of it when the thing changes. We are now to think of the change as falling 'between' the thing and the percipient, not inside the thing. The case of more or less in number or size may be introduced partly because it is easier to see in that case how a change can occur 'between' a thing and a percipient.[1] The six dice will *appear* more to me when I compare them with four, less when I compare them with twelve, but they have not become more or fewer in themselves. This will help us to understand how a thing can appear or become white for me, without that implying that whiteness in it has replaced some other colour.

It is not safe, however, to infer that Plato has 'abandoned Ideas (Forms) of relations', if that implies that he had drawn any clear distinction between relations and qualities. It is rather probable that he still sees no important distinction between 'large' and 'hot' or 'white'. And he nowhere explicitly states that he has abandoned Forms of both relative terms and sensible qualities.[2]

155D–157C. *Theory of the nature of Sense-perception*

Socrates now expands the analysis of the process of sense-perception, which was briefly announced before the passage on size and number.

155D. SOCR. (*continues*). Do you now begin to see the explanation of all this which follows from the theory we are attributing to Protagoras? Or is it not yet clear?

THEAET. I can't say it is yet.

SOCR. Then perhaps you will be grateful if I help you to

---

[1] Note that Plato's illustrations are perceptible things—dice, not abstract numbers. He is not talking about mathematical 'relations' between the numbers 4, 6, 12.

[2] The treatment by Plato and Aristotle of 'relative terms' will be further discussed below, p. 282. It is one thing to say (with Plato) that 'larger' and 'more' are relative terms because what is larger or more is always larger *than something* or more *than something* or '*in comparison with something*' (πρός τι), and another to say (with Campbell) that 'size and number are wholly relative'. What is number, or any number (say 7), wholly relative to?

155D. penetrate to the truth concealed in the thoughts of a man
 E. —or, I should say, of men—of such distinction.[1]

THEAET. Of course I shall be very grateful.

SOCR. Then just take a look round and make sure that none of the uninitiate overhears us. I mean by the uninitiate the people who believe that nothing is real save what they can grasp with their hands and do not admit that actions or processes or anything invisible can count as real.

THEAET. They sound like a very hard and repellent sort
156. of people.[2]

SOCR. It is true, they are remarkably crude. The others, into whose secrets I am going to initiate you, are much more refined and subtle. Their first principle, on which all that we said just now depends, is that the universe really is motion and nothing else. And there are two kinds of motion. Of each kind there are any number of instances, but they differ in that the one kind has the power of acting, the other of being acted upon.[3] From the intercourse and friction of these with one another arise offspring, endless in
 B. number, but in pairs of twins. One of each pair is something perceived, the other a perception, whose birth always coincides with that of the thing perceived. Now, for the perceptions we have names like ' seeing ', ' hearing ', ' smelling ', ' feeling cold ', ' feeling hot ', and again pleasures and pains and desires and fears, as they are called, and so on. There are any number that are nameless, though names have been found for a whole multitude. On the other side, the brood of things perceived always comes to birth at the same moment with one or another of these—with instances
 C. of seeing, colours of corresponding variety ; with instances of hearing, sounds in the same way ; and with all the other perceptions, the other things perceived that are akin to them. Now, what light does this story throw on what has gone before, Theaetetus ? Do you see ?

[1] Observe the hints that the coming theory is one that ' we are attributing ' to Protagoras, and not to him alone.

[2] Like the physical bodies in whose reality they believe, with their essential property of hardness and resistance to touch.

[3] The two kinds of motion here meant are : (1) physical objects considered as agents with the power of acting upon or affecting our senses ; (2) sense-organs, as patients with the capacity of being affected in the way peculiar to sensation or perception. Later (156c) both kinds are distinguished, as ' slow motions (qualitative changes) occurring in the same place ', from the rapid movements which pass between them—the offspring mentioned in the next sentences.

156C. THEAET. Not very clearly, Socrates.

SOCR. Well, consider whether we can round it off. The point is that all these things are, as we were saying, in motion ; but there is a quickness or slowness in their motion. The slow sort has its motion without change of place and with respect to what comes within range of it, and that is

D. how it generates offspring ; but the offspring generated are quicker, inasmuch as [1] they move from place to place and their motion consists in change of place. As soon, then, as an eye and something else whose structure is adjusted to the eye come within range and give birth to the whiteness together with its cognate perception—things that would never have come into existence if either of the two had approached anything else—then it is that, as the

E. vision from the eyes and the whiteness from the thing that joins in giving birth to the colour pass in the space between, the eye becomes filled with vision and now sees, and becomes, not vision, but a seeing eye ; while the other parent of the colour is saturated with whiteness and becomes, on its side, not whiteness, but a white thing, be it stock or stone or whatever else may chance to be so coloured.

And so, too, we must think in the same way of the rest— 'hard', 'hot' and all of them—that no one of them has

157. any being just by itself (as indeed we said before), but that it is in their intercourse with one another that all arise in all their variety as a result of their motion ; since it is impossible to have any ' firm notion ' (as they say) of either what is active or what is passive in them, in any single case, as having any being.[2] For there is no such thing as an agent until it meets with a patient, nor any patient until it meets with its agent.[3] Also what meets with something and behaves as agent, if it encounters something different at another time, shows itself as patient.[4]

The conclusion from all this is, as we said at the outset, that nothing *is* one thing just by itself, but is always in

B. process of becoming for someone, and being is to be ruled

---

[1] Taking οὕτω δή (γεννώμενα) as referring forward and explained by the following clause with γάρ. There should be a colon after ἐστίν (so Diès). But perhaps this οὕτω δή should be omitted, with Peipers.

[2] The ambiguity of εἶναί τι is discussed below, p. 50. For τὸ ποιοῦν . . . αὐτῶν, cf. αὐτὸ τοῦτο αὐτῶν, 163B, 8.

[3] Strictly the present participles mean a thing which *is acting, is being acted on*. It is not denied that there exists beforehand something with the *power* to act or be acted on.

[4] The eyeball can be seen by another eye, the flesh touched, etc.

157B.   out altogether, though, needless to say, we have been
        betrayed by habit and inobservance into using the word
        more than once only just now.   But that was wrong, these
        wise men tell us ; and we must not admit the expressions
        ' something ' or ' somebody's ' or ' mine ' or ' this ' or ' that '
        or any other word that brings things to a standstill, but
        rather speak, in accordance with nature, of what is ' be-
        coming ', ' being produced ', ' perishing ', ' changing '.   For
        anyone who talks so as to bring things to a standstill is
        easily refuted.   So we must express ourselves in each
        individual case and in speaking of an assemblage of many—

   c.   to which assemblage people give the name of ' man ' or
        ' stone ' or of any living creature or kind.[1]

Whose is this theory ?   Modern critics usually say that Socrates
attributes it to ' certain unnamed thinkers ', and many have
proceeded to identify these with the Cyrenaics.   For this there is
no warrant in the text.   The theory is first introduced (152C) as a
secret doctrine revealed by Protagoras to his disciples.   Its fundamental thesis—the flux doctrine—is then ascribed to the whole
series of philosophers, with the exception of Parmenides, and to
Homer and Epicharmus.   At 155D it is called ' the theory we are
attributing to Protagoras ', and once more described as a secret
' concealed in the thoughts of a man—or rather men—of distinction '.   Materialists, who identify the real with the tangible and do
not reckon actions and processes as real at all, are excluded from the
mystery, which reduces the tangible bodies they believe in precisely
to actions and processes.[2]   ' The others '[3] are more refined, and
now their secret doctrine is fully revealed.   ' The others ' means
simply the distinguished men just mentioned, Protagoras himself
and all the philosophers (except Parmenides, who denied the existence of motion) and poets who recognised the flux of all things—

---

[1] The text is doubtful : καὶ ἕκαστον ζῷόν τε καὶ εἶδος is hard to construe.
Does ἕκαστον ζῷον mean ' an individual animal ', εἶδος a ' kind ' of animal ?
What sort of ' assemblage ' is meant ?   Perhaps a physical object considered
merely as an aggregate of what are commonly regarded as its sensible qualities
—all the qualities (white, hard, etc.) we should name in describing a stone
that we saw.   The whole theory is confined to the discussion of sensible
qualities.   Cf. Burnet, G.P. i, 241.

[2] We shall meet with the materialists again in the Sophist (p. 231, infra).
Probably no particular school is directly aimed at, though the Atomists who
identified the real with (essentially tangible) body would come within the
condemnation.

[3] Reading ἄλλοι δὲ with Burnet at 156A, 2.   But the reading does not
affect my argument.

all who have been wise enough to acknowledge the reality of actions and processes. There are no ' unnamed thinkers ' to be identified ; nor is there any evidence that any Cyrenaics or other contemporaries existed who held the doctrine of sense-perception here set forth.

No one would take seriously the suggestion that this very advanced theory of the nature of perception and its objects was really taught in secret by any of the distinguished philosophers and poets. Socrates is, in fact, himself in the act of constructing it by a dialectical combination of elements borrowed, with important modifications and restrictions, from Protagoras and Heracleitus. Jackson [1] pointed out that the theory is not refuted in the sequel, but on the contrary taken as a true account of the matter, and that it is repeated elsewhere in Plato's writings. He inferred that it originated with Plato himself. There is a conclusive argument (not urged by Jackson) in favour of this inference. Plato intends to refute the claim of perception (in spite of its infallibility) to be knowledge on the ground that its objects have no real being, but are always becoming and changing and therefore cannot be known. For that purpose he is bound to give us what he believes to be a true account of the nature of those objects. It would be futile to prove that what some other individual or school, perhaps wrongly, supposed to be the nature of perception was inconsistent with its claim to yield knowledge. Accordingly he states his own doctrine and takes it as established for the purposes of the whole subsequent criticism of perception. To preserve the dramatic proprieties of dialogue, he uses the transparent device of making Socrates state it as a secret doctrine of a whole succession of wise men who notoriously had never taught anything of the kind.

Assured that the theory must be Plato's own, we may now look at it more closely. Contemporaries must have found it extremely daring. The physical objects which yield our sensations and perceptions are described as actually being ' slow motions '. No permanent quality resides in them. The only other thing we know about them is that they have the power ($\delta\acute{v}\nu\alpha\mu\iota\varsigma$) of acting upon our organs and (it may be added) upon one another. What we call a hot thing is a change that can make us ' feel hot ' and can make another thing we call ' cold ' hotter. This change, as opposed to locomotion, is a modification or qualitative change. [2] On the other side, the subject of perception is here treated as if it were, not the

---

[1] *Journal of Philology* xiii, pp. 250 ff. Burnet (*Greek Philosophy* i, 242) agrees with the attribution to Plato.

[2] This is clear from 181D and *Parm.* 138B, where it is said that the two kinds of change are locomotion ($\phi o\rho\acute{a}$) and qualitative change ($\dot{a}\lambda\lambda o\acute{\iota}\omega\sigma\iota\varsigma$). The conception of the $\delta\acute{v}\nu\alpha\mu\iota\varsigma$ will be further discussed below, pp. 234 ff.

mind, but the sense-organ [1]—the eye from which issues the stream of visual ' fire ' or light (called ' vision ', ὄψις)—to encounter the rapid motion coming from the object. The eye which sees, or the flesh which feels, is itself a physical object which can be seen or touched, and therefore itself a qualitative change, a ' slow motion in the same place '. Thus, before the act of perception takes place, there are, on both sides, changes going on all the time in physical objects, unperceived and capable of giving rise to actual perceptions. But nothing that can properly be called an agent or patient exists until the two come within range of one another.

When they do come within range, the powers of acting and being acted upon come into play. Quick motions pass between organ and external object. A stream of visual light flows out from the eye to meet a stream of light whose structure corresponds in such a way that the two streams can interpenetrate one another and coalesce.[2] The marriage of these two motions generates seeing and colour. Physically, ' the eye becomes filled with vision '— a mixture of visual fire and the fiery particles coming from the object. The external thing ' becomes white ' ; its surface is ' saturated with whiteness '. This last statement is more difficult ; the object is described as affected by the act of sight and acquiring colour. The meaning may be that the ' flame ' or light belonging to the object cannot until this moment be called ' colour ' or ' white '. At other times the object ought not to be spoken of as if it possessed in itself any quality with a fixed name.

When perception is not taking place, we are finally told, one cannot have any ' firm notion ' of either agent or patient as ' having any being ' or ' being any definite thing ' (εἶναί τι). The last words are ambiguous. ' Being any definite thing ' means having any definite quality, such as white. ' Having any being ' means that there is strictly no such thing as an agent or patient *as such* : there is nothing that is acting or being acted upon, but only two things or changes with a capacity of acting and being acted upon. This capacity must imply that my pen and this paper have some difference of property when not perceived, which would explain why, when I do see them, the pen looks black, the paper white. Plato's point

---

[1] Later (184B) it will be pointed out that there is a central mind which perceives rather *through* than *with* the several sense-organs, but this addition does not invalidate the present account of the commerce between organs and objects.

[2] The *Timaeus* explains the process in terms of the theory which there assigns particles of regular form to each of the four elements. Colours are ' a flame streaming off any and every body, having its particles so adjusted (σύμμετρα) to those of the visual current as to excite sensation ' (67C). Cf. συμμέτρων here, 156D. The coalescence is described at *Tim.* 45B ff. See p. 327.

is that these properties, whatever they are, are always changing, however slightly, and that they are not the qualities I perceive—my sense-objects—and so should not be called ' black ' or ' white '.[1]

157C–D. *Theaetetus accepts the theory of Perception*

In a short interlude, Theaetetus accepts the theory, while Socrates disclaims the authorship.

157C. SOCR. (*continues*). Does all this please you, Theaetetus? Will you accept it as palatable to your taste?

THEAET. Really, I am not sure, Socrates. I cannot even make out about you, whether you are stating this as something you believe or merely putting me to the test.

SOCR. You forget, my friend, that I know nothing of such matters and cannot claim to be producing any offspring of my own. I am only trying to deliver yours, and to that end uttering charms over you and tempting your appetite

D. with a variety of delicacies from the table of wisdom,[2] until by my aid your own belief shall be brought to light. Once that is done, I shall see whether it proves to have some life in it or not. Meanwhile, have courage and patience, and answer my questions bravely in accordance with your convictions.

THEAET. Go on with your questioning.

SOCR. Once more, then, tell me whether you like this notion that nothing is, but is always becoming, good or beautiful or any of the other things we mentioned?

THEAET. Well, when I hear you explaining it as you have, it strikes me as extraordinarily reasonable, and to be accepted as you have stated it.

The theory so accepted stands henceforth as a satisfactory account of that perception which Theaetetus has identified with knowledge. The word has now received a clearer meaning, more restricted than Theaetetus, perhaps, at first intended. He apparently feels no qualm when Socrates slips in the words ' good ' and ' beautiful ', as if these qualities were on the same footing with ' hot ' or ' white ' or ' large ', and since his identification of knowledge with perception implies that there is no knowledge other than perception, he would have no right to object.

[1] There is no question here of a ' solipsist epistemology ' or of a relativism asserting that, if every sentient creature were annihilated, nothing would exist

[2] The allusion seems to be rather to the fastidious appetite of pregnant women than to drugs, which are not ' set before ' the patient to be ' tasted of '.

157E–160E.   *The claim of Perception, so defined, to be infallible*

The next section completes the case on behalf of Theaetetus' identification of knowledge with perception.   At the outset Protagoras' assertion that 'what appears to each man *is* to him' was construed as meaning that what he perceives has being (at any rate 'for him') and that his perception is infallible.   Plato's theory of perception has now denied that the object has 'being' apart from the percipient, and has interpreted '*is* for him' as meaning '*becomes* for him'.   This interpretation, though it will finally prove fatal to the claim of perception to be knowledge of true reality, leaves untouched the claim to infallibility.   Socrates, whose present business is to make the best of Theaetetus' hypothesis that perception is knowledge, now brings forward this latter claim and upholds it against the objections commonly based on so-called delusions of sense, the unreality of dream images, the vitiated sensations of the diseased, and the hallucinations of insanity.

157E.   SOCR.   Then let us not leave it incomplete.   There remains the question of dreams and disorders, especially madness and all the mistakes madness is said to make in seeing or hearing or otherwise misperceiving.   You know, of course, that in all these cases the theory we have just stated is supposed to be admittedly disproved, on the ground that in these
158.   conditions we certainly have false perceptions, and that so far from its being true that what appears to any man also is, on the contrary none of these appearances is real.
THEAET.   That is quite true, Socrates.
SOCR.   What argument, then, is left for one who maintains that perception is knowledge, and that what appears to each man also 'is' for him to whom it appears?
THEAET.   I hesitate to say that I have no reply, Socrates, because just now you rebuked me for saying that.   Really,
B.   I cannot undertake to deny that madmen and dreamers believe what is false, when madmen imagine they are gods or dreamers think they have wings and are flying in their sleep.
SOCR.   Have you not taken note of another doubt that is raised in these cases, especially about sleeping and waking? [1]
THEAET.   What is that?
SOCR.   The question I imagine you have often heard asked:

[1] The reply our theory will make to dispose of the objection does not begin till 158E.   Here Socrates makes a sort of preliminary answer : Who is to judge between the dreamer's conviction that his experience is real and the waking man's, that it is unreal?

158B.   what evidence could be appealed to, supposing we were
        asked at this very moment whether we are asleep or awake

C.   —dreaming all that passes through our minds or talking
        to one another in the waking state.

THEAET.   Indeed, Socrates, I do not see by what evidence
it is to be proved ; for the two conditions correspond in
every circumstance like exact counterparts. The conversation we have just had might equally well be one that we
merely think we are carrying on in our sleep ; and when
it comes to thinking in a dream that we are telling other
dreams, the two states are extraordinarily alike.

SOCR.   You see, then, that there is plenty of room for

D.   doubt, when we even doubt whether we are asleep or awake ;
and in fact, our time being equally divided between waking
and sleeping, in each condition our mind strenuously con-
tends that the convictions of the moment are certainly
true ; so that for equal times we affirm the reality of the one
world and of the other, and are just as confident of both.

THEAET.   Certainly.

SOCR.   And the same holds true of disorders and madness,
except that the times are not equal.

THEAET.   That is so.

SOCR.   Well, is the truth to be decided by length or shortness
of time ?

E.   THEAET.   No, that would be absurd in many ways.

SOCR.   Have you any other certain test to show which of
these beliefs is true ?

THEAET.   I don't think I have.

The word *aesthesis* is here still used in a sense wide enough to
include awareness of inner sensations and feelings and of dream-
images. All these are, in Protagoras' phrase, ' things that appear '
to me. Since, as Socrates will point out, I cannot be aware and yet
aware of nothing (160A), these objects must have some sort of
existence ; and there is no ground for saying that my direct awareness of them is ' false '.

It is true that Theaetetus (158B), instead of keeping to Socrates'
expressions ' perceptions,' ' what appears ', speaks of the dreamer
and the madmen as ' thinking ' (δοξάζειν, διανοεῖσθαι) or ' believing ' (οἴεσθαι) what is false. This is no doubt intentional. It
stirs in the reader the suggestion that, although there may be no such
thing as a false awareness of sensation, there is such a thing as
false belief. But the vital distinction between direct awareness
and belief is not yet drawn, and Theaetetus, like most people, would

say indifferently of the dreamer that he 'has the sensation of flying', 'seems to himself to be flying', and 'imagines or believes he is flying'. When the distinction is drawn, the claim of direct awareness to be infallible is not shaken. No one can deny that the dreamer has just that experience which he does have.

After this glimpse of the distinction between sensation or perception and belief or judgment, the argument returns to the case of 'perception' and is confined to that. Socrates now disposes of the popular notion that the healthy or the sane man is the only measure of what is or appears—that wine really is in itself sweet because it seems sweet to the normal palate, sour only to the unhealthy. Since the sense-organ co-operates in producing the sensation, its condition at least partly determines the character of the sensation. The unhealthy man is not 'misperceiving' a fixed quality inherent in the external object, which the normal man perceives as it really is. The two percipient organs are different, and these differences will necessarily modify the joint product of the marriage of subject and object.

158E. SOCR. Then let me tell you what sort of account would be given of these cases by those who lay it down that whatever at any time seems to anyone is true to him. I imagine they would ask this question : 'Tell us, Theaetetus ; when one thing is entirely different from another, it cannot be in any respect capable of behaving [1] in the same way as that other, can it ? We are not to understand that the thing we speak of is in some respects the same though different in others, but that it is entirely different.'

159. THEAET. If so, it can have nothing in common, either in its capabilities of behaviour or in any other respect, when it is altogether different.

SOCR. Must we not admit, then, that such a thing is unlike the other ?

THEAET. I agree.

SOCR. So if it happens that something comes to be like or unlike either itself or something else, we shall say that when it is made like it becomes the *same*, when unlike, *different*.

THEAET. Necessarily.

SOCR. And we said earlier that there was no limit to the number of things that are active or of things that are acted upon by them.

THEAET. Yes.

---

[1] By δύναμις the capacity of acting or being acted upon, mentioned at 156A, is specially meant, though the word has vaguer senses.

159. SOCR. And further, that when one of these is married to a succession of different partners, the offspring produced will be not the same but different.

B. THEAET. Certainly.

SOCR. Now let us take you or me or any other instance to which the principle applies—Socrates in health and Socrates ill : are we to call one of these *like* the other or unlike ?

THEAET. You mean : Is the ill Socrates taken as a whole like Socrates in health taken as a whole ?

SOCR. You understand me perfectly : that is just what I mean.

THEAET. Then of course he is unlike.

SOCR. And consequently, inasmuch as he is unlike, a different thing ?

THEAET. Necessarily.

C. SOCR. And you would say the same of Socrates asleep or in any other of the conditions we mentioned ?

THEAET. Yes.

SOCR. Then any one of the objects whose nature it is to act upon something will, according as it finds Socrates well or ill, treat me as a different thing ?

THEAET. Of course it will.

SOCR. And consequently the pair of us—I who am acted upon and the thing that acts on me—will have different offspring in the two cases ?

THEAET. Naturally.

SOCR. Now when I am in health and drink wine, it seems pleasant to me and sweet.

THEAET. Yes.

SOCR. Because, in accordance with the account we accepted earlier, agent and patient give birth to sweetness and a

D. sensation, both movements that pass simultaneously. The sensation, on the patient's side, makes the tongue percipient, while, on the side of the wine, the sweetness, moving in the region of the wine,[1] causes it both to be and to appear sweet to the healthy tongue.

THEAET. Certainly that was what we agreed upon.

SOCR. But when it finds me in ill health, to begin with, the person it finds is not really the same ; for the one it now meets with is unlike the other.

THEAET. Yes.

E. SOCR. And so this pair—Socrates in this condition and the

---

[1] περὶ αὐτὸν φερομένη seems to mean, as it were, ' spreading itself over the wine ' as whiteness saturated the surface of the thing seen (156E).

55

159E.   drinking of the wine—produce a different offspring : in the
region of the tongue a sensation of sourness, and in the region
of the wine a sourness that arises as a movement there.   The
wine becomes, not sourness, but sour ; while I become, not
a sensation, but sentient.

THEAET.   Undoubtedly.

The assertion here that Socrates-ill is a totally different person
from Socrates-well may seem fallacious.   But the whole argument
is confined within the limits of the earlier account of sense-perception.   Socrates is for this purpose nothing more than a bundle of
sense-organs.   If these sense-organs are perpetually changing (as
the theory maintains), then the whole of Socrates is different at any
two moments.   So at 166B Protagoras is made to say that we have
no right to speak of a single person continuously existing, but only
of an infinite number, if change of quality is always taking place,
as it is on our Heracleitean premiss.   Socrates is, accordingly,
justified in drawing the three conclusions that follow : (1) No
percipient can have the same sensation or perception twice, since
both subject (organ) and object will be different ; (2) No two
percipients can have precisely similar sensations or perceptions from
the same object ; (3) Neither percipient nor sense-object can exist
independently of the other.   These conclusions will yield the final
result, that no one can challenge the truth of my perception on the
grounds that he perceives an object different from mine, and that
that object is a quality which resides in the thing independently of
either percipient, so that one of us must be ' misperceiving ' it.

159E.   SOCR.   It follows, then, (1) that, on my side, I shall never
become percipient in just this way of any other thing ; for to
a different object belongs a different perception, and in acting
on its percipient it is acting on [1] a person who is in a different
condition and so a different person.   Also (2) on its side,
160.   the thing which acts on me can never meet with someone else
and generate the same offspring and come to be of just this
quality ; for when it brings to birth another thing from
another person, it will itself come to be of another quality.

----

[1] ποιεῖ ' is acting on ' (cf. τὸ ποιοῦν ἐμὲ in the next clause and 160c, 4), not
' makes him a different person ' ; it *finds* a different person, since the sense-
organ is, on our Heracleitean principle, perpetually changing.   The agent
itself is different ; so the combination of a different object and a different
subject must produce a different sensation.   The expression ποιεῖν τινα for
' doing something to a person ' is a slight extension of the common usages,
εὖ ποιεῖν τινα, οὐκ οἶδ' ὅτι χρῆμά με ποιεῖς (Ar., *Wasps* 697), ταῦτα τοῦτον
ἐποίησα (Hdt.).

160. THEAET. That is so.

SOCR. Further, (3) I shall not come to have this sensation *for myself*,[1] nor will the object come to be of such a quality *for itself.*

THEAET. No.

SOCR. Rather, when I become percipient, I must become percipient *of something*; for I cannot have a perception and have it of nothing; and equally the object, when it

B. becomes sweet or sour and so on, must become so *to someone*: it cannot become sweet and yet sweet to nobody.

THEAET. Quite so.

SOCR. Nothing remains, then, I suppose, but that it and I should be or become—whichever expression we are to use—*for each other*; necessity binds together our existence, but binds neither of us to anything else, nor each of us to himself[2]; so we can only be bound to one another. Accordingly, whether we speak of something ' being ' or of its ' becoming ', we must speak of it as being or becoming *for someone*, or *of something* or *towards something*; but

C. we must not speak, or allow others to speak, of a thing as either being or becoming anything just in and by itself. That is the conclusion to which our argument points.

THEAET. Certainly, Socrates.

SOCR. And so, since what acts upon me is for me and for no one else, I, and no one else, am actually perceiving it.

THEAET. Of course.

SOCR. Then my perception is true for me; for its object at any moment is my reality,[3] and I am, as Protagoras says, a judge of what is for me, that it is, and of what is not, that it is not.

THEAET. So it appears.

D. SOCR. If, then, I am infallible and make no mistake in my state of mind about what is or becomes, how can I

---

[1] Without the co-operation of an object *of* which I am percipient, as the next speech explains. τοιοῦτος = οὕτως αἰσθανόμενος (159E, 7-8).

[2] i.e. neither subject nor object can produce just that sensation and quality in conjunction with any other object or subject; and neither of the two can produce offspring ' for itself ' without the other.

[3] τῆς ἐμῆς οὐσίας = τῶν ἐμοὶ ὄντων, what is real for me. Socrates is here stating the claim that perception is true as having the real (τὸ ὄν) for its object, as well as its claim to infallibility, next mentioned. The weak point is that ' my reality ' is in fact only ' what becomes for me ', not genuinely real in Plato's sense. Note that in his next speech Socrates speaks of what ' is *or becomes* '.

160D. fail to have knowledge of the things of which I have perception ?

THEAET. You cannot possibly fail.

SOCR. So you were perfectly right in saying that knowledge is nothing but perception ; and it has turned out that these three doctrines coincide : the doctrine of Homer and Heracleitus and all their tribe that all things move like flowing streams ; the doctrine of Protagoras, wisest of men, that Man is the measure of all things ; and Theaetetus'

E. conclusion that, on these grounds, it results that perception is knowledge.

Is it not so, Theaetetus ? May we say that this is your newborn child which I have brought to birth ? What do you say ?

THEAET. I can only agree, Socrates.

Thus Socrates claims to have brought to light the full meaning of Theaetetus' identification of knowledge with perception. The first step was to analyse the nature of perception. Plato was forced to give his own account of the process, based on the Heracleitean principle which he accepted so far as sensible things are concerned. He has also adopted Protagoras' doctrine as applied to my immediate awareness of sense-objects, including dream images and hallucinations. In this field I am the measure of what ' becomes for me ' or ' appears to me ' ; if wine tastes sour to me, no one can say I am mistaken because the wine really is sweet in itself. So perception has one of the two marks of knowledge, infallibility. And, if we can accept Protagoras' identification of what appears to me with what is, or is real, ignoring the addition ' for me ' or ' to me ' and the distinction between being and becoming, the case will be complete. Socrates has, at any rate, dealt fairly with Theaetetus in making the best case for his candidate that can be made.

160E–161B. *Interlude. Criticism begins*

A short interlude marks that the first stage of the dialectical process is now complete. Socrates has drawn out the full meaning of Theaetetus' suggested definition of knowledge. The second stage, criticism, is now to begin. What follows has sometimes been misunderstood through a failure to see what the scope of the criticism precisely is.

First, it is not directed against the theory of perception as a whole, or against those elements in the theory which Plato has adopted from Heracleitus and Protagoras. If the account of the nature of perception were now to be rejected, obviously we should not know what we were denying when we finally deny that perception is knowledge. This fabric stands unshaken. The process of perception is such as it has been described. The question is whether, being such, it possesses all the marks of knowledge.

At the same time, Plato has to explain exactly how much he has taken from Heracleitus and Protagoras, and exactly where he refuses to follow them further. The Heracleitean dogma ' All things are in motion ' can be accepted if ' all things ' is restricted (as it is in the theory of perception) to sensible physical objects. But there are other things—intelligible objects—to which it does not apply ; and these are, for Plato, the true realities. If these were always changing, no true statement could ever be made and there could be no such thing as knowledge or discourse. Similarly, the Protagorean maxim, man the measure of all things, can be accepted if ' all things ' is restricted (as our theory restricts it) to the immediate objects of our awareness in sensation or perception, in which no element of judgment is supposed to be involved. But Protagoras' phrase ' what appears to me ' was not so restricted ; it included what appears *true* to me, what I judge or think or believe to be true. Plato will deny that whatever I judge to be true must be true, simply, or even true *to me* or *for me*. Hence, in the following argument, criticism is directed partly against the claim of perception, as Plato has defined it, to be knowledge ; partly against those elements of Heracleitean and Protagorean doctrine which go beyond what Plato has accepted.

160E. SOCR. Here at last, then, after our somewhat painful labour, is the child we have brought to birth, whatever sort of creature it may be. His birth should be followed by the ceremony of carrying him round the hearth [1] ; we must look at our offspring from every angle to make sure we
161. are not taken in by a lifeless phantom not worth the rearing. Or do you think an infant of yours must be reared in any case and not exposed ? Will you bear to see him put to the proof, and not be in a passion if your first-born should be taken away ?

THEOD. Theaetetus will bear it, Socrates ; he is thoroughly good-tempered. But do explain what is wrong with the conclusion.

SOCR. You have an absolute passion for discussion, Theodorus. I like the way you take me for a sort of bag

[1] The Amphidromia was held a few days after birth. The infant received its name and was associated with the family cult by being carried round the central hearth.

161. full of arguments, and imagine I can easily pull out a proof
B. to show that our conclusion is wrong. You don't see what is happening : the arguments never come out of me, they always come from the person I am talking with. I am only at a slight advantage in having the skill to get some account of the matter from another's wisdom and entertain it with fair treatment. So now, I shall not give any explanation myself, but try to get it out of our friend.

THEOD. That is better, Socrates ; do as you say.

161B–163A. *Some objections against Protagoras*

Theodorus is here drawn into the discussion, to mark that the first objections will be made against his personal friend, Protagoras.

161B. SOCR. Well then, Theodorus, shall I tell you a thing that surprises me in your friend Protagoras ?
C. THEOD. What is that ?

SOCR. The opening words of his treatise. In general, I am delighted with his statement that what seems to anyone also is ; but I am surprised that he did not begin his *Truth* with the words : The measure of all things is the pig, or the baboon, or some sentient creature still more uncouth. There would have been something magnificent in so disdainful an opening, telling us that all the time, while we were admiring him for a wisdom more than mortal,
D. he was in fact no wiser than a tadpole, to say nothing of any other human being. What else can we say, Theodorus ? If what every man believes as a result of perception is indeed to be true for him ; if, just as no one is to be a better judge of what another experiences, so no one is better entitled to consider whether what another thinks is true or false, and (as we have said more than once) every man is to have his own beliefs for himself alone and they are all right and true—then, my friend, where is the wisdom of
E. Protagoras, to justify his setting up to teach others and to be handsomely paid for it, and where is our comparative ignorance or the need for us to go and sit at his feet, when each of us is himself the measure of his own wisdom ? Must we not suppose that Protagoras speaks in this way to flatter the ears of the public ? I say nothing of my own case or of the ludicrous predicament to which my art of midwifery is brought, and, for that matter, this whole business of philosophic conversation ; for to set about overhauling and testing one another's notions and opinions when

162.   those of each and every one are right, is a tedious and monstrous display of folly, if the Truth of Protagoras is really
truthful and not amusing herself with oracles delivered
from the unapproachable shrine of his book.

THEOD. Protagoras was my friend, Socrates, as you were
saying, and I would rather he were not refuted by means
of any admissions of mine. On the other hand, I cannot
resist you against my convictions ; so you had better go
back to Theaetetus, whose answers have shown, in any case,
how well he can follow your meaning.

B.   SOCR. If you went to a wrestling-school at Sparta, Theodorus, would you expect to look on at the naked wrestlers,
some of them making a poor show, and not strip so as to
let them compare your own figure ?

THEOD. Why not, if they were likely to listen to me
and not insist, just as I believe I shall persuade you to
let me look on now ? The limbs are stiff at my age ; and
instead of dragging me into your exercises, you will try
a fall with a more supple youth.

SOCR. Well, Theodorus, as the proverb says, ' what likes
you mislikes not me.' So I will have recourse to the
C.   wisdom of Theaetetus.

Tell me, then, first, Theaetetus, about the point we have
just made : are not *you* surprised that you should turn
out, all of a sudden, to be every bit as wise as any other
man and even as any god ? Or would you say that Protagoras' maxim about the measure does not apply to gods
just as much as to men ?

THEAET. Certainly I think it does ; and, to answer your
question, I am very much surprised. When we were dis-
D.   cussing what they mean by saying that what seems to
anyone really is to him who thinks it so,[1] that appeared
to me quite satisfactory ; but now, all in a moment, it has
taken on a very different complexion.

SOCR. That, my friend, is because you are young ; so you
lend a ready ear to clap-trap and it convinces you. Protagoras or his representative will have an answer to this.
He will say : ' You good people sitting there, boys and
old men together, this is all clap-trap. You drag in the
gods, whose existence or non-existence I expressly refuse
E.   to discuss in my speeches and writings, and you count

---

[1] The ambiguity of δοκεῖν, including ' what *seems* ' (τὸ δοκοῦν), which might
mean only perception, and ' he who *thinks* ' or ' *judges* ' (ὁ δοκῶν), is here neatly
illustrated.

162E.   upon appeals to the vulgar such as this : how strange that
         any human individual is to be no wiser than the lowest
         of the brutes ! You go entirely by what looks probable,
         without a word of argument or proof. If a mathematician
         like Theodorus elected to argue from probability in geometry,
         he wouldn't be worth an ace. So you and Theodorus might
         consider whether you are going to allow questions of this
163.   importance to be settled by plausible appeals to mere
         likelihood.'
         THEAET.   Well, you would not think that right, Socrates,
         any more than we should.
         SOCR.   It seems, then, we must attack the question in
         another way. That is what you and Theodorus think.
         THEAET.   Certainly we must.

Socrates has brought against Protagoras two objections, which
are not of equal cogency. (1) Why not ' Pig the measure of all
things ' ? On the level of mere sensation, man has no privileged
position. The pig, or the anthropomorphic god (if such a being
exists), is just as much the measure of his own sensations. Plato,
who confined his acceptance of the maxim to that level, would
admit this. But Protagoras went beyond sensation and perception to include under ' what seems to me ' what I think or
judge to be true. The serious objection is : (2) ' If what every
man believes as the result of perception is to be true for him ',
how can any man be wiser than another ? Here Plato parts
company with Protagoras. When we return to these objections,
we shall deny that every man is the measure of the truth of his
own judgments.

163A–164B. *Objections to a simple identification of Perceiving and
         Knowing*

Meanwhile, Protagoras having registered his protest against
clap-trap, the question of judgment is dropped. Socrates turns
to some preliminary criticisms of Theaetetus' proposition : Perception is knowledge. These criticisms are made here because
Protagoras will be able to answer them presently in his Defence.
They take ' perception ', as we have now analysed it, in the strictest
and narrowest sense, and point out that we shall find ourselves in
curious difficulties if we assert that such perception is the only
form of knowledge. The objections are later called captious or
' eristic ', not because they are invalid, but because they take
Theaetetus' statement more literally than he intended. They
serve a purpose by calling attention to various meanings of the

word 'know' (ἐπίστασθαι). (1) I am said to 'know' Syriac [1]
when I *understand the meaning* of written or spoken symbols.
(2) I 'know' Socrates when I have *become acquainted with* a certain
person by sense-perception and possess a record of this acquaintance
in *memory*. In neither of these senses can 'I know' be simply
equated with 'I am perceiving'. It is necessary and fair to make
Theaetetus see what a simple identification of perceiving and
'knowing' commits him to.

163A. SOCR. Let us look at it in this way, then—this question
whether knowledge and perception are, after all, the same
thing or not. For that, you remember, was the point to
which our whole discussion was directed, and it was for
its sake that we stirred up all this swarm of queer doctrines,
wasn't it ?

THEAET. Quite true.

B. SOCR. Well, are we going to agree that, whenever we
perceive something by sight or hearing, we also at the same
time know it ? Take the case of a foreign language we
have not learnt. Are we to say that we do not hear the
sounds that foreigners utter, or that we both hear and
know what they are saying ? Or again, when we don't
know our letters, are we to maintain that we don't see
them when we look at them, or that, since we see them,
we do know them ?

THEAET. We shall say, Socrates, that we know just so
much of them as we do see or hear. The shape and colour
of the letters we both see and know ; we hear and at the
C. same time know the rising and falling accents of the voice ;
but we neither perceive by sight and hearing nor yet know
what a schoolmaster or an interpreter could tell us about
them.

SOCR. Well done, Theaetetus. I had better not raise
objections to that, for fear of checking your growth.[2] But
look, here is another objection threatening. How are we
going to parry it ?

THEAET. What is that ?

D. SOCR. It is this. Suppose someone to ask : 'Is it possible

---

[1] Συριστὶ ἐπίστασθαι (Xenophon), γράμματα ἐπίστασθαι.

[2] Socrates might object that to 'know' a language does not mean hearing
unintelligible sounds or seeing black marks on paper, but to know the meaning,
which we do not see or hear. But Plato does not want to embark on a discussion of what it is we know when we know the meaning of words. That
would involve bringing in the Forms, which he is determined, so far as possible,
to leave out of account. So the point is not pressed.

163D. for a man who has once come to know something and
still preserves a memory of it, not to know just that thing
that he remembers at the moment when he remembers
it ? ' This is, perhaps, rather a long-winded way of putting
the question. I mean : Can a man who has become acquainted [1] with something and remembers it, not know it ?
THEAET. Of course not, Socrates ; the supposition is
monstrous.
SOCR. Perhaps I am talking nonsense, then. But consider : you call seeing ' perceiving ', and sight ' perception ',
don't you ?
THEAET. I do.

E.   SOCR. Then, according to our earlier statement,[2] a man
who sees something acquires from that moment knowledge
of the thing he sees ?
THEAET. Yes.
SOCR. Again, you recognise such a thing as memory ?
THEAET. Yes.
SOCR. Memory of nothing, or of something ?
THEAET. Of something, surely.
SOCR. Of what one has become acquainted with and per-
ceived—that sort of things ?
THEAET. Of course.
SOCR. So a man sometimes remembers what he has seen ?
THEAET. He does.
SOCR. Even when he shuts his eyes ? Or does he forget
when he shuts them ?
THEAET. No, Socrates ; that would be a monstrous thing
to say.

164.   SOCR. All the same, we shall have to say it, if we are to
save our former statement. Otherwise, it goes by the
board.
THEAET. I certainly have a suspicion that you are right,
but I don't quite see how. You must tell me.
SOCR. In this way. One who sees, we say, acquires knowledge of what he sees, because it is agreed that sight or
perception and knowledge are the same thing.
THEAET. Certainly.
SOCR. But suppose this man who sees and acquires knowledge of what he has seen, shuts his eyes ; then he remembers
the thing, but does not see it. Isn't that so ?

---

[1] μανθάνειν here is wider than ' learn ', and equivalent to the phrase ' come
to know something ' (ἐπιστήμων γενέσθαι) above.
[2] The simple identification of perceiving with knowing, recalled at 163A.

164. THEAET. Yes.

B.   SOCR. But 'does not see it' means 'does not know it', since 'sees' and 'knows' mean the same.

THEAET. True.

SOCR. Then the conclusion is that a man who has come to know a thing and still remembers it does not know it, since he does not see it; and we said that would be a monstrous conclusion.

THEAET. Quite true.

SOCR. Apparently, then, if you say that knowledge and perception are the same thing, it leads to an impossibility.

THEAET. So it seems.

SOCR. Then we shall have to say they are different.

THEAET. I suppose so.

In this argument memory first comes into sight. Remembering is a kind of knowing different from perceiving as we have analysed it. We seem to have immediate awareness of past objects not now given in the actual process of perception. If Theaetetus' definition of knowledge as perception is to be saved, 'perception' must be stretched to cover awareness of memory-objects. Since there would be no objection to that, Socrates here breaks off what threatens to become a mere dispute about words. The conclusion stands, however, that 'I know' has other meanings than 'I am (now) perceiving'. And the nature of memory will call for analysis later.

164C–165E. *Socrates undertakes to defend Protagoras*

In an interlude Socrates consents to state, on Protagoras' behalf, a reply to the criticism urged against Man the measure of all things. Incidentally, he adds another 'eristic' objection to Theaetetus' equation of perceiving with knowing.

164C.   SOCR. What, then, can knowledge be? Apparently we must begin all over again. But wait a moment, Theaetetus. What are we doing?

THEAET. Doing about what?

SOCR. It seems to me we are behaving towards our theory like an ill-bred gamecock who springs away from his adversary and starts crowing over him before he is beaten.

THEAET. How so?

SOCR. It looks as if we were content to have reached an agreement resting on mere verbal consistency and to have got the better of the theory by the methods of a professional controversialist. We profess to be seeking wisdom, not

164D. competing for victory, but we are unconsciously behaving just like one of those redoubtable disputants.

THEAET. I still don't understand what you mean.

SOCR. Well, I will try to make the point clear, so far as I can see it. We were asking whether one who had become acquainted with something and remembered it could fail to know it. Then we pointed out that a man who shuts his eyes after seeing something, remembers but does not see ; and so concluded that at the same moment he both remembers the thing and does not know it. That, we said, was impossible. And so no one was left to tell Protagoras' tale [1], or yours either, about knowledge and perception being the same thing.

E. THEAET. So it appears.

SOCR. I fancy it would be very different if the author of the first story were still alive. He would have put up a good fight for his offspring. But he is dead, and here are we trampling on the orphan. Even its appointed guardians, like Theodorus here, will not come to the rescue. However, we will step into the breach ourselves and see that it has fair play.

THEOD. In point of fact, Socrates, it is rather Callias, son
165. of Hipponicus,[2] who is Protagoras' trustee. My own inclinations diverted me at rather an early age from abstract discussions to geometry. All the same, I shall be grateful for any succour you can give him.

SOCR. Very good, Theodorus. You shall see what my help will amount to. For one might commit oneself to even stranger conclusions, if one were as careless in the use of language as we commonly are in our assertions and denials. Am I to enlarge upon this to you or to Theaetetus ?

THEOD. To the company in general ; but let the younger man answer your questions. It will not be such a disgrace
B. to him to be caught tripping.

SOCR. Let me put, then, the most formidable poser of all, which I take to be this : Can the same person know something and also not know that which he knows ?

THEOD. Well, Theaetetus, what are we to answer ?

THEAET. That it is impossible, I suppose.

SOCR. Not if you say that seeing is knowing. How are you going to deal with a question that leaves no loophole,

[1] A proverbial expression.

[2] A wealthy amateur of sophistry, who had entertained Protagoras on his visit to Athens.

165B. when you are trapped like a beast in a pit and an imperturbable gentleman puts his hand over one of your eyes and asks

C. if you can see his coat with the eye that is covered ?

THEAET. I suppose I should say : No, not with that one, but I can with the other.

SOCR. So you both see and do not see the same thing at the same time ?

THEAET. Yes, in a sort of way.

SOCR. Never mind about the sort of way, he will reply ; that was not the question I set you, but whether, when you know a thing, you also do not know it. In this instance you are obviously seeing something you don't see, and you have agreed that seeing is knowing and not seeing is not knowing. Now draw your conclusion. What is the consequence ?

D. THEAET. Well, I conclude that the consequence contradicts my thesis.

SOCR. Yes, and you might have been reduced to the same condition by a number of further questions : whether knowing can be keen or dim ; whether you can know from close at hand what you cannot know from a distance, or know the same thing with more or less intensity. A mercenary skirmisher in the war of words might lie in wait for you armed with a thousand such questions, once you have identified knowledge and perception. He would make his assaults upon hearing and smelling and suchlike senses and put you

E. to confusion, sustaining his attack until your admiration of his inestimable skill betrayed you into his toils ; and thereupon, leading you captive and bound, he would hold you to ransom for such a sum as you and he might agree upon.[1]

And now, perhaps, you may wonder what argument Protagoras will find to defend his position. Shall we try to put it into words ?

THEAET. By all means.

The ' most formidable ' objection here added is, like the earlier ones, valid against Theaetetus' position, since he has accepted the account of perception as the commerce between a sense-organ and an external object. If that is what perception is, then to identify it with knowledge does lead to these absurdities. The objections

---

[1] Protagoras, if a pupil objected to the fee he charged, made him swear in a temple how much he thought what he had learnt was worth. *Protag.* 328B ; Ar., *E.N.* 1164a, 24.

do not touch Protagoras, who did not limit knowledge to perception. They are called captious because they only apply to Theaetetus' statement when that is taken more literally than he meant, and do not apply to Protagoras, upon whom Socrates has seemed to father all this complex of doctrines he has constructed by his dialectical combinations. Such cavils do not dispose of the whole point of view which Theaetetus meant to bring forward, and we do not want to quarrel about words. Further, they do not impair Plato's own doctrine of the nature of sense-perception, or shake the claim of perception, as so defined, to yield *infallible* awareness of a private object, an element in that doctrine borrowed from Protagoras himself. It still remains to be shown why Plato refuses to call such awareness ' knowledge '. Accordingly, he admits frankly that the whole position has not been disposed of by means of a few essays in sophistical disputation.

165E–168C. *The Defence of Protagoras*

The Defence now put by Socrates into the mouth of Protagoras falls into three main divisions. First comes a protest against the ' captious ' objections and a reply to them. The central and most important part attempts to meet the really damaging criticism of Protagoras himself : If every man is the measure of his own *judgments*, how can Protagoras set up to be wiser than others ? Finally, in a peroration, the sophist is (ironically) represented as exhorting the dialectician to argue seriously, not catching at words, but trying to understand what the opponent really means.

SOCR. No doubt, then, Protagoras will make all the points we have put forward in our attempt to defend him, and 166. at the same time will come to close quarters with the assailant, dismissing us with contempt.[1] ' Your admirable Socrates ', he will say, ' finds a little boy who is scared at being asked whether one and the same person can remember and at the same time not know one and the same thing. When the child is frightened into saying No, because he cannot foresee the consequence, Socrates turns the conversation so as to make a figure of fun of my unfortunate self. You take things much too easily, Socrates. The truth of the matter is this : when you ask someone questions in order to canvass some opinion of mine and he is found tripping, then I am

[1] Protagoras will both (τε) urge, as we have done for him, that we are talking clap-trap (162D), that verbal disputation is futile (164B) and we must use words more carefully (165A), and (καὶ) will come to grips (not with us, but) with the sophistic skirmisher and his armoury of eristic cavils, despising us for our feeble surrender to such weapons.

166.   refuted only if his answers are such as I should have given ;
B.   if they are different, it is he who is refuted, not I. For
instance, do you think you will find anyone to admit that
one's present memory of a past impression is an impression
of the same character as one had during the original experience, which is now over ? It is nothing of the sort. Or
again, will anyone shrink from admitting that it is possible
for the same person to know and not to know the same thing ?
Or, if he is frightened of saying that, will he ever allow that
a person who is changed is the *same* as he was before the
change occurred ; or rather, that he is *one* person at all,
and not several, indeed an infinite succession of persons,
C.   provided change goes on happening—if we are really to be
on the watch against one another's attempts to catch at
words ?

Protagoras here makes three replies : (1) The first is to the objection (163D) : You admit I can remember and so ' know ' an object
I am not now seeing ; but you say ' I do not see ' = ' I do not
know ' ; therefore I do not know what I remember, and we have
the contradiction : I know and do not know the same thing. Protagoras replies : The image before my memory is not the *same thing*
as a present sense-impression or even like it. So it is not true that
I know (remember) and do not know (see) the *same thing*. All
that the objection in fact established was that ' perception ' must
be stretched to include awareness of memory images.

(2) ' No one will shrink from admitting that the same person can
know and not know the same thing.' This replies to the ' most
formidable ' puzzle of the man with one eye open, one shut (166B).
Theaetetus did suggest the answer : If we identify perception with
the physical commerce between organ and object, one of my eyes
does know the object, the other does not. This reply was brushed
aside ; and if we shrink from it, Protagoras says, another answer
is ready.

(3) We have no right to speak of a person as *the same* at different
moments. This reply is based on the theory of perception itself,
which holds that the subject (organ) never remains the same for
two moments together. Socrates himself has used this premiss for
his conclusion at 160A : No one can have the same perception twice.
We have, in fact, spoken all through as if the physical organ were
the subject that perceives, and the person a mere bundle of sense-
organs. Hence we could argue that Socrates-well was ' totally
different ', as a measure of the sweetness or sourness of wine, from
Socrates-ill. If the subject, as well as the object, is perpetually

changing, objections which turn upon the *same* person knowing a
not knowing the *same* thing fall to the ground.

Thus the captious objections to Theaetetus' position are disposed
of. We now turn to Protagoras' own doctrine and Socrates' criticisms of that (161C ff.).

166C. SOCR. (*continues*). ' No,' he will say; ' show a more
generous spirit by attacking what I actually say ; and prove,
if you can, that we have not, each one of us, his peculiar
perceptions, or that, granting them to be peculiar, it would
not follow that what appears to each becomes—or is, if we
may use the word ' is '—for him alone to whom it appears.
With this talk of pigs and baboons, you are behaving like
a pig yourself,[1] and, what is more, you tempt your hearers
D. to treat my writings in the same way, which is not fair.

So much for the objection : ' Why not pig the measure of all
things ? ' That really needs no answer. For the rest, Socrates
will not attempt to disprove the propositions here asserted : that
each man has his private sensations and perceptions, which are
infallible. This was precisely the Protagorean element adopted by
Plato himself. Protagoras is not responsible for Theaetetus' suggestion, interpreted as asserting that knowledge consists solely of such
perceptions. On the other hand, the doctrine ' man the measure '
was not confined to perception, but included judgment. To this
extension it was objected : If each man is the measure of his own
judgments or beliefs, how can one be wiser than another ? Here
we come to the core of the Defence, which attempts to explain how
one man can be wiser than another, although every man's judgments
are true for him.

166D. SOCR. (*continues*). ' For I do indeed assert that the truth
is as I have written : each one of us is a measure of what is
and of what is not ; but there is all the difference in the
world between one man and another just in the very fact
that what is and appears to one is different from what is
and appears to the other. And as for wisdom and the
wise man, I am very far from saying they do not exist.
By a wise man I mean precisely a man who can change
any one of us, when what is bad appears and is to him, and
make what is good appear and be to him. In this statement,
again, don't set off in chase of words, but let me explain

---

[1] The pig, in Greek, is an emblem of stupidity (ἀμαθία). *Lach.* 169D : ' Would
not any pig know . . .' Cic., *Ac. Post.* i, 5, 18 : *non sus docet Minervam.*
This remark is less offensive than the English sounds.

166E. still more clearly what I mean. Remember how it was put earlier in the conversation : to the sick man his food appears sour and is so ; to the healthy man it is and appears the opposite. Now there is no call to represent either of the two as wiser—that cannot be—nor is the sick man to be

167. pronounced unwise because he thinks[1] as he does, or the healthy man wise because he thinks differently. What is wanted is a change to the opposite condition, because the other state is better.

' And so too in education a change has to be effected from the worse condition to the better ; only, whereas the physician produces a change by means of drugs, the sophist does it by discourse. It is not that a man makes someone who previously thought what is false think what is true (for it is not possible either to think the thing that is not or to think anything but what one experiences, and all

B. experiences are true) ; rather, I should say, when someone by reason of a depraved condition of mind has thoughts of a like character, one makes him, by reason of a sound condition, think other and sound thoughts, which some people ignorantly call true, whereas I should say that one set of thoughts is better than the other, but not in any way truer.[2] And as for the wise, my dear Socrates, so far from calling them frogs, I call them, when they have to do with the body, physicians, and when they have to do with plants, husbandmen. For I assert that husbandmen too, when plants are sickly and have depraved sensations, substitute

C. for these sensations that are sound and healthy[3] ; and moreover that wise and honest public speakers substitute in the community sound for unsound views of what is

---

[1] ' Thinks ', ' judges ' (δοξάζει), here replaces ' appears ' (φαίνεσθαι). What is meant is the judgment stating the fact of a sense-impression : ' This food seems and is to me sour.' If Socrates' earlier expression, ' what every man believes as the result of perception ' (ὃ ἂν δι' αἰσθήσεως δοξάζῃ, 161D) is restricted to such judgments, they are not ignorant or foolish judgments ; nor are they false.

[2] The text is doubtful. The best sense is obtained by taking τίς (167A, 7) as the subject of a single sentence from ἐπεὶ (A, 6) to οὐδέν (B, 4). Read πονηρᾷ and χρηστῇ (sc. ψυχῆς ἕξει, with W.) and omit τὰ φαντάσματα (with Diels, Vors.⁴ ii, 225). It is the sophist, not the χρηστὴ ἕξις, that ' makes ' the change to sound thoughts. The reading χρηστὴ will then be explained as an attempt to provide the ἐποίησε following it with a subject, made by someone who did not see that τίς (governing the earlier ἐποίησε, A. 7) is still the subject.

[3] Omitting τε καὶ ἀληθεῖς. Diels' suggestion (Vors.⁴ ii, 225) ὥστε καὶ ἀληθεῖς gives a wrong sense, for the unhealthy sensations are also true. The conjectures ἀληθείας (Schleiermacher), ἕξεις (Diès), πάθας (Richards) are not convincing.

167C.   right. For I hold that whatever practices seem right and
laudable to any particular State are so, for that State, so
long as it holds by them. Only, when the practices are, in
any particular case, unsound for them, the wise man substitutes others that are and appear sound. On the same
principle the sophist, since he can in the same manner guide
his pupils in the way they should go, is wise and worth a
D.   considered fee to them when their education is completed. In this way it is true both that some men are wiser
than others and that no one thinks falsely ; and you,
whether you like it or not, must put up with being a measure,
since by these considerations my doctrine is saved from
shipwreck.[1]

In this central section there is no reason to doubt that Socrates
is doing what he professes to do—defending Protagoras' thesis as
Protagoras, if he were alive, would himself have defended it.[2]
The form of the argument is necessarily adapted to the context ;
but the contents are, in all probability, Protagorean. Protagoras
was the first to claim the title of ' Sophist ', with its suggestion of a
superior wisdom.[3] He must have reconciled this claim with his
doctrine that all opinions are equally true, and can only have done
so by arguing, as he does here, that some opinions are ' better ',
though not truer, than others, and that his own business, as an educator, was to substitute better opinions for worse. The analogy
of the husbandman substituting sound and healthy sensations in
plants is an archaic touch,[4] suggesting that Plato may be drawing
on Protagoras' own writings. Protagoras' special profession was
to educate men and make them good citizens ; and he taught the
art of Rhetoric, which was to enable the public speaker to offer
good counsel to the assembly in an effective form. He must have
held the corresponding view, here stated, about the laws and cus-
toms of States, considered as the judgments or decisions ($\delta\delta\xi\alpha\iota$) of
the community. Such laws and customs are ' right ' for that
community so long as it holds by them ; but a wise statesman can
try to substitute others that are ' better ' or ' sounder '. We may
conclude that Plato here is fairly reproducing the standpoint of the
historic Protagoras.

---

[1] σώζεται ὁ λόγος seems to allude to μῦθος ἀπώλετο ὁ Πρωταγόρειος, 164D. Cf.
Rep. 621B μῦθος ἐσώθη καὶ οὐκ ἀπώλετο.
   [2] Cf. H. Gomperz, Sophistik u. Rhetorik, p. 261.   [3] Protag. 317B.
   [4] Ps.-Arist., de plant 815a, 15, attributes to Anaxagoras and Empedocles
the view that plants have sensation and pleasure and pain. The analogy
between physician, husbandman, and educator recurs at Protag. 334, and
Symp. 187A, both places where Plato is using earlier material.

What, then, does the Defence actually maintain ? The argument advances, by stages, from the position where Plato has already agreed with Protagoras to the position which he will challenge in the sequel.

(1) At the level of physical sensations or perceptions, it has been admitted (159–160) that a sick man's abnormal sensations are not less ' true ' than the healthy man's normal ones, and that they are partly determined by his own state of body. The physician, Protagoras argues, is called in to change that state, because it is generally agreed, by physicians and patients alike, that the healthy sensations are ' better '. ' Better ' presumably means ' more pleasant ' ; and each man is the sole judge of what he finds pleasant. The physician can be called ' wise ' because he knows how to change the worse state to a better. The point that remains obscure is what sort of knowledge enables him to do this.

(2) The position of the educator is said to be analogous to the physician's ; it is his business to change our mental condition from unsound to sound, so that our judgments, beliefs, opinions, may be sounder, though not truer. The crucial statement is : ' It is not that a man makes someone who previously thought what is false think what is true ; for it is not possible either to think the thing that is not or to think anything beyond what one experiences, and all experiences are true.' The last words refer to Socrates' objection : ' If what every man believes as a result of perception is indeed to be true for him ; if, just as no one is to be a better judge of what another *experiences* (πάθος), so no one is better entitled to consider whether what another *thinks* (δόξαν) is true or false ', where is the superior wisdom of Protagoras ? Protagoras' reply, ' No one can think anything beyond what he experiences, and all experiences are true ', refers primarily to judgments which are supposed merely to register the fact of a present sensation : I judge that this wine seems sour to me. No one can challenge the truth of such a judgment. But in the same breath Protagoras extends this claim to all judgments or beliefs in the general statement : ' It is impossible to think the thing that is not ', *i.e.*, to think what is false. The educator cannot, therefore, substitute truer beliefs ; but only ' sounder ' ones. What ' sounder ' means is left obscure. It does not mean ' normal ', for that would set up the majority as a norm or measure for the minority. It can only mean more useful or expedient : a sound belief is one that *will* produce better effects in the future.[1] ' Better effects ', again, must mean effects that will seem better to me when the sophist has trained me.

[1] Protagoras' position should not be confused with modern Pragmatism, which does not assert that all beliefs must be equally true.

I shall then prefer my new beliefs to those which I now prefer.
The same argument applies to the laws and customs of the State.
'Whatever practices seem right (δίκαια) and laudable (καλά) to
any particular State are so, for that State, so long as it holds by
them '. Thus it is legally right and socially approved that Moham-
medans should have several wives, Englishmen one only. But a
statesman may try to substitute ' sounder ' customs. This again
can only mean ' more expedient ' : an Englishman persuading
Turks to adopt monogamy can only urge that the results will seem
better to the converted Turk.

Such is Protagoras' position. The Defence now ends with a
peroration, in which Protagoras lectures Socrates for frivolity and
the points outstanding for serious criticism are recalled.

167D. SOCR. (*continues*). ' Now if you can dispute this doctrine in
principle, do so by argument stating the case on the other
side, or by asking questions, if you prefer that method,
which has no terrors for a man of sense ; on the contrary
it ought to be specially agreeable to him. Only there is
E. this rule to be observed : do not conduct your questioning
unfairly. It is very unreasonable that one who professes
a concern for virtue should be constantly guilty of unfairness in argument. Unfairness here consists in not observing
the distinction between a debate and a conversation. A
debate need not be taken seriously and one may trip up an
opponent to the best of one's power ; but a conversation
should be taken in earnest ; one should help out the other
party and bring home to him only those slips and fallacies
168. that are due to himself or to his earlier instructors. If
you follow this rule, your associates will lay the blame for
their confusions and perplexities on themselves and not on
you ; they will like you and court your society, and disgusted with themselves, will turn to philosophy, hoping to
escape from their former selves and become different men.
But if, like so many, you take the opposite course, you will
reach the opposite result : instead of turning your com-
B. panions to philosophy, you will make them hate the whole
business when they get older.. So, if you will take my
advice, you will meet us in the candid spirit I spoke of,
without hostility or contentiousness, and honestly consider
what we mean when we say that all things are in motion
and that what seems also is, to any individual or community. The further question whether knowledge is, or
is not, the same thing as perception, you will consider as a

168B. consequence of these principles, not (as you did just now)
C. basing your argument on the common use of words and phrases, which the vulgar twist into any sense they please and so perplex one another in all sorts of ways.'

So the Defence ends. The central part was confined to genuine Protagorean doctrine ; but here we are reminded that Socrates' dialectical construction has included also the Heracleitean flux and Theaetetus' claim that perception is the same thing as knowledge. All three elements still await serious criticism, and they are dealt with separately in the sequel. (1) The Protagorean thesis—Every judgment true for him who makes it—is refuted for the individual (169D–171C) and for the State (177C–179B) ; next (2) the unrestricted doctrine—All things are in motion—is denounced as fatal to all discourse (179C–183B) ; and (3) the identification of perception with knowledge is finally rejected (184B–186E).

168C–169D. *Interlude*

In an interlude Theodorus is again drawn into the discussion. This marks that the next section of the argument is directed against his friend Protagoras, who is not held responsible for the two other theses.

168C. SOCR. (*continues*). Such, Theodorus, is my contribution to the defence of your friend—the best I can make from my small means. Were he alive to speak for himself, it would be a much more impressive affair.
THEOD. You are not serious, Socrates ; your defence was most spirited.
SOCR. Thank you, my friend. And now, did you notice how Protagoras was reproaching us for taking a child to
D. argue with and using the boy's timidity to get the better of his own position in what he called a mere play of wit, in contrast to the solemnity of his measure of all things, and how he exhorted us to be serious about his doctrine ?
THEOD. Of course I did, Socrates.
SOCR. What then ? Do you think we should do as he says ?
THEOD. Most certainly.
SOCR. Well, the company, as you see, are all children, except yourself. If we are to treat his doctrine seriously,
E. as he enjoins, you and I must question one another. So we shall at any rate escape the charge of making light of it by discussing it with boys.
THEOD. Why, surely Theaetetus can follow up such an

168E.   investigation better than a great many men with long
        beards.
            SOCR. But not better than you, Theodorus. So don't
        imagine that you have no duty to your departed friend, but
        can leave it to me to make the best defence for him.   Please
169.   come with us a little of the way at any rate—just until we
        know whether, in the matter of mathematical demonstrations,
        you cannot help being a measure, or everybody is just as
        competent as you in geometry and astronomy and all the
        other subjects you are supposed to excel in.
            THEOD. It is no easy matter to escape questioning in your
        company, Socrates. I was deluded when I said you would
        leave me in peace and not force me into the ring like the
        Spartans : you seem to be as unrelenting as Skiron.   The
B.   Spartans tell you to go away if you will not wrestle, but
        Antaeus is more in your line : you will let no one who comes
        near you go until you have stripped him by force for a trial
        of strength.
            SOCR. Your comparisons exactly fit what is wrong with me,
        Theodorus ; but my capacity for endurance is even greater.
        I have encountered many heroes in debate, and times
        without number a Heracles or a Theseus has broken my head ;
C.   but I have so deep a passion for exercise of this sort that
        I stick to it all the same.   So don't deny me the pleasure
        of a trial, for your own benefit as well as mine.
            THEOD. I have no more to say ; lead me where you will.
        You are like Fate : no one can elude the toils of argument you
        spin for him.   But I shall not be able to oblige you beyond
        the point you have proposed.
            SOCR. Enough, if you will go so far.   And please be on
        the watch for fear we should be betrayed into arguing
D.   frivolously and be blamed for that again.
            THEOD. I will try as well as I can.

169D–171D. *Criticism of Protagoras' doctrine as extended to all
        judgments*

Socrates now opens the attack on the genuinely Protagorean
doctrine put forward in the central part of the Defence—the extension of the maxim, Man the measure, beyond the field of immediate
perception (where we accepted it) to all judgments.

Our original objection (161D) was : If all judgments are true to
him who makes them, how can one man be wiser than another ?
In the Defence Protagoras was represented as ' conceding ' that some
are wiser than others, and this might seem to weaken his case.

76

Socrates now observes that we ought to make sure of this step by deducing it formally from what Protagoras certainly did say, namely, that 'what seems to each man is to him'. Presumably, Plato wishes to avoid the imputation of attributing to Protagoras a statement which did not appear just in that form in his writings.

169D. SOCR. Let us begin, then, by coming to grips with the doctrine at the same point as before. Let us see whether or not our discontent was justified, when we criticised it as making every individual self-sufficient in wisdom. Protagoras then conceded that some people were superior in the matter of what is better or worse, and these, he said, were wise. Didn't he ?

THEOD. Yes.

SOCR. If he were here himself to make that admission,
E. instead of our conceding it for him in our defence, there would be no need to reopen the question and make sure of our ground ; but, as things are, we might be said to have no authority to make the admission on his behalf. So it will be more satisfactory to come to a more complete and clear agreement on this particular point ; for it makes a considerable difference, whether this is so or not.

THEOD. That is true.

SOCR. Let us, then, as briefly as possible, obtain his agreement, not through any third person, but from his
170. own statement.

THEOD. How ?

SOCR. In this way. He says—doesn't he ?—that what seems true [1] to anyone is true for him to whom it seems so ?

THEOD. He does.

SOCR. Well now, Protagoras, we are expressing what seems true to a man, or rather to all men, when we say that everyone without exception holds that in some respects he is wiser than his neighbours and in others they are wiser than he. For instance, in moments of great danger and distress, whether in war or in sickness or at sea, men regard as a god anyone who can take control of the situation and look to him
B. as a saviour, when his only point of superiority is his knowledge. Indeed, the world is full of people looking for those who can instruct and govern men and animals and direct their doings, and on the other hand of people who think themselves quite competent to undertake the teaching

---

[1] τὸ δοκοῦν here, as the context shows, mean 'what seems true'. Since Protagoras' maxim covered judgment, the interpretation is perfectly fair.

170B.   and governing. In all these cases what can we say, if not that men do hold that wisdom and ignorance exist among them?

THEOD.   We must say that.

SOCR.   And they hold that wisdom lies in thinking truly, and ignorance in false belief?

C.   THEOD.   Of course.

SOCR.   In that case, Protagoras, what are we to make of your doctrine? Are we to say that what men think is always true, or that it is sometimes true and sometimes false? From either supposition it results that their thoughts are not always true, but both true and false. For consider, Theodorus. Are you, or is any Protagorean, prepared to maintain that no one regards anyone else as ignorant or as making false judgments?

THEOD.   That is incredible, Socrates.

D.   SOCR.   That, however, is the inevitable consequence of the doctrine which makes man the measure of all things.

THEOD.   How so?

SOCR.   When you have formed a judgment on some matter in your own mind and express an opinion about it to me, let us grant that, as Protagoras' theory says, it is true for you; but are we to understand that it is impossible for us, the rest of the company, to pronounce any judgment upon your judgment; or, if we can, that we always pronounce your opinion to be true? Do you not rather find thousands of opponents who set their opinion against yours on every occasion and hold that your judgment and belief are false?

E.   THEOD.   I should just think so, Socrates; thousands and tens of thousands, as Homer says; and they give me all the trouble in the world.

SOCR.   And what then? Would you have us say that in such a case the opinion you hold is true for yourself and false for these tens of thousands?

THEOD.   The doctrine certainly seems to imply that.

SOCR.   And what is the consequence for Protagoras himself? Is it not this: supposing that not even he believed in man being the measure and the world in general did not believe it either—as in fact it doesn't—then this Truth which he

171.   wrote would not be true for anyone? If, on the other hand, he did believe it, but the mass of mankind does not agree with him, then, you see, it is more false than true by just so much as the unbelievers outnumber the believers.

171. THEOD. That follows, if its truth or falsity varies with each individual opinion.

SOCR. Yes, and besides that it involves a really exquisite conclusion.[1] Protagoras, for his part, admitting as he does that everybody's opinion is true, must acknowledge the truth of his opponents' belief about his own belief, where they think he is wrong.

THEOD. Certainly.

B. SOCR. That is to say, he would acknowledge his own belief to be false, if he admits that the belief of those who think him wrong is true?

THEOD. Necessarily.

SOCR. But the others, on their side, do not admit to themselves that they are wrong.

THEOD. No.

SOCR. Whereas Protagoras, once more, according to what he has written, admits that this opinion of theirs is as true as any other.

THEOD. Evidently.

SOCR. On all hands, then, Protagoras included, his opinion will be disputed, or rather Protagoras will join in the general consent—when he admits to an opponent the truth

C. of his contrary opinion, from that moment Protagoras himself will be admitting that a dog or the man in the street is not a measure of anything whatever that he does not understand. Isn't that so?

THEOD. Yes.

SOCR. Then, since it is disputed by everyone, the Truth of Protagoras is true to nobody—to himself no more than to anyone else.

THEOD. We are running my old friend too hard, Socrates.

SOCR. But it is not clear that we are outrunning the truth, my friend. Of course it is likely that, as an older man, he

D. was wiser than we are; and if at this moment he could pop his head up through the ground there as far as to the neck, very probably he would expose me thoroughly for talking such nonsense and you for agreeing to it, before he sank out of sight and took to his heels. However, we must do our best with such lights as we have and continue to say what we think.

[1] Sextus, *Math.* vii, 389, says that an argument of this form, known as 'turning the tables' (περιτροπή), was used against Protagoras by Democritus, as well as by Plato here.

Socrates' last words probably do not mean that Protagoras would, in Plato's opinion, have had any valid answer to make. The argument has fairly deduced, on Protagoras' own principles, the consequences of asserting that what every man thinks true is true for him. It does follow for Protagoras' opponents that his doctrine is not true, and, for Protagoras himself, that their belief in its falsity is true for them.

171D–172B. *Restatement of the question : wherein lies the superiority of the wise ?*

This argument, however, is *ad hominem*. The real issue between Protagoras and Plato is too serious to be disposed of so lightly, and Socrates now gives the conversation a graver turn. He begins by restating the premiss on which all, including Protagoras, are agreed : that one man can be wiser than another. Wherein can such superiority lie ? Not in the field of immediate perception of sense-qualities : there (as Plato is careful to note once more) we have agreed with Protagoras that each man is the measure of what is, or rather ' becomes ', for him. But the Defence itself claimed a superiority in wisdom for the physician, the educator, and the statesman. All these undertake to change our condition and make ' better ' things ' appear and be ' to the individual or to the State. We have still to inquire what this profession implies.

171D. SOCR. (*continues*). Now, for instance, must we not say that everyone would agree at least to this : that one man can be wiser or more ignorant than another ?

THEOD. I certainly think so.

SOCR. And further, shall we say that the doctrine would find its firmest footing in the position we traced out in

E. our defence of Protagoras : that most things—hot, dry, sweet, everything of that sort—are to each person as they appear to him ? Whereas, if there is any case in which the theory would concede that one man is superior to another, it might consent to admit that, in the matter of good or bad health, not any woman or child—or animal, for that matter —knows what is wholesome for it and is capable of curing itself ; but that here, if anywhere, one person is superior to another.

THEOD. I should certainly say so.

172. SOCR. And again in social matters, the theory will say that, so far as good and bad customs or rights and wrongs or matters of religion are concerned, whatever any State makes up its mind to enact as lawful for itself, really is

172.   lawful for it, and in this field no individual or State is wiser
than another. But where it is a question of laying down
what is for its advantage or disadvantage, once more there,
if anywhere, the theory will admit a difference between
two advisers or between the decisions of two different
States in respect of truth, and would hardly venture to
assert that any enactment which a State supposes to be
B.   for its advantage will quite certainly be so.

The position taken up in the Defence is here restated fairly.
The doctor has some wisdom or knowledge justifying his offer to
change my condition to one in which things he calls ' better ' will
appear and be to me. His case is parallel to that of the statesman,
who uses his eloquence to recommend a change of custom or of
law or a practical policy. If ' right ' means simply what is enjoined by law and a ' good custom ' one that is in fact socially
approved, no State can claim to be wiser than another. But
anyone who comes forward to recommend a change must claim
that it will produce ' better ' results, that is to say, results which
will appear as more advantageous when the change has been
effected. When we return to this point later, it will be argued
that the doctor's or the statesman's present judgment about what
will be more advantageous in the future conflicts, *ex hypothesi*,
with the judgment of his unconverted hearers, and that both cannot
be true. This argument, however, is not developed until after
the ' digression ', which now follows.

172B–177C. *Digression : the contrast of Philosophy and Rhetoric*

The occasion of this digression has not been well understood.
Socrates breaks off at this point to suggest that some who ' do not
argue altogether as Protagoras does ' may not accept the analogy
that has just been drawn between the doctor's concern with the
bodily health of the individual and the statesman's concern with
questions of right and wrong. They will deny that ' right ' has
any meaning at all other than what is publicly decreed at any
time. This, as Socrates says, raises a larger issue than the argument we were just embarking upon with Protagoras.

172B.   SOCR. (*continues*). But, in that field I am speaking of—in
right and wrong and matters of religion—people [1] are ready
to affirm that none of these things is natural, with a reality
of its own, but rather that the public decision becomes true

---

[1] The subject of the plural ἐθέλουσι is not the same as the singular subject
(ὁ λόγος) of the previous sentences, and accordingly not Protagoreans but (as
Campbell says) ' certain persons who are presently defined '.

172B. at the moment when it is made and remains true so long
as the decision stands ; and those who do not argue altogether as Protagoras does carry on their philosophy on
these lines.[1]

But cne theory after another is coming upon us, Theo-
c. dorus, and the last is more important than the one before.

Editors have net seen clearly that this sentence does not amplify
the preceding one, but introduces a new position held, not by
Protagoras, but by people who do not state their position
altogether as Protagoras stated his. Their view is the ' more
important' theory, involving larger issues than the restricted
position we have just ascribed to Protagoras, the consideration of
which is accordingly postponed.

What is this larger theory ? Those who hold it are not ' incomplete Protagoreans ', but go further than Protagoras himself. They
deny the analogy between physical qualities (hot, dry, sweet, etc.)
and moral qualities like ' just '. The hot and the cold, the dry
and the moist, they will say, exist ' by nature ' ; and they would
agree with Protagoras that the fact that one contrary appears to
me, the other to you, is consistent with their having an objective
being of their own. But ' just ' and ' unjust ', they say, have no
status in Nature ; they are mere creations of convention or of the
public decision of the community. We have no evidence that
Protagoras went so far as this.[2] It is the extreme position formulated in the *Republic* by Thrasymachus, who denies that ' right '
has any natural validity : the word means nothing more than what
the most powerful element in the State decrees for its own advantage (τὸ τοῦ κρείττονος συμφέρον). He would reject the distinction
Socrates has just drawn between what is laid down as lawful and
what is decided upon as advantageous (συμφέροντα). When
Socrates argued in the *Republic* (as he will later in the *Theaetetus*)
that the strongest element in the State may be mistaken about
its own advantage, Thrasymachus was not convinced. The
atheists of *Laws* X (889 ff.) draw the same contrast between Nature
and convention. Fire, Air, Water, and Earth exist by nature and

[1] Reading καὶ ὅσοι γε δή. . . . λέγουσι. Ὅσοι ἂν λέγωσι would mean ' *all* who
do not argue ', and we should then have to understand (with M. Diès and
others) all who do *not go so far* as Protagoras. But these people go further.
It is not true that everyone who stops short of Protagoras' position holds the
extreme view here stated.

[2] His speech in the *Protagoras* 320 ff. recognises innate moral instincts of
αἰδώς and δίκη, existing in all men before society is formed. Education
in virtue is a development of these natural instincts by a socialising process,
making men good citizens of their own States.

chance, without design ; and by the interplay of their active powers—hot, cold, dry, moist, etc.—produce the whole physical cosmos. But art or design arises only later ; it is mortal and of mortal origin. The whole of legislation, custom, and religion is ' not by nature, but by art '. Conventions differ in different communities. ' What is right (τὰ δίχαια) has no natural existence at all ; but men are perpetually disputing about it and altering it, and whatever alteration they make at any time is at that time authoritative, owing its existence to design and the laws, not in any way to nature ' (889E). This is precisely the position stated here, the extreme consequence of making man the measure of all things, but a consequence never, so far as we know, drawn by Protagoras himself, who did not dream of subverting the basis of morality.

To Plato this thesis is the position of the arch-enemy ; the whole of the *Republic* is a reply to it. Here, acknowledging that it cannot be attributed to Protagoras, Socrates drops for a time the criticism of Protagoras' own theory, and replies indirectly in the ' digression ' that follows. A direct treatment would demand a repetition of the contents of the *Republic* and arguments supporting the Platonic thesis that the moral Forms, Justice and the rest, do ' exist by nature with a being of their own '. But the Forms are to be excluded, so far as possible, from this conversation, which discusses the claim of the world of appearances to yield knowledge without invoking the intelligible world. So Plato is content to indicate his answer by reviving the contrast drawn in the *Gorgias* and the *Republic* between the orator of the law court or the Assembly and the true statesman, the philosopher whose knowledge lies in that other realm of reality. The whole digression is studded with allusions to the *Republic*, and in the course of it the moral Forms are plainly, though unobtrusively, mentioned.

172C. THEOD. Well, Socrates, we have time at our disposal.

SOCR. Evidently. And it strikes me now, as often before, how natural it is that men who have spent much time in philosophical studies [1] should look ridiculous when they appear as speakers in a court of law.

THEOD. How do you mean ?

SOCR. When you compare men who have knocked about from their youth up in law courts and such places with others bred in philosophical pursuits, the one set seem to

D. have been trained as slaves, the others as free men.

---

[1] Φιλοσοφία has often a wide meaning covering all liberal studies (as at 143D) or ' culture ' (as in Isocrates).

172D. THEOD. In what way ?

SOCR. In the way you spoke of : the free man always has time at his disposal to converse in peace at his leisure. He will pass, as we are doing now, from one argument to another—we have just reached the third ; like us, he will leave the old for a fresh one which takes his fancy more ; and he does not care how long or short the discussion may be, if only it attains the truth. The orator is always talking

E. against time, hurried on by the clock ; there is no space to enlarge upon any subject he chooses, but the adversary stands over him ready to recite a schedule of the points to which he must confine himself. He is a slave disputing about a fellow-slave before a master sitting in judgment with some definite plea in his hand ; and the issue is never indifferent, but his personal concerns are always at stake,

173. sometimes even his life. Hence he acquires a tense and bitter shrewdness ; he knows how to flatter his master and earn his good graces, but his mind is narrow and crooked. An apprenticeship in slavery has dwarfed and twisted his growth and robbed him of his free spirit, driving him into devious ways, threatening him with fears and dangers which the tenderness of youth could not face with truth and honesty ; so, turning from the first to lies and the requital of wrong

B. with wrong, warped and stunted, he passes from youth to manhood with no soundness in him and turns out, in the end, a man of formidable intellect—as he imagines.

So much for the orator, Theodorus. Shall I now describe the philosophic quire to which we belong, or would you rather leave that and go back to our discussion ? We must not abuse that freedom we claimed of ranging from one subject to another.

THEOD. No, Socrates ; let us have your description first.

C. As you said quite rightly, we are not the servants of the argument, which must stand and wait for the moment when we choose to pursue this or that topic to a conclusion. We are not in a court under the judge's eye, nor in the theatre with an audience to criticise our philosophic evolutions.

SOCR. Then, if that is your wish, let us speak of the leaders in philosophy ; for the weaker members may be neglected.

D. From their youth up they have never known the way to market-place or law court or council chamber or any other place of public assembly ; they never hear a decree read out or look at the text of a law ; to take any interest in

173D. the rivalries of political cliques, in meetings, dinners, and merrymakings with flute-girls, never occurs to them even in dreams. Whether any fellow-citizen is well or ill born or has inherited some defect from his ancestors on either side, the philosopher knows no more than how many pints of water there are in the sea. He is not even aware that

E. he knows nothing of all this; for if he holds aloof, it is not for reputation's sake, but because it is really only his body that sojourns in his city, while his thought, disdaining all such things as worthless, takes wings, as Pindar says, 'beyond the sky, beneath the earth', searching the heavens and measuring the plains, everywhere seeking the true

174. nature of everything as a whole, never sinking to what lies close at hand.

THEOD. What do you mean, Socrates?

SOCR. The same thing as the story about the Thracian maidservant who exercised her wit at the expense of Thales, when he was looking up to study the stars and tumbled down a well. She scoffed at him for being so eager to know what was happening in the sky that he could not see what lay at his feet. Anyone who gives his life to philo-

B. sophy is open to such mockery. It is true that he is unaware what his next-door neighbour is doing, hardly knows, indeed, whether the creature is a man at all; he spends all his pains on the question, what man is, and what powers and properties distinguish such a nature from any other.[1] You see what I mean, Theodorus?

THEOD. Yes; and it is true.

SOCR. And so, my friend, as I said at first, on a public

C. occasion or in private company, in a law court or anywhere else, when he is forced to talk about what lies at his feet or is before his eyes, the whole rabble will join the maid-servants in laughing at him, as from inexperience he walks blindly and stumbles into every pitfall. His terrible clumsiness makes him seem so stupid. He cannot engage in an exchange of abuse,[2] for, never having made a study of anyone's peculiar weaknesses, he has no personal scandals to bring up; so in his helplessness he looks a fool. When

D. people vaunt their own or other men's merits, his unaffected laughter makes him conspicuous and they think he is frivolous. When a despot or king is eulogised, he fancies

---

[1] A clear allusion to the theory of Forms. The real object of knowledge is the Form 'Man', not individual men.

[2] A constant feature of forensic speeches at Athens.

174D. he is hearing some keeper of swine or sheep or cows being congratulated on the quantity of milk he has squeezed out of his flock; only he reflects that the animal that princes tend and milk is more given than sheep or cows to nurse a sullen grievance, and that a herdsman of this sort, penned up in his castle, is doomed by sheer press of

E. work to be as rude and uncultivated as the shepherd in his mountain fold. He hears of the marvellous wealth of some landlord who owns ten thousand acres or more; but that seems a small matter to one accustomed to think of the earth as a whole. When they harp upon birth—some gentleman who can point to seven generations of wealthy ancestors—he thinks that such commendation must come from men of purblind vision, too uneducated to keep their

175. eyes fixed on the whole or to reflect that any man has had countless myriads of ancestors and among them any number of rich men and beggars, kings and slaves, Greeks and barbarians. To pride oneself on a catalogue of twenty-five progenitors going back to Heracles, son of Amphitryon, strikes him as showing a strange pettiness of outlook. He laughs at a man who cannot rid his mind of foolish vanity

B. by reckoning that before Amphitryon there was a twenty-fifth ancestor, and before him a fiftieth, whose fortunes were as luck would have it. But in all these matters the world has the laugh of the philosopher, partly because he seems arrogant, partly because of his helpless ignorance in matters of daily life.

THEOD. Yes, Socrates, that is exactly what happens.

SOCR. On the other hand, my friend, when the philosopher drags the other upwards to a height at which he may

C. consent to drop the question ' What injustice have I done to you or you to me ? ' and to think about justice and injustice in themselves, what each is, and how they differ from one another and from anything else [1]; or to stop quoting poetry about the happiness of kings or of men with gold in store and think about the meaning of kingship and the whole question of human happiness and misery, what their nature is, and how humanity can gain the one and escape the other—in all this field, when that small, shrewd,

D. legal mind has to render an account, then the situation is reversed. Now it is he who is dizzy from hanging at such an unaccustomed height and looking down from mid-air.

---

[1] The moral Forms are here openly mentioned, and there are allusions to the allegory of the Cave in *Rep.* vi.

175D. Lost and dismayed and stammering, he will be laughed at, not by maidservants or the uneducated—they will not see what is happening—but by everyone whose breeding has been the antithesis of a slave's.

E. Such are the two characters, Theodorus. The one is nursed in freedom and leisure, the philosopher, as you call him. He may be excused if he looks foolish or useless when faced with some menial task, if he cannot tie up bed-clothes into a neat bundle or flavour a dish with spices and a speech with flattery. The other is smart in the dispatch of all such services, but has not learnt to wear his cloak like

176. a gentleman, or caught the accent of discourse that will rightly celebrate the true life of happiness for gods and men.

THEOD. If you could convince everyone, Socrates, as you convince me, there would be more peace and fewer evils in the world.

SOCR. Evils, Theodorus, can never be done away with, for the good must always have its contrary ; nor have they any place in the divine world ; but they must needs haunt this region of our mortal nature. That is why we should make all speed to take flight from this world to the other ; and

B. that means becoming like the divine so far as we can, and that again is to become righteous with the help of wisdom. But it is no such easy matter to convince men that the reasons for avoiding wickedness and seeking after goodness are not those which the world gives. The right motive is not that one should seem innocent and good—that is no better, to my thinking, than an old wives' tale—but let us state the truth in this way. In the divine there is no

C. shadow of unrighteousness, only the perfection of righteousness ; and nothing is more like the divine than any one of us who becomes as righteous as possible. It is here that a man shows his true spirit and power or lack of spirit and nothingness. For to know this is wisdom and excellence of the genuine sort ; not to know it is to be manifestly blind and base. All other forms of seeming power and intelligence in the rulers of society are as mean and vulgar as the

D. mechanic's skill in handicraft. If a man's words and deeds are unrighteous and profane, he had best not persuade himself that he is a great man because he sticks at nothing, glorying in his shame as such men do when they fancy that others say of them : They are no fools, no useless burdens to the earth, but men of the right sort to weather the storms

176D. of public life. Let the truth be told : they are what they fancy they are not, all the more for deceiving themselves ; for they are ignorant of the very thing it most concerns them to know—the penalty of injustice. This is not, as they imagine, stripes and death, which do not always fall on the

E.   wrong-doer, but a penalty that cannot be escaped.

THEOD.. What penalty is that ?

SOCR. There are two patterns, my friend, in the unchange-able nature of things, one of divine happiness, the other of godless misery—a truth to which their folly makes them

177. utterly blind, unaware that in doing injustice they are grow-ing less like one of these patterns and more like the other. The penalty they pay is the life they lead, answering to the pattern they resemble. But if we tell them that, unless they rid themselves of their superior cunning, that other region which is free from all evil will not receive them after death, but here on earth they will dwell for all time in some form of life resembling their own and in the society of things as evil as themselves, all this will sound like foolishness to such strong and unscrupulous minds.

THEOD. So it will, Socrates.

B.   SOCR. I have good reason to know it, my friend. But there is one thing about them : when you get them alone and make them explain their objections to philosophy, then, if they are men enough to face a long examination without running away, it is odd how they end by finding their own arguments unsatisfying ; somehow their flow of eloquence runs dry, and they become as speechless as an infant.

All this, however, is a digression ; we must stop now,

C.   and dam the flood of topics that threatens to break in and drown our original argument. With your leave, let us go back to where we were before.

THEOD.. For my part, I rather prefer listening to your digressions, Socrates ; they are easier to follow at my time of life. However, let us go back, if you like.

The tone of this digression goes beyond the *Gorgias* and the *Phaedo* and is far removed from the humanity of Socrates, who certainly knew the way to the market-place, though he deliberately kept out of politics. There is a foretaste of Cynicism in the emphatic contempt of wealth and high birth. The main contrast is not between the life of contemplation and the active life, to which, in a reformed society, the philosopher king would acknow-ledge his duty to descend. Many saints, like Teresa, have led very active lives without abandoning the joys of contemplation. The life contrasted with the philosopher's is at first that of the rhetorician, and towards the end that of the man trained in rhetoric to be the ruler of society, the strong-minded man who will stick at nothing and thinks himself a ' realist ' because he has no conception of the reality of ideals—a familiar figure in the post-war world of Plato's manhood, as in our own. It is an easy conjecture that some part of this tirade was inspired by Plato's experiences at the court of Syracuse.

The allusions to the allegory of the Cave, the passage about the true meaning of kingship, happiness, and justice, are intended to recall the whole argument of the *Republic*, with its doctrine of the divine, intelligible region of Forms, the true objects of knowledge. This is no mere digression ; it indicates—what cannot be directly stated—the final cleavage between Platonism and the extreme consequences of the Protagorean thesis. The *Theaetetus* here opens a window upon the world of true being ; but the vision must be closed. Our concern at present is only with the world of appearances and its claim to yield knowledge.

177C–179C. *Refutation of the Defence of Protagoras*

The argument is now resumed at the point where it was dropped (172A), when the genuinely Protagorean position had been isolated from extraneous elements. That position is now stated again, to mark that we have been straying beyond it. Socrates proceeds to refute the defence he put forward earlier on Protagoras' behalf.

177C. SOCR. Very well. I think the point we had reached was this. We were saying that the believers in a perpetually changing reality and in the doctrine that what seems to an individual at any time also is for him would, in most matters, strongly insist upon their principle, and not least in the case of what is right they would maintain that any

D. enactments a State may decide on certainly are right for that State so long as they remain in force ; but when it comes to what is good, we said that the boldest would not go to the length of contending that whatever a State may believe and declare to be advantageous for itself is in fact advantageous for so long as it is declared to be so—unless he meant that the name ' advantageous ' would continue to be so applied ; but that would be turning our subject into a joke.

THEOD. Certainly.

177E. SOCR. We will suppose, then, that he does not mean the name, but has in view the thing that bears it.

THEOD. We will.[1]

SOCR. Whatever name the State may give it, advantage is surely the aim of its legislation, and all its laws, to the full extent of its belief and power, are laid down as being for its own best profit. Or has it any other object in view when it makes laws?

178. THEOD. None.

SOCR. Then does it also hit the mark every time? Or does every State often miss its aim completely?

THEOD. I should say that mistakes are often made.

SOCR. We may have a still better chance of getting every-one to assent to that, if we start from a question covering the whole class of things which includes the advantageous. It is, I suggest, a thing that has to do with future time. When we legislate, we make our laws with the idea that they *will be* advantageous in time to come. We may call this class ' what is going to be '.

B. THEOD. Certainly.

SOCR. Here, then, is a question for Protagoras or anyone else who agrees with him : According to you and your friends, Protagoras, man is the measure of all things—of white and heavy and light and everything of that sort. He possesses in himself the test of these things, and believing them to be such as he experiences them, he believes what is true and real for him. Is that right?

THEOD. Yes.

SOCR. Is it also true, Protagoras (we shall continue), that
C. he possesses within himself the test of what is going to be in the future, and that whatever a man believes will be, actually comes to pass for him who believes it? Take heat, for example. When some layman believes that he is going to catch a fever [2] and that this hotness is going to exist, and another, who is a physician, believes the contrary, are we to suppose that the future event will turn out in accordance with one of the two opinions, or in accordance with both opinions, so that to the physician the patient will not be hot or in a fever, while he will be both these things to himself?

---

[1] It is not a question of the State giving the name ' advantageous ' to any class of actions it enjoins. Legislation must be understood to imply a judg-ment that the conduct prescribed will have good effects.

[2] πυρετὸν is subject of λήψεσθαι, cf. *Phaedr.* 251A, ἱδρὼς καὶ θερμότης ἀήθης λαμβάνει.

178C. THEOD. That would be absurd.

SOCR. And on the question whether a wine is going to be
D. sweet or dry, I imagine the vine-grower's judgment is authoritative, not a flute-player's.

THEOD. Of course.

SOCR. Or again, on the question whether a piece of music is going to be in tune or not, a gymnastic trainer would not have a better opinion than a musician as to what the trainer himself will later judge to be in good tune.

THEOD. By no means.

SOCR. And when a feast is being prepared, the guest who is to be invited, supposing him not to be an expert in cookery, will have a less authoritative opinion than the confectioner upon the pleasure that will result. We will not dispute yet
E. about what already is or has been pleasant to any individual; but about what will in the future seem and be to anyone, is every man the best judge for himself, or would you, Protagoras,—at least in the matter of the arguments that any one of us would find convincing for a court of law —have a better opinion beforehand than any untrained person?

THEOD. Certainly, Socrates, in that matter he did emphatically profess to be superior to everybody.

SOCR. Bless your soul, I should think he did. No one
179. would have paid huge sums to talk with him, if he had not convinced the people who came to him that no one whatever, not even a prophet, could judge better than he what was going to be and appear in the future.

THEOD. Quite true.

SOCR. And legislation, too, and the question of advantageousness are matters concerned with the future; and everyone would agree that a State, when it makes its laws, must often fail to hit upon its own greatest advantage?

THEOD. Assuredly.

SOCR. Then we may quite reasonably put it to your master
B. that he must admit that one man is wiser than another and that the wiser man is the measure, whereas an ignorant person like myself is not in any way bound to be a measure, as our defence of Protagoras tried to make me, whether I liked it or not.

THEOD. I think that is the weakest point in the theory, Socrates, though it is also assailable in that it makes other people's opinions valid when, as it turns out, they hold Protagoras' assertions to be quite untrue.

179C.   SOCR.   There are many other ways, Theodorus, of assailing such a position and proving that not every opinion of every person is true.

The Defence of Protagoras is thus refuted.   The argument which ' turns the tables ' is reaffirmed by Theodorus ; and it has been shown that not all judgments can be true.   When the patient and the doctor disagree about what the patient's experiences will be at some future time, they are disagreeing about the same fact, which is not at the moment part of the private experience of either, so that he might claim to be the only possible judge.   They cannot both be right.   No more can two politicians who dispute whether some law or decree will have good effects for the State.   Protagoras' own profession as an educator of good citizens rested entirely on his claim to be a better judge than his pupils of what they would, when educated, find to be good for them.

179C–181B. *The extreme Heracleitean position, contrasted with Parmenides' denial of all motion and change*

Plato has now shown why he will not accept the Protagorean position as extended by its author to judgments which go beyond the individual's immediate and private experience of his present sensations.   But within this narrower field he has himself accepted the position, and built it into his own account of the nature of perception.   We must now return to that account and consider the second element, drawn from the flux doctrine of Heracleitus.   With what reservations and restrictions are we to adopt the principle that all things are perpetually in motion ?

179C.   SOCR. (*continues*).   But with regard to what the individual experiences at the moment—the source of his sensations and the judgments in accordance with them—it is harder to assail the truth of these.   Perhaps it is wrong to say ' harder ' ; maybe they are unassailable, and those who assert that they are transparently clear [1] and are instances of knowledge may be in the right, and Theaetetus was not beside the mark when he said that perception and know-
D.   ledge were the same thing.

We must, then, look more closely into the matter, as our defence of Protagoras enjoined, and study this moving

---

[1] Cf. *Phaedrus* 250C, ' through the *clearest* of the senses, sight, we apprehend beauty in the perfect *clearness* of its radiance ' (διὰ τῆς ἐναργεστάτης αἰσθήσεως στίλβον ἐναργέστατα).   Plato will contend that perception of sensible qualities, though infallible in the sense above defined, does not reveal true reality and is therefore not knowledge.

179D.   reality, ringing its metal to hear if it sounds true or cracked. However that may be, there has been no inconsiderable battle over it and not a few combatants.

THEOD.   Anything but inconsiderable ; in Ionia, indeed, it is actually growing in violence. The followers of Heracleitus lead the quire of this persuasion with the greatest vigour.

SOCR.   All the more reason, my dear Theodorus, to look into it carefully and to follow their lead by tracing it to its
E.   source.

THEOD.   By all means. For there is no discussing these principles of Heracleitus—or, as you say, of Homer or still more ancient sages—with the Ephesians themselves, who profess to be familiar with them ; you might as well talk to a maniac. Faithful to their own treatises they are literally in perpetual motion ; their capacity for staying still to attend to an argument or a question or for a quiet
180.   interchange of question and answer amounts to less than nothing, or rather even a minus quantity is too strong an expression for the absence of the least modicum of repose in these gentry.[1] When you put a question, they pluck from their quiver little oracular aphorisms to let fly at you ; and if you try to obtain some account of their meaning, you will be instantly transfixed by another, barbed with some newly forged metaphor. You will never get anywhere with any of them ; for that matter they cannot get anywhere with one another, but they take very good care to leave
B.   nothing settled either in discourse or in their own minds ; I suppose they think that would be something stationary —a thing they will fight against to the last and do their utmost to banish from the universe.

SOCR.   Perhaps, Theodorus, you have seen these gentlemen in the fray and never met them in their peaceable moments ; indeed they are no friends of yours. I dare say they keep such matters to be explained at leisure to their pupils whom they want to make like themselves.

THEOD.   Pupils indeed ! My good friend, there is no such
C.   thing as a master or pupil among them ; they spring up like mushrooms. Each one gets his inspiration wherever he can, and not one of them thinks that another understands any-thing. So, as I was going to say, you can never bring them

---

[1] Taking τὸ οὐδ᾽ οὐδέν (' not even nothing ' = a minus quantity) as the subject of ὑπερβάλλει, ' is excessive (an exaggerated estimate) with respect to the absence of even a little quietness in them '. For πρὸς, cf. *Soph.* 258A, 5 ; *Phaedo* 75A, 9.

180c. to book, either with or without their consent. We must
take over the question ourselves and try to solve it like a
problem.

Socr. That is a reasonable proposal. As to this problem,
then, have we not here a tradition from the ancients who
D. hid their meaning from the common herd in poetical figures,
that Ocean and Tethys, the source of all things, are flowing
streams and nothing is at rest ; and do not the moderns,
in their superior wisdom, declare the same quite openly,
in order that the very cobblers may hear and understand
their wisdom and, abandoning their simple faith that some
things stand still while others move, may reverence those
who teach them that everything is in motion ?

But I had almost forgotten, Theodorus, another school
E. which teaches just the opposite, that reality ' is one, immovable : " Being " is the name of the All ',[1] and much else that
men like Melissus and Parmenides maintain in opposition to
all those people, telling us that all things are a Unity which
stays still within itself, having no room to move in. How are
we to deal with all these combatants ? For, little by little, our

---

[1] Reading οἷον (for οἶον), ἀκίνητον τελέθει. τῷ παντὶ ὄνομ' εἶναι. There is
no reason to doubt that this verse stood in the text of Parmenides used
by Plato and Simplicius, who twice quotes it, without reference to the *Theaetetus*, at *Phys.* 29, 15 and 143, 8. Both must have understood it as above
translated. The sense is good and relevant. I cannot believe that Plato
concocted the verse from the two halves of frag. 8, 38, ἐπεὶ τό γε Μοῖρ'
ἐπέδησεν | οὖλον ἀκίνητόν τ' ἔμεναι· τῷ πάντ(α) ὄνομ' ἔσται | ὅσσα βροτοὶ κατέθεντο,
κτλ, which belong to different sentences and have a quite different meaning.

I suggest, however, that Parmenides' text itself was corrupt. τελέθειν
is not used by the Pre-Socratics in the sense ' to be '. I conjecture τε θέλει,
and supply as the only possible subject of θέλει logical Necessity ('Ἀνάγκη
or Δίκη or Μοῖρα). Cf. Heracl. 65 : ἐν τὸ σοφὸν μοῦνον λέγεσθαι οὐκ ἐθέλει καὶ
ἐθέλει Ζηνὸς ὄνομα. The verse can then be placed after frag. 19 at the end
of the poem :

> οὕτω τοι κατὰ δόξαν ἔφυ τάδε καί νυν ἔασι
> καὶ μετέπειτ' ἀπὸ τοῦδε τελευτήσουσι τραφέντα·
> τοῖς δ' ὄνομ' ἄνθρωποι κατέθεντ' ἐπίσημον ἑκάστῳ.
> ⟨τούτων οὐδενὶ πίστις ἔνι· μοῦνον γὰρ Ἀνάγκη⟩
> οἷον ἀκίνητόν τε θέλει τῷ παντὶ ὄνομ' εἶναι.

' Men have given many names to changing things ; but all these names are
false ; for Necessity is willing that the All should *only* be called one and
immovable.' This makes a good ending. If we now suppose that the text
used by Plato and Simplicius had been corrupted and corrected into μοῦνον
γὰρ ἀνάγκη | οἷον, ἀκίνητον τελέθει. τῷ παντὶ ὄνομ' εἶναι, we have the verse
quoted, independently and correctly, by Plato and Simplicius, as Parmenides' last word on the unity and changelessness of Being (see *Classical
Review*, 1935, A New Fragment of Parmenides).

180E. advance has brought us, without our knowing it, between
the two lines ; and, unless we can somehow fend them off and
181. slip through, we shall suffer for it, as in that game they play
in the wrestling schools, where the players are caught by
both sides and dragged both ways at once across the line.
The best plan, I think, will be to begin by taking a look at
the party whom we first approached, the men of Flux ; and
if there seems to be anything in what they say, we will
help them to pull us over to their side and try to elude the
others ; but if we find more truth in the partisans of the
immovable whole, we will desert to them from these revolu-
B. tionaries who leave no landmark unremoved. If both sides
turn out to be quite unreasonable, we shall merely look
foolish if we suppose that nobodies like ourselves can make
any contribution after rejecting such paragons of ancient
wisdom. Do you think it worth while to go further in the
teeth of such danger, Theodorus ?

THEOD. Certainly, Socrates ; I could not bear to stop before
we have found out what each of the two parties means.

Theodorus' vigorous outburst perhaps expresses Plato's impatience
with the later followers of Heracleitus, who appear to have copied
with exaggeration their master's use of cryptic aphorisms and reiter-
ated his doctrine of flux without contributing anything more than
emphasis. The Heracleitean position that is to be examined is
the extreme position, comparable to the equally extreme denial of
all motion and change by Parmenides. Plato's own task was to
discover what elements of truth each party was trying to express.
Parmenides will be reserved for the *Sophist*. The *Theaetetus*, being
concerned with the sensible world, deals with Heracleitus, whose
doctrine has its application in that world.

181B–183C. *Criticism of extreme Heracleiteanism*

Socrates opens his criticism of Heracleitus by drawing the distinction between two kinds of change : local motion and change of
quality. At *Parmenides* 138B these were declared to be the only
two species of change. The word for change of quality ($\dot{a}\lambda\lambda o\iota o\tilde{v}\sigma\theta a\iota$)
occurs in Heracleitus himself : ' God is day and night, winter and
summer, war and peace, surfeit and hunger ; he changes ($\dot{a}\lambda\lambda o\iota o\tilde{v}\tau a\iota$)
just as fire, when blended with spices, is named according to the
savour of each ' (36 Byw., 67 Diels). Whether the later Heracleiteans drew this distinction or not, they appear to have denied any
kind of rest or fixity.

95

181B. SOCR. Well, if you feel so strongly about it, we must look into the matter. I think our study of change should begin

C. with the question : What after all do they mean when they say all things are in change ? What I mean is this : Do they recognise one kind of change or two ? I think there are two ; but I must not be alone in my opinion ; you must take your share in the risk, so that we may meet together whatever fate shall befall us. Tell me : do you call it change when something removes from place to place or revolves in the same place ?

THEOD. Yes.

SOCR. Let that be one kind, then. Now suppose a thing

D. stays in the same place but grows old or turns black instead of white or hard instead of soft or alters in some other way, isn't it proper to call that a different kind of change ?

THEOD. Yes, it must be.

SOCR. So I should recognise these as two kinds of change —alteration and local movement.

THEOD. And you are right.

SOCR. Having made that distinction, then, let us now begin our talk with these people who say that everything is in change and ask them : Do you say everything is in

E. both sorts of change—both moving in place and altering —or that part changes in both ways, part in only one of the two ?

THEOD. I really cannot tell ; but I think they would say ' in both ways '.

SOCR. Yes, my friend ; otherwise they will find things at rest as well as things in change, and it will be no more correct to say that everything is changing than to say that everything is at rest.

THEOD. Quite true.

SOCR. So, since they are to be in change and unchangingness

182. must be impossible anywhere, all things are always in every kind of change.

THEOD. That follows.

The theory of the nature of sense-perception, stated earlier, is now included in the position we are examining. Judgment, as distinct from sense-perception, has already been disposed of in the criticism of Protagoras. Being fallible, judgment (as Theaetetus will remark later, 187B) cannot be simply identified with knowledge. So the discussion has now been narrowed down to the question : Can sense-perception, whose infallibility has been admitted, give us know-

ledge ?   Plato stands by his analysis of sense-perception, which is
now recalled.   It is still attributed to those more refined thinkers
who have been alleged to hold the doctrine of flux.   That doctrine
was originally stated without any reservation as applying to ' all
things '.   Plato has now to point out that, if the objects of perception (to which it does, in his opinion, apply) are taken to be ' all
things ', there can be no such thing as knowledge at all, since no
statement we make about these perpetually changing things can
remain true for two moments together.   All discourse will be impossible, since there will be no fixed and stable things for our words
to refer to.

182A.   SOCR.   Now consider this point in their theory.   The
account they gave of the genesis of hotness or whiteness or
whatever it may be, we stated—didn't we ?—in this sort of
way : that any one of these things is something that moves
in place, simultaneously with a perception, between agent
and patient ; and that the patient becomes perceptive, not
a perception, while the agent comes to have a quality, rather
than to be a quality.   Perhaps this word ' quality ' strikes
you as queer and uncouth and you don't understand it as
a general expression [1] ; so let me give particular instances.

B.   The agent does not become hotness or whiteness, but hot
or white, and so on with all the rest.   No doubt you remember how we put this earlier : that nothing has any being
as one thing just by itself, no more has the agent or patient,
but, as a consequence of their intercourse with one another,
in giving birth to the perceptions and the things perceived,
the agents come to be of such and such a quality, and the
patients come to be percipient.

THEOD.   I remember, of course.

The reference is to the statement (156E) that ' white ', ' hot ',
' hard ', etc., have no being just by themselves, and that the agent
(as such) and the patient (as such) do not exist until the external
object and the sense-organ come within range of one another and the
' quick movements ' begin to pass between them.   Such being the
process of perception, Socrates now takes objects and perceptions
separately, beginning with objects.

[1] This is the first occurrence in Greek of the substantive ποιότης, though the
corresponding adjective ποῖος, ' of what sort ', or ' nature ' or ' character ',
was in common use.   The word was coined as a general term for all characters
like ' hotness ', ' whiteness ', ' heaviness ', etc., the termination -της corresponding to ' -ness ' in English.

182C. SOCR. Very well, then, we will not inquire into other parts of their theory, whether they mean this or that, but keep to the point we have in view and ask them this : All things, by your account, are in a perpetual stream of change. Is that so ?

THEOD. Yes.

SOCR. With both the kinds of change we distinguished—both moving in place and altering ?

THEOD. Certainly, if they are to be completely in change.

SOCR. Well now, if they only moved in place without altering in quality, we should be able to say what qualities they have as they move in this stream, shouldn't we ?

THEOD. Yes.

D. SOCR. Since, however, there is nothing constant here either —the flowing thing does not flow white but changes, so that the very whiteness itself flows and shifts into another colour, in order that the thing may escape the charge of constancy in that respect—can we ever give it the name of any colour and be sure that we are naming it rightly ?

THEOD. How can that be done, Socrates ? Or how can anything else of the kind you mean be called by its right name, if, while we are speaking, it is all the time slipping away from us in this stream ?

SOCR. And again, what are we to say of a perception of any sort ; for instance, the perception of seeing or hearing ?

E. Are we to say that it ever abides in its own nature as seeing or hearing ?

THEOD. It certainly ought not, if all things are in change.

SOCR. Then it has no right to be called seeing, any more than not-seeing, nor is any other perception entitled to be called perception rather than not-perception, if everything is changing in every kind of way.

THEOD. No, it hasn't.

SOCR. And moreover perception is knowledge, according to Theaetetus and me.

THEOD. Yes, you did say so.

SOCR. In that case, our answer to the question, what knowledge is, did not mean knowledge any more than not-knowledge.

183. THEOD. So it appears.

The latter part of this argument, dealing with perception, seems at first sight less cogent than the part concerned with objects. It might be objected that, though the organ of sight and the perception (seeing) may be changing all the time, that does not mean that seeing ceases to be seeing and might as well be called ' not-seeing '. Theaetetus' identification of perception with knowledge meant that every individual act of perception is infallible awareness of something that exists. This is not disproved by pointing out that the perception and its object are always changing. The total complex —perception + object—may be changing, but if it yields knowledge at any moment, it does so at all moments. We are merely aware of slightly different objects in a slightly different way from moment to moment ; but each new perception is just as infallible as the last. The fact of change does not make perception cease to be perception, or, if it ever is knowledge, cease to be knowledge.

The extreme Heracleitean, however, cannot make this reply. It would mean that my perception, though changing in content, remains the same in so far as it always has the character of being perception and knowledge. But the Heracleitean says that nothing ever remains the same. Plato's point is that, if ' all things ' without exception are always changing, language can have no fixed meaning. In the statement ' Perception is knowledge ' the meanings of the words must be constantly shifting. So the statement cannot remain true or the same statement.

The Heracleitean Cratylus, who influenced Plato in his youth, did in fact reach this conclusion. Aristotle says that thinkers who identified the real with the sensible world concluded that ' to seek truth would be to chase a flying bird '. ' They saw that all this world of nature is in movement and that about that which changes no true statement can be made ; at least, regarding that which everywhere in every respect is changing nothing could be truly affirmed. It was this belief that blossomed into the most extreme of the views above mentioned, that of the professed Heracleiteans, such as was held by Cratylus, who finally did not think it right to say anything but only moved his finger, and criticised Heracleitus for saying that it is impossible to step twice into the same river ; for *he* thought one could not do it even once.'[1] The conclusion Plato means us to draw is this : unless we recognise some class of knowable entities exempt from the Heracleitean flux and so capable of standing as the fixed meanings of words, no definition of knowledge can be any more true than its contradictory. Plato is determined to make us feel the need of his Forms without mentioning them. Without the Forms, as his Parmenides said,[2] there can be no discourse. The same conclusion had already been stated at the end of the *Cratylus.*

[1] Ar., *Metaph.* 1010a, 7, trans. Ross.
[2] See Introd., p. 11.

182A. SOCR. That would be a pretty result of the improvement we made upon that first answer,[1] when we were so eager to prove it right by showing that everything is in change. Now it seems that what has in fact come to light is that, if all things are in change, any answer that can be given to any question is equally right : you may say it is so and it is not so—or ' becomes ', if you prefer to avoid any term that would bring these people to a standstill.

THEOD. You are right.

SOCR. Except, Theodorus, that I used the words ' so ' and ' not so ', whereas we have no right to use this word ' so '— what is ' so ' would cease to be in change—nor yet ' not so ' :

B. there is no change in that either. Some new dialect will have to be instituted for the exponents of this theory, since, as it is, they have no phrases to fit their fundamental proposition—unless indeed it were ' not even no-how '.[2] That might be an expression indefinite enough to suit them.

THEOD. A most appropriate idiom.

SOCR. So, Theodorus, we are quit of your old friend, and not yet ready to concede to him that every man is the

C. measure of all things, if he is not a wise man. Also, we shall not admit that knowledge is perception, at least on the basis of the theory that all things are in change, unless Theaetetus has some objection.

THEOD. That is excellent, Socrates ; for now these questions are disposed of, it was agreed that I should be quit of answering your questions, as soon as the discussion of Protagoras' theory should come to an end.

Two conclusions are here carefully stated. By the argument that the wise man is a better judge of what will be in the future we have disposed of Protagoras' doctrine as extended to judgments ; but in the restricted sphere of sense-perception our application of his principle still stands. Theaetetus' proposition, that perception is knowledge, has been refuted ' *on the basis of the theory that all things*

---

[1] Viz. that knowledge is the same as perception.

[2] The text is corrupt. οὐδ' οὕτως (W) cannot be right, since οὐχ οὕτω has already been rejected as not indefinite enough. οὐδ' ὅπως (BT) is not Greek for ' No-how ' (οὐδ' ὁπωσοῦν, or ὁπωστιοῦν). If some still more negative expression is needed—' not even nohow ' (cf. τὸ οὐδ' οὐδέν, 180A)—we might conjecture οὐδ' οὐδέπως, a form as possible as οὐδέποτε or οὐδέπω, which Plato might coin for this occasion (οὔπως being poetic). Another possibility is οὐ< κ οἱ >δ' ὅπως, *nescio quomodo*, involving a pun on ἄπειρον = ' indefinite 'and ἄπειρον = ' ignorant' (as at *Tim.* 55C and *Phileb.* 17E). Pending a better suggestion, δ' οὕτως after μάλιστα should be retained.

are in change'—the extreme Heracleitean position—but only on that basis. The theory of the nature of perception is not abandoned ; on the contrary it is used to disprove the claim of perception to be knowledge. It is true that the organs and objects of perception are always changing ; and if this were (as Theaetetus held) the only form of cognition, there would be no knowledge. Knowledge requires terms that will have a fixed meaning and truths that will remain true.

The upshot of this section is that Plato has disentangled the application of the flux doctrine to sensible things, which he accepts, from the unrestricted assertion, ' All things whatsoever are in change ', which he rejects. The conclusion would be more obvious, if it were not his plan to exclude mention of the Forms—the things which are not in change and can be known.

183C–184B. *Interlude. Socrates declines to criticise Parmenides*

Socrates now declines to discuss the equally extreme Eleatic doctrine that all motion and change is an illusion. The criticism of Parmenides is reserved for the *Sophist*, where the world of un-changing reality will be allowed to come into view.

183C. THEAET. No, Theodorus, you must not be released until
   D. you and Socrates, as you proposed just now, have discussed those others who assert that the whole of things is at rest.
   THEOD. Would you teach your elders, Theaetetus, to dis-honour their agreements ? No, for what remains you must prepare yourself to carry on the argument with Socrates.
   THEAET. Yes, if he wishes ; though I would much rather have been a listener while this subject is discussed.
   THEOD. To invite Socrates to an argument is like inviting cavalry to fight on level ground. You will have something to listen to, if you question him.
   SOCR. Well, but, Theodorus, I think I shall not comply
   E. with Theaetetus' request.
   THEOD. Not comply ? What do you mean ?
   SOCR. A feeling of respect keeps me from treating in an unworthy spirit Melissus and the others who say the uni-verse is one and at rest ; but there is one being [1] whom I respect above all : Parmenides himself is in my eyes, as Homer says, a ' reverend and awful ' figure. I met him when I was quite young and he quite elderly, and I thought there

---

[1] I suspect a sort of pun on ἕνα ὄντα Παρμενίδην and the ἓν ὄν he believed in. (So Diès, p. 123.)

184. was a sort of depth in him that was altogether noble.[1] I am afraid we might not understand his words and still less follow the thought they express. Above all, the original purpose of our discussion—the nature of knowledge— might be thrust out of sight, if we attend to these impor- tunate topics that keep breaking in upon us. In par- ticular, this subject we are raising now is of vast extent. It cannot be fairly treated as a side issue ; and an adequate handling would take so long that we should lose sight of our question about knowledge. Either course would be wrong. My business is rather to try, by means of my
B. midwife's art, to deliver Theaetetus of his conceptions about knowledge.

THEOD. Well, do so, if you think that best.

184B–186E. *'Perception is Knowledge' finally disproved*

Plato has now eliminated those elements in Protagoras' doctrine and in Heracleiteanism which he will not accept. There remain those which he does accept and has included in his own theory of the nature of perception. He can now consider the claim of perception to be identical with knowledge. This claim, as advanced by Theaetetus, strictly implies not only that perception is know- ledge, but that it is the whole of knowledge. The following refuta- tion proves (1) that perception cannot be the whole of knowledge, for a great part of what is always called knowledge consists of truths involving terms which are not objects of perception ; and (2) that, even within its own sphere, the objects of perception have not that true reality which the objects of knowledge must possess. Hence, so far from being co-extensive with knowledge, perception is not knowledge at all.

(1) *Perception is not the whole of knowledge.*—The first argument does not depend on the details of Plato's theory of sense-perception. Such a theory, he would hold, can never be more than a probable account which might need amendment. But even if it be not accepted, he can still show that perception, in the strict sense which is taken to exclude judgment, cannot be the whole of knowledge.

184B. SOCR. Well then, Theaetetus, here is a point for you to consider. The answer you gave was that knowledge is perception, wasn't it ?
THEAET. Yes.

[1] For this reference to the meeting described in the *Parmenides*, see Introd., p. 1.

184B. SOCR. Now suppose you were asked : ' When a man sees white or black things or hears high or low tones, what does he see or hear with ? ' I suppose you would say : ' With eyes and ears '.

THEAET. Yes, I should.

C. SOCR. To use words and phrases in an easy-going way without scrutinising them too curiously is not, in general, a mark of ill-breeding ; on the contrary there is something low-bred in being too precise. But sometimes there is no help for it, and this is a case in which I must take exception to the form of your answer. Consider : is it more correct to say that we see and hear *with* our eyes and ears or *through* them ?

THEAET. I should say we always perceive through them, rather than with them.

D. SOCR. Yes ; it would surely be strange that there should be a number of senses ensconced inside us, like the warriors in the Trojan horse, and all these things should not converge and meet in some single nature—a mind, or whatever it is to be called—*with* which we perceive all the objects of perception *through* the senses as instruments.

THEAET. Yes, I think that is a better description.

SOCR. My object in being so precise is to know whether there is some part of ourselves, the same in all cases, with which we apprehend black or white through the eyes, and

E. objects of other kinds through the other senses. Can you, if the question is put to you, refer all such acts of apprehension to the body ? Perhaps, however, it would be better you should speak for yourself in reply to questions, instead of my taking the words out of your mouth. Tell me : all these instruments through which you perceive what is warm or hard or light or sweet are parts of the body, aren't they ?—not of anything else.

THEAET. Of nothing else.

SOCR. Now will you also agree that the objects you per-

185. ceive through one faculty cannot be perceived through another—objects of hearing, for instance, through sight, or objects of sight through hearing ?

THEAET. Of course I will.

SOCR. Then, if you have some thought about both objects at once, you cannot be having a perception including both at once through either the one or the other organ.

THEAET. No.

SOCR. Now take sound and colour. Have you not, to

185.   begin with, this thought which includes both at once—that
they both *exist* ?

THEAET.   I have.

SOCR.   And, further, that each of the two is *different* from
the other and the *same* as itself ?

B.   THEAET.   Naturally.

SOCR.   And again, that both together are *two*, and each
of them is *one* ?

THEAET.   Yes.

SOCR.   And also you can ask yourself whether they are
unlike each other or *alike* ?

THEAET.   No doubt.

SOCR.   Then through what organ do you think all this
about them both ?   What is common to them both cannot
be apprehended either through hearing or through sight.
Besides, here is further evidence for my point.   Suppose
it were possible to inquire whether sound and colour were
both brackish or not, no doubt you could tell me what

C.   faculty you would use—obviously not sight or hearing,
but some other.

THEAET.   Of course : the faculty that works through the
tongue.

SOCR.   Very good.   But now, through what organ does
that faculty work, which tells you what is common not
only to these objects but to all things—what you mean
by the words ' exists ' and ' does not exist ' and the other
terms applied to them in the questions I put a moment
ago ?   What sort of organs can you mention, corresponding
to all these terms, through which the perceiving part of us
perceives each one of them ?

THEAET.   You mean existence and non-existence, likeness
and unlikeness, sameness and difference, and also unity

D.   and numbers in general as applied to them ; and clearly
your question covers ' even ' and ' odd ' and all that kind
of notions.   You are asking, through what part of the body
our mind perceives these ?

SOCR.   You follow me most admirably, Theaetetus ; that
is exactly my question.

THEAET.   Really, Socrates, I could not say, except that
I think there is no special organ at all for these things, as
there is for the others.   It is clear to me that the mind

E.   in itself is its own instrument for contemplating the common
terms that apply to everything.

SOCR.   In fact, Theaetetus, you are handsome, not ugly

185E.   as Theodorus said you were ; for in a discussion handsome
is that handsome does. And you have treated me more
than handsomely in saving me the trouble of a very long
argument, if it is clear to you that the mind contemplates
some things through its own instrumentality, others through
the bodily faculties. That was indeed what I thought
myself ; but I wanted you to agree.

186.   THEAET. Well, it is clear to me.

In this argument, for the first time, we go behind the earlier
account of sense-perception, which regarded the subject as no
more than a bundle of distinct sense-organs, and sense-perception
as a process occurring between organ and external object. That
account stands ; but it is now added that, behind the separate
organs, there must be a mind, centrally receiving their several
reports and capable of reflecting upon the data of sense and making
judgments. In these judgments the thinking mind uses terms
like 'exists', 'is the same as', 'is different from', which are not
objects of perception reaching the mind through the channel of
any special sense, but are 'common' to all the objects of sense.
The mind gains its acquaintance with the meaning of such terms
through its own instrumentality, not by the commerce between
bodily organs and objects.

These terms are called 'common' ($\varkappa o\iota v\acute{a}$) in contrast with the
'private' ($\emph{ἴδια}$) or 'peculiar' objects of the several senses.
'Common' means no more than that. They are not to be confused with the 'common sensibles' which Aristotle regarded as
the objects of a common sensorium seated in the heart, namely
objects perceptible by more than one sense, such as motion, shape,
number, size, time. Plato does not speak of a 'common sense'
($\varkappa o\iota v\acute{\eta}\ a\emph{ἴσθησις}$), but on the contrary insists that his common terms
are apprehended, not by any sense, but by thought. The judg-
ments involving them are made by the mind, thinking by itself,
without any special bodily organ. The terms are 'common',
not in Aristotle's sense, but in the sense in which a name is common
to any number of individual things. Thus 'exists' is 'applied
in common to all things' ($\varkappa o\iota v\grave{o}v\ \emph{ἐπὶ}\ \pi\tilde{a}\sigma\iota$, 185C) ; it can occur
in a statement about any subject you like. Existence, we are
presently told (186A), 'attends on' or 'belongs to' all things.
These common terms are, in fact, the meanings of common names
—what Plato calls 'Forms' or 'Ideas'. The instances given here
correspond to the instances given by Socrates in the *Parmenides*
(129D), where he says that Zeno's dilemmas could be escaped by
'separating apart by themselves Forms such as likeness and un-

likeness, plurality and unity, rest and motion and all such things '.
The terms there mentioned happen to be those which occurred in
Zeno's arguments against plurality and motion; Socrates adds
later (130B) the moral Forms ' beautiful, good, and all such things ',
just as he will presently add them here (186A).[1]   In the *Theaetetus*
Plato is determined to say as little as possible about the Forms,
and he here avoids using the word ; but that these ' common '
terms simply are Forms should be obvious to anyone who has
read the *Parmenides*.   The avoidance of the word has misled many
critics into asserting that the Forms are not mentioned in the
Theaetetus, and miscalling these common terms ' categories '.[2]

Plato could not press the argument further in this direction
without openly discussing the Forms as the true objects of knowledge.   But the inference is clear : that percepts cannot be the
only objects of knowledge, as the identification of knowledge with
perception implied.   Any statement we can make about the objects
of perception, and therefore any truth, must contain at least one
of these common terms.   Therefore all knowledge of truths, as
distinct from immediate acquaintance with sense-data, involves
acquaintance with Forms, which are not private objects of perception, not individual existents, not involved in the Heracleitean
flux.   The reader can now draw the first conclusion : Perception
is not the whole of knowledge.

The argument next proceeds to the second conclusion : (2) *Perception, even within its own sphere, is not knowledge at all.*

186A.   SOCR. Under which head, then, do you place existence ?
    For that is, above all, a thing that belongs to everything.
    THEAET. I should put it among the things that the mind
    apprehends by itself.
    SOCR.   And also likeness and unlikeness and sameness and
    difference ?
    THEAET. Yes.
    SOCR. And how about ' honourable ' and ' dishonourable '
    and ' good ' and ' bad ' ?
    THEAET. Those again seem to me, above all, to be things

---

[1] See Introd., p. 8.

[2] The entirely gratuitous confusion, traceable to Plotinus, of Plato's common
terms with Aristotle's categories will be dealt with later (p. 274), where some
of the common terms come up again for discussion.   The moderns add a
further confusion with the quite different use of ' categcry ' by Kant and
others.   Campbell (p. liii), for instance, speaks of ' necessary forms of thought
which are as inseparable from perception as from reasoning '.   The common
terms are not forms of thought, but objects of thought (νοητά), and they are
separable from perception.

186A. whose being is considered, one in comparison with another, by the mind, when it reflects within itself upon the past
B. and the present with an eye to the future.[1]

SOCR. Wait a moment. The hardness of something hard and the softness of something soft will be perceived by the mind through touch, will they not?

THEAET. Yes.

SOCR. But their existence and the fact that they both exist, and their contrariety to one another and again the existence of this contrariety are things which the mind itself undertakes to judge for us, when it reflects upon them and compares one with another.

THEAET. Certainly.

SOCR. Is it not true, then, that whereas all the impressions which penetrate to the mind through the body are things
C. which men and animals alike are naturally constituted to perceive from the moment of birth, reflections about them with respect to their existence and usefulness only come, if they come at all, with difficulty through a long and troublesome process of education?

THEAET. Assuredly.

SOCR. Is it possible, then, to reach truth when one cannot reach existence?

THEAET. It is impossible.

SOCR. But if a man cannot reach the truth of a thing, can he possibly know that thing?

D. THEAET. No, Socrates, how could he?

SOCR. If that is so, knowledge does not reside in the impressions, but in our reflection upon them. It is there, seemingly, and not in the impressions, that it is possible to grasp existence and truth.

THEAET. Evidently.

SOCR. Then are you going to give the same name to two things which differ so widely?

THEAET. Surely that would not be right.

SOCR. Well then, what name do you give to the first one —to seeing, hearing, smelling, feeling cold and feeling warm?

---

[1] Theaetetus seems to be thinking of the recent argument against Protagoras, turning on the question of judgments about the comparative goodness or badness of future effects, and what *will* seem honourable (laudable) or dishonourable customs to a State. Socrates stops him short and applies his statement to the contrasts of sense qualities. Touch can show us that this is hard, that soft ; but it is thought, not sense, that reflects upon the contrast of hard and soft.

186E.   THEAET.   Perceiving.   What other name is there for it ?
        SOCR.   Taking it all together, then, you call this perception ?
        THEAET.   Necessarily.
        SOCR.   A thing which, we agree, has no part in apprehending
        truth, since it has none in apprehending existence.
        THEAET.   No, it has none.
        SOCR.   Nor, consequently, in knowledge either.
        THEAET.   No.
        SOCR.   Then, Theaetetus, perception and knowledge cannot
        possibly be the same thing.
        THEAET.   Evidently not, Socrates.   Indeed, it is now perfectly
        plain that knowledge is something different from perception.

   Such is the final disproof of the claim of perception to be knowledge.   Though admitted to be, in a sense, infallible, perception
has not the second mark of knowledge : it cannot apprehend
existence and truth.   There is a certain ambiguity about the words
' existence ' (οὐσία) and ' truth ' (ἀλήθεια) : both are commonly
used by Plato to mean that true reality which he ascribes to Forms
and denies to sensible objects.   If we keep to the sense suggested
by the previous context, the statement should mean that the
simplest judgment, such as ' Green exists here ', is beyond the
scope of perception proper, our immediate awareness of green.
The faculty of perception has no cognizance of the meaning of the
word ' exists ' ; and, since only judgments or statements can be
true, all truths are beyond its scope.
   To the Platonist, however, who is familiar with the associations
of ' reality ' and ' truth ', the passage will mean more than this.
The statement that reflections on the existence or usefulness of
our sense-impressions come only, if at all, after a long and troublesome education seems at first sight to conflict with the argument
for Recollection in the *Phaedo*, where it was asserted that from the
time when we first begin to use our senses we make judgments
involving Forms, which we must therefore have known before
birth.   All judgments involve the use of some common term ; and
Plato cannot mean to deny here that uneducated people make
judgments.   Plainly he means that they have not such knowledge
of Forms as the dialectician gains by the long process of education
described in *Republic* vii.   And the *Phaedo* may only mean that,
though children do make judgments such as ' This is like that '
and mean something by them, they have only a dim and confused
apprehension of Forms such as likeness.   The advance to knowledge
is a gradual recovery of clear vision, possible only by a training in
dialectic.

II. THE CLAIM OF TRUE JUDGMENT

The conclusion suggested earlier was that perception cannot be the whole of knowledge because there are other objects—the common terms—which the mind must know if it is to reflect at all. If we now take account of the Platonic sense of ' reality and truth ', we can add a further inference. Even my direct perception of my own sense-object cannot be called ' knowledge ', because the object is not a thing which is unchangingly real, but only something that becomes and is always changing. Some might say that they are more certain of the sensations and perceptions they have at any moment than they are of anything else ; and to deny the name of knowledge to such direct acquaintance is, in a sense, a matter of terminology. But to Plato knowledge, by definition, has the real for its object, and these objects have not true and permanent being. This point, however, cannot be elaborated without entering on an account of the intelligible world. Hence a certain ambiguity is allowed to remain about the meaning of ' reaching truth (reality) and existence '.

II. THE CLAIM OF TRUE JUDGMENT TO BE KNOWLEDGE

187A–C. *Theaetetus states the claim of True Judgment*

In the foregoing argument against Protagoras the distinction between direct perception and judgment has gradually emerged. Theaetetus has been led to see that knowledge must be sought above the level of mere sensation or perception, somewhere in the field of that ' thinking ' or ' judging ' which has been described as an activity of the mind ' by itself ', exercised upon the reports of the senses and using the common terms. Judgments may be true or false. Theaetetus' next suggestion is that any judgment that is true is entitled to be called knowledge.

187A. SOCR. But when we began our talk it was certainly not our object to find out what knowledge is not, but what it is. Still, we have advanced so far as to see that we must not look for it in sense-perception at all, but in what goes on when the mind is occupied with things by itself, whatever name you give to that.

THEAET. Well, Socrates, the name for that, I imagine, is ' making judgments '.

SOCR. You are right, my friend. Now begin all over
B.   again. Blot out all we have been saying, and see if you can get a clearer view from the position you have now reached. Tell us once more what knowledge is.

THEAET. I cannot say it is judgment as a whole, because

187B. there is false judgment; but perhaps true judgment is knowledge. You may take that as my answer. If, as we go further, it turns out to be less convincing than it seems now, I will try to find another.

SOCR. Good, Theaetetus; this promptness is much better than hanging back as you did at first. If we go on like

C. this, either we shall find what we are after, or we shall be less inclined to imagine we know something of which we know nothing whatever; and that surely is a reward not to be despised. And now, what is this you say: that there are two sorts of judgment, one true, the other false, and you define knowledge as judgment that is true?

THEAET. Yes; that is the view I have come to now.

The word (δοξάζειν) above translated ' making judgments ' has been loosely used earlier for thinking or reflection of any sort that goes on in the mind ' by itself '. Judgment (δόξα) will be more precisely defined presently (190A) as the decision terminating the mind's inward debate with itself. But the verb continues to be used as a synonym for thinking generally and even for ' thinking of ' some object. The translation will follow Plato in using whatever expression seems most natural in each context.

187C-E. *How is false judgment possible?*

Instead of developing and criticising Theaetetus' new suggestion, Socrates here goes back to a point that arose in the Defence of Protagoras. Almost the whole of this section of the dialogue will be devoted to attempts to account for the possibility of false judgment. At 167A Protagoras said that no one can judge falsely; ' for it is not possible either to think the thing that is not or to think anything but what one experiences, and all experiences are true '. So far, our only reply to this has been to argue *ad hominem* that if all judgments are true, Protagoras refutes himself, and that two contradictory judgments about a future fact which is not now part of ' what one experiences ', cannot both be true. We have not shown that it is possible to ' think the thing that is not '; and if it is not possible, Protagoras could reply that then all judgments must be true and his position is unassailable by such arguments.

In the next dialogue, the Sophist whom we attempt to define will be found taking refuge in this position; and he is not finally dislodged from it till near the end, where the introduction of the theory of Forms at last provides a satisfactory definition of false statement and judgment. The *Theaetetus* is leaving the Forms out of account so far as possible, and the long analysis here given of the problem of false judgment cannot, accordingly, yield a complete solution. Its object is to explore the ground within the field of the present discussion and to see how far we can get towards an explanation of false judgment without invoking the Forms.

187C. SOCR. Then, had we better go back to a point that came up about judgment?

THEAET. What point do you mean?

D. SOCR. A question that worries me now, as often before, and has much perplexed me in my own mind and also in talking to others. I cannot explain the nature of this experience we have, or how it can arise in our minds.

THEAET. What experience?

SOCR. Making a false judgment. At this moment I am still in doubt and wondering whether to let that question alone or to follow it further, not as we did a while ago, but in a new way.

THEAET. Why not, Socrates, if it seems to be in the least necessary? Only just now, when you and Theodorus were speaking of leisure, you said very rightly that there is no pressing hurry in a discussion of this sort.

E. SOCR. A good reminder; for this may be the right moment to go back upon our track. It is better to carry through a small task well than make a bad job of a big one.

THEAET. Certainly it is.

187E–188C. *False Judgment as thinking that one thing (known or unknown) is another thing (known or unknown)*

Socrates opens up this new problem with two arguments showing that false judgment cannot be explained if we limit the discussion to the terms in which it was commonly debated by contemporary Sophists. Plato, as often, begins with a simple and naïve view which ignores certain relevant factors, and gradually brings these factors in. The whole discussion, however, as we shall see, is limited by certain fundamental premises, which are not Plato's own. He is criticising other people's attempts to account for the existence of false judgments, and the conclusion is negative: they have failed to explain it, and must fail so long as those premises are assumed.

(1) If we accept the dilemma that anything must be either known to us or (totally) unknown, it is hard, Socrates argues, to see how we can ever think that one thing (whether known to us or not) can be another thing (whether known to us or not), i.e. *mistake* one thing for another.

187E. SOCR. How shall we set about it, then ? What is it that
we do mean ? Do we assert that there is in every case a
false judgment, and that one of us thinks what is false,
another what is true, such being the nature of things ?

THEAET. Certainly we do.

188. SOCR. And, in each and all cases, it is possible for us either
to know a thing or not to know it ? I leave out of account
for the moment becoming acquainted with things and forgetting, considered as falling between the two. Our argument is not concerned with them just now.

N THEAET. Well then, Socrates, there is no third alternative
left in any case, besides knowing and not knowing.

SOCR. And it follows at once that when one is thinking
he must be thinking either of something he knows or of
something he does not know ?

THEAET. Necessarily.

SOCR. And further, if you know a thing, you cannot also
B. not know it ; and if you do not know it, you cannot also
know it ?

THEAET. Of course.[1]

N SOCR. Then is the man who thinks what is false supposing
that things he knows are not those things but other things
he knows, so that, while he knows both, he fails to recognise
either ? [2]

THEAET. No, that is impossible, Socrates.

SOCR. Well then, is he supposing that things he does *not*
know are other things he does not know ? Is this possible—
N that a man who knows neither Theaetetus nor Socrates
should take it into his head that Socrates is Theaetetus or
Theaetetus Socrates ?

C. THEAET. No. How could he ?

SOCR. But surely a man does not imagine that things he
does know are things he does not know, or that things he
does not know are things he knows ?

THEAET. No, that would be a miracle.

SOCR. What other way is there, then, of judging falsely ?
There is, presumably, no possibility of judging outside these
alternatives, granted that everything is either known by us

---

[1] This apparently obvious admission is retracted later (191A). There is
a sense in which you do not know (are not now conscious of) what you do
know (have become acquainted with and possess stored somewhere in your
memory).

[2] ἀγνοεῖν means both ' fail to recognise ' and ' be ignorant of '. No English
expression covers both meanings.

188C. or not known ; and inside them there seems to be no room
for a false judgment.

THEAET. Quite true.

The limitations of this argument are obvious. As the illustration
shows, ' to know ' is used in the sense in which I am said to know,
not a truth, but a person or an object formerly seen and now remembered. We can divide all things into those we know in this sense
and those we do not ; and we can ignore any processes of becoming
acquainted and forgetting. The argument is that I cannot think
that a friend is a total stranger, or that one stranger is another
stranger, or that one friend is another friend. False judgments are
never of that pattern. Three points are to be noted.

(1) The field is limited to judgments of the form asserting that
one thing is (identical with) another—that Theaetetus is Socrates.
Very few false judgments consist in mistaking one thing for another ;
but this limitation was characteristic of sophistic discussion of the
question, partly because, as Apelt observes, the formula ' one thing
is another ' (τὸ ἕτερον ἕτερον εἶναι) was the Greek equivalent for
our ' x is A ', where x is subject, A predicate. This led to the
confusion of commoner types of proposition with assertions of
identity. It is not to be supposed, however, that Plato was guilty
of this confusion.

(2) The discussion is psychological, rather than logical. It is
argued that we never in fact think that Theaetetus whom we know
is Socrates whom we also know. It is true that when two known
objects are clearly before the mind we do not judge that one is the
other. Logicians, however, might maintain that there is a false
' proposition ' : ' Theaetetus is identical with Socrates ', which
has a meaning, though I cannot believe it. With that we are not
concerned, but only with judgments and statements that can be
actually made and believed by some rational being. Plato never
discusses ' propositions ' that no one propounds.[1]

(3) When we come to objects that are unknown (things I have
never been acquainted with), it may be urged that I can identify
one unknown object with another : I can judge (truly or falsely)
that Sir Philip Francis was the author of the Letters of Junius.
Nearly all historical knowledge is about things unknown to us in
the present sense. But the argument assumes that, unless I ' know '
an object, my mind must be a complete blank with respect to it,
as it is with respect to a person I have never seen or heard of.

[1] Hence in translating Plato the unhappy word ' proposition ' should be
avoided where modern associations are likely to obtrude themselves. See
below, p. 265.

Plato was not blind to these considerations. The only conclusion, so far, is that so long as we confine the question to these very narrow limits, we cannot explain the occurrence of false judgment.

188c–189b. *False Judgment as thinking the thing that is not*

The second argument develops the current objection to the possibility of 'thinking the thing that is not'—a phrase which Protagoras used as equivalent to 'judging falsely' (167a).

188c.   SOCR.   Perhaps, then, we had better approach what we are looking for by way of another alternative.   Instead of
  D.   'knowing or not knowing', let us take 'being or not being'.

THEAET.   How do you mean?

SOCR.   May it not simply be that one who thinks *what is not* about anything cannot but be thinking what is false, whatever his state of mind may be in other respects?

THEAET.   There is some likelihood in that, Socrates.

SOCR.   Then what shall we say, Theaetetus, if we are asked : 'But is what you describe possible for anyone?   Can any man think what is not, either about something that is or absolutely?'   I suppose we must answer to that : 'Yes,
  E.   when he believes something and what he believes is not true.'   Or what are we to say?

THEAET.   We must say that.

SOCR.   Then is the same sort of thing possible in any other case?

THEAET.   What sort of thing?

SOCR.   That a man should see something, and yet what he sees should be nothing.

THEAET.   No.   How could that be?

SOCR.   Yet surely if what he sees is something, it must be a thing that is.   Or do you suppose that 'something'[1] can be reckoned among things that have no being at all?

THEAET.   No, I don't.

SOCR.   Then, if he sees something, he sees a thing that is.

THEAET.   Evidently.

189.   SOCR.   And if he hears a thing, he hears something and hears a thing that is.

THEAET.   Yes.

---

[1] The Greek εἷς γέ τις, 'at least some one', is the contradictory of οὐδείς, not even one', 'no one'.   ἕν γέ τι means 'a (= one) thing' (*ein Ding*, *une chose*), as the opposite of 'no-thing'; and τὸ ἕν here means 'what is one' (or 'a thing' in this sense), while τοῖς μὴ οὖσιν means the opposite, 'nothings'.

189. SOCR. And if he touches a thing, he touches something, and if something, then a thing that is.

THEAET. That also is true.

SOCR. And if he thinks,[1] he thinks something, doesn't he ?

THEAET. Necessarily.

SOCR. And when he thinks something, he thinks a thing that is ?

THEAET. I agree.

SOCR. So to think what is not is to think nothing.

THEAET. Clearly.

SOCR. But surely to think nothing is the same as not to think at all.

THEAET. That seems plain.

B.   SOCR. If so, it is impossible to think what is not, either about anything that is, or absolutely.

THEAET. Evidently.

SOCR. Then thinking falsely must be something different from thinking what is not.

THEAET. So it seems.

SOCR. False judgment, then, is no more possible for us on these lines than on those we were following just now.

THEAET. No, it certainly is not.

The problem developed in this argument is not a mere sophistic paradox, but a very real problem that is still being discussed. It will recur in the *Sophist*, where Plato, having brought the Forms upon the scene, will be able to offer a solution.[2] The statement of it is attributed to Protagoras elsewhere [3] : to think what is false is to think what is not ; but that is to think nothing ; and that, again, is not to think at all : therefore we can only think the thing that is, and all judgments must be true. Such was Protagoras' conclusion. Plato's is different, namely that, since there is such a thing as thinking falsely, it cannot be ' thinking what is not ', if that means (as the argument implies) having nothing at all before the mind. But the real significance of ' thinking what is not ' cannot be followed up here. It would involve drawing the necessary distinctions between various meanings of the terms ' is ' and ' is not ', and a discussion of the whole question of reality and unreality. All this is reserved for the *Sophist*, where the inquiry will start again from the problem as stated here, and follow the only line that can lead to a satisfactory conclusion.

---

[1] Or ' makes a judgment '.   ' Thinks something ', again, is not distinguished from ' thinks of something '.

[2] See pp. 212 and 299 ff.   [3] *Euthydemus* 286c and 283E.

Since the limits of the *Theaetetus* exclude a discussion of reality, the present argument has to be left where it is, and the transition to Socrates' next suggestion seems somewhat abrupt. We may, however, find a link, if we observè that the terms in which the debate had been carried on were too simple. Protagoras has been represented earlier (167A) as asserting that ' one cannot think anything but what one experiences, and all experiences are true '. He saw no important distinction between what appears *real* to me in direct perception and what appears *true* to me, what I believe or judge to be true. ' Appears ' covered both. So he assumed that belief was like direct acquaintance with a sense-object, and must be infallible in the same way. What I believe, what I have before my mind when I think, must be *something* ; so there must *be* just that object or fact ; and there are no false facts, any more than non-existent objects.

To escape this conclusion, further analysis is needed to bring out the distinction between direct acquaintance with sense-objects (which Plato has admitted to be infallible) and the process of making a judgment, which is not so simple and immediate as seeing a colour. It will be indicated that judgments of the type so far considered—thinking that one thing is another thing—involve two terms, not to mention the connecting term ' is '. The act of making a judgment is not the same thing as perceiving this whole complex— perceiving a fact as we perceive a colour—but involves an operation of the mind which puts the terms together in a certain way. There may be room for mistakes to occur in this process, the nature of which Socrates will attempt tο bring out gradually and to illustrate by images.

189B–190E. *The apparent impossibility of false judgment as mistaking one thing for another*

Socrates now recurs to the conception of false judgment as mistaking one thing for another, or thinking that one thing is another. We are to examine what this can mean and in what circumstances it can occur. Our first conclusion (188C) that it was impossible resulted from the assumption that we must either ' know ' a thing (be acquainted with it and have it clearly before our minds) or not know it (be totally unacquainted with it). This dilemma does not really exhaust the possibilities. By taking memory into account, we can find a sense in which an object can be both known and not known.

189B. SOCR. Well, does the thing we call false judgment arise in this way ?

THEAET. How ?

189B. SOCR. We do recognise the existence of false judgment as a sort of misjudgment,[1] that occurs when a person inter-
C. changes in his mind two things, both of which are, and asserts that the one is the other. In this way he is always thinking of something which is, but of one thing in place of another, and since he misses the mark he may fairly be said to be judging falsely.

THEAET. I believe you have got it quite right now. When a person thinks ' ugly ' in place of ' beautiful ' or ' beautiful ' in place of ' ugly ', he is really and truly thinking what is false.

SOCR. I can see that you are no longer in awe of me, Theaetetus, but beginning to despise me.

THEAET. Why, precisely?

SOCR. I believe you think I shall miss the opening you give me by speaking of ' *truly* thinking what is *false* ', and not
D. ask you whether a thing can be slowly quick or heavily light or whether any contrary can desert its own nature and behave like its opposite. However, I will justify your bold-ness by letting that pass. So you like this notion that false judgment is mistaking.

THEAET. I do.

Theaetetus' phrase ' thinking (or judging) " ugly " in place of " beautiful " ' is vague and ambiguous. We should expect it to mean : thinking that some object which is in fact beautiful is ugly, or (in the language of later logic) assigning a wrong predicate to a subject. But this is not the sense taken in the following context. A discussion of what we call ' predicates ' would inevitably lead to the Forms. Possibly Theaetetus' remark is intended to remind us of their existence ; but Socrates will not bring them in. The field is still limited to judgments asserting that one (individual) thing is (identical with) another, as when I mistake Theaetetus for Socrates.[2] We are to consider how and when such a mistake can be made.

189D. SOCR. According to you, then, it is possible for the mind to take one thing for another, and not for itself.

THEAET. Yes, it is.

---

[1] Plato coins a word ἀλλοδοξία, ' misjudgment ', analogous to ἀλλογνοεῖν, meaning to mistake one person for another.

[2] Accordingly this hypothesis that false judgment is ' mistaking ' must not be confused with Plato's own analysis in the *Sophist*, which depends on the recognition of Forms. See p. 317.

189E. SOCR.   And when the mind does that, must it not be thinking either of both things or of one of the two ?

THEAET.   Certainly it must, either at the same time or one
after the other.

SOCR.   Excellent.   And do you accept my description of the
process of thinking ?

THEAET.   How do you describe it ?

SOCR.   As a discourse that the mind carries on with itself
about any subject it is considering.   You must take this
explanation as coming from an ignoramus ; but I have a
notion that, when the mind is thinking, it is simply talking
to itself, asking questions and answering them, and saying
190. Yes or No.   When it reaches a decision—which may come
slowly or in a sudden rush—when doubt is over and the two
voices affirm the same thing, then we call that its ' judgment '.   So I should describe thinking as discourse, and
judgment as a statement pronounced, not aloud to someone
else, but silently to oneself.[1]

THEAET.   I agree.

SOCR.   It seems, then, that when a person thinks of one
thing as another, he is affirming to himself that the one is
the other.

B. THEAET.   Of course.

The effect of this account of thinking and judgment is to equate
the act of ' mistaking ' one thing for another (' misjudgment ', the
suggested equivalent of false judgment) with making the silent
statement (λόγος) that one thing is the other.   So Theaetetus' phrase
' judging " ugly " in place of " beautiful " ' is reduced to making
the statement that the beautiful (*or* what is beautiful) is ugly, or
is the same thing as the ugly.[2]   We are still considering only judgments of this type, which assert that one thing is another thing.
We are supposed to have both things clearly before our minds
(memory not having yet come into the discussion).   Socrates proceeds to point out that, within the limits of these assumptions,
we never do judge that one thing is another.

190B. SOCR.   Now search your memory and see if you have ever
said to yourself ' Certainly, what is beautiful is ugly ', or

[1] This account of the process of thinking and judgment is repeated in the
Sophist (see p. 318).

[2] Since the Forms are excluded from discussion, this expression ' the
beautiful ' is left ambiguous.   It can mean (1) anything that is beautiful
(and recognised as such at the moment), or (2) Beauty itself (the Form).
The ambiguity does not matter, because we never judge either that what we
now see to be beautiful is ugly or that Beauty itself is Ugliness.

190B. 'what is unjust is just'. To put it generally, consider if you have ever set about convincing yourself that any one thing is certainly another thing, or whether, on the contrary, you have never, even in a dream, gone so far as to say to yourself that odd numbers must be even, or anything of that sort.

THEAET. That is true.

c. SOCR. Do you suppose anyone else, mad or sane, ever goes so far as to talk himself over, in his own mind, into stating seriously that an ox must be a horse or that two must be one?

THEAET. Certainly not.

SOCR. So, if making a statement to oneself is the same as judging, then, so long as a man is making a statement or judgment about both things at once and his mind has hold of both, he cannot say or judge that one of them is the
D. other. You, in your turn, must not cavil at my language [1]; I mean it in the sense that no one thinks: 'the ugly is beautiful' or anything of that kind.

THEAET. I will not cavil, Socrates. I agree with you.

SOCR. So long, then, as a person is thinking of both, he cannot think of the one as the other.

THEAET. So it appears.

SOCR. On the other hand, if he is thinking of one only and not of the other at all,[2] he will never think that the one is the other.

THEAET. True; for then he would have to have before his mind the thing he was not thinking of.

SOCR. It follows, then, that 'mistaking' is impossible, whether he thinks of both things or of one only. So
E. there will be no sense in defining false judgment as 'mis-

---

[1] Burnet's text. In Greek 'the one' and 'the other' happen to be expressed by the same word, ἕτερον. Socrates means: 'You must not cavil at my saying no one thinks one thing (τὸ ἕτερον) is another (ἕτερον), on the verbal ground that ἕτερον is the same word as ἕτερον. I mean all the particular cases (such as 'the ugly is beautiful') covered by this general formula.' The words ἐπὶ τῶν ἐν μέρει, ἐπειδὴ τὸ [ῥῆμα] ἕτερον τῷ ἑτέρῳ κατὰ ῥῆμα ταὐτόν ἐστιν (B) may be a gloss on τῇδε, inserted in the wrong place; or, if retained where they stand, they must mean 'You must let this phrase pass as applied to the particular cases (covered by them); for verbally the word ἕτερον (one) is the same as the word ἕτερον (other).' Cf. Madvig, Adv. Crit. i (1871), 377; Peipers, Erkenntnisstheorie Plato's 694. The καὶ σοὶ (with ἑατέον) means: You must pass my expression as I passed your 'ἀληθῶς ψευδοῦς' (at 189D).

[2] This sentence shows clearly that δοξάζειν (with accus.) here, as in other places in the context, means 'thinking of' a thing, not making a judgment about it; though δοξάσει in the next line does mean making the judgment that the one is the other. This is a good example of Plato's deliberate refusal to use terms as fixed technicalities.

190E. judgment '. It does not appear that false judgment exists in us in this form any more than in those we dismissed earlier.
THEAET. So it seems.

The upshot, so far, is that the notion of mistaking or interchanging one object for another will not explain how we can make a false judgment, so long as it is assumed that the objects must either be ' known ' (clearly present to the mind) or else ' unknown ' (completely absent from the mind).

190E–195B. *One class of mistakes can be explained by taking into account memory. The Wax Tablet*

The notion of ' mistaking ', however, need not be abandoned, if the assumption can be evaded ; and it can be evaded by introducing what has hitherto been excluded—the contents of the memory. We shall find that there is one class of false judgments that can be described as ' mistaking '. These are judgments in which the two things wrongly identified are objects of different sorts—one a present object of perception, the other a memory-image. So the scope of the discussion is now enlarged to include memory.

190E. SOCR. And yet, Theaetetus, if we cannot show that false judgment does exist, we shall be driven into admitting all sorts of absurdities.
THEAET. For instance ?
SOCR. I will not mention them until I have tried to look at the question from every quarter. So long as we cannot see our way, I should feel some shame at our being forced
191. into such admissions. But if we find the way out, then, as soon as we are clear, it will be time to speak of others as caught in the ludicrous position we shall have ourselves escaped ; though, if we are completely baffled, then, I suppose, we must be humble and let the argument do with us what it will, like a sailor trampling over sea-sick passengers. So let me tell you where I still see an avenue open for us to follow.
THEAET. Do tell me.
SOCR. I shall say we were wrong to agree that a man cannot think that things he knows are things he does not know and
B. so be deceived. In a way it is possible.
THEAET. Do you mean something that crossed my mind at the moment when we said that was impossible ? It occurred to me that sometimes I, who am acquainted with Socrates, imagine that a stranger whom I see at a distance is

191B. the Socrates whom I know. In a case like that a mistake of the kind you describe does occur.

SOCR. And we were shy of saying that, because it would have made us out as both knowing and not knowing what we know ?

THEAET. Exactly.

SOCR. We must, in fact, put the case in a different way. Perhaps the barrier will yield somewhere, though it may

C. defy our efforts. Anyhow, we are in such straits that we must turn every argument over and put it to the test. Now, is there anything in this ? Is it possible to become acquainted with something one did not know before ?

THEAET. Surely.

SOCR. And the process can be repeated with one thing after another ?

THEAET. Of course.

SOCR. Imagine, then, for the sake of argument, that our minds contain a block of wax, which in this or that individual may be larger or smaller, and composed of wax that is com-

D. paratively pure or muddy, and harder in some, softer in others, and sometimes of just the right consistency.

THEAET. Very well.

SOCR. Let us call it the gift of the Muses' mother, Memory, and say that whenever we wish to remember something we see or hear or conceive in our own minds, we hold this wax under the perceptions or ideas and imprint them on it as we might stamp the impression of a seal-ring. Whatever is so imprinted we remember and know so long as the image remains ; whatever is rubbed out or has not succeeded in

E. leaving an impression we have forgotten and do not know.

THEAET. So be it.

The word ' know ' has now received a new meaning : I know a thing when I have had direct acquaintance with it and an image of it remains stored in my memory. This gives a fuller range of possibilities than we have so far had. I may know Socrates in this sense and yet fail to recognise or identify him when I see him ; and I may mistake a stranger whom I see at a distance for the Socrates whom I know. This possibility of ' mistaking ' was excluded in the earlier argument by the false assumption that I must either know Socrates, in the sense of clearly perceiving him or having the thought of him clearly before my mind, or else my mind must be a complete blank concerning him.

It may be noted that ideas or notions (ἔννοιαι) are spoken of as

stamped on the memory, as well as perceptions. An idea is something we ' conceive in our own minds ' (αὐτοὶ ἐννοήσωμεν), but do
not perceive. Its nature and origin are left obscure ; but the
mention of such objects prepares the way for our knowledge of
numbers, which are not perceived but are treated as images stamped
in the memory (195E).

191E.   SOCR.   Now take a man who knows things in this way, and
is attending to something that he sees or hears. Is·there
not here a possibility of his making a false judgment ?
THEAET.   How ?
SOCR.   By thinking that things he knows are other things
he knows, or sometimes things he does not know. We
were wrong when we agreed earlier that this was impossible.
THEAET.   What do you think about it now ?

Socrates' next speech (192A, 1–C, 5) contains a list of all the cases
in which it is impossible to mistake one thing for another. He
takes all the possible combinations of two objects which are (a)
known (and now remembered) or (b) unknown (completely), (c) now
perceived or (d) not now perceived. The conclusion is that there
are only three combinations in which mistaking is possible. The
reader would find the same difficulty as Theaetetus in following
the statement and may prefer a summary to a translation. It
will be simplest to use ' an acquaintance ' to mean a person (or
thing) whom I know and of whom I have a memory image now before
my mind ; and ' a stranger ' to mean a person (or thing) with which
I have never been acquainted at all, a *total* stranger.

Mistake, then, is impossible in the following cases :

(1) If neither object is now perceived, I cannot mistake an
acquaintance for another acquaintance, or confuse him with a
stranger, or confuse two strangers.   (These cases will be illustrated
by examples at 193A–B.)

(2) If perception only is involved, I cannot confuse two things
which I see, or an object seen with an object not seen, or two objects
neither of which is seen.

(3) Where both knowledge and perception are involved, I cannot
confuse two acquaintances both now seen and recognised [1] ; or
confuse an acquaintance now seen and recognised with an absent
acquaintance or with a stranger who is present. And there can be
no confusion of two total strangers, whether I now see one of them
or not.

[1] To recognise is to fit the new perception to the right memory-image, left
by a former perception of the same object.

Socrates now gives a summary statement of the three cases where mistake is possible, and these are illustrated in detail.

192C, 5. SOCR. (*continues*). There remain, then, the following cases in which, if anywhere, false judgment can occur.

THEAET. What are they ? Perhaps they may help me to understand better. At present I cannot follow.

SOCR. Take things you know : you can suppose them to be other things which you both know and perceive ; or to be things you do not know, but do perceive ; or you can confuse

D. two things which you both know and perceive.

THEAET. Now I am more in the dark than ever.

SOCR. Let me start again, then, and put it in this way. I know Theodorus and have a memory in my mind of what he is like, and the same with Theaetetus. At certain moments I see or touch or hear or otherwise perceive them ; at other times, though I have no perception of you and Theodorus, I nevertheless remember you both and have you before my mind. Isn't that so ?

E. THEAET. Certainly.

SOCR. That, then, is the first point I want to make clear— that it is possible either to perceive or not to perceive something one is acquainted with.

THEAET. True.

SOCR. And it is also possible, when one is not acquainted with a thing, sometimes not to perceive it either, sometimes merely to perceive it and nothing more.

THEAET. That is possible too.

Socrates now takes, for illustration, three cases from his list, where mistake is impossible. They are cases in which no present perception is involved. (1) When nothing is before my mind except images of things I have formerly become acquainted with, I cannot judge that one of these remembered things is the other. (2) If I have an image of one only, I cannot judge that the thing is something I have never known. (3) Still less can I identify or confuse two things, neither of which I have ever known.

192E. SOCR. Then see if you can follow me better now. If
193. Socrates knows Theodorus and Theaetetus, but sees neither and has no sort of present perception of them, he can never think in his own mind that Theaetetus is Theodorus. Is that good sense ?

THEAET. Yes, that is true.

SOCR. Well, that was the first of the cases I mentioned.

193.   THEAET. Yes.

SOCR. And the second was this : if I know one of you but not the other and perceive neither, once more I could never think that the one I know is the other whom I do not know.

THEAET. True.

B.   SOCR. And thirdly, if I neither know nor perceive either of you, I cannot think that one unknown person is another unknown person. And now take it as if I had gone over the whole list of cases again, in which I shall never judge falsely about you and Theodorus, whether I know both or neither or only one of you. And the same applies to perceiving, if you follow me.

THEAET. I follow now.

' The same applies to perceiving ' refers to the second class of cases, where perception only is involved. If there is nothing but two objects of perception, you cannot mistake the one for the other, whether you perceive both or neither or one only. There remains the third class of cases, where both previous acquaintance and present perception are concerned. Among these Socrates now illustrates the three cases in which mistake is possible.

193B.   SOCR. It remains, then, that false judgment should occur in a case like this : when I, who know you and Theodorus and possess imprints of you both like seal-impressions in
C.   the waxen block, see you both at a distance indistinctly and am in a hurry to assign the proper imprint of each to the proper visual perception, like fitting a foot into its own footmark to effect a recognition [1] ; and then make the mistake of interchanging them, like a man who thrusts his feet into the wrong shoes, and apply the perception of each to the imprint of the other. Or my mistake might be illustrated by the sort of thing that happens in a mirror
D.   when the visual current transposes right to left.[2] In that case mistaking or false judgment does result.

THEAET. I think it does, Socrates. That is an admirable description of what happens to judgment.

SOCR. Then there is also the case where I know both and perceive only one, and do not get the knowledge I

[1] An allusion to the recognition of Orestes by his footmark tallying with his sister Electra's, Aeschylus, *Choephori*, 205 ff.

[2] Plato explains reflection by supposing that a stream of light (the visual current) from the eye coalesces at the surface of the mirror with a stream of light (colour) from the object. How the transposition occurs will be explained below, p. 327.

193D. have of that one to correspond with my perception. That is the expression I used before, which you did not understand.

THEAET. No, I did not.

The first of these two cases might be called the mistake of double transposition. The second is really similar, but simpler, involving only a single transposition of the same type. Instead of two false judgments : ' Yonder man (Theodorus) is Theaetetus, and that other man (Theaetetus) is Theodorus ', we now have only one. There is also the third case (192c) where I mistake a stranger whom I see for someone I remember. This is of the same pattern : I wrongly identify something now perceived (whether formerly known or not known, does not matter) with something I know. Socrates does not illustrate this, but now repeats his explanation of the two cases he has illustrated.

193D. SOCR. Well, that is what I was saying : if you know
E.   one of two people and also perceive him and if you get the knowledge you have to correspond with the perception of him, you will never think he is another person whom you both know and perceive, if your knowledge of him likewise is got to correspond with the perception. That was so, wasn't it ?

THEAET. Yes.

SOCR. But there was left over the case I have been describing now, in which we say false judgment does occur : the possibility that you may know both and see or otherwise
194.   perceive both, but not get the two imprints to correspond each with its proper perception. Like a bad archer, you may shoot to one side and miss the mark—which is indeed another phrase we use for error.

THEAET. With good reason.

SOCR. Also, when a perception is present which belongs to one of the imprints, but none which belongs to the other, and the mind fits to the present perception the imprint belonging to the absent one, in all such cases it is in error. To sum up : in the case of objects one does not
B.   know and has never perceived, there is, it seems, no possibility of error or false judgment, if our present account is sound ; but it is precisely in the field of objects both known and perceived that judgment turns and twists about and proves false or true—true when it brings impressions straight to their proper imprints ; false when it misdirects them crosswise to the wrong imprint.

194B.   THEAET. Surely that is a satisfactory account, isn't it, Socrates ?

C.   SOCR. You will think still better of it when you hear the rest. To judge truly is a fine thing and there is something discreditable in error.

THEAET. Of course.

SOCR. Well, they say the differences arise in this way. When a man has in his mind a good thick slab of wax, smooth and kneaded to the right consistency, and the impressions that come through the senses are stamped on these tables of the ' heart '—Homer's word hints at the

D.   mind's likeness to wax [1]—then the imprints are clear and deep enough to last a long time. Such people are quick to learn and also have good memories, and besides they do not interchange the imprints of their perceptions but think truly. These imprints being distinct and well-spaced are quickly assigned to their several stamps—the ' real things ' as they are called—and such men are said to be clever. Do you agree ?

THEAET. Most emphatically.

E.   SOCR. When a person has what the poet's wisdom commends as a ' shaggy heart ', or when the block is muddy or made of impure wax, or over soft or hard, the people with soft wax are quick to learn, but forgetful, those with hard wax the reverse. Where it is shaggy or rough, a gritty kind of stuff containing a lot of earth or dirt, the impressions obtained are indistinct ; so are they too when the stuff is hard, for they have no depth. Impressions in

195.   soft wax also are indistinct, because they melt together and soon become blurred. And if, besides this, they overlap through being crowded together into some wretched little narrow mind, they are still more indistinct. All these types, then, are likely to judge falsely. When they see or hear or think of something, they cannot quickly assign things to their several imprints. Because they are so slow and sort things into the wrong places, they constantly see and hear and think amiss, and we say they are mistaken about things and stupid.

[1] The Homeric word for heart ($\kappa\acute{\epsilon}\alpha\rho$) resembles $\kappa\eta\rho\acute{o}s$ (wax). Beare (*Gk. Theories of Elem. Cognition* 267) remarks that, had Plato chosen any physical organ to correspond to the wax as the seat of memory, it would probably have been the heart, the brain being the instrument of reason. There is no satisfactory evidence that the comparison of memory to a waxen block had ever been used before, except as a poet's metaphor (Aesch. *P.V.* 81 $\mu\nu\acute{\eta}\mu\sigma\sigma\iota\nu$ $\delta\acute{\epsilon}\lambda\tau\sigma\iota s$ $\phi\rho\epsilon\nu\tilde{\omega}\nu$, *Eum.* 275, etc.).

195B. THEAET. Your description could not be better, Socrates.

SOCR. We are to conclude, then, that false judgments do exist in us?

THEAET. Most certainly.

SOCR. And true ones also, I suppose?

THEAET. True ones also.

SOCR. At last, then, we believe we have reached a satis-factory agreement that both these kinds of judgments certainly exist?

THEAET. Most emphatically.

It does not appear that Plato offers his waxen block as anything more than an illustration, a mechanical model which helps us to distinguish a memory-image from a fresh impression of sense, and to imagine the process of fitting the one to the other correctly or incorrectly. The conclusion, that true and false judgments of this type do exist, rests simply on familiar experience. The illus-tration serves to bring out the point that error comes in, not in the act of direct perception, but in judgments we make about what we perceive. This is an advance on Protagoras, who drew no distinction between what ' appears ' to me to be true (what I believe or think) and what ' appears ' to me as real in perception. But his account of false judgment as ' thinking the thing that is not ' and his denial that such a thing is possible have been shelved. This thesis is reserved for the *Sophist*.

195B–196C. *False judgment in general cannot, however, be defined as the misfitting of perception to thought*

The weak point, however, is this. Only a small class of false judgments, even about things we now perceive, consist in identify-ing them with things we formerly perceived and now remember. This is the only type of judgment so far considered and described. It has been agreed, as a matter of common experience, that such judgments do exist. But there is an immense class of judgments, true and false, about things I do not now perceive and never have perceived. All historical judgments about events outside my own experience belong to this class. There are also, as Socrates now observes, true and false judgments about things that never can be perceived. Hence all that has been established is that false judgment does exist in a very small class of cases where we wrongly identify something we perceive. This is important, as contradicting Protagoras' doctrine that false judgment is impossible. But it has now to be pointed out that this ' mistaking ' or wrong ' fitting together of thought and perception ' is not a definition of false judgment in general. It will not cover cases where no perception is involved. We can make mistakes about numbers, which are not objects of perception but are said to be ' known ' in the sense we have just given to that term, *i.e.* registered as imprints in the memory. We must accordingly retract the earlier statement that mistakes cannot occur between two objects both known but not perceived.

195B. SOCR. It really does seem to be true, Theaetetus that a garrulous person is a strange and disagreeable creature.[1]

THEAET. Why, what makes you say that ?

C. SOCR. Disgust at my own stupidity. I am indeed garrulous : what else can you call a man who goes on bandying arguments to and fro because he is such a dolt that he cannot make up his mind and is loath to surrender any one of them ?

THEAET. But why are you disgusted with yourself ?

SOCR. I am not merely disgusted but anxious about the answer I shall make if someone asks : ' So, Socrates, you have made a discovery : that false judgment resides, not in our perceptions among themselves nor yet in our thoughts,

D. but in the fitting together of perception and thought ? ' I suppose I shall say, Yes, and plume myself on this brilliant discovery of ours.

THEAET. I don't see anything to be ashamed of in what you have just pointed out, Socrates.

SOCR. ' On the other hand,' he will continue, ' you also say that we can never imagine that a man whom we merely think of and do not see is a horse which again we do not see or touch but merely think of without perceiving it in any way ? ' I suppose I shall say, Yes, to that.

THEAET. And rightly.

E. SOCR. ' On that showing,' he will say, ' a man could never imagine that 11, which he merely thinks of, is 12, which again he merely thinks of.' Come, you must find the answer now.

THEAET. Well, I shall answer that, if he saw or handled eleven things, he might suppose they were twelve ; but he will never make that judgment about the 11 and the 12 he has in his thoughts.

SOCR. Well now, does a man ever consider in his own
196. mind 5 and 7—I don't mean five men and seven men or anything of that sort, but just 5 and 7 themselves, which

---

[1] ' Garrulity ' or ' babbling ' was an abusive term applied to the conversations of Socrates and his associates. See below, p. 176, on *Soph.* 225D.

196   we describe as records in that waxen block of ours, among which there can be no false judgment—does anyone ever take these into consideration and ask himself in his inward conversation how much they amount to; and does one man believe and state that they make 11, another that they make 12, or does everybody agree they make 12?

B.   THEAET. Far from it; many people say 11; and if larger numbers are involved, the more room there is for mistakes; for you are speaking generally of any numbers, I suppose.

SOCR. Yes, that is right. Now consider what happens in this case. Is it not thinking that the 12 itself that is stamped on the waxen block is 11?

THEAET. It seems so.

SOCR. Then haven't we come round again to our first argument? For when this happens to someone, he is thinking that one thing he knows is another thing he knows; and that, we said, was impossible. That was the very ground on which we were led to make out that there could be no such thing as false judgment: it was in order C.   to avoid the conclusion that the same man must at the same time know and not know the same thing.

THEAET. Quite true.

SOCR. If so, we must account for false judgment in some other way than as the misfitting of thought to perception. If it were that, we should never make mistakes among our thoughts themselves. As the case stands now, either there is no such thing as false judgment, or it is possible not to know what one does know. Which alternative do you choose?

THEAET. I see no possible choice, Socrates.

The Platonist may here be surprised to find our knowledge of a number regarded as the record in the memory-tablet of an impression, as if we became acquainted with the number 12 in the same way as with a colour or a sound or a person. Has Plato abandoned his doctrine of Recollection, according to which our knowledge of Forms, including numbers and their relations, is always latent in the soul, not acquired through the senses during this life, but only revived on the occasion of sense-experience? There is no ground for such a conclusion. The whole dialogue examines the claim of the world of external sensible objects to be the sole source of knowledge. This claim is taken as implying that outside us there are physical objects which can yield us sense-data through the several organs, and inside us a *tabula rasa* on which impressions so received can be stamped and recorded. This mechanism is based on the empiricist assumption that all our knowledge must be derived somehow from the external objects of perception. On this assumption (which Plato himself does not accept) our idea of the number 12 must be supposed to be extracted from a series of sense-impressions and added to our memory records. As Campbell remarks, ' memory is made to do the work of abstraction '. This is all the apparatus that has so far come into view. It has sufficed to illustrate one class of mistakes—the wrong fitting-together of old records and new impressions. But we have now seen that this formula will not cover the mistaking of one memory record for another, and so it will not do as a general account of false judgment. We cannot admit mistakes about numbers, unless we can find a sense in which we can not know something we do know. The empiricist's apparatus will have to be enlarged.

196D–199C. *Memory compared to an aviary, to provide for mistaken judgments not involving perception*

Objection might be taken to the statement (196B) that, when we make the mistake, we ' think that the 12 on our wax-tablet is 11 ', or that ' one thing we know (12) is another thing we know (11) '. It is still presumed that a false judgment must consist in wrongly identifying one thing with another. Even if that were so, what we identify with 11 is, not 12, but ' the sum of 5 and 7 ' —a number which at the moment we do not know (in a sense). We are wondering what number it is, and wrongly conclude that it is 11. The number 12, although we are familiar with it, is not present to our mind. We do not judge that 12 is 11.

This objection, it is true, does not invalidate the only conclusion stated : that the misfitting of thought and perception cannot be a definition of false judgment in general. But it serves to bring out the need for some enlargement of the empiricist apparatus— some further distinction between the meanings of the word ' know '. The misleading statement that ' we judge the 12 in our waxen block to be 11 ' is a consequence of the too narrow use of ' know ' in terms of that image. To ' know ' meant to have become acquainted with a thing and to ' remember ' it in the sense of having the memory of it now before the mind. If I remember both 11 and 12 in that way, to confuse them is as impossible as we said it was to confuse two absent friends when I now remember them both. Socrates, accordingly, goes on to distinguish yet another sense of ' know '. The image of an object may be registered in the memory without being present to our consciousness. It is possible not to know (have before our minds) what we do know (possess somewhere registered in memory). A new simile, the aviary, is now substituted for the waxen block to provide for this latent knowledge. We shall no longer need to speak as if the number 12 were present to our minds and confused with 11.

196D. SOCR. But the argument is not going to allow both alternatives. However, we must stick at nothing : suppose we try being quite shameless.

THEAET. In what way ?

SOCR. By making up our minds to describe what knowing is like.

THEAET. How is that shameless ?

SOCR. You seem to be unaware that our whole conversation from the outset has been an inquiry after the nature of knowledge on the supposition that we did not know what it was.

THEAET. No, I am quite aware of that.

SOCR. Then, doesn't it strike you as shameless to explain what knowing is like, when we don't know what knowledge

E. is ? The truth is, Theaetetus, that for some time past there has been a vicious taint in our discussion. Times out of number we have said : 'we know ', 'we do not know ', 'we have knowledge ', 'we have no knowledge ', as if we could understand each other while we still know nothing about knowledge. At this very moment, if you please, we have once more used the words ' know nothing ' and ' understand ', as if we had a right to use them while we are still destitute of knowledge.

THEAET. Well, but how are you going to carry on a discussion, Socrates, if you keep clear of those words ?

197. SOCR. I cannot, being the man I am, though I might if I were an expert in debate. If such a person were here now, he would profess to keep clear of them and rebuke us severely for my use of language. As we are such bunglers, then, shall I be so bold as to describe what knowing is like ? I think it might help us.

THEAET. Do so, then, by all means. And if you cannot avoid those words, you shall not be blamed.

SOCR. Well, you have heard what ' knowing ' is commonly said to be ?

THEAET. Possibly ; but I don't remember at the moment.

B. SOCR. They say it is ' having knowledge '.[1]

---

[1] This is of course not a ' definition ' of knowing, but a verbal paraphrase, which occurs at *Euthyd.* 277B. It may be due to Prodicus or some other writer on the correct use of language (περὶ ὀνομάτων ὀρθότητος). Prodicus is cited in the context at *Euthyd.* 277E.

197B. THEAET. True.

SOCR. Let us make a slight amendment and say : ' possessing knowledge '.

THEAET. What difference would you say that makes ?

SOCR. None, perhaps ; but let me tell you my idea and you shall help me test it.

THEAET. I will if I can.

SOCR. ' Having ' seems to me different from ' possessing '. If a man has bought a coat and owns it, but is not wearing it, we should say he possesses it without having it about him.[1]

THEAET. True.

c. SOCR. Now consider whether knowledge is a thing you can possess in that way without having it about you, like a man who has caught some wild birds—pigeons or what not—and keeps them in an aviary he has made for them at home. In a sense, of course, we might say he ' has ' them all the time inasmuch as he possesses them, mightn't we ?

THEAET. Yes.

SOCR. But in another sense he ' has ' none of them, though he has got control of them, now that he has made them captive in an enclosure of his own ; he can take and have hold of them whenever he likes by catching any bird he

D. chooses, and let them go again ; and it is open to him to do that as often as he pleases.

THEAET. That is so.

SOCR. Once more then, just as a while ago we imagined a sort of waxen block in our minds, so now let us suppose that every mind contains a kind of aviary stocked with birds of every sort, some in flocks apart from the rest, some in small groups, and some solitary, flying in any direction among them all.[2]

E. THEAET. Be it so. What follows ?

SOCR. When we are babies we must suppose this receptacle empty, and take the birds to stand for pieces of knowledge. Whenever a person acquires any piece of

---

[1] Ἔχειν is commonly used of ' wearing ' a garment. It also means ' to have hold of '—the phrase used below for holding the bird that has been caught inside the aviary.

[2] Some classification of the objects of knowledge seems to be hinted at. Comparison with the *Sophist* (252E ff.) may suggest that the large and small groups of birds are generic and specific Forms, the solitary birds which fly among all the rest, Forms of universal application like Existence, Sameness, Difference. But nothing turns on such conjectures.

197E. knowledge and shuts it up in his enclosure, we must say he has learnt or discovered the thing of which this is the knowledge, and that is what ' knowing ' means.

THEAET. Be it so.

198. SOCR. Now think of him hunting once more for any piece of knowledge that he wants, catching and holding it, and letting it go again. In what terms are we to describe that —the same that we used of the original process of acquisition, or different ones ? An illustration may help you to see what I mean. There is a science you call ' arithmetic '.

THEAET. Yes.

SOCR. Conceive that, then, as a chase after pieces of knowledge about all the numbers, odd or even.

THEAET. I will.

SOCR. That, I take it, is the science in virtue of which

B. a man has in his control pieces of knowledge about numbers and can hand them over to someone else.

THEAET. Yes.

SOCR. And when he hands them over, we call it ' teaching ', and when the other takes them from him, that is ' learning ', and when he has them in the sense of possessing them in that aviary of his, that is ' knowing '.

THEAET. Certainly.

SOCR. Now observe what follows. The finished arithmetician knows all numbers, doesn't he ? There is no number the knowledge of which is not in his mind.

THEAET. Naturally.

C. SOCR. And such a person may sometimes count either the numbers themselves in his own head or some set of external things that have a number.

THEAET. Of course.

SOCR. And by counting we shall mean simply trying to find out what some particular number amounts to ?

THEAET. Yes.

SOCR. It appears, then, that the man who, as we admitted, knows every number, is trying to find out what he knows as if he had no knowledge of it. No doubt you sometimes hear puzzles of that sort debated.

THEAET. Indeed I do.

D. SOCR. Well, our illustration from hunting pigeons and getting possession of them will enable us to explain that the hunting occurs in two ways: first, before you possess your pigeon in order to have possession of it; secondly, after getting possession of it, in order to catch and hold

198D.   in your hand what you have already possessed for some
time. In the same way, if you have long possessed pieces
of knowledge about things you have learnt and know, it
is still possible to get to know the same things again, by
the process of recovering the knowledge of some particular
thing and getting hold of it. It is knowledge you have
possessed for some time, but you had not got it handy in
your mind.

THEAET. True.

E.   SOCR. That, then, was the drift of my question, what
terms should be used to describe the arithmetician who
sets about counting or the literate person who sets about
reading ; because it seemed as if, in such a case, the man
was setting about learning again from himself what he
already knew.

THEAET. That sounds odd, Socrates.

SOCR. Well, but can we say he is going to read or count
199.   something he does *not* know, when we have already granted
that he knows all the letters or all the numbers ?

THEAET. No, that is absurd too.

SOCR. Shall we say, then, that we care nothing about
words, if it amuses anyone to turn and twist the expressions
' knowing ' and ' learning ' ? Having drawn a distinction
between possessing knowledge and having it about one,
we agree that it is impossible not to possess what one does
possess, and so we avoid the result that a man should not
know what he does know ; but we say that it is possible
for him to get hold of a false judgment about it. For
B.   he may not have about him the knowledge of that thing,
but a different piece of knowledge instead, if it so happens
that, in hunting for some particular piece of knowledge,
among those that are fluttering about, he misses it and
catches hold of a different one. In that case, you see, he
mistakes 11 for 12,[1] because he has caught hold of the
knowledge of 11 that is inside him, instead of his knowledge
of 12, as he might catch a dove in place of a pigeon.

THEAET. That seems reasonable.

SOCR. Whereas, when he catches the piece of knowledge
he is trying to catch, he is not mistaken but thinks what

[1] Literally ' thinks 11 is 12 '. This cannot now mean that he has both
numbers before his mind and judges one of them to be the other. This was
agreed to be impossible (195E). It means that he *mistakes* the number 11,
which he lays hold of for the number 12 which he was really looking for,
when he asked : What is the sum of 7 and 5 ?

199B.   is true. In this way both true and false judgments can
  C.   exist, and the obstacles that were troubling us are removed.
       You will agree to this, perhaps? Or will you not?
       THEAET. I will.
       SOCR. Yes; for now we are rid of the contradiction about
       people not knowing what they do know. That no longer
       implies our not possessing what we do possess, whether
       we are mistaken about something or not.

The aviary has enlarged the machinery of the waxen block by
providing for the process of hunting out latent pieces of knowledge
and bringing them before the mind. So it has led to the suggestion
that false judgment occurs when we get hold of the wrong piece
of knowledge and ' interchange ' it for the right one. An important
difference between the two images is that the process of originally
acquiring knowledge is differently conceived. The waxen block
was thought of as a receptacle for sense-impressions which left
their imprint as memory-images. It seemed hard to imagine how
one such imprint should ever be mistaken for another; and no
provision was made for historical knowledge or any knowledge
not immediately derived from the senses. The aviary, on the other
hand, represents knowledge as acquired from a teacher who ' hands
over ' pieces of information to the learner. Such information would
not consist in a series of separate imprints, but rather of statements
offered for our belief. It would cover historical and abstract
knowledge, as well as our notions of such things as numbers.

Now, from the *Meno* onwards, Plato has repeatedly declared
that what he calls ' knowledge ' is not a thing that can be ' handed
over ' by one person to another. The true objects of knowledge
must be directly seen by the eye of the soul; the professors of
education who claim to put into the mind knowledge that is not
there are like one who should claim to put sight into blind eyes.[1]
The sophists are condemned for offering to ' hand over ' ' excellence '
(*areté*) of various sorts to their hearers.[2] In Plato's view all
mathematical knowledge and knowledge of the Forms cannot, in
the ordinary sense, be ' taught '. It is always in the soul and
needs to be ' recollected '. The intervention of a teacher is not
necessary, though the process may be directed and assisted by
conversation (' dialectic ') with a wiser person who will act as
midwife. The Platonist will see at once that what is here called
a ' piece of knowledge ' can be nothing more than a belief ($\delta \acute{o} \xi a$),
conveyed from one mind to another. All this cannot be openly
said here, because the Forms are excluded from the discussion,

---

[1] *Rep.* 518C.   [2] *Meno* 93B; *Euthyd.* 273D, 287A.

which is confined to the empiricist claim that all knowledge comes from the external world of sense, either directly or by teaching as commonly conceived. But Plato is careful to note that we are still working on the empiricist assumption that the aviary is empty at birth—a *tabula rasa*—and gradually filled with contents derived from sensible experience and learning. The reader, guided by the long description of Socratic midwifery, is left to infer that these so-called 'pieces of knowledge' are not knowledge at all. It is perhaps with intention that Plato, while describing the recovery of latent 'knowledge', never uses his own word for recollection (*anamnesis*).

199C–200D. *Rejection of 'interchange of pieces of knowledge' as an account of False Judgment*

The aviary has enabled us to imagine how a man who has learnt that the sum of 7 and 5 is 12, may sometimes ask himself what the sum of 7 and 5 is, and get hold of a wrong ' piece of knowledge ', viz. the number 11, which he is also acquainted with. He mistakes this for the 'piece of knowledge' he wants, namely 12. This 'interchange' may seem to be an unobjectionable description of such a mistake. Socrates, however, at once raises an objection, which turns upon the unexplained term 'piece of knowledge '.

199C. SOCR. (*continues*). But it strikes me that a still stranger consequence is coming in sight.

THEAET. What is that ?

SOCR. That the interchange of pieces of knowledge should ever result in a judgment that is false.

THEAET. How do you mean ?

D. SOCR. In the first place, that a man should have knowledge of something and at the same time fail to recognise [1] that very thing, not for want of knowing it but by reason of his own knowledge ; and next that he should judge that thing to be something else and *vice versa*—isn't that very unreasonable : that when a piece of knowledge presents itself, the mind should fail to recognise anything and know nothing ? On this showing, the presence of ignorance might just as well make us know something, or the presence of blindness make us see—if knowledge can ever make us fail to know.

This objection is obscure, and the language ambiguous : ἀγνοεῖν can mean either ' to be ignorant of ' or ' to fail to recognise ' (the

[1] For ἀγνοεῖν, meaning ' fail to recognise ', cf. 188B.

opposite of γνῶναι, 'to recognise'). The 'piece of knowledge that presents itself' must mean the number 11, which I have laid hold of instead of the number 12 which I was looking for and have not found. In what sense does the interchange involve that I should 'fail to recognise (ἀγνοεῖν) that very thing, not for want of knowing it (ἀγνωμοσύνη) but by reason of my own knowledge'? 'Fail to recognise that very thing' (the number 11) can only mean that I fail to recognise the fact that it is not the number I want; hence Socrates says I judge it to be 12, *i.e.* mistake it for 12. But 'not for want of knowing it' (ἀγνωμοσύνη) means 'not for want of *be ingacquainted with* it'. The situation is analogous to what was described earlier: I see an acquaintance and, failing to recognise him, mistake him for another acquaintance. But there perception was involved, and the mistake was explained as the fitting-together of the fresh impression and the wrong memory-image. Here no perception is involved. Socrates' point seems to be that the aviary contains nothing but 'pieces of knowledge'. I am acquainted with both the numbers, 11 and 12. One of them (11) is now before my mind. How can I mistake that number for the other which I am also acquainted with? If I have been taught and know the truth that $7 + 5 = 12$, how can I substitute 11 for 12 and believe that I have got hold of the right number? There is no question here of seeing something dimly at a distance; only 'pieces of knowledge' are involved.

To this we might reply that an analogous explanation by the misfitting of two pieces of knowledge could be given, if the unexplained term 'piece of knowledge' were taken in a sufficiently wide sense. The expression covers objects (such as numbers) that I am acquainted with, as well as truths that I have been taught. All these are in my aviary. Does it also include a complex object such as 'the sum of 7 and 5'? This ought to be included; it consists of terms I am acquainted with and it is before my mind when I ask: what is the sum of 7 and 5? It is this object that I identify with 11 when I make my false judgment. If it is a 'piece of knowledge' and contained in the aviary, then the false judgment can be explained as the wrong putting-together of two pieces of knowledge, as in the waxen block false judgment was the putting-together of a fresh impression and the wrong memory imprint. The result will be a false judgment entirely composed of 'pieces of knowledge' (terms I am acquainted with). It thus seems that the aviary apparatus is, after all, as adequate to explain false judgment where no perception is involved as the waxen block was to explain false judgment involving perception.

It is hard to resist the impression that Plato has overlooked this explanation, because he does not recognise ' the sum of 7 and 5 ' as a ' piece of knowledge ', but persists in speaking as if we judged not that ' the sum of 7 and 5 is 11 ' but that ' 12 (the number we are seeking) is 11 (the number we lay hold of) '. If such objects as ' the sum of 7 and 5 ' are excluded, then the difficulty Socrates raises does exist : how can I mistake the 11 which I have before my mind for the 12 which I know but have not before my mind ?

Theaetetus, at any rate, does not put forward the explanation above offered. He takes up Socrates' word for ' ignorance ' or ' failure to recognise ' (ἀγνωμοσύνη), and suggests that our minds may contain ' pieces of ignorance ' as well as ' pieces of knowledge '.

199E. THEAET. Perhaps, Socrates, we were wrong in making the birds stand for pieces of knowledge only, and we ought to have imagined pieces of ignorance flying about with them in the mind. Then, in chasing them, our man would lay hold sometimes of a piece of knowledge, sometimes of a piece of ignorance ; and the ignorance would make him judge falsely, the knowledge truly, about the same thing.

What is a ' piece of ignorance ' ? Evidently not an object I am unacquainted with, for then it would not be in the aviary at all. It can only be a false belief which I have somehow formed or been taught, such as that $7 + 5 = 11$. There is no reason why false beliefs should not be in the aviary ; in fact our aviaries contain only too many. In so far as they consist of terms I am acquainted with and are things that I have learnt and possess stored in my memory, they satisfy the description of ' pieces of knowledge '. But they are not knowledge in the sense in which whatever is knowledge must be true. That they are simply false beliefs is practically stated in Theaetetus' last words : ' the ignorance would make him judge falsely '. Theaetetus' suggestion means that what I lay hold of is an old false belief which I bring up into consciousness.

An obvious answer to Theaetetus' suggestion would be this : ' You explain my making a false judgment now as my getting hold of an old false belief which I have acquired and have in my memory ; but that does not explain how I could acquire that false belief originally. You merely push back to an earlier stage the same problem : how could I ever judge that $7 + 5 = 11$? ' Socrates, however, does not raise that objection. Taking Theaetetus' suggestion that I call up and affirm an old false belief, he asks how it is that I fail to recognise it as false and mistake it for a true piece of knowledge.

199E. SOCR. It is not easy to disapprove of anything you say, Theaetetus ; but think again about your suggestion. Sup-

199E.
200.

 pose it is as you say ; then the man who lays hold of the
piece of ignorance will judge falsely. Is that right ?

THEAET. Yes.

SOCR. But of course he will not think he is judging falsely.

THEAET. Of course not.

SOCR. No ; he will think he is judging truly ; and his
attitude of mind will be the same as if he knew the thing
he is mistaken about.

THEAET. Naturally.

SOCR. So he will imagine that, as a result of his chase, he
has got hold of a piece of knowledge, not a piece of ignorance.

THEAET. Clearly.

SOCR. Then we have gone a long way round only to find
ourselves confronted once more with our original difficulty.
Our destructive critic will laugh at us. ' You wonderful

B. people,' he will say, ' are we to understand that a man
knows both a piece of knowledge and a piece of ignorance,
and then supposes that one of these things he knows is the
other which he also knows ?   Or does he know neither, and
then judge that one of these unknown things is the other ?
Or does he know only one, and identify this known thing
with the unknown one, or the unknown one with the known ?
Or are you going to tell me that there are yet further pieces
of knowledge *about* your pieces of knowledge and ignorance,
and that their owner keeps these shut up in yet another of

C. your ridiculous aviaries or waxen blocks, knowing them so
long as he possesses them, although he may not have them
at hand in his mind ?   On that showing you will find your-
selves perpetually driven round in a circle and never getting
any further.' What are we to reply to that, Theaetetus ?

THEAET. Really, Socrates, I don't know what we are to say.

SOCR. Maybe, my young friend, we have deserved this
rebuke, and the argument shows that we were wrong to

D. leave knowledge on one side and look first for an explanation
of false judgment. That cannot be understood until we
have a satisfactory account of the nature of knowledge.

THEAET. As things now stand, Socrates, one cannot avoid
that conclusion.

The critic objects that it is as hard to explain how I can fail to
recognise a false belief as false and mistake it for the true belief
which I possess stored in my mind, as it is to explain how I can
mistake an object before my mind for another object which is in
my memory. As Socrates indicates, that leads on to the question :

How can I know that I know? How can I recognise knowledge when I have it and be sure that it is knowledge? This is an old problem inconclusively discussed in the *Charmides* (167 ff.). Plato refuses to pursue it here, or to carry any further the attempt to account for false belief.

What has emerged is that the term 'knowledge' is very ambiguous. Until we have discovered all its meanings, we cannot really explain false judgment. The discussion has been fruitful in bringing to light some of these meanings. But the scope of the dialogue excludes all that Plato calls knowledge in the full sense. He breaks off here because he cannot go further without invoking the true objects of knowledge. Plato's own analysis of false judgment will be given in the *Sophist*, when the Forms have been brought into view.

200D–201C. *Conclusion : Knowledge cannot be defined as True Belief*

It has become clear that the so-called ' pieces of knowledge ' which I have learnt from a teacher and stored in my memory are nothing better than true beliefs. When I recall one to consciousness my attitude of mind towards it is, as Socrates says, indistinguishable from my attitude to a false belief. This consideration leads us to the next point : the final refutation of the claim of true belief to be knowledge. My confidence in a mere belief is not grounded in reason. The teaching which consists in ' handing over ' beliefs, whether true or false, is no better than the rhetorical persuasion of a barrister. Knowledge is not so gained ; and when it is gained, it cannot be shaken by persuasion.

200D. SOCR. To start all over again, then : what is one to say that knowledge is? For surely we are not going to give up yet.

THEAET. Not unless you do so.

SOCR. Then tell me: what definition can we give with the least risk of contradicting ourselves?

E. THEAET. The one we tried before, Socrates. I have nothing else to suggest.

SOCR. What was that?

THEAET. That true belief is knowledge. Surely there can at least be no mistake in believing what is true and the consequences are always satisfactory.[1]

---

[1] It has been pointed out in the *Meno* (97A) that for practical purposes it is as useful to believe that a road leads to a certain place as to know that it does. Cf. also *Rep.* 506c : belief without knowledge is at the best like a blind man who takes the right road.

TRUE BELIEF IS NOT KNOWLEDGE

200E.　SOCR.　Try, and you will see, Theaetetus, as the man said when he was asked if the river was too deep to ford. So here, if we go forward on our search, we may stumble upon

201.　something that will reveal the thing we are looking for. We shall make nothing out, if we stay where we are.

THEAET. True ; let us go forward and see.

SOCR. Well, we need not go far to see this much : you will find a whole profession to prove that true belief is not knowledge.

THEAET. How so ? What profession ?

SOCR. The profession of those paragons of intellect known as orators and lawyers. There you have men who use their skill to produce conviction, not by instruction, but by making people believe whatever they want them to believe. You

B.　can hardly imagine teachers so clever as to be able, in the short time allowed by the clock, to instruct their hearers thoroughly in the true facts of a case of robbery or other violence which those hearers had not witnessed.

THEAET. No, I cannot imagine that ; but they can convince them.

SOCR. And by convincing you mean making them believe something.

THEAET. Of course.

SOCR. And when a jury is rightly convinced of facts which can be known only by an eye-witness, then, judging by hear-

C.　say and accepting a true belief, they are judging without knowledge, although, if they find the right verdict, their conviction is correct ?

THEAET. Certainly.

SOCR. But if true belief and knowledge were the same thing, the best of jurymen could never have a correct belief without knowledge. It now appears that they must be different things.

This argument is repeated in a later dialogue, the *Timaeus* (51D), where the existence of the Forms is said to follow from the distinction between knowledge or rational understanding (νοῦς) and true belief. Knowledge is produced by instruction, always accompanied by a true account of its grounds (ἀληθὴς λόγος), unshakable by persuasion, and possessed by gods and only a few among men. True belief is produced by persuasion, not based on rational grounds (ἄλογον), can be changed by persuasion, and is possessed by all mankind.

In our passage Socrates has not spoken of the absence of rational

grounds, such as he has in mind in the *Meno* and the *Timaeus*.
In both those dialogues Plato is thinking of what he himself calls
knowledge. In the *Meno* mathematical knowledge is in question.
After his experiment with the slave, Socrates remarks that the
slave has now a true belief about the solution ; but it will not be
knowledge until he has been taken repeatedly through all the steps
of the proof. He will then see for himself, with unshakable conviction, that the conclusion must be true. His belief will now be
assured by reflection on the grounds or reasons (αἰτίας λογισμῷ).
Such is the ' true account of the grounds ' (ἀληθὴς λόγος) to which
the *Timaeus* refers. But here the real objects of knowledge are
not to be mentioned, and Socrates is only allowed his analogous
contrast between the juryman's second-hand belief and the direct
' knowledge ' of the eye-witness, who has seen the fact for himself.

III. THE CLAIM OF TRUE BELIEF ACCOMPANIED BY AN ACCOUNT OR EXPLANATION TO BE KNOWLEDGE

201C–202C. *Socrates states this theory as he has heard it*

Theaetetus' next suggestion is that the addition of some kind of
' account ' or ' explanation ' (*logos*) [1] will convert true belief into
knowledge. Various possible senses of ' account ' are distinguished
and considered, and the suggestion is finally rejected. It will
appear, however, that no one of these senses is the sense which
' account ' bears in the *Meno* and the *Timaeus*. Why that sense
is ignored will become clear as we proceed.

201C. THEAET. Yes, Socrates, I have heard someone make the
distinction.[2] I had forgotten, but now it comes back to me.

D. He said that true belief with the addition of an account
(*logos*) was knowledge, while belief without an account was
outside its range. Where no account could be given of a
thing, it was not ' knowable '—that was the word he used
—where it could, it was knowable.

SOCR. A good suggestion. But tell me how he distinguished
these knowable things from the unknowable. It may turn
out that what you were told tallies with something I have
heard said.

---

[1] English provides no single equivalent for *logos*, a word which covers
(1) statement, speech ; (2) expression, definition, description, formula ;
(3) ' tale ' or enumeration ; (4) explanation, account, ground. A translator
is forced to use now one, now another of these expressions. In the text the
word remains ambiguous until Socrates distinguishes some of its chief
meanings.

[2] Between knowledge and true belief.

III. TRUE BELIEF WITH AN ACCOUNT

201D. THEAET. I am not sure if I can recall that ; but I think I should recognise it if I heard it stated.

SOCR. If you have had a dream, let me tell you mine in return. I seem to have heard some people say that what
E. might be called the first elements [1] of which we and all other things consist are such that no account can be given of them. Each of them just by itself can only be named ; we cannot attribute to it anything further or say that it exists or does
202. not exist ; for we should at once be attaching to it existence or non-existence, whereas we ought to add nothing if we are to express just it alone. We ought not even to add ' just ' or ' it ' or ' each ' or ' alone ' or ' this ' [2], or any other of a host of such terms. These terms, running loose about the place, are attached to everything, and they are distinct from the things to which they are applied. If it were possible for an element to be expressed in any formula exclusively belonging to it, no other terms ought to enter into that expression ; but in fact there is no formula in which any
B. element can be expressed : it can only be named, for a name is all there is that belongs to it. But when we come to things composed of these elements, then, just as these things are complex, so the names are combined to make a description (*logos*), a description being precisely a combination of names. Accordingly, elements are inexplicable and unknowable, but they can be perceived ; while complexes (' syllables ') are knowable and explicable, and you can have a true notion of them. So when a man gets hold of the true notion of
C. something without an account, his mind does think truly of it, but he does not know it ; for if one cannot give and receive an account of a thing, one has no knowledge of that thing. But when he has also got hold of an account, all this becomes possible to him and he is fully equipped with knowledge.

Does that version represent the dream as you heard it, or not ?

THEAET. Perfectly.

The theory here put forward was certainly never held by Plato himself. On the other hand, it is obviously a philosophic theory,

---

[1] στοιχεῖα meant letters of the alphabet, or the ' rudiments ' of a subject. This is said to be its first occurrence as applied to the elements of physical things. Presently συλλαβαί (syllables) is used for the complex things composed of elements.

[2] Buttmann's conjecture τὸ ' τὸ ' for τοῦτο (here and at 205C) may be supported by *Soph.* 239A. See note there (p. 207).

which would not occur to common sense. It must belong to some contemporary of Socrates or Plato, whom Plato does not choose to name.[1] Possibly, Socrates is represented as ' dreaming ' it because the theory was really advanced after his death. There seems to be no evidence sufficient to identify the author.[2]

The theory may be considered under the three heads : (a) Things ; (b) Language ; (c) Cognition.

(a) *Things.*—The only things recognised are ' ourselves and everything else ', *i.e.* concrete individual natural objects. These are composed of simple unanalysable elements. There is no question of immaterial things, for the elements are said to be perceptible. This also shows that atoms are not intended. Since no examples are given, we cannot say whether ' elements ' means simple primary substances, such as gold, or simple qualities, like yellow, or even whether the author drew this distinction. He may have meant any simple constituent that we should name in enumerating all the parts we can perceive and distinguish in a complex thing.

(b) *Language.*—The element, being simple, has a name only. We can refer to or indicate it by this name. But it ' has no *logos* '. This appears to cover two meanings which we should distinguish. (1) We cannot make any *statement* about the element, such as that it exists. If we are to speak of it alone, we must not add, or ascribe, to it any second ' name ' (word). The element is completely indicated by uttering the single word ' gold ' or ' yellow '. We may not even say ' this is yellow ', since ' this ' and ' is ' express something different from the simple name ' yellow ', which already expresses all there is to be expressed and all that I perceive. Also, ' this ' and ' is ' do not belong exclusively to the element I now perceive. (2) The name of an element is *indefinable,* just as the element itself is unanalysable. The nature is simple and no ' account ' consisting of several names (words) can be given of it.

The definition of *logos* as a ' combination of names (words) ' will cover statements about a thing as well as the definition of a definable name. But probably the author was not thinking about defining names (which he would not rank among complex ' things ') but only about describing things. The simple name indicates the elementary

---

[1] Theaetetus (at 201c) and Socrates (202E, τὸν εἰπόντα) both speak of the author in the singular.

[2] The case for Antisthenes was most fully stated by Gillespie (*Arch. Gesch. Philos.* xxvi, 479 ff. ; xxvii, 17 ff.). See also Ross, *Metaph. of Aristotle* i, 346. A. Levi (*Revue Hist. Philos.* 1930, pp. 16 ff.), among others, has disputed this attribution. Prof. G. C. Field has given a judicious account of Antisthenes in *Plato and His Contemporaries* (1930), 160 ff. I can see little resemblance between the doctrine and the atomism attributed to Ecphantus, who is suggested by Burnet and Prof. Taylor.

part ; the full description or ' account ' of a complex thing consists of as many names as there are elements. All statements about the thing he would regard as giving it names, each of which should belong to one of its parts. In the *Sophist* (p. 253) we shall meet again with this view of what was later called ' predication '. The effect is that the distinction between the definition and other statements about the thing is not drawn ; and this appears to be the case in our passage.

(*c*) *Cognition.*—The theory distinguishes between perception (αἴσθησις), a true notion (ἀληθὴς δόξα), and knowledge (ἐπιστήμη).

Of the element we have only a simple direct perception, not ' knowledge '. Of the complex thing we have at first a true notion (ἀληθὴς δόξα) without a *logos*. *Logos*, as the later argument shows, means enumerating by name the simple components of the complex. When I have done this, I have ' given an account ' of the complex thing and am now said to ' know ' it. I have expressed what the thing is by giving a list of all its simple parts. But it is hard to be sure what is meant by the ' true δόξα ' which I have before I enumerate the parts. Presumably it means a complex unanalysed presentation of the whole object. In defence of the translation ' true notion ' it may be remarked that Plato uses the phrase ' get hold of the true δόξα *of a thing* without a *logos* '.[1] ' Notion ' or ' impression ' seems to be meant. It may be conjectured that such a notion would be expressed by a definable name, such as ' man ', or (to use Socrates' later illustration, 207A) ' wagon '. Possibly δόξα includes the judgment ' That is a man '. This judgment may be true (perhaps, *must* be true) ; but I shall not have knowledge till I have enumerated all the parts of the object, which is the same thing as defining the name.

The theory mentions only *true* notions, not false ones. It is not unlikely that the author held that every notion is true. If the notion is composed of simple perceptions, each of which is an impression directly given by some simple property of the thing, and if there can be no error in the perceptions, there can be none in the complex notion. The theory may hold that there must be just that thing I perceive or have a notion of ; otherwise I should be perceiving something else or nothing at all. It is quite possible that the author of the theory agreed (as Antisthenes did) with those who denied the possibility of false beliefs and statements.

---

[1] 202B : ὅταν ἄνευ λόγου τὴν ἀληθῆ δόξαν τινός τις λάβῃ. We have already noted (p. 119) Plato's use of δοξάζειν with an accusative for 'thinking *of* a thing '. Again ἔχων δόξαν περὶ σοῦ (209A, 1) and σὲ ἐδόξαζον (209B, 2) are used interchangeably for ' having a notion of you '

202C–206C.   *The Theory criticised for making Elements unknowable*

For the understanding of the following argument, it is essential to grasp that the theory is materialistic, in the sense that the only ' things ' it recognises as the objects of any sort of cognition are concrete individual things, and the perceptible parts of which such things are aggregates.

Socrates first disposes of the theory on its own ground, where the statement that elements are unknowable proves fatal.

202C.   SOCR.   So this dream finds favour and you hold that a true notion with the addition of an account is knowledge ?

THEAET.   Precisely.

D.   SOCR.   Can it be, Theaetetus, that, all in a moment, we have found out to-day what so many wise men have grown old in seeking and have not found ?

THEAET.   I, at any rate, am satisfied with our present statement, Socrates.

SOCR.   Yes, the statement just in itself may well be satisfactory ; for how can there ever be knowledge without an account and right belief ? [1]   But there is one point in the theory as stated that does not find favour with me.

THEAET.   What is that ?

SOCR.   What might be considered its most ingenious

E.   feature : it says that the elements are unknowable, but whatever is complex (' syllables ') can be known.

THEAET.   Is not that right ?

SOCR.   We must find out.   We hold as a sort of hostage for the theory the illustration in terms of which it was stated.

THEAET.   Namely ?

SOCR.   Letters—the elements of writing—and syllables. That and nothing else was the prototype the author of this theory had in mind, don't you think ?

THEAET.   Yes, it was.

203.   SOCR.   Let us take up that illustration, then, and put it to the question, or rather put the question to ourselves : did we learn our letters on that principle or not ? [2]   To begin with : is it true that an account can be given of syllables, but not of letters ?

THEAET.   It may be so.

---

[1] This may mean that the formula ' true belief with an account ' is a satisfactory description at least of some knowledge, provided that the right meaning be given to *logos*, not any of the meanings discussed in the following context.

[2] Socrates goes back to this question at 206A.

203. SOCR. I agree, decidedly. Suppose you are asked about the first syllable of 'Socrates': 'Explain, Theaetetus; what is SO?' How will you answer?

THEAET. S and O.

SOCR. And you have there an account of the syllable?

THEAET. Yes.

B. SOCR. Go on, then; give me a similar account of S.

THEAET. But how can one state the elements of an element? The fact is, of course, Socrates, that S is one of the consonants, nothing but a noise, like a hissing of the tongue; while B not only has no articulate sound but is not even a noise, and the same is true of most of the letters. So they may well be said to be inexplicable, when the clearest of them, the seven vowels themselves, have only a sound, and no sort of account can be given of them.[1]

SOCR. So far, then, we have reached a right conclusion about knowledge.

THEAET. Apparently.

The 'right conclusion' is that, if *logos* means an account or explanation consisting in the enumeration of the components of a complex thing, we must finally reach simple parts which cannot be so 'explained'. (So in mathematics the ultimate terms used in definitions must be indefinable.) But if such analysis is to yield knowledge, these ultimate components must be knowable. The weak point of the theory is that it says they are unknowable, and can only be perceived. So the process of acquiring knowledge will be a process of analysing a complex which is not yet known into components which cannot be known.

The argument exposing this weakness is in the form of a dilemma. A syllable (complex) must be either (1) the mere aggregate of the letters, or (2) a single entity which comes into being when the letters are combined and vanishes when they are separated. Socrates easily disposes of the first alternative.

203C. SOCR. But now, have we been right in declaring that the letter cannot be known, though the syllable can?

THEAET. That seems all right.

SOCR. Take the syllable then: do we mean by that both the two letters or (if there are more than two) all the letters?

---

[1] At *Philebus* 18B we find the same classification: (1) *vowels* (φωνήεντα), (2) *consonants* (ἄφωνα, without articulate sound), (3) *mutes* (ἄφθογγα, which are not even noises).

203C. Or do we mean a single entity that comes into existence from the moment when they are put together?

THEAET. I should say we mean all the letters.

SOCR. Then take the case of the two letters S and O. The two together are the first syllable of my name. Anyone who knows that syllable knows both the letters, doesn't he?

D. THEAET. Naturally.

SOCR. So he knows the S and the O.

THEAET. Yes.

SOCR. But has he, then, no knowledge of *each* letter, so that he knows both without knowing either?

THEAET. That is a monstrous absurdity, Socrates.

SOCR. And yet, if it is necessary to know each of two things before one can know both, he simply must know the letters first, if he is ever to know the syllable ; and so our fine theory will vanish and leave us in the lurch.

E. THEAET. With a startling suddenness.

SOCR. Yes, because we are not keeping a good watch upon it.

This argument is not verbal, but quite fair. If the syllable is exactly the same thing as its two letters, then to know the syllable is to know the letters. It may be added that the theory distinguished knowledge from perception, and evidently regarded knowledge as superior. Since the syllable is nothing more than the aggregate of the two letters, of each of which I have a perception, ' the addition of the account ' which was to yield knowledge can in fact only lead to two perceptions, side by side, of two unknowable objects.

(2) The second alternative—that the syllable is something other than the aggregate of the letters—requires some more subtle distinctions.

203E. SOCR. (*continues*). Perhaps we ought to have assumed that the syllable was not the letters but a single entity that arises out of them with a unitary character of its own and different from the letters.

THEAET. By all means. Indeed, it may well be so rather than the other way.

SOCR. Let us consider that. We ought not to abandon an imposing theory in this poor-spirited manner.

THEAET. Certainly not.

204. SOCR. Suppose, then, it is as we say now : the syllable arises as a single entity from any set of letters which can

204.   be combined [1] ; and that holds of every complex, not only
in the case of letters.

THEAET. By all means.

SOCR. In that case, it must have no parts.

THEAET. Why ?

SOCR. Because, if a thing has parts, the whole thing must
be the same as all the parts.

The term ' whole ' is here limited to mean a thing composed of
parts into which it can be divided up, in such a way that the parts
so arrived at account for the whole thing. Thus the sum of money
called a shilling can be divided into twelve pence which completely
represent its value. Nothing evaporates in the process of division.
So the whole here is said to be exactly equivalent to ' all the parts '.
Accordingly, if the syllable or complex is something over and above
the letters, the letters will not be parts of that something (and it
can have no other parts) ; so it will not be the ' whole '. From this
statement we might pass straight to the conclusion (205c) : Since
a syllable is a unitary thing, having no parts into which it can be
analysed, it is simple, inexplicable, and unknowable for the same
reason as the letter. This is the conclusion which completes the
dilemma. It is fatal to the theory, if we keep to the theory's own
assumptions. But here Socrates turns aside to meet the objection
that a whole consisting of parts may not be simply the ' sum ' of
those parts (τὸ πᾶν) or ' all the parts ' (τὰ πάντα), but a single entity
arising out of them and distinct from them. It is true that even
a jigsaw puzzle, when completed, has a unity as forming a picture,
which disappears when the parts are separated. But Socrates is
justified in arguing that that resulting entity is not properly
described as ' the whole '. It is an additional element which super-
venes on the putting together of the parts which make the whole.
He urges that the whole cannot be distinguished from the ' sum ',
which itself cannot be distinguished from ' all the parts '.

204A.   SOCR. (continues). Or do you say that a whole likewise [2]
is a single entity that arises out of the parts and is different
from the aggregate of the parts ?

THEAET. Yes, I do.

SOCR. Then do you regard the sum (τὸ πᾶν) as the same
thing as the whole, or are they different ?

---

[1] συναρμοττόντων is not ' harmonious '. It means that only some letters
will ' fit together ' to form a syllable : one of them must always be a vowel
(Soph. 253A). Other combinations of letters, e.g. two or three consonants
without a vowel, are impossible.

[2] ' likewise ' (καί), i.e. as well as the syllable, of which this has been said.

204B. THEAET. I am not at all clear ; but you tell me to answer boldly, so I will take the risk of saying they are different.

SOCR. Your boldness, Theaetetus, is right ; whether your answer is so, we shall have to consider.

THEAET. Yes, certainly.

SOCR. Well, then, the whole will be different from the sum, according to our present view.

THEAET. Yes.

SOCR. Well but now, is there any difference between the sum and all the things it includes ? For instance, when we say, ' one, two, three, four, five, six ', or ' twice three ' or

C. ' three times two ' or ' four and two ' or ' three and two and one ', are we in all these cases expressing the same thing or different things ?

THEAET. The same.

SOCR. Just six, and nothing else ?

THEAET. Yes.

SOCR. In fact, in each form of expression we have expressed all the six.[1]

THEAET. Yes.

SOCR. But when we express them all, is there no sum [2] that we express ?

THEAET. There must be.

SOCR. And is that sum anything else than ' six ' ?

THEAET. No.

D. SOCR. Then, at any rate in the case of things that consist of a number, the words ' sum ' and ' all the things ' denote the same thing.

THEAET. So it seems.

SOCR. Let us put our argument, then, in this way. The number of (square feet in) an acre, and the acre are the same thing, aren't they ?

THEAET. Yes.

SOCR. And so too with the number of (feet in) a mile ?

THEAET. Yes.

SOCR. And again with the number of (soldiers in) an army and the army, and so on, in all cases. The total number is the same as the total thing in each case.

THEAET. Yes.

E. SOCR. But the number of (units in) any collection of things cannot be anything but *parts* of that collection ?

---

[1] Reading πάντα τὰ ἕξ with BT.

[2] The word ' sum ' (πᾶν) here is necessary to the argument. The manuscripts have πάλιν.

204E. THEAET. No.

SOCR. Now, anything that has parts consists of parts.

THEAET. Evidently.

SOCR. But all the parts, we have agreed, are the same as the sum, if the total number is to be the same as the total thing.

THEAET. Yes.

SOCR. The whole, then, does not consist of parts; for if it were all the parts it would be a sum.

THEAET. Apparently not.

SOCR. But can a part be a part of anything but its whole?

THEAET. Yes; of the sum.

205. SOCR. You make a gallant fight of it, Theaetetus. But does not ' the sum ' mean precisely something from which nothing is missing?

THEAET. Necessarily.

SOCR. And is not a whole exactly the same thing—that from which nothing whatever is missing? Whereas, when something is removed, the thing becomes neither a whole nor a sum : it changes at the same moment from being both to being neither.

THEAET. I think now that there is no difference between a sum and a whole.

Plato is not denying that there are wholes which contain an additional element that arises when the parts are put together and disappears when they are separated. He was aware of this,[1] but his point is that such an additional element is not what we mean by ' the whole '. It may also be remarked that he is arguing within the limits of the theory he is criticising. That theory holds that the only things we can perceive or know or talk about are concrete individual things in nature, complex or simple, and that a complex thing is no more than an aggregate of simple things or elements, which can be enumerated in the only account we can give of it. When the enumeration is complete we know all that we can know about the thing. So the whole is nothing but the sum of its parts. A man is, for this theory, a trunk and a head and limbs. There is no substance or essence ' Man ', over and above the separable ' material ' parts, such as Plato and Aristotle would recognise and make the subject of a definition (*logos*) by genus and specific difference.

Having ruled out the suggestion that ' the whole ' can be a single entity distinct from all the parts, Socrates can now return to the

---

[1] Cf. Aristotle's discussion, inspired by the *Theaetetus*, at *Metaph.* z, 17.

argument interrupted at 204A, namely the second alternative:
that the syllable or complex is a unity over and above its letters or
elements. He can now reaffirm the statement there made, that if
the syllable is such a unity, it is not a whole and can have no parts.

205A. SOCR. Well, we were saying—were we not?—that when
a thing has parts, the whole or sum will be the same thing
as all the parts?

THEAET. Certainly.

SOCR. To go back, then, to the point I was trying to make
B. just now; if the syllable is not the same thing as the letters,
does it not follow that it cannot have the letters as parts
of itself; otherwise, being the same thing as the letters, it
would be neither more nor less knowable than they are?

THEAET. Yes.

SOCR. And it was to avoid that consequence that we supposed the syllable to be different from the letters.

THEAET. Yes.

SOCR. Well, if the letters are not parts of the syllable,
can you name any things, other than its letters, that are
parts of a syllable?

THEAET. Certainly not, Socrates. If I admitted that it
had any parts, it would surely be absurd to set aside the
letters and look for parts of any other kind.

C. SOCR. Then, on the present showing, a syllable will be a
thing that is absolutely one and cannot be divided into parts
of any sort? [1]

THEAET. Apparently.

SOCR. Do you remember then, my dear Theaetetus, our
accepting a short while ago a statement that we thought
satisfactory: that no account could be given of the primary
things of which other things are composed, because each of
them, taken just by itself, was incomposite; and that it
was not correct to attribute even ' existence ' to it, or to
call it ' this ', on the ground that these words expressed
different things that were extraneous to it; and this was
the ground for making the primary thing inexplicable
and unknowable?

THEAET. I remember.

D. SOCR. Then is not exactly this, and nothing else, the
ground of its being simple in nature and indivisible into
parts? I can see no other.

---

[1] παντάπασι, put first for emphasis, should be construed with μία τις ἰδέα
ἀμέριστος.

205D. THEAET. Evidently there is no other.

SOCR. Then has not the syllable now turned out to be a thing of the same sort, if it has no parts and is a unitary thing ?

THEAET. Certainly.

SOCR. To conclude, then : if, on the one hand, the syllable is the same thing as a number of letters and is a whole with the letters as its parts, then the letters must be neither more nor less knowable and explicable than syllables, since we made out that all the parts are the same thing as the whole.

E. THEAET. True.

SOCR. But if, on the other hand, the syllable is a unity without parts, syllable and letter likewise are equally incapable of explanation and unknowable. The same reason will make them so.

THEAET. I see no way out of that.

SOCR. If so, we must not accept this statement : that the syllable can be known and explained, the letter cannot.

THEAET. No, not if we hold by our argument.

Putting aside the illustration from letters, it has now been established that knowledge cannot be gained, as the theory holds, by analysing a concrete thing, presented in a complex notion, into its simple parts, each presented in a simple perception which is not knowledge.

It is finally pointed out that the illustration itself tells against the theory. Our knowledge of letters must actually be clearer than our knowledge of syllables, whereas the theory evidently regards our perception of elements as inferior to the knowledge we are alleged to gain by giving an account of the complex.

206. SOCR: And again, would not your own experience in learning your letters rather incline you to accept the opposite view ?

THEAET. What view do you mean ?

SOCR. This : that all the time you were learning you were doing nothing else but trying to distinguish by sight or hearing each letter by itself, so as not to be confused by any arrangement of them in spoken or written words.

THEAET. That is quite true.

SOCR. And in the music school the height of accomplish-

B. ment lay precisely in being able to follow each several

206B. note and tell which string it belonged to ; and notes, as everyone would agree, are the elements of music.[1]
THEAET. Precisely.
SOCR. Then, if we are to argue from our own experience of elements and complexes to other cases, we shall conclude that elements in general yield knowledge that is much clearer than knowledge of the complex and more effective for a complete grasp of anything we seek to know. If anyone tells us that the complex is by its nature knowable, while the element is unknowable, we shall suppose that, whether he intends it or not, he is playing with us.
THEAET. Certainly.

206C–E. *Three possible meanings of ' account '. (1) Expression of thought in speech (irrelevant)*

The refutation of the theory ' dreamt ' by Socrates is now complete. It turns upon the allegation that the simple and unanalysable is unknowable. But Theaetetus' suggestion that knowledge is true judgment or belief combined with an account or explanation may have other meanings not involving this fatal flaw. Socrates accordingly turns to consider these possible meanings. The discussion still proceeds, however, on certain assumptions of the refuted theory, namely that the only things to be known are concrete individual things, and that knowledge accordingly must consist in giving some account of such things. This limitation is in accordance with the scope of the whole dialogue, which asks whether knowledge can be extracted from the world of concrete natural things, yielding perceptions and complex notions, without invoking other factors. The three meanings of *logos* now considered are determined by these assumptions, which exclude Plato's own view, that the objects of which knowledge must give an account are not concrete individuals but objects of thought, and that the simpler terms in which the account must be stated are not material parts but higher concepts.

206C. SOCR. Indeed we might, I think, find other arguments to prove that point. But we must not allow them to distract our attention from the question before us, namely, what can really be meant by saying that an account added to true belief yields knowledge in its most perfect form.

[1] The appeal to music and (earlier) to numbers and measures lends no support to Campbell's suggestion that the theory is due to ' some Pythagorean ' (p. xxxix). These examples are brought forward, not by the author of the theory, but by Socrates in refuting it.

(1) EXPRESSION OF THOUGHT IN SPEECH

206C. THEAET. Yes, we must see what that means.

SOCR. Well then, what is this term ' account ' intended to convey to us ? I think it must mean one of three things.

THEAET. What are they ?

D. SOCR. The first will be giving overt expression to one's thought by means of vocal sound with names and verbs, casting an image of one's notion on the stream that flows through the lips, like a reflection in a mirror or in water. Do you agree that expression of that sort is an ' account ' ?

THEAET. I do. We certainly call that expressing ourselves in speech (λέγειν).

SOCR. On the other hand, that is a thing that anyone can do more or less readily. If a man is not born deaf or dumb, he can signify what he thinks on any subject. So in this sense anyone whatever who has a correct

E. notion evidently will have it ' with an account ', and there will be no place left anywhere for a correct notion apart from knowledge.

THEAET. True.

Logos here does not mean a ' verbal definition ' such as a dictionary gives, but simply ' statement ', ' speech '—the utterance of the notion or judgment in our minds. This common meaning of the word is mentioned only for the sake of clearness. It is obviously not what Theaetetus intended.

206E–208B. (2) *Enumeration of elementary parts. This will not convert a true notion into knowledge*

The second meaning is the enumeration of elementary parts. This is now considered on its own merits, apart from the further feature which proved fatal to the earlier theory, namely, the doctrine that an element must be unknowable.

206E. SOCR. Then we must not be too ready to charge the author of the definition of knowledge now before us [1] with talking nonsense. Perhaps that is not what he meant. He may have meant : being able to reply to the question,

207. what any given thing is, by enumerating its elements.

THEAET. For example, Socrates ?

SOCR. For example, Hesiod says about a wagon, ' In a wagon are a hundred pieces of wood.' I could not name

---

[1] The author of the definition originally quoted by Theaetetus (201D), who is now regarded as not responsible for the doctrine, in the theory ' dreamt ' by Socrates, that elements are unknowable.

207. them all ; no more, I imagine, could you. If we were asked what a wagon is, we should be content if we could mention wheels, axle, body, rails, yoke.

THEAET. Certainly.

SOCR. But I dare say he would think us just as ridiculous as if we replied to the question about your own name by

B. telling the syllables. We might think and express ourselves correctly, but we should be absurd if we fancied ourselves to be grammarians and able to give such an account of the name Theaetetus as a grammarian would offer. He would say it is impossible to give a scientific account of anything, short of adding to your true notion a complete catalogue of the elements, as, I think, was said earlier.

THEAET. Yes, it was.

SOCR. In the same way, he would say, we may have a correct notion of the wagon, but the man who can give a complete statement of its nature by going through those

C. hundred parts has thereby added an account to his correct notion and, in place of mere belief, has arrived at a technical knowledge of the wagon's nature, by going through all the elements in the whole.

THEAET. Don't you approve, Socrates ?

SOCR. Tell me if you approve, my friend, and whether you accept the view that the complete enumeration of elements is an account of any given thing, whereas description in terms of syllables or of any larger unit still leaves it un-

D. accounted for. Then we can look into the matter further.

THEAET. Well, I do accept that.

SOCR. Do you think, then, that anyone has knowledge of whatever it may be, when he thinks that one and the same thing is a part sometimes of one thing, sometimes of a different thing ; or again when he believes now one and now another thing to be part of one and the same thing ?

THEAET. Certainly not.

SOCR. Have you forgotten, then, that when you first began learning to read and write, that was what you and your schoolfellows did ?

THEAET. Do you mean, when we thought that now one

E. letter and now another was part of the same syllable, and when we put the same letter sometimes into the proper syllable, sometimes into another ?

SOCR. That is what I mean.

THEAET. Then I have certainly not forgotten ; and I do

207E. not think that one has reached knowledge so long as one is in that condition.

Socr. Well then, if at that stage you are writing ' Theaetetus ' and you think you ought to write T and H and E and do so, and again when you are trying to write ' Theo-

208. dorus ', you think you ought to write T and E and do so, can we say that you know the first syllable of your two names ?

Theaet. No ; we have just agreed that one has not knowledge so long as one is in that condition.

Socr. And there is no reason why a person should not be in the same condition with respect to the second, third, and fourth syllables as well ?

Theaet. None whatever.

Socr. Can we, then, say that whenever in writing ' Theaetetus ' he puts down all the letters in order, then he is in possession of the complete catalogue of elements together with correct belief ?

Theaet. Obviously.

B. Socr. Being still, as we agree, without knowledge, though his beliefs are correct ?

Theaet. Yes.

Socr. Although he possesses the ' account ' in addition to right belief. For when he wrote he was in possession of the catalogue of the elements, which we agreed was the ' account '.

Theaet. True.

Socr. So, my friend, there is such a thing as right belief together with an account, which is not yet entitled to be called knowledge.

Theaet. I am afraid so.

Socr. Then, apparently, our idea that we had found the perfectly true definition of knowledge was no better than a golden dream.

Socrates has now disposed of the theory that the addition of a complete enumeration of elements to a correct, but previously unanalysed, notion of a complex thing will convert true belief into knowledge. Even if we reject the doctrine that the element is unknowable, and suppose it to be at least as knowable as the complex, still the complete enumeration may fail to give us anything better than true belief. The analysis, though it be carried as far as possible, will not yield knowledge of any different kind from the true notion we started with, or the correct beliefs about the parts of a wagon which stopped short at five parts instead of all the hundred. So the schoolboy may have a correct belief about every letter in the name ' Theaetetus ' and write it correctly, without having that assured knowledge which would save him from writing it incorrectly on another occasion.

If we go behind the illustration and beyond the limits of the theory that is being criticised, we see further into Plato's mind. In the *Meno* the slave who is ignorant of geometry is led through a problem till he reaches the correct solution. But Socrates points out that he still has only true belief, not knowledge, because he does not understand the proof or see how the conclusion necessarily follows from the premises. Even if he were taken back through the earlier propositions, axioms, and definitions to the primitive indefinables, he might still possess no more than an exhaustive catalogue of true beliefs leading to the solution. He will not know even this much of geometry until he has grasped the necessary connexion which will make all these beliefs abiding and unshakable. All this, however, lies outside the presuppositions of the theory under examination, which contemplates only the analysis of a concrete thing into elementary parts.

208B–210B. (3) *The statement of a distinguishing mark. This will not convert a true notion into knowledge*

Socrates now suggests a third possible meaning of *logos*—' being able to state some mark by which the thing in question differs from everything else '. Will this addition convert true belief into knowledge ? *Logos* will now mean the ' account ' of a thing given by a description which serves to distinguish the thing we wish to indicate from all other things.

208B. Socr. (*continues*). Or shall we not condemn the theory
c. yet ? Perhaps the meaning to be given to ' account ' is not this, but the remaining one of the three, one of which we said must be intended by anyone who defines knowledge as correct belief together with an account.

Theaet. A good reminder ; there is still one meaning left. The first was what might be called the image of thought in spoken sound ; and the one we have just discussed was going all through the elements to arrive at the whole. What is the third ?

Socr. The meaning most people would give : being able to name some mark by which the thing one is asked about differs from everything else.

Theaet. Could you give me an example of such an account of a thing ?

208D.   SOCR.   Take the sun as an example. I dare say you will
be satisfied with the account of it as the brightest of the
heavenly bodies that go round the earth.
THEAET.   Certainly.
SOCR.   Let me explain the point of this example. It is
to illustrate what we were just saying : that if you get
hold of the difference distinguishing any given thing from
all others, then, so some people say, you will have an
' account ' of it ; whereas, so long as you fix upon something common to other things, your account will embrace
all the things that share it.

E.   THEAET.   I understand. I agree that what you describe
may fairly be called an ' account '.
SOCR.   And if, besides a right notion about a thing, whatever it may be, you also grasp its difference from all other
things, you will have arrived at knowledge of what, till
then, you had only a notion of.
THEAET.   We do say that, certainly.
SOCR.   Really, Theaetetus, now I come to look at this
statement at close quarters, it is like a scene-painting :
I cannot make it out at all, though, so long as I kept at
a distance, there seemed to be some sense in it.
THEAET.   What do you mean ? Why so ?

209.   SOCR.   I will explain, if I can. Suppose I have a correct
notion about you ; if I add to that the account of you,
then, we are to understand, I know you. Otherwise I have
only a notion.
THEAET.   Yes.
SOCR.   And ' account ' means putting your differentness [1]
into words.
THEAET.   Yes.
SOCR.   So, at the time when I had only a notion, my
mind did not grasp any of the points in which you differ
from others ?
THEAET.   Apparently not.
SOCR.   Then I must have had before my mind one of those
common things which belong to another person as much
as to you.

B.   THEAET.   That follows.
SOCR.   But look here ! If that was so, how could I possibly

---

[1] Plato seems deliberately to avoid the term διαφορά here and henceforward
(though it occurred at 208D), perhaps because of its technical use for the
differentia of a species, which is irrelevant to this context. Διαφορότης is a
Platonic word which occurs again at *Rep.* 587E.

209B. be having a notion of you rather than of anyone else?
Suppose I was thinking : Theaetetus is one who is a man
and has a nose and eyes and a mouth and so forth, enumerating every part of the body. Will thinking in that way
result in my thinking of Theaetetus rather than of Theodorus or, as they say, of the man in the street?

THEAET. How should it?

SOCR. Well, now suppose I think not merely of a man

C. with a nose and eyes, but of one with a snub nose and
prominent eyes, once more shall I be having a notion of
you any more than of myself or anyone else of that description?

THEAET. No.

SOCR. In fact, there will be no notion of Theaetetus in
my mind, I suppose, until this particular snubness has
stamped and registered within me a record distinct from
all the other cases of snubness that I have seen ; and so
with every other part of you. Then, if I meet you to-
morrow, that trait will revive my memory and give me
a correct notion about you.

THEAET. Quite true.

D. SOCR. If that is so, the correct notion of anything must
itself include the differentness of that thing.

THEAET. Evidently.

SOCR. Then what meaning is left for getting hold of an
' account ' in addition to the correct notion? If, on the
one hand, it means adding the notion of how a thing differs
from other things, such an injunction is simply absurd.

THEAET. How so?

SOCR. When we have a correct notion of the way in which
certain things differ from other things, it tells us to add a
correct notion of the way in which they differ from other

E. things. On this showing, the most vicious of circles would
be nothing to this injunction. It might better deserve to
be called the sort of direction a blind man might give : to
tell us to get hold of something we already have, in order
to get to know something we are already thinking of, suggests a state of the most absolute darkness.

THEAET. Whereas, if —— ? The supposition you made
just now implied that you would state some alternative ;
what was it? [1]

---

[1] Reading εἰ δέ γε — τί νυνδὴ ὡς ἐρῶν ⟨ἔτι⟩ ὑπέθου ; The objection to reading
(with Burnet and others) εἰπὲ δὴ τί νυνδὴ ὡς ἐρῶν ἐπύθου is that Socrates' last
question (τὸ οὖν προσλαβεῖν . . . εἴη ; 209D, 4) did not suggest that he had

209E. SOCR. If the direction to add an 'account' means that we are to get to *know* the differentness, as opposed to merely having a notion of it, this most admirable of all definitions of knowledge will be a pretty business ; because

210. 'getting to know' means acquiring knowledge, doesn't it ?

THEAET. Yes.

SOCR. So, apparently, to the question, What is knowledge ? our definition will reply : 'Correct belief together with knowledge of a differentness' ; for, according to it, 'adding an account' will come to that.

THEAET. So it seems.

SOCR. Yes ; and when we are inquiring after the nature of knowledge, nothing could be sillier than to say that it is correct belief together with a *knowledge* of differentness or of anything whatever.

So, Theaetetus, neither perception, nor true belief, nor

B. the addition of an 'account' to true belief can be knowledge.

THEAET. Apparently not.

Some critics have imagined that the above argument is concerned with the definition of species by genus and specific difference, and even that Plato is here criticising himself. But it is clearly presumed throughout that the object to be defined and known is a concrete individual thing—' ourselves and other things ', Hesiod's wagon, a person (Theaetetus), the sun. The ' differentness ' is a perceptible individual peculiarity, such as ' this particular snubness which I have seen ', distinguishing this individual person from other individuals, not a specific difference distinguishing a species from other species and common to all individuals of the species.

something more to say. What did suggest this was the εἰ μὲν (209D, 5), implying that an alternative supposition (εἰ δὲ) was to follow—the supposition stated in Socrates' next speech (εἰ τὸ λόγον . . . 209E, 6). Badham saw this and tried to restore the necessary sense to Theaetetus' inquiry by reading εἰ δέ γε—τί νυνδὴ ὡς ἕτερον ὑπέθου ; ' Whereas if—what was it you suggested just now as the alternative ? ' The sense is better, if it could be got out of the words. But (as Campbell noted) ὑποτίθεσθαι, though it can mean to *put* an explicit suggestion *to* a person, cannot mean to *imply* something not stated at all ; and the imperfect would be required.

The reading I propose (*Class. Rev.* xliv (1930), 114) means : ' Whereas if—what was it (the " whereas if ") that your supposition just now (" if on the one hand ") implied (ὡς) that you were going on to state ? ' For εἰπεῖν ἔτι, cf. Soph., *O.T.* 748, δείξεις δὲ μᾶλλον, ἢν ἐν ἐξείπῃς ἔτι.

The rather obscure form of the question is (like the rest of these concluding pages) in the manner of the *Sophist*; *e.g.* 217A, τί δὲ μάλιστα καὶ τὸ ποῖον τι περὶ αὐτῶν διαπορηθεὶς ἐρέσθαι διενοήθης ; 226C, τὸ ποῖον αὐτῶν πέρι βουληθεὶς δηλῶσαι παραδείγματα προθεὶς ταῦτα κατὰ πάντων ἤρου ;

Socrates argues : Suppose I have a correct notion of Theaetetus. If my notion contains only traits he shares with all or some other men, then it is not a notion of him any more than of them. It must include his individual and peculiar characteristics. Thus my notion of his individual ' differentness ' is already included in my notion of just that person, and I am acquainted with that differentness in just the same way as I am with his common characteristics. It is absurd to tell me to add it to my notion of the person as a whole or to suppose that such an addition could convert a correct notion into some higher kind of cognition called ' knowledge '.

The instance of the sun recalls Aristotle's argument that it is impossible to define an individual sensible substance.[1] A definition must consist of words whose established meanings can all apply to other actual or possible individuals. Even if you take an eternal substance which is in fact unique, such as the sun or moon, it is still impossible to define it. Some attributes of the sun (going round the earth, invisible at night) might be removed, and yet the sun would still be the sun. Any description such as ' the brightest of the heavenly bodies ' must consist of attributes that might belong to another subject. There can, at any time, be only one body which is ' the brightest ', but if a brighter body should appear in the heavens, the description would transfer itself to that.

There is no question here of the definition of species, which are definable precisely because no two species are conceptually identical, as any number of individuals may be. The whole discussion is confined to the level of the theory ' dreamt ' by Socrates, which contemplates only our acquaintance with individual sensible things. The point is that we cannot get ' knowledge ', supposed to be somehow superior to mere beliefs or notions, by adding a *logos* in any of the senses considered. These senses appear to exhaust the possible ways in which an ' account ' can be given of an individual thing. (1) We may name it (express our notion of it in speech) ; (2) we may enumerate the material parts of which it is composed ; or (3) we may point it out by a description which will serve to distinguish the thing we indicate from other things. But none of these ' accounts ' will yield any ' clearer ' or more certain kind of cognition than we started with.

The Platonist will draw the necessary inference. True knowledge has for its object things of a different order—not sensible things, but intelligible Forms and truths about them. Such objects are necessarily unique ; they do not become and perish or change

---

[1] *Metaph.* z, 15. Aristotle took the example of the Sun from our passage and evidently understood Plato's meaning correctly.

in any respect. Hence we can know them and eternal truths about them. The *Theaetetus* leads to this old conclusion by demonstrating the failure of all attempts to extract knowledge from sensible objects.

210B–D. *Epilogue. All these attempts to define knowledge have failed.*

It only remains to point out that all these attempts have failed and no others are forthcoming.

210B. SOCR. Are we in labour, then, with any further child, my friend, or have we brought to birth all we have to say about knowledge ?

THEAET. Indeed we have ; and for my part I have already, thanks to you, given utterance to more than I had in me.

SOCR. All of which our midwife's skill pronounces to be mere wind-eggs and not worth the rearing ?

THEAET. Undoubtedly.

SOCR. Then supposing you should ever henceforth try to
C. conceive afresh, Theaetetus, if you succeed, your embryo thoughts will be the better as a consequence of to-day's scrutiny ; and if you remain barren, you will be gentler and more agreeable to your companions, having the good sense not to fancy you know what you do not know. For that, and no more, is all that my art can effect ; nor have I any of that knowledge possessed by all the great and admirable men of our own day or of the past. But this midwife's art is a gift from heaven ; my mother had it for women,
D. and I for young men of a generous spirit and for all in whom beauty dwells.[1]

Now I must go to the portico of the King Archon to meet the indictment which Meletus has drawn up against me. But to-morrow morning, Theodorus, let us meet here again.

[1] καλοί refers to beauty of mind, such as Theaetetus has, rather than bodily beauty. Cf. 185E.

THE SOPHIST

216A–218D. *Introductory Conversation*

THE introductory conversation announces the subject of the discussion begun in this dialogue and continued in the *Statesman* :
How are the Sophist and the Statesman to be defined and distinguished (if they are to be distinguished) from the Philosopher ?
A second purpose is to describe the philosophic position of the
Stranger from Elea, who here takes Socrates' place as leader of the
conversation.

THEODORUS.   SOCRATES.   A STRANGER FROM ELEA.   THEAETETUS

216.   THEODORUS.   Here we are, Socrates, faithful to our appointment of yesterday ; and, what is more, we have brought a
guest with us.   Our friend here is a native of Elea ; he
belongs to the school of Parmenides and Zeno, and is
devoted to philosophy.

SOCRATES.   Perhaps, Theodorus, it is no ordinary guest
but some god that you have brought us unawares.   Homer [1]

B.   tells us that gods attend upon the goings of men of mercy
and justice ; and not least among them the God of Strangers
comes to mark the orderly or lawless doings of mankind.
Your companion may be one of those higher powers, who
intends to observe and expose our weakness in philosophic
discourse, like a very spirit of refutation.

THEOD.   That is not our friend's way, Socrates ; he is
more reasonable than the devotees of verbal dispute.   I
should not call him a god by any means ; but there is some-

C.   thing divine about him : I would say that of any philosopher.

SOCR.   And rightly, my friend ; but one might almost say
that the type you mention is hardly easier to discern than
the god.   Such men—the genuine, not the sham philosophers—as they go from city to city surveying from a height
the life beneath them, appear, owing to the world's blindness,
to wear all sorts of shapes.   To some they seem of no
account, to others above all worth ; now they wear the guise

D.   of statesmen, now of sophists ; and sometimes they may
give the impression of simply being mad.   But if our guest

---

[1] *Odyssey* ix, 270, and xvii, 483.

165

216D. will allow me, I should like to ask him what his countrymen
217. thought and how they used these names.

THEOD. What names?

SOCR. Sophist, Statesman, Philosopher.

THEOD. What is your question exactly? What sort of
difficulty about these names have you in mind?

SOCR. This: did they think of all these as a single type,
or as two, or did they distinguish three types and attach
one of the three corresponding names to each?

THEOD. I imagine you are quite welcome to the information. Is not that so, sir?

B. STRANGER. Yes, Theodorus, perfectly welcome; and the
answer is not difficult. They thought of them as three
different types; but it is not so short and easy a task to
define each one of them clearly.

THEOD. As luck would have it, Socrates, you have hit upon
a subject closely allied to one on which we were pressing
him with questions before we came here. He tried to put
us off with the same excuse he has just made to you, though
he admits he has been thoroughly instructed and has not
forgotten what he heard.

C. SOCR. Do not deny us, then, the first favour we ask. Tell
us this much [1] : which do you commonly prefer—to discourse at length by yourself on any matter you wish to
make clear, or to use the method of asking questions, as
Parmenides himself did on one occasion in developing some
magnificent arguments in my presence, when I was young
and he quite an elderly man? [2]

D. STR. When the other party to the conversation is tractable
and gives no trouble, to address him is the easier course;
otherwise, to speak by oneself.

SOCR. Then you may choose any of the company you will;
they will all follow you and respond amenably. But if you
take my advice, you will choose one of the younger men—
Theaetetus here or any other you may prefer.

STR. I feel some shyness, Socrates, at the notion that, at
my first meeting with you and your friends, instead of
exchanging our ideas in the give and take of ordinary

---

[1] It may be an accident that μὴ . . . τήν γε πρώτην . . . χάριν ἀπαρνηθεὶς
γένῃ, | τοσόνδε δ' ἡμῖν φράζε scans as iambic verse; but the last words do not
perfectly fit what follows (for the information whether the Stranger prefers
speaking at length or asking questions is not *part* of the favour asked, as
τοσόνδε suggests). Plato may be adapting a quotation from Tragedy. Otherwise language and rhythm together seem slightly too tragic for the occasion.

[2] For this reference to the *Parmenides*, see Introd., p. 1.

217E. conversation, I should spin out a long discourse by myself
or even address it to another, as if I were giving a display of
eloquence.[1] For indeed the question you have just raised
is not so easy a matter as one might suppose, on hearing it
so simply put, but it calls for a very long discussion. On
the other hand, to refuse you and your friends a request,
especially one put to me in such terms as you have used,
strikes me as a breach of civility in a guest.[2] That

218. Theaetetus should be the other party to our conversation
is a proposal which my earlier talk with him, as well as
your recommendation, makes exceedingly welcome.

THEAETETUS. Then do as you say, sir ; you will, as Socrates said, be conferring a favour on us all.

STR. On that point, Theaetetus, no more need be said ;
the discussion from now onwards must, it seems, be carried
on with you. But if the long task should after all weigh
heavy on you, your friends here, not I, must bear the blame.

B. THEAET. I do not feel at this moment as if I should sink
under it ; but should something of that sort happen, we will
call in Socrates' namesake here, who is of my own age and
shares my pursuits. He is quite used to working out most
questions with me.

STR. A good suggestion : that shall be for you to consider
as our conversation goes forward. What now concerns us
both is our joint inquiry. We had better, I think, begin
by studying the Sophist and try to bring his nature to light

C. in a clear formula. At present, you see, all that you and I
possess in common is the name. The thing to which each
of us gives that name we may perhaps have privately before
our minds [3] ; but it is always desirable to have reached an

---

[1] Three alternative procedures are suggested : (1) an unbroken monologue,
such as the rhetorical Sophists preferred ; (2) an exposition ' addressed to
another ', i.e. cast in the form of questions, to which the respondent merely
answers ' yes ' or ' no ' as required (ὑπακούειν), like the young Aristotle in the
Parmenides ; (3) a genuine conversation, to which the respondent makes a
real contribution. The Stranger's preference for the third marks that he
understands ' dialectic ' as Plato understood it.

[2] Read ἄγροικον, ' rude ', for ἄγριον, ' wild, savage, fierce ', which is too
strong a word. At Aristotle E.N. 1128a, 9, ἄγροικοι Kᵇ (Byw. Burnet) is the
true reading : ἄγριοι vulg. At 1128b, 2, ἄγροικος was restored by Coraes
for the MSS. ἄγριος. Mr. W. D. Ross has kindly supplied me with other
instances of the confusion : Euthyd. 285A, 2, ἀγριωτέρως BT : ἀγροικοτέρως W.
Phaedrus 268D, 6, ἀγροίκως. E1 ἀγρίως (ἀγροίκως Osann).

[3] ἔργον, ' thing ' = πρᾶγμα, as at 221B and Theaet. 177E. (cf. Apelt). I
think the meaning is : ' We may each have a private view of the same thing
which we both call by the same name, but we shall not be sure that we are

167

218C.   agreement about the thing itself by means of explicit statements, rather than be content to use the same word without
formulating what it means.   It is not so easy to com-
prehend this group we intend to examine or to say what
it means to be a sophist.   However, when some great task
is to be properly carried through, everyone has long
since found it a good rule to take something compara-
D.   tively small and easy and practise on that, before
attempting the big thing itself.   That is the course I
recommend for us now, Theaetetus.   Judging the Sophist
to be a very troublesome sort of creature to hunt down, let
us first practise the method of tracking him on some easier
quarry—unless you have some readier means to suggest?
THEAET.   No, I have none.

This introduction serves both for the *Sophist* and for the *Statesman*, in which the same company continue the conversation, the
young Socrates taking Theaetetus' place as respondent.   It is still
debated whether or not Plato contemplated a third dialogue, the
Philosopher.   Scholars have collected certain indications of such an
intention.[1]   (1) At *Soph.* 253E, after the description of Dialectic,
the Stranger says : ' In some such region as this we shall find the
philosopher now *and hereafter*, if we look for him.'   (2) That Plato
did not think of this account of Dialectic as sufficiently describing
the philosopher seems to be implied at the beginning of the *Statesman* (257A–C), where Theodorus speaks as if the *Sophist* had accomplished only one-third of the task and asks the Stranger whether
he will now take the Statesman first or the Philosopher.   (3) Later
(258A), Socrates, discussing who shall act as respondent in the *Statesman*, remarks that Theaetetus has already served in the *Theaetetus*
as Socrates' respondent and in the *Sophist* as the Stranger's,
and suggests that the young Socrates should answer the Stranger
in the *Statesman* (as he does), and ' myself on another occasion '.
If this other occasion was to be the *Philosopher*, the four dialogues
would be tied together in a symmetrical scheme :

	Theaetetus	*Sophist*	*Statesman*	*Philosopher*
Questioner :	Socrates	Stranger	Stranger	Socrates
Respondent :	Theaetetus	Theaetetus	Young Socr.	Young Socr.

meaning the same thing by that name until we have explicitly defined it,'
not that we may each have a *different thing* before our minds.   In any case
ἔργον means the thing, not a ' notion ' of the thing, and λόγος means a statement in words (a defining formula), not a ' conception '.

[1] See Diès, *Parménide* (Paris, 1923), p. xv.

The alleged ' eclipse of Socrates ' by the Eleatic Stranger (of which critics have made too much) would then be only temporary ; he would reappear as leader in the *Philosopher*. It is hard to see why these expressions should be there at all, if the intention had never been in Plato's mind.

Why the *Philosopher* was never written, we can only conjecture. The *Statesman* is concerned with the Philosopher in active life. as the royal shepherd of mankind, the guardian who has come down from the vision of the Good to serve his fellow-men in the Cave as lawgiver. We might expect the picture to be completed by an account of the region of contemplation, his proper home, and of the nature of the reality he contemplates. This would be the place for that final account of the relation of reality to appearance which is called for in the *Parmenides* and again in the *Sophist*, but is not given in any of these dialogues. The *Philosopher*, if it could have been written, might have gathered up these loose ends in that doctrine which Plato adumbrated in the Lecture on the Good, but never published in writing. But, as we know from his Seventh Letter, Plato's final decision was that the ultimate truth could never be set down on paper, and ought not to be, even if it could.

In what appears on the surface to be a graceful exchange of compliments Plato has contrived to define precisely the philosophic standpoint of the Stranger from Elea. On hearing that he is ' of the school of Parmenides and Zeno ', Socrates at once fears he may be an exponent of that verbal disputation (' Eristic ') which disregards truth and aims solely at refuting an opponent. This type of Sophistry, analysed below (224E ff.), was associated with the Megarian school, which, though founded by the Socratic Euclides, took its main doctrine from the Eleatics. Zeno had supplied Eristic sophistry with one of its methods—the *reductio ad absurdum*, which refutes an opponent's thesis by asserting that it involves a dilemma, either horn of which leads to a contradiction. The description of the Stranger makes clear that he does not stand for this negative and destructive element in the Eleatic tradition. The reader is not to expect an exhibition of Zenonian dialectic, such as we had in the *Parmenides*. An open reference to the conversation in that dialogue emphasises the contrast between Eleatic methods of argument and the genuine dialectic of Socrates and Plato, already illustrated by the *Theaetetus*.

The Stranger, then, is not, as Socrates feared, a ' very spirit of refutation ', but a genuine philosopher ; and the philosopher is the ' divine ' or inspired man who looks down from above on human life and is taken by the world for a madman. These traits recall the *Phaedrus* (249) and the *Theaetetus* (173E). All this means that the Stranger stands for the genuinely philosophic element in the Parmenidean tradition. He understands dialectic as the co-operative search for truth, and, once the conversation is started, his manner is distinguished by no individual trait from that of the Platonic Socrates. He is an abstract figure, a representative of Parmenides, because Parmenides had set the problem that is to be attacked : How can what appears, but is not real, exist at all ? Since he holds a theory of Forms which no one hesitates to ascribe to Plato himself, it seems as if Plato claimed to be the true heir of Parmenides.[1]

The purpose of the dialogue is to define ' the Sophist '. Here, at the threshold, we cross the boundary between the sensible world, to which the *Theaetetus* was confined, and the world of Forms. We are to define by a formula (*logos*) an object of which both interlocutors have a notion before their minds. The object or ' thing ' is no longer an individual concrete thing. The last conclusion of the *Theaetetus* was that the addition of a *logos* of such a thing to a true notion of it could not yield knowledge. ' The Sophist ' is not an individual, but a species ; and the addition of a *logos* in a new sense—a definition by genus and specific differences—can lead to knowledge of the nature of a species.

218D–221C. *Illustrative Division, defining the Angler.*

The Stranger now proceeds to illustrate by a trivial example the method to be used in defining the Sophist. The species is to be defined by systematically dividing the genus that is taken to include it. The method was new to Plato's public ; but the modern reader, familiar with classifications all ultimately derived from the model here set up, might be wearied by a translation. I shall, therefore, give only a summary of the illustrative Division defining the Angler, and of the six following Divisions defining the Sophist under various aspects. Something must also be said about the method itself, which Plato evidently regarded as a very valuable engine of dialectic.

Although the classification of the Angler is the first long and formal Division in Plato, no preliminary account of the method is given and no rules are laid down. The only earlier description of the method (*Phaedrus* 265D) tells us that a Division should be preceded by a Collection (συναγωγή) or survey of the ' widely scattered ' terms (species) which are to be brought under a single (generic) Form. The object of such a review is to divine the generic Form which is to stand at the head of the subsequent Division. As we shall see (p. 186), all hope of a correct definition depends on the right choice of the genus. Here, however, there is

---

[1] As Prof. Taylor remarks, *Plato* (1926), 375.

no systematic Collection. Plato prefers to introduce the method by giving an illustrative Division, reserving what needs to be said about rules of procedure to be added later, chiefly in the *Statesman*.

Angling being obviously a species of Hunting, it would be natural to begin with Hunting as the genus to be divided. But the Stranger starts farther back with the genus ' Art '. The earlier stages, before Hunting is reached, provide starting-points for the first five attempts to define the Sophist, as appears from the following table :

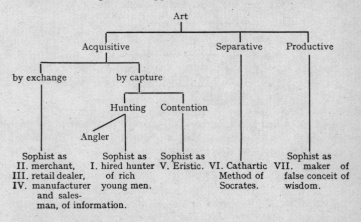

Sophist as II. merchant, III. retail dealer, IV. manufacturer and sales-man, of information.	Sophist as I. hired hunter of rich young men.	Sophist as V. Eristic. VI. Cathartic Method of Socrates.	Sophist as VII. maker of false conceit of wisdom.

The classification of Arts is not meant to be systematic or complete : the ' Separative ' class (διακριτική) is added later (226B), not mentioned here. The Acquisitive class includes ' learning and knowing ' with money-making, contention, and hunting : all these are arts ' which produce nothing, but merely get hold of things that already exist and prevent others from getting hold of them ' (219C). Nothing more will be heard of ' learning and knowing ' till the first Division of the *Statesman* (258E) which opens with ' knowledge ', divided into ' theoretical ' and ' practical '—a contrast relevant to the distinction between the Philosopher and the practical Statesman.

The method of Division may be used for two distinct objects : (1) the classification of all the species falling under a genus in a complete table, or (2) the definition of a single species only. Plato seems to contemplate sometimes one purpose, sometimes the other, though the rules to be observed will be somewhat different. A complete classification may exhibit more than two subordinate classes on the same level, and if these are to be subdivided, they must be described in positive terms. In biology, for instance, animals

must not be classified as 'vertebrate' and 'invertebrate'. To
lump together whole genera and families as 'invertebrate' tells us
nothing of positive importance about their structure ; and 'inverte-
brateness' is not a character that can be subdivided. But if our
object is to define a single species of vertebrate animal, we can cut
out all invertebrates at a blow and subdivide only the vertebrate.
The illustrative division here is of this kind. It proceeds through
two sets of stages. Angling is catching (*a*) a certain kind of prey
(*b*) by a certain method. (*a*) The division of the prey :

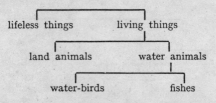

would be absurd in a classification : there is no provision for birds
which live and are caught in the air. Only the second set of stages
—the division of methods (netting or striking : by a fish-spear or
by hook and line) makes any pretence to a complete classification.
Also the shift of principle from prey to method would vitiate the
scheme as a classification of hunting : land animals and birds
may equally well be netted or struck. Considerations of this sort
are pointed out in the *Statesman*. The upshot here is a definition
of the species Angling in terms of the genus 'Art' and all the
specific differences (as they were later called), formally enumerated
at 221B.

The Seven Divisions defining the Sophist

The Stranger next (221C) sets out 'to discover the nature of the
Sophist on the pattern of this illustration'. Six Divisions follow
immediately and are summarised at 231C–E. The results are then
criticised. The seventh and final Division is preceded by a discussion leading to the choice of a new genus, the image-making
branch of Productive (as distinct from Acquisitive) art. It is
interrupted by the long discussions justifying the assumption that
there can be such a thing as an unreal 'image' : the whole problem
of appearance and falsity is involved. At the end of the dialogue
(264B) this Division is continued and yields the final definition of
the Sophist.

This procedure suggests the questions : Why are we given seven
definitions ? Is one of them meant to be right, the rest wrong ?
Who is the Sophist ? What class, or classes, of persons are defined ?

I. THE SOPHIST AS HUNTER

Some have held that all the Divisions define one class of historical persons from different approaches, and even that all the definitions are ' adequate '. A fatal objection to this view is that there never existed any class of persons who could be characterised by the sixth definition as well as by the first five and the seventh. The Cathartic art of the sixth Division was practised by Socrates alone. Its purpose is to purge the soul of the false conceit of wisdom. This flatly contradicts the final definition of the Sophist as the creator of a false appearance of wisdom ; and the Stranger himself says that he is afraid to call the practitioners of the Cathartic art Sophists : they only resemble the Sophist as the dog resembles the wolf (231A).

Plato was not primarily concerned to describe the character of any class of persons with historical accuracy. What interested him was the spirit of Sophistry, which might be incarnate in many persons or groups with a variety of superficial characteristics. The view I shall recommend is briefly this. Divisions I and II–IV characterise, superficially and with a considerable element of satire, the rhetorical sophists and lecturers on advanced subjects of the type represented in the fifth century by Protagoras, Gorgias, and Hippias. They are ' hired hunters of rich young men ', or ' salesmen ' of alleged wisdom and of the arts of succeeding in life. Division V starts from a different genus, the art of Contention, and defines the Eristic—the man who disputes for victory, not for truth. This class had its professional representatives in men like Euthydemus and his brother ; but Eristic was also a feature of the dialectic of the Eleatic school and of the Megarians. Division VI does not define any type of Sophist, but gives a serious and even eloquent analysis of the purifying *elenchus* as practised by Socrates himself. Division VII is the only one that goes to the heart of the matter and starts from the right genus. It defines, not any particular class of persons, but a whole tendency of thought, the essence of Sophistry. It is based on the metaphysical distinction of appearance from reality. Sophistry is the false counterfeit of philosophy and of statesmanship and has its being in the world of *eidola* that is neither real nor totally unreal. The claim of that world to yield knowledge has been rejected in the *Theaetetus*. The *Sophist* will raise the question, what sort of existence it can have.

221C–223B. *Division I. The Sophist as Hunter.*

Division I starts, with no explicit justification, from the Angler's genus, Hunting, and begins by distinguishing the Sophist's prey—the tame animal, man. The significant part is the further sub-

division according to method. What follows is an analysis of that
rhetorical Sophistry which had been attacked in the *Gorgias* and the
Phaedrus. (1) Man-hunting may be violent (piracy, slave-hunting,
tyranny, and warfare in general) or persuasive (πιθανουργική) including forensic and political oratory and displays of rhetoric in
private company. The *Gorgias* had defined Rhetoric as ' the producer of persuasion ', and the violent methods here contrasted with
it recall Polus' idealisation of the tyrant and of the political orator,
as men who can do what they like, and also Socrates' description
of Callicles' ideal of unlimited egoism as the life of a robber and
an outlaw. (2) The next division—public or private (ἰδιοθηρευτική)
—separates the rhetorical displays of the Sophist to a private
audience from the public oratory of the politician and the lawyer.
(3) Then the taking of fees (μισθαρνητική) is introduced. The
Sophist demands a wage, in contrast with the false lover who,
as described in the *Phaedrus*, offers bribes to his prey to induce
him to yield. (4) Finally, the Sophist professes to seek the company of his victims ' for the sake of goodness ' as the exponent
of a ' spurious education ' (δοξοπαιδευτική). He is contrasted with
the parasite, whose bait is pleasure. This echoes the elaborate
parallel drawn in the *Gorgias* between the rhetorician and the
parasite. The profession to teach ' virtue ', or the successful
conduct of public and private life, was characteristic of Protagoras.
The genus chosen for this Division throws an initial emphasis on
rhetoric, rather to the exclusion of sophists like Hippias, who
mainly taught advanced subjects to youths who had left their
elementary school. But this type finds a place in the next Divisions.

223C–224E. *Divisions II–IV. The Sophist as Salesman*

In Divisions II–IV, the taking of money, a minor feature in
Division I, comes to the front in the genus, ' acquisition by exchange ', the alternative to ' hunting '. (1) The distinction of
selling (ἀγοραστική) from giving presents characterises the Sophist
as fundamentally a salesman. (2) The difference of methods—
the manufacturer selling his own produce (αὐτοπωλική), the local
retail dealer (καπηλική), the merchant who goes from city to city
(ἐμπορική)—though it leads to three definitions, is of less importance
than the description of the wares. (3) The Sophist trades in commodities that are to nourish the soul (ψυχεμπορική), not the body.
He is grouped at first with the artists—the painter, the musician,
the puppet-showman (who in the *Laws*, 658B, is classed with the
dramatist and the reciter). The Sophist's wares are knowledge
(μαθηματοπωλική), and in particular the knowledge of ' goodness '
(*aretê*). All this has a close parallel in the introductory conversa-

tion of the *Protagoras* (313), where Socrates warns the young Hippocrates against entrusting the care of his soul to ' a merchant or retail dealer in those commodities whereby the soul is nourished '.

These Divisions repeat many of the traits which occurred in Division I, only in a different order, throwing into relief the taking of money for teaching ' goodness ', which in Division I holds a subordinate place. There is no objection to a teacher being paid for imparting a store of knowledge or information which can be transferred to another person. The other receives something he desires to possess and gets value for his money.[1] Much of the Sophists' teaching was of this kind. What Socrates and Plato denounce is the taking of fees for teaching ' goodness '. Goodness, although according to Socrates it consists in a certain kind of ' knowledge ', is not a thing that anyone can teach ; not a stock of information that can be transferred [2] from one man to another. Moreover, the men who professed to sell ' goodness ' did not possess it themselves or even know what it was. To offer for sale what you do not possess, and, if you did possess it, could not transfer, is fraudulent. The professor of ' goodness ' demanding a fee excited in Plato the same sort of disgust as would be felt by a man who should summon a priest to give him spiritual consolation and then receive from the physician of souls a bill charging him five shillings for each visit.

Divisions I–IV may, then, be taken as analysing the practice of the great fifth-century Sophists, considered as rhetoricians and paid teachers of ' goodness '. The treatment is satirical and superficial ; we have not yet found the essence of Sophistry.

224E–226A. *Division V. Eristic*

The next Division, defining Eristic, is, like its predecessors, ultimately derived from the Acquisitive (as opposed to the Productive) class of Art ; but it follows a different branch. The fundamental character of this type is not ' hunting ' or ' selling ' but ' contention ' (ἀγωνιστική). The taking of fees comes in only at the end, to mark off the Eristic who is a professional Sophist from others who are not.

First, fighting (μαχητική) is distinguished from friendly competi-

---

[1] *Gorgias*, 520. It is no disgrace to the teacher of any ordinary art to stipulate for a fee. The trainer only teaches you to run fast, not to be honest. But the sophist professes to make you virtuous ; and if he succeeds, he will have made you honest and there will be no need of a previous contract for payment.

[2] *Meno* 93B, παραδοτὸν καὶ παραληπτὸν ἄλλῳ παρ' ἄλλου. *Euthyd.* 273D, 287A, ἀρετὴν παραδοῦναι. *Protag.* 319E, Pericles could not παραδίδοναι ἀρετήν to his sons. See above, p. 135.

tion ; then fighting in the form of verbal disputation (ἀμφιβητητική) from the violence of physical warfare. The disputation of forensic oratory, carried on in ' long speeches in public about rights and wrongs ', is marked off from private disputation ' in the small change of question and answer ' (ἀντιλογική).[1] Finally, there are the ' random and artless ' disputes of ordinary life ; but if disputation is conducted by rules of art we call it *Eristic*.

In the final summary of all the first six Divisions (231E), this type will be simply called the Eristic ; but here (225D) a further subdivision is added. The Eristic Sophist (like Euthydemus) is distinguished from other Eristics by taking fees and called a ' money-maker ' (χρηματιστικός). But there are other Eristics who ' waste their money ' (χρηματοφθορικοί). Their sort of disputation ' which makes one neglect one's own affairs for the pleasure of spending time in that way, but is carried on in a style that gives no pleasure to the ordinary hearer, can only be called a sort of babbling ' (ἀδολεσχικόν). Who are these ' babblers ' ? I cannot agree with Campbell that Socrates is meant, though he did neglect his affairs and become poor in pursuit of his mission ; nor with Diès that the babbler is the true dialectician. This would make the true philosopher a species of Eristic, arguing for fame or victory. It is true that the term ' babbling ' was applied to philosophy by its enemies and in particular to Socratic conversation.[2] Plato himself adopts it as a left-handed compliment, together with μετεωρολόγος, the term of reproach for Ionian science.[3] This suggests that the babblers here, who do not take fees, must be some followers of Socrates who could also be described as Eristics. There can be little doubt that the Megarians are meant, as Susemihl suggested.[4]

---

[1] This contrast recalls *Rep.* 499A : Many are sceptical about the value of the true philosopher, never having seen one or heard ' noble and free discourse ' aiming only at truth. They have only listened to displays of eristic cleverness, whose sole object is reputation and strife, whether in lawsuits (forensic oratory) or in private company (eristic sophistry).

[2] Eupolis 352 : Σωκράτην, τὸν πτωχὸν ἀδολέσχην. Aristophanes, *Clouds* 1485 : τὴν οἰκίαν τῶν ἀδολεσχῶν.

[3] *Phaedo* 70C, Socrates : ' No one can say I ἀδολεσχῶ in discussing death at this moment.' *Theaet.* 195B, Socrates calls himself ἀνὴρ ἀδολέσχης. *Phaedrus* 270A, All great arts require ἀδολεσχία and μετεωρολογία. *Statesman* 270A ; *Rep.* 488C.

[4] Diog. L. ii, 106 : Euclides (of Megara) applied himself to the writings of Parmenides, and his followers were called Megarians, then *Eristics*, and later Dialecticians, because they put their arguments in the form of question and answer. Timon (frag. 28D, D.L. ii, 107) : ' I care not for these babblers (φλεδόνων) . . . nor for Euclides the wrangler (ἐριδάντεω), who inspired the Megarians with a frenzy of controversy (ἐρισμοῦ).' A comic fragment (D.L. ii, 107) calls the Megarian Eubulides ὁ ἐριστικός ; Diogenes says he kept up a controversy with Aristotle. D.L. ii, 30 : Socrates ' seeing Euclides

They were also followers of the Eleatic School, and at *Phaedrus* 261C disputation (ἀντιλογική) includes, together with political and forensic oratory, the dialectical arguments of Zeno,[1] ' the Eleatic Palamedes '—his art of ' making the same things appear to his hearers both like and unlike, one and many, at rest and moving '. The whole is condemned as an art of deception.

The main contrast in Plato's mind is between Dialectic, the true art of philosophic conversation, and the technique of verbal dispute for victory which had been derived by the Megarians from the controversial methods of Zeno. This had enough resemblance to the Socratic *elenchus* for the two to be deliberately confused by Isocrates, who, as the champion of Gorgias' tradition of rhetorical sophistry, persistently brackets the Socratics in general with the ' devotees of verbal disputation '.[2] It may be for this reason that the Eristic strain in philosophical schools—the Eleatic and the Megarian—stands here in close contrast with the Cathartic procedure of Socrates himself.

226A–231B. *Division VI. Cathartic Method of Socrates*

In the sixth Division satire is dropped. The tone is serious and sympathetic ; towards the close it becomes eloquent. The type defined is ' the purifier of the soul from conceits that stand in the way of knowledge ' (231E)—a description which (as Jackson and others have seen) applies to Socrates and to no one else.

This Division, unlike the others, is preceded by a Collection. From a survey of various domestic operations—filtering, sifting, winnowing, and the combing and dividing of the warp in weaving—we collect the notion of an art of Separating (διακριτική). The effect is to dissociate this Division completely from the earlier ones, which were all derived from the art of Acquisition. The forms of Sophistry they defined were fundamentally arts of gain, acquiring influence over rich young men, or money by selling knowledge, or victory in argument instead of truth. All such

keenly interested in eristic arguments, said : " You will be able to get on with sophists, but not with men " ; for he thought such hair-splitting useless, as Plato shows in the *Euthydemus*.'

[1] Von Arnim (*Platos Jugenddialoge* (1914), 193) thinks that not Zeno, but a contemporary Megarian is here meant ; but I agree with Taylor, *Plato* (1926), 311, and others. At *Parm.* 135D Parmenides himself describes the display of Eleatic dialectic that is to follow as ' what the world calls useless babbling '.

[2] οἱ περὶ τὰς ἔριδας ἐσπουδακότες —the phrase which Theodorus has said (216B) does *not* apply to the Eleatic Stranger—is taken from Isocrates (κατὰ σοφ. i, 291B) ; *Helena* 1 and 6 (after references to Antisthenes and Plato) ; *Antid.* 258 (aimed at Plato).

motives are ruled out by going back to a distinct branch of art, not recognised at all where Art was at first divided into Acquisitive and Productive. The Separative arts are not productive either. Their function is negative.

The arts collected in this survey are introduced abruptly with no hint of their relevance. The normal Collection takes into consideration the term proposed for definition together with others which can plausibly be thought to resemble it. The object is to discern some common property with a claim to be the most important or essential and so to stand as the genus to be divided. Here Sophistry is not included, and the reader is left entirely without a clue to the connection between Sophistry and these homely operations. There is no sort of promise that by dividing the generic notion of Separation we shall ever arrive at a definition of the Sophist. Nor can the reader guess that what we shall, in fact, define is not Sophistry but the Socratic *elenchus*.

The art of Separating (διακριτική) is now divided. Things separated may be alike ; but we are concerned with purification (καθαρμός) which expels what is worse and retains what is better. One kind of purification is the physical cleansing of lifeless things and of the living body, ' including those internal separations and purgations effected by gymnastic and medicine '. The other kind is the purification which ' removes evil from the soul ' (ἀφαίρεσις κακίας ψυχῆς, 227D). (It should be noted that Purification is a negative notion—the riddance of evil.[1] Medicine and gymnastic are not regarded positively as creating health and strength, but classed with washing. They will presently be described more definitely under their negative aspect—medicine as the riddance of disease, gymnastic as the riddance of ugliness. Similarly purification of the soul is not the production of goodness but the ' removal of evil '.)[2]

At the next step an analogy is drawn between two kinds of bodily, and two kinds of mental, purification :

Purification

out of the body

of disease (Medicine)

of ugliness (Gymnastic)

out of the soul

of wickedness (Chastisement)

of ignorance (Instruction)

---

[1] The passive substantive κάθαρμα (offscouring, outcast) means the impurity removed, not the thing purified.

[2] Hence Apelt's assertion (note on 226B) that διακριτική is to be subordinated to ποιητική (τέχνη) must be rejected.

VI. CATHARTIC METHOD OF SOCRATES

Disease is regarded, not in the usual way as lack of balance that needs to be redressed, but as faction, sedition, or civil warfare (στάσις) among things naturally ' akin '. This is for the sake of its counterpart, ' wickedness ' (πονηρία) in the soul, where there is ' mutual dissension everywhere—judgments at variance with desires, courage with pleasures, reflection with pains '. The description of wickedness recalls passages in the *Republic* where the conflict between the three parts of the soul is compared to political strife. Thus at 440B the ' spirited ' part takes the side of reason against desire ' in the faction-fight of the soul '. This is Platonic, rather than Socratic. Vice is not here identified with ignorance (as by Socrates), but distinguished from it. The counterpart of medicine as the remedy for bodily disease is ' the justice that chastises '[1] vice. Chastisement (κολαστική) is introduced for the sake of its negative meaning. The *Gorgias* had used the same analogy between the doctor and the judge who chastises the wrong-doer to ' rid ' him of his vice.[2]

Gymnastic is the parallel remedy for physical ugliness, the deformity due to lack of proportion. This is, somewhat strangely, treated as analogous to a lack of proportion or co-ordination between impulses in the soul, causing them to miss their mark. Ignorance (ἄγνοια) is the swerving aside of the soul's impulse towards truth, and (as Socrates had taught) is always ' involuntary '—against the true wish for the right end. The remedy for ignorance in all its many forms is Instruction (διδασκαλική).

Instruction is next divided. Setting aside technical instruction (which is obviously positive), we take, as the other branch, moral education (παιδεία), conceived negatively as the deliverance of the soul from that conceit of wisdom which renders it unable to under-stand (ἀμαθία).[3] (This education is directly contrary to the ' spurious education ' offered by the Sophists in the earlier Divisions, which resulted precisely in producing the conceit of wisdom). Next the method of rebuke and admonition practised by parents

---

[1] ἡ κολαστικὴ . . . δίκη (229A) is the manuscript reading. The epithet is intended to distinguish justice as chastisement from the more common view of it as the vengeance of the community. (In the next sentence τὸ γοῦν εἰκὸς ὡς εἰπεῖν differs only in emphasis from ὡς γοῦν τὸ εἰκὸς εἰπεῖν. Cf. ὡς συντόμως εἰπεῖν.)

[2] *Gorg.* 478A, δικαιοσύνῃ τινὶ χρώμενοι κολάζουσιν οἱ ὀρθῶς (*i.e.* ' in the true sense ') κολάζοντες.

[3] Ἀμαθία is not ignorance in the sense of a blank absence of knowledge, to be cured by imparting information. It is due to the positive presence of the false belief that you already know or understand. It was Socrates' discovery that true moral education must begin with casting out popular beliefs about right and wrong, derived from parents and teachers.

is contrasted with the method of those who have ' convinced themselves upon reflection that all inability to understand is involuntary '
and that ' admonition yields little result for much pains '. ' They
press a person with questions about some matter on which he
fancies he has something valuable to say, when really he is talking
nonsense. Then, when such persons begin to waver, they readily
hold a muster of their opinions, collect them in argument and
confront them with one another, and thereby show that they are
in contradiction on the same subjects, at the same moment, from
the same point of view. When the others see this, they are vexed
with themselves, and become gentler towards others ; so by this
means they are delivered from their lofty and obstinate conceit
of themselves—of all deliverances the most pleasant to witness
and of the most lasting benefit to the patient. Their purifiers are
of the same mind as those physicians who hold that the body can
get no benefit from the food it takes until all inward obstructions
are removed. These others have observed that the same is true
of the soul, which will not profit by the instruction it receives until
cross-examination has reduced the man to a modest frame of mind,
and has cleared away the conceits that obstruct learning and so
purged him and convinced him that he knows only what he does
know and nothing more.' This examination (*elenchus*) is ' the
highest and most sovran method of purification '.[1] All this passage
is in the tone and manner of the *Republic*. It describes the method
of Socrates, who declares in the *Apology* that the life not subject to
examination is not worth living.

But are these purifiers of the soul ' Sophists ' ?

230E. STRANGER (*continues*). Well, what name shall we give to
the practitioners of this art ? For my part I shrink from
231.   calling them Sophists.

THEAET. Why so ?

STR. For fear of ascribing to them too high a function.[2]

THEAET. And yet your description has some resemblance
to that type (the Sophist).

STR. So has the dog to the wolf—the fiercest of animals to
the tamest. But a cautious man should above all be on
his guard against resemblances ; they are a very slippery
sort of thing. However, be it so (*i.e.* let them pass for
Sophists) ; for should they ever set up an adequate defence

---

[1] 230B–D. The language here closely resembles the description of the
effect of Socrates' art on Theaetetus, *Theaet.* 210C (p 163).

[2] As Jackson and others have seen, ' them ' can only mean the practitioners
(not the sophists). This echoes Socrates' habit of disclaiming any title that
implies the possession of wisdom ; he is only a ' lover of wisdom ', a philosopher.

231B. of their confines, the boundary in dispute will be of no small importance.

THEAET. That is likely enough.

STR. Let us take it, then, that under the art of Separation there is a method of Purification ; that we have distinguished that kind of purification which is concerned with the Soul ; and under that, Instruction ; and under that again, Education. Within the art of education, the Examination which confutes the vain conceit of wisdom we will allow to pass, in the argument which has now come in by a side wind,[1] by no other name than the Sophistry that is of noble lineage (ἡ γένει γενναία σοφιστική).

It is hard to see why this analysis of Socrates' Cathartic method should stand here as the last of these preliminary attempts to define the Sophist. The whole argument has admittedly ' come in by a side wind '. From the outset the Division has no link or point of contact with first five or with the seventh ; it starts from an entirely new genus—a point that may be emphasised by the final phrase, ' the Sophistry that is of noble lineage ' (γένει).[2] The fundamental aim of the Cathartic method is the precise opposite of the production of the false conceit of wisdom, characteristic of the Sophist in the earlier Divisions and in the seventh, which is taken as final.

Where the Stranger says he would shrink from calling the purifier of the soul a Sophist, Theaetetus remarks that they have a certain resemblance. It is true that the negative *elenchus* of Socrates, pressing the respondent with questions, reviewing his beliefs and confuting them by exposing their contradictions, did superficially resemble the controversy practised by Euthydemus, the Eleatics, and the Megarians ' in the private exchange of question and answer ' (225B)—a style of ' babbling ' which ' most hearers do not find agreeable to listen to ', whereas the Socratic deliverance of men ' from a lofty and stubborn conceit of themselves ' was ' of all deliverances the most agreeable to listen to '.[3] Isocrates persistently encouraged

---

[1] ἐν τῷ νῦν λόγῳ παραφανέντι. Παραφαίνεσθαι is used at *Theaet.* 199C of a difficulty that shows itself in a fresh quarter, where we were not looking. The construction with λεγέσθω is awkward. Perhaps we should read παραφανέν τι : ' And (as a part) of education, the examination which confutes the vain conceit of wisdom—a thing that has come by a side wind into our present argument—we will allow to pass,' etc.

[2] There is no trace in the text of the link with Eristic suggested by Campbell (Introd., p. li) : ' Controversy is, or should be, an art of separating the false from the true, of determining what propositions are not tenable.'

[3] 225D, περὶ δὲ τὴν λέξιν τοῖς πολλοῖς τῶν ἀκουόντων οὐ μεθ' ἡδονῆς ἀκουόμενον (of Eristic) in designed contrast with 230C, πασῶν ἀπαλλαγῶν ἀκούειν τε ἡδίστην. Plato may (with some moderns) have understood ἀδο-λέσχης as = ἀηδολέσχης.

the popular confusion of Socratic conversation with verbal dispute
for victory. As Socrates remarked at the outset (216D), the genuine
philosopher sometimes seems to wear the guise of the Sophist.
Here, moreover, Plato has been careful to analyse only the negative
side of Socrates' practice—the side on which the resemblance
lies.

But the resemblance, as the Stranger says, is as misleading as
that of the dog to the wolf. In the *Republic* (375A and E ff.), the
dog is the symbol of the Guardian of society. The watch-dog of
generous breed is gentle to those whom he knows, and this friendli-
ness to what is known is taken to be a genuinely ' philosophic '
trait.[1] The wolf is the typical enemy of society. The sophist
Thrasymachus breaks in upon the conversation with a wolf's
ferocity.[2] The tyrant is like the man who has tasted human
flesh and turned into a wolf.[3] The sensual passion of the false
lover in the *Phaedrus* is the passion of the wolf for the lamb ; his
kinship with the Sophist as a man-hunter was remarked in the
first Division.[4] The upshot is that the purifier of the soul is not
a Sophist in the sense of this dialogue. The whole Division has no
point of contact with any of the others.

Why then does it stand here ? Perhaps it can be explained as
a feature in the whole design of these dialogues, which remains
obscure because never completed. Another element in the pattern
is added in the *Statesman* where the ' art of Combining ' (συγκριτική)
is contrasted with the ' art of Separating ' (διακριτική). The
Statesman opens with a long Division defining the art of shepherd-
ing mankind. To illustrate its defects, an exemplary Division, to
define weaving, reviews and classifies a number of household operations, including the use of comb and rod mentioned in the Collection
of the Separative arts at *Soph.* 226B. Separation and Combination
(from which Weaving is derived) are described as ' two great arts
of universal application ' (282B). Just as in the *Sophist* Hunting,
the genus of the Angler, turns out to be relevant to the first definition
of the Sophist, so in the *Statesman* Weaving symbolises the art of
the Statesman, whose function is to combine in harmony the
various elements of society. It is perhaps to prepare the way for
this conception of statesmanship that Plato in our passage regards

---

[1] In the Stranger's speech the phrases ποιεῖσθαι τὴν φυλακήν and φυλάττωσιν
suggest that the Guardian is in Plato's thoughts.

[2] *Rep.* 336D, καί μοι δοκῶ, εἰ μὴ πρότερος ἑωράκη αὐτὸν ἢ ἐκεῖνος ἐμέ, ἄφωνος ἂν
γενέσθαι.

[3] *Rep.* 565D. Cf. Glotz, *Solidarité de la famille* (1904), p. 23. *Phaedo* 82A,
the tyrant and the robber are reincarnated as wolves or birds of prey.

[4] *Phaedrus* 241D, ὡς λύκοι ἄρν' ἀγαπῶσ', ὡς παῖδα φιλοῦσιν ἐρασταί. *Soph.* 222D.

VI. CATHARTIC METHOD OF SOCRATES

vice, not as ignorance, but as a political sedition in the soul, to be remedied by ' the justice that chastens ', the analogue of medical purgation of disease. So in the *Statesman* (308E) the Royal Art ' casts out by death or exile and chastens with the severest disfranchisement ' those natures which cannot take a place in the pattern of the community.

The parallel elaborately drawn in the *Statesman* between the combining operations of weaving and statesmanship has its counterpart elsewhere [1] in an analogy between the separating operations of weaving and dialectic. The suggestion is being discussed, that there may be a ' right ' way of naming things in words whose form will somehow express their natures. The name, like the weaver's rod (κερκίς), is a tool. The use of the rod is to *separate* (διακρίνειν) the web or the warp. A name has two uses : to convey information and to distinguish (separate, διακρίνειν) the natures of things. The rod is made by the carpenter under the directions of the weaver, who understands its use. So the skilled name-maker fashions names for the use of the dialectician (philosopher), who, it is implied, has the ability to distinguish those natures which are the meanings of names. It is no accident that the operations of weaving should thus be used in analogy with dialectic in the *Cratylus* and with statesmanship in the *Statesman*.

Plato may have intended to derive the dialectical method of Division more openly than he has done from that branch of Separation which distinguishes things that are ' alike ' (226D, in contrast with the branch separating the worse from the better, leading to Cathartic). Dialectic is ' to divide according to kinds ',[2] not mistaking one Form for another, or ' to separate by kinds ' (διακρίνειν κατὰ γένος, 253DE). It discovers differences separating things that are ' alike ' in being of the same genus. The task of philosophy is regarded in the *Sophist* as mainly analytical—the mapping out of the realm of Forms in all its articulations by Division. The practical task of the philosopher as statesman is synthetic. Possibly the *Philosopher*, had it been written, would have completed the account of philosophic method by recognising the synthetic or intuitive moment in dialectic, which the *Sophist* leaves in the background. If the Collection and Division of the Separative arts had some such intended relation to a larger design, its apparent irrelevance ceases to be a problem.

[1] *Cratylus*, 386E, ff.

[2] τὸ κατὰ γένη διαιρεῖσθαι. At 226C the separative domestic operations were called διαιρετικά, and at 227B the task of philosophic discourse was ' to discern what is of the same kind and what is not ' (τὸ συγγενὲς καὶ τὸ μὴ συγγενές).

The Methods of Collection and Division

But the purpose served by these six Divisions in the economy of the whole dialogue is still not perfectly clear. Some light may be gained by considering the nature of Plato's methods of Collection and Division in contrast with the Socratic method sometimes called ' Induction ' (*Epagogé*).

Socrates had been the first to realise clearly that, both in common life and in science, men constantly use words without knowing the ' essence ' of the thing named or being able to ' give an account ' (λόγον διδόναι) of it.[1] The Socratic and Platonic view is that, in such a case, we have the same object before our minds, but see it only indistinctly. We ' have only the name in common ', until we express its meaning in an explicit formula. Such a name as ' Justice ' has one true meaning, more or less dimly present to our minds when we hear the name. If one of us can give the right account of it, the other will be able to see it too.

Plato's early dialogues illustrate Socrates' attempts to give an account of the meaning of terms, and, without any parade of technique, formulate a method that is regularly applied. In its full form the method has two stages. (1) The first is Cathartic. The questioner elicits from the respondent what he thinks he knows. His ' suggestions ' (' hypotheses ') are criticised in the *elenchus*, often by deducing consequences conflicting with other opinions he holds. The result is the riddance of the false conceit of knowledge. Conscious of ignorance and in perplexity (ἀπορία), the respondent is now ready for the co-operative search.[2] (2) This further inquiry normally proceeds by the same method : a series of suggestions criticised and amended by bringing in fresh considerations. The end should be the correct definition of the meaning or ' Form ' which has all along been coming more clearly into view.

Contrast with this Socratic procedure the new method of Collection and Division. It is twofold. The preliminary Collection is to fix upon the genus to be divided. The Division is a downward process from that genus to the definition of a species. This process has nothing in common with the deductive movement of the Socratic *elenchus*, which terminates in the rejection of a suggested definition.

[1] It is a curious fact that, not only in physical science, but even in mathematics, men have made great advances and discoveries without being able to define the most important concepts correctly, *e.g.* the concept of Number.

[2] A good illustration is the rejection of Meno's suggested definitions of Virtue, followed by his complaint that Socrates reduces men to perplexity. Meno had thought he knew what virtue is ; now he is puzzled. Socrates replies that he does not know either, but is willing to undertake the co-operative search (συζητῆσαι), *Meno* 80A ff. The *Theaetetus*, again, is Cathartic, rejecting all suggested definitions and ending in ἀπορία.

In the Socratic procedure the clear vision of the Form and the true account of it are reached as the goal of series of upward leaps (to use Plato's metaphor). But in Collection and Division the goal is reached at the end of the downward process, when an indivisible species is defined in terms of genus and specific differences. In a word, the Socratic method approaches the Form to be defined from below, the new method descends to it from above.

The reason lies in the difference between the groups of objects with which the two methods are severally concerned. The Socratic method contemplates a single Form (such as The Beautiful Itself) and the many individual things which partake of that Form. Only one Form is in view, and the definition is to be gained by a survey of individual instances. We seek to isolate and apprehend the common character ($\epsilon \hat{\iota} \delta o \varsigma$) which, in ordinary language, would be said to be ' present ' in all the instances, as white hair is white ' by the presence of whiteness '. [1] One expedient is to ' adduce ' ($\epsilon \pi \acute{\alpha} \gamma \epsilon \sigma \theta \alpha \iota$) fresh instances that have been overlooked and, when produced, are seen not to be covered by the respondent's suggested account. If he has implied that it is always right to tell the truth, you may bring forward the lie told to deceive an enemy in war or an insane friend. This is one sense of *Epagogé*.

Another use of the verb $\epsilon \pi \acute{\alpha} \gamma \epsilon \iota \nu$, to ' lead on ', also fits the Socratic procedure. Aristotle speaks of ' leading on from individual instances to the universal, and from the familiar to the unknown ', and defines ' Induction ' ($\epsilon \pi \alpha \gamma \omega \gamma \acute{\eta}$) as ' the approach from particulars to the universal.' [2] His illustration is an argument of obviously Socratic pattern : ' If the skilled pilot is most effective, and likewise the skilled charioteer, then in general the skilled man is best at his particular task.' The process is confined to the Socratic group of objects ; from observation of individual cases, an act of insight discerns the universal latent in them and disengages it in a generalisation.

But, as the *Parmenides* showed,[3] Plato's attention is now transferred from the group of individuals with its common Form to the relations of Forms among themselves, and in particular to the relations between the Forms which occur in the definition of a, specific Form. The earliest passage betraying any interest in this question is in the *Meno* (75A ff.), where a definition of ' Figure '

---

[1] *Lysis* 217D.

[2] Plato, *Pol.* 278A : A certain device for teaching children their letters is the easiest way to " *lead them on* to what they do not yet know " ($\epsilon \pi \acute{\alpha} \gamma \epsilon \iota \nu$ $\alpha \grave{\upsilon} \tau o \grave{\upsilon} \varsigma$ $\epsilon \pi \grave{\iota}$ $\tau \grave{\alpha}$ $\mu \acute{\eta} \pi \omega$ $\gamma \iota \gamma \nu \omega \sigma \kappa \acute{o} \mu \epsilon \nu \alpha$). Ar., *Top.* 152a, 4, $\epsilon \pi \acute{\alpha} \gamma o \nu \tau \alpha$ $\dot{\alpha} \pi \grave{o}$ $\tau \hat{\omega} \nu$ $\kappa \alpha \theta'$ $\epsilon \kappa \alpha \sigma \tau o \nu$ $\epsilon \pi \grave{\iota}$ $\tau \grave{o}$ $\kappa \alpha \theta \acute{o} \lambda o \upsilon$ $\kappa \alpha \grave{\iota}$ $\tau \hat{\omega} \nu$ $\gamma \nu \omega \rho \acute{\iota} \mu \omega \nu$ $\epsilon \pi \grave{\iota}$ $\tau \grave{\alpha}$ $\check{\alpha} \gamma \nu \omega \sigma \tau \alpha$, *ibid*. 105a, 13, $\epsilon \pi \alpha \gamma \omega \gamma \acute{\eta}$, $\dot{\eta}$ $\dot{\alpha} \pi \grave{o}$ $\tau \hat{\omega} \nu$ $\kappa \alpha \theta'$ $\epsilon \kappa \alpha \sigma \tau o \nu$ $\epsilon \pi \grave{\iota}$ $\tau \grave{\alpha}$ $\kappa \alpha \theta \acute{o} \lambda o \upsilon$ $\epsilon \phi o \delta o \varsigma$.

[3] See Introd , p. 11.

—'that which always accompanies colour'—is rejected as containing the unknown term 'colour'. Terms should be defined by other terms admitted to be already known. Socrates obtains Meno's admission that he understands 'boundary' and 'solid' before substituting the correct definition of Figure as 'the boundary of a solid'. It is significant that the illustration should be taken from mathematics. Geometry may have supplied the first formal examples of definition by genus and specific difference, such as the division of triangle into equilateral, isosceles, and scalene. Here all the terms are Forms. The study of their mutual relations takes no account of individual instances, indefinite in number and beneath the level of knowledge. Triangular objects in the world of sense, which partake more or less perfectly of the triangular character, drop out of sight. The question how an indefinite number of individual things can partake of a single Form gives place to that other question raised in the *Parmenides*: Can many Forms partake of a single Form?

The new method of Collection and Division is thus wholly confined to the world of Forms; and Collection must not be confused with the Socratic muster of individual instances (ἐπαγωγή). Collection is a survey of specific Forms having some *prima facie* claim to be members of the same genus. As usual, Plato avoids a rigid terminology, and uses 'Form' (εἶδος, ἰδέα), and 'kind' (γένος) indifferently for genus and species alike.[1] His only distinctive word for species is 'part' (μέρος, μόριον). The method of Division exhibits Forms arranged in systematic classification, spreading downwards from a single genus, through a definite number of specific differences, to the indivisible species at the bottom. Below that there is nothing but the indefinite number of individual things which may or may not partake of the indivisible specific Form. They are below the horizon of science; the method considers only the *One* which is divided and the definite *Many* which are its 'parts'.[2]

The Division should be preceded by a Collection, to fix upon the genus we are to divide. This is done by 'taking a comprehensive view and gathering a number of widely scattered terms into a unity'.[3] Here no methodical procedure is possible. The generic Form must be divined by an act of intuition, for which no rules can be given. The survey will include the Form we wish ultimately

---

[1] For instance, at *Soph.* 227D, the Stranger says there are 'two forms (εἴδη) of evil in the soul', and at 228E Theaetetus remarks 'there are, as you said, two kinds (γένη) of evil in the soul'

[2] Cf. *Philebus* 16B ff.

[3] *Phaedrus* 265D.

to define, with others that may be 'widely scattered' and have
little superficial resemblance to it or to one another.

The need for a preliminary Collection is, as we have seen, ignored
in all but one of the early Divisions of the *Sophist*, and where it
does occur it is abnormal. What I would now suggest is that
these first six Divisions actually, though not formally, serve the
purpose of a Collection preliminary to the seventh. They bring
before us the types to be surveyed before we can fix upon the
really fundamental character of Sophistry. The name 'Sophist'
had been loosely applied to various classes : the rhetoricians, like
Protagoras and Gorgias ; teachers of advanced subjects, like
Hippias ; professional disputants, like Euthydemus. All these had
called themselves 'Sophists'. Isocrates and the public had also
applied the name to Socrates himself and to his followers, including
the Megarians, whose methods of argument did resemble the
dialectic of Zeno and the eristic of Euthydemus. The early
Divisions analyse and characterise each of these types and so provide a survey of the field within which we must discover the really
fundamental trait, the generic Form that will finally yield the
correct definition of the essence of Sophistry.

The Collection is disguised in the misleading form of a series of
tentative Divisions. The definitions in which they terminate are
not definitions of 'the Sophist', but analytical descriptions of
easily recognisable classes to whom the name had been attached.
By this device Plato avoids mentioning the names of individuals
or of schools, and can amuse himself with satire. At the same
time he can familiarise the reader with the method of Division
before giving the final serious analysis of the essential Sophist.
If these six earlier Divisions are in effect a Collection, that explains
why no one of them is preceded by a Collection of the normal
pattern. Plato may also mean to indicate that, when a difficult
idea is to be defined, it may be well to begin by making a number
of tentative Divisions, each starting from some salient character,
and then compare the results. The same character may be found
at different points in the various tables ; and reflection may discover which is the really fundamental trait that ought to stand
as genus. This, at any rate, is the result now to be reached in
the next section of the dialogue.

231B–235A. *Survey yielding the genus ' Image-making '*

The translation will now be resumed. The following section
opens with a summary, mustering for review the six types that
have been characterised. Further analysis then leads to the discovery of a new generic character, Image-making, which is taken

as a starting-point for the final Division. At 235B the Division
is begun, but is soon arrested by the problem : how can there be
such a thing as an image or false appearance ? So we reach the
metaphysical kernel of the dialogue.

To the Stranger's suggestion that we may let the purification
of the soul from the conceit of wisdom pass by the name of ' the
Sophistry of noble lineage ', Theaetetus replies :

231B. THEAET. Let it pass by that name. But by this time
C. the Sophist has appeared in so many guises that for my
part I am puzzled to see what description one is to maintain as truly expressing his real nature.

STR. You may well be puzzled. But we may suppose
that by now the Sophist too is very much puzzled to see
how he is once more to slip through the meshes of our
argument ; for it is a true saying that you cannot easily
evade all the wrestler's grips. So now is the moment of
all others to set upon him.

THEAET. Well and good.

STR. First, then, let us stand and take breath ; and while
D. we are resting let us reckon up between ourselves in how
many guises the Sophist has appeared. First, I think, he
was found as the hired hunter of rich young men.

THEAET. Yes.

STR. And secondly as a sort of merchant of learning as
nourishment for the soul.

THEAET. Certainly.

STR. Thirdly, he showed himself as a retail-dealer in the
same wares, did he not ?

THEAET. Yes ; and fourthly as selling the products of his
own manufacture.

STR. Your memory serves you well. His fifth appearance
E. I will myself try to recall. He was an athlete in debate,
appropriating that subdivision of contention which consists in the art of Eristic.

THEAET. He was.

STR. His sixth appearance was open to doubt ; however,
we conceded his claim to be described as a purifier of the
soul from conceits that block the way to understanding.

THEAET. Quite so.

The Sophist has ' appeared in many guises ' [1]—as many things,
not a unity. As Theaetetus suggests, we have not yet defined

---

[1] The word ' appear ' is repeated many times : διὰ τὸ πολλὰ πεφάνθαι (231B) ;
ὅποσα ἡμῖν ὁ σοφιστὴς πέφανται; ἀνεφάνη (D) ; φαίνηται, φάντασμα (232A).

his real or essential nature. In reckoning precisely the number of these appearances, we are in effect collecting the ' many scattered terms ' which must be ' comprehensively surveyed ', if we are to divine the genus that will yield the true definition. The Stranger now remarks that we have not divined it yet. We have given the Sophist the names of many arts (hunter, salesman, Eristic, etc.) ; but ' Sophistry ' is a single name for a single art. There must be some fundamental feature common to all these many arts, and our next business to ' see it clearly ' ($\varkappa a\tau\iota\delta\epsilon\tilde{\iota}\nu$)—Plato's favourite word for that act of insight or intuition ($\nu\acute{o}\eta\sigma\iota\varsigma$) which *sees* directly, without any process of discursive reasoning.[1]

232.   STR. Now does it strike you that, when one who is known by the name of a single art appears to be master of many,[2] there is something wrong with this appearance ? If one has that impression of any art, plainly it is because one cannot see clearly that feature of it in which all these forms of skill converge, and so one calls their possessor by many names instead of one.

THEAET. I dare say that is the gist of the situation.

B. STR. If so, we must not be so lazy as to let that happen to us in our inquiry. Let us begin by going back to one among the characteristics we attributed to the Sophist. There was one that struck me particularly as revealing his character.

THEAET. What was that ?

STR. We said, I believe, that he was a controversialist.

THEAET. Yes.

STR. And further that he figures as an instructor of others in controversy.

THEAET. Certainly.

The term ' controversialist ' ($\dot{a}\nu\tau\iota\lambda o\gamma\iota\varkappa\acute{o}\varsigma$) actually occurred in the analysis of Eristic (Division V, 225B), and was there given the limited sphere of ' private debates about rights and wrongs in the small change of question and answer '. Such controversy differed from the public debates about rights and wrongs carried on by the forensic orator, only in the superficial circumstance that it was conducted in private conversation. The wider term ' disputation ' ($\dot{a}\mu\varphi\iota\sigma\beta\eta\tau\eta\tau\iota\varkappa\acute{\eta}$) covered both. Reduced to rules of art, controversy

---

[1] In *Rep.* vii, $\varkappa a\theta o\rho\tilde{a}\nu$ is frequently used as a synonym of $\nu o\epsilon\tilde{\iota}\nu$ in this sense of immediate intuitive vision of a prior truth or premiss to be used in the proof of a desired conclusion. See F. M. Cornford, Mathematics and Dialectic in *Republic* vi–vii, Mind xli, pp. 37 ff, 173 ff.

[2] Note the introduction at the outset of the phrase which will presently receive a deeper significance : ' one who *appears as knowing many things* '.

included the verbal disputation of the Eristic Sophist and the Megarian, and the dialectic of Zeno. Of all the arts described it came nearest in externals to the genuine dialectic of Socrates—a resemblance that caused the confusion of Socrates and his followers with the Eristics. But in fundamental motive controversy, which neglects truth to gain victory, is diametrically opposed to the philosophic art of conversation.[1] Victory is gained by producing a belief in the audience that you are in the right as against your opponent. Hence the term ' controversy ' is used in the *Phaedrus* (261C ff.) to embrace both Zenonian dialectic and the public forms of rhetoric (political and forensic), as a single art which makes things *seem* right at one time, wrong at another, according as the orator chooses. It is a practice of deception leading on those who do not know the true nature of things to false beliefs. It is the art of one ' who does not know the truth, but has gone hunting after opinions '. That passage enlarges the meaning of ' controversy ' so as to include the rhetorical Sophists,[2] the hunters of Division I, the ' producers of persuasion ' ($\pi\iota\theta\alpha\nu o\nu\rho\gamma\iota\kappa\dot{\eta}$) and professors of spurious education in goodness, who were alternatively regarded as salesmen of the soul's nourishment in Divisions II–IV. Protagoras himself will presently be named. Because of this wider sense, ' controversy ' is pitched upon as a character common to all the types described in the earlier Divisions (except the purifier of the soul) and as the ' most revealing ' trait. Nothing that is said here has any relevance to Cathartic.

The next point is that the art of controversy in which the Sophist instructs others, covers the whole field of knowledge. It is a formal technique of debate (whether conversational or rhetorical), supposed to make men capable of disputing on any subject without really knowing anything about it.

232B. STR. Let us consider, then, in what field these people profess to turn out controversialists. Let us go to the root of the matter and set about it in this way. Tell me, does

c. their pupils' competence extend to divine things that are hidden from common eyes ?[3]

---

[1] Cf. *Rep.* 455A : Many people unwittingly fall into controversy ($\dot{\alpha}\nu\tau\iota\lambda o\gamma\iota\kappa\dot{\eta}$) and mistake Eristic dispute for philosophic conversation ($o\check{\iota}\epsilon\sigma\theta\alpha\iota\ o\dot{\upsilon}\kappa\ \dot{\epsilon}\rho\dot{\iota}\zeta\epsilon\iota\nu$ $\dot{\alpha}\lambda\lambda\dot{\alpha}\ \delta\iota\alpha\lambda\dot{\epsilon}\gamma\epsilon\sigma\theta\alpha\iota$), because they cannot think about meanings and ' divide them by kinds ', but are misled by words to go in chase of verbal contradictions, $\dot{\epsilon}\rho\iota\delta\iota,\ o\dot{\upsilon}\ \delta\iota\alpha\lambda\dot{\epsilon}\kappa\tau\omega\ \pi\rho\dot{o}s\ \dot{\alpha}\lambda\lambda\dot{\eta}\lambda o\upsilon s\ \chi\rho\dot{\omega}\mu\epsilon\nu o\iota$.

[2] Forensic Oratory was actually grouped with private Controversy under the wider term Disputation ($\dot{\alpha}\mu\phi\iota\sigma\beta\eta\tau\eta\tau\sigma\iota\kappa\dot{\eta}$, 225B), a word used here (232D) as synonymous with ' Controversy '.

[3] ' Divine things ' may mean religion ; but possibly the vague phrase is meant to cover the divine and invisible entities of Plato's system, the Forms,

232C. THEAET. So it is said of them, at any rate.

STR. And also to all that is visible in sky and earth and everything of that sort.

THEAET. Surely.

STR. And in private circles, whenever any general statement is made about becoming or reality, we are aware how cleverly they can controvert it and make others able to do the same.

THEAET. Certainly.

D. STR. And then again where laws are in question or any political matter, do they not promise to produce debaters?

THEAET. If they did not hold out that promise, hardly anyone would take part in their discussions.[1]

STR. And about the crafts in general and each particular craft, the arguments to be used in controversy with any actual craftsman have been published broadcast for all who choose to learn.

THEAET. I take it you mean what Protagoras wrote on E. wrestling and the other arts.[2]

STR. Yes, and on many other things. In fact, the pretensions of this art of controversy amount, it seems, to a capacity for disputation on any subject whatsoever.

THEAET. It certainly seems that nothing worth speaking of is beyond its scope.[3]

STR. Do you, then, my young friend, really think that

---

which are meanings of words in common use, though their true nature is unknown to the many. The *Philebus* 62A calls the eternal Form of the circle ' the divine circle ' as opposed to the ' human '. The ' divine things ' are contrasted in the next speech with the visible parts of the universe, and the terms ' reality ' and ' becoming ' just below suggest the intelligible and sensible worlds. So at 254B the region of true reality is called ' the divine ' (τὸ θεῖον), on which the eye of the vulgar soul cannot fix its gaze.

[1] Theaetetus echoes Socrates' remark about Protagoras at *Theaet.* 178E (p. 91).

[2] Protagoras published criticisms of special arts, probably in the two books of *Controversies* ('Ἀντιλογίαι, Diels, *Vors.*[4] ii, 231ⁿ .) or in the 'Ἀλήθεια, which Bernays identified with the *Controversies*. His attack on mathematics is mentioned by Aristotle (*Met.* 997b, 32). Diels (*ibid.*) quotes Hippocrates π. νουσῶν I (*L.* vi, 140), 'Whoever wishes to ask and answer questions correctly and to dispute (ἀντιλέγειν) about medicine, should bear in mind the following truths,' etc. This suggests Eristic debate about Medicine.

[3] Plato has not exaggerated the historical sophists' claim to wisdom on all subjects. Apelt cites a passage in the *Dialexeis*, an anonymous summary of arguments, which some believe to have been based on the lectures of some fifth-century sophist : ' I hold that it belongs to the same person and to the same art to be able to converse ; to know the truth of things ; to under-

232E.   possible ?   You young people may perhaps see more clearly ;
         my eyes are too dim.

233.   THEAET.   Is what possible ?   What am I meant to see ?
         I don't clearly understand what you are asking me.
         STR.   Whether it is possible for any human being to know
         everything.
         THEAET.   Mankind would indeed be happy, if it were so.
         STR.   Then if a man who has no knowledge controverts
         one who does know, how can there be any sound sense in
         what he says ?
         THEAET.   There cannot be.
         STR.   Then what can be the secret of this magical power of
         Sophistry ?
         THEAET.   In what respect ?

B.   STR.   I mean, how they can ever create a belief in the minds
         of young men that they are the wisest of men on all subjects ?
         For clearly if they were not in the right in their controversies
         or did not appear to be so in the young men's eyes, and if
         that appearance did not enhance the belief that they are
         wise because they can dispute, then, to quote your own
         remark, it is hard to see why anyone should want to pay
         their fees and be taught this art of disputation.
         THEAET.   Hard indeed.
         STR.   But in actual fact there is a demand.
         THEAET.   Quite a brisk one.

C.   STR.   No doubt because the Sophists are believed to possess
         a knowledge of their own in the subjects they dispute
         about.
         THEAET.   No doubt.
         STR.   And, we say, there is no subject they do not dispute
         about.
         THEAET.   Yes.
         STR.   So they appear to their pupils to be wise on all
         subjects.
         THEAET.   Certainly.
         STR.   Although they are not really wise ; for that, we saw,
         is impossible.
         THEAET.   It must be impossible.

---

stand how to give a right verdict in court ; to be able to speak in public ;
to understand the arts of discourse ; and to give instruction on the nature
of all things, how they are and how they came to be. He who knows the
nature of all things must surely be able to instruct his city to act rightly
in all matters. He who understands the arts of discourse will know how to
speak rightly on any subject ', and so on (*Dialexeis* 8 ; Diels, *Vors.*⁴ ii, 344).

233C. STR. The upshot is, then, that the Sophist possesses a sort of reputed and apparent knowledge on all subjects, but not the reality.

D. THEAET. I quite agree ; and perhaps this is the truest thing that has yet been said about them.

We are, in fact, at last approaching the essential feature of Sophistry. Controversy in the wide sense, a technique of debate applied to any subject, implies the false conceit of wisdom in the Sophist himself and a false belief in that wisdom created in his pupils. This links with the ' spurious education ' of Division I (δοξοπαιδευτική 223AB), producing that ' vain conceit of wisdom ' (δοξοσοφία) which the true education of the Cathartic *elenchus* was designed to expel (231B).

The next speeches bring into view the genus, Productive Art, that will yield the final Division. The Sophist's power of producing an illusory belief in his own wisdom and a false appearance of universal knowledge reveals him as a creator of appearances, an illusionist, one who produces an imitation of real things in play, comparable with the artist who can make images of all things in heaven and earth.

233D. STR. Let us, then, take an analogy that will throw more light on their position.

THEAET. What is that ?

STR. It is this. Try to give me your closest attention in answering.

THEAET. What is your question ?

STR. Suppose a man professed to know, not how to speak or dispute about everything, but how to produce all things in actual fact by a single form of skill.

E. THEAET. What do you mean by ' all things ' ?

STR. My meaning is beyond your comprehension at the very outset. It seems you do not understand what is meant by ' all things '.

THEAET. No.

STR. Well, ' all things ' is meant to include you and me and, besides ourselves, all other animals and plants.

THEAET. How do you mean ?

STR. Suppose a man should undertake to produce you and me and all creatures.

234. THEAET. What sort of production do you mean ? You cannot mean some sort of farmer, for you spoke of him as producing animals as well.

STR. Yes, and besides that, sea and sky and earth and gods

234.   and everything else there is.   What is more, after producing
any one of them with a turn of the hand he sells them for
quite a moderate sum.

THEAET.   You mean in some kind of play ?

STR.   Well, a man who says he knows everything and could
teach it to another for a small fee in a short time can hardly
be taken in earnest.

THEAET.   Assuredly not.

B.   STR.   And of all forms of play, could you think of any
more skilful and amusing than imitation ?

THEAET.   No.   When you take that one form with all that
it embraces, it covers a very large variety.

STR.   Well, we know this about the man who professes to
be able, by a single form of skill, to produce all things, that
when he creates with his pencil representations bearing the
same name as real things, he will be able to deceive the
innocent minds of children, if he shows them his drawings
at a distance, into thinking that he is capable of creating,
in full reality, anything he chooses to make.

C.   THEAET.   Of course.

STR.   Then must we not expect to find a corresponding form
of skill in the region of discourse, making it possible to impose
upon the young who are still far removed from the reality
of things, by means of words that cheat the ear, exhibiting
images of all things in a shadow-play of discourse, so as to
make them believe that they are hearing the truth and
that the speaker is in all matters the wisest of men ?

D.   THEAET.   There may well be such an art as you describe.

STR.   And is it not inevitable that, after a long enough
time, as these young hearers advance in age and, coming
into closer touch with realities, are forced by experience to
apprehend things clearly as they are, most of them should
abandon those former beliefs, so that what seemed important
will now appear trifling and what seemed easy, difficult,
and all the illusions created in discourse will be completely

E.   overturned by the realities which encounter them in the
actual conduct of life ?

THEAET.   Yes, so far as I can judge at my age ; but I suppose I am one of those who are still at a distance.

STR.   That is why all of us here must try, as we are in fact
trying, to bring you as close as possible to the realities and
spare you the experience.

But about the Sophist : tell me, is it now clear that he

235.   is a sort of wizard, an imitator of real things—or are we still

235. uncertain whether he may not possess genuine knowledge of all the things he seems capable of disputing about ?

THEAET. He cannot, sir. It is clear enough from what has been said that he is one of those whose province is play.

STR. Then we may class him as a wizard and an imitator of some sort.

THEAET. Certainly.

The imagery of this passage is intended to recall the allegory of the Cave in the *Republic*. The young who are far removed from reality and can be deluded by the images (*eidola*) exhibited in the Sophist's discourse are like the prisoners bound in the darkness who watch on the wall of the Cave the shadows cast by firelight from images behind their backs. The images are shown above a wall which screens the men carrying them as the puppet-showman is screened from his audience.[1] The allegory goes on to describe, in language recalling the cathartic ministry of Socrates, a liberator who turns the prisoners round and tries to convince them that the actual images they can now see are nearer to reality than the shadows they watched before. So in our passage the Stranger speaks of bringing Theaetetus and his young friends closer to the realities.

235A-236C. *Division of Image-making into two species*

We have now completed the analytical survey of the collection of types, rightly or wrongly called ' Sophists ', provided by the six earlier Divisions. The train of thought has led us away from the Acquisitive class of Arts, the starting-point of all the first five Divisions, to the other class which was set aside at the very outset (219A), the Productive class. Acquisitiveness is not the fundamental trait in Sophistry. The Sophist is a creator, but a creator of illusions. We shall ultimately define his essence by dividing the Productive branch of Art in the complete table given at the end of the dialogue. Here, however, we start with the genus Image-making, which stands at a point some way down that table. The Sophist has just been grouped with the fine artist as a mere imitator of actual things, a maker of images or semblances. In the next section Image-making or Imitation is divided into two forms, before the Division is broken off in order to examine all the problems connected with appearance and falsity.

---

[1] *Rep.* vii, 514B : ὥσπερ τοῖς θαυματοποιοῖς πρὸ τῶν ἀνθρώπων πρόκειται τὰ παραφράγματα, ὑπὲρ ὧν τὰ θαύματα δεικνύασι. The Sophist is called, 'a kind of θαυματοποιός' at *Soph.* 235B and 268D.

235A.   STR.   Come then, it is now for us to see that we do not
   B.   again relax the pursuit of our quarry.   We may say that
         we have him enveloped in such a net as argument provides
         for hunting of this sort.   He cannot shuffle out of this.
         THEAET.   Out of what ?
         STR.   Out of being somewhere within the class of illu-
         sionists.[1]
         THEAET.   So far I quite agree with you.
         STR.   Agreed then that we should at once quarter the
         ground by dividing the art of Image-making, and if, as soon
         as we descend into that enclosure, we meet with the Sophist
   C.   at bay, we should arrest him on the royal warrant of reason,
         report the capture, and hand him over to the sovereign.[2]
         But if he should find some lurking-place among the sub-
         divisions of this art of imitation, we must follow hard upon
         him, constantly dividing the part that gives him shelter,
         until he is caught.   In any event there is no fear that he or
         any other kind shall ever boast of having eluded a process
         of investigation so minute and so comprehensive.
         THEAET.   Good ;   that is the way to go to work.
         STR.   Following, then, the same method of division as
   D.   before, I seem once more to make out two forms of imitation ;
         but as yet I do not feel able to discover in which of the two
         the type we are seeking is to be found.
         THEAET.   Make your division first, at any rate, and tell us
         what two forms you mean.
         STR.   One art that I see contained in it is the making of
         likenesses (eikastiké).   The perfect example of this consists
         in creating a copy that conforms to the proportions of the
         original in all three dimensions and giving moreover the
   E.   proper colour to every part.
         THEAET.   Why, is not that what all imitators try to do ?

[1] θαυματοποιῶν means specially the puppet-showman, but it is used here to
cover all species of ' imitators '—artists and poets as well as Sophists (cf. 224A).
They are all ' creators of eidola '.
    [2] Apelt illustrates the allusion to the Persian method (called ' draw-netting ',
σαγηνεία) of sweeping up the whole population of a district by means of a line
of soldiers holding hands and marching across it.   It is several times mentioned by Herodotus (e.g. vi, 31) ;   and Plato (Laws 698D) says that Datis,
ten years before Salamis, sent word to Athens that he had captured all the
Eretrians by this method, under Darius' orders (the ' royal warrant ') to
transport all Eretrians and Athenians to Persia.   The method is an admirable
image for the procedure of the last section which has drawn the notion of
Image-making or Imitation like a net round all the types called ' Sophists '
collected for review.   The net also includes other ' imitators ', all the varieties
of artist.

235E.   STR.   Not those sculptors or painters whose works are of
colossal size.   If they were to reproduce the true proportions
of a well-made figure,[1] as you know, the upper parts would

236.   look too small, and the lower too large, because we see the
one at a distance, the other close at hand.

THEAET.   That is true.

STR.   So artists, leaving the truth to take care of itself,
do in fact put into the images they make, not the real proportions, but those that will appear beautiful.

THEAET.   Quite so.

STR.   The first kind of image, then, being like the original,
may fairly be called a likeness (*eikon*).

THEAET.   Yes.

B.   STR.   And the corresponding subdivision of the art of
imitation may be called by the name we used just now—
Likeness-making.

THEAET.   It may.

STR.   Now, what are we to call the kind which only appears
to be a likeness of a well-made figure because it is not seen
from a satisfactory point of view, but to a spectator with
eyes that could fully take in so large an object would not
be even like the original it professes to resemble ?   Since it
seems to be a likeness, but is not really so, may we not
call it a semblance (*phantasma*) ?

THEAET.   By all means.

STR.   And this is a very extensive class, in painting and

C.   in imitation of all sorts.

THEAET.   True.

STR.   So the best name for the art which creates, not a likeness, but a semblance will be Semblance-making (*phantastiké*).

THEAET.   Quite so.

STR.   These, then, are the two forms of image-making I
meant—the making of likenesses and the making of
semblances.

THEAET.   Good.

At this point the Division is broken off.   It is not at once clear
why images should be divided here into 'likenesses' and 'semblances'.

---

[1] 'Well-made' (καλῶν), because what is in question is not improving the
proportions of an ill-made model to conform to canons of beauty, but altering
the proportions which are really beautiful so as to keep the appearance of
beauty.   Apelt mentions that, in the Epicurean inscription on a wall at
Oenoanda, the letters in the top lines are cut larger than those in the lower,
so that all may look the same size from below.

The whole description of the Sophist as Imitator is meant to
recall the attack on fine art as ' imitation ' in *Republic* x ; an
attack based on metaphysical grounds which will reappear when
our present Division is fully stated at the end of the dialogue. The
object of that attack is to show that the representations of fine art,
considered as imitations of actual things, are at two removes from
true reality. The carpenter who makes an actual bed works with
reference to a unique Form, a model not made by any carpenter,
but fixed in the nature of things and made by God. This Form is
real in the full sense ; the carpenter's bed is ' something like this
reality, but not perfectly real ' ; it belongs to the world of sensible
things, which are only images of the real. The painter is farther
still from reality. He copies, not the Form, but the craftsman's
product, and that not as it is, but only as it appears from one point
of view. He does not produce a second actual bed, a replica of the
craftsman's work, but only ' an imitation of an appearance (*phantasma*)', which may deceive a distant spectator. So a man might
claim to ' make ' all things in heaven and earth by turning a mirror
in his hands and catching their reflections—a marvellous virtuoso
(θαυμαστὸς σοφιστής) ! The painter's, or the poet's, work is only
' play '.

This part of the *Republic* has already been recalled by the description of the man who should profess to produce all things (233D ff.) ;
and it throws light on the present distinction between ' likenesses '
and ' semblances ', which is mentioned again in the full Division
at 266D. Both here and in the *Republic* the whole of fine art, considered as ' imitative ', falls under the art of making 'semblances ',
not ' likenesses '. Plato does not mean that there is a good and
honest kind of art which makes ' likenesses ' reproducing the actual
proportions in all three dimensions and the natural colours of the
original—a production of waxworks—and a dishonest kind, including the Parthenon sculptures, which distorts the true proportions.
The term ' likeness ' is here used in a narrower sense than usual.[1]
It means a reproduction or replica, such as the making of a second
actual bed, reproducing exactly the first bed made by the carpenter.
If I make a plaster cast of a plaster cast, there is nothing to choose
between the ' likeness ' (copy) and the original. The two are
exactly alike and either can be called the ' very image ' of the other.
In this case there is no element of deceit or illusion. This is the
production of ' likenesses '. It lies outside the scope of fine art and

---

[1] Plato is never rigid in his use of terms. At *Cratylus* 432B, ' likeness '
(*eikon*) has its more usual sense of the painter's portrait, which is *not* a complete
replica but is contrasted with a duplicate of the sitter, such as a god might
create, a second actual person.

of Sophistry. The Sophist creates ' images (*eidola*) in discourse '
(234C) ; but if there is such a thing in discourse as the production
of exact replicas, we are not concerned with it. All the ' images '
we are going to consider fall under the inferior branch, the production of semblances, that are not complete reproductions of the
original, but involve an element of deceit and illusion. This means
that the class of ' images ' (*eidola*) we are concerned with—semblances—imply two relations between image and original. The
image is more or less *like* the original, though not wholly like it,
not a reproduction. But it is also conceived as possessing in some
sense a *lower grade of reality*, as illusory, phantom-like. We are
to think of the work of ' semblance-makers ' (artists and sophists)
as analogous to shadows and reflections of natural objects, ' appearances ' of things that are themselves only images of the real world of
Forms.

236C–237B. *Statement of the problems of unreal appearances and of
falsity in speech and thought*

Here the Division is interrupted. The Sophist has been taxed
with creating a false belief in his own wisdom by false statements.
But, he will object, it is impossible to think or state ' the thing that
is not '. The *Theaetetus* failed to meet this objection with a satisfactory definition of false judgment. The present dialogue will supply
one.

At the same time, many allusions to the *Republic* have recalled
that the whole visible world is only an image of the real. The
Demiurge himself is an image-maker. The long discussion which
here intervenes before the division of Image-making can be resumed,
is not confined to proving the possibility of false judgment and
clearing up misconceptions as to the meaning of negative statements.
It has a bearing on the metaphysical status of a world of appearances. Parmenides denied that there could be a world intermediate
between the perfectly real and the totally non-existent. This problem of the *eidolon* soon comes into view, alongside the problem of
false judgment.

236C. STR. Yes ; but even now I cannot see clearly how to settle
the doubt I then expressed : under which of the two arts
(likeness-making and semblance-making) we must place the
D. Sophist. It is really surprising how hard it is to get a clear
view of the man. At this very moment he has, with admirable cleverness, taken refuge in a class [1] which baffles
investigation.

[1] Namely ' unreal appearance and falsity '.

236D. THEAET. So it seems.

STR. You assent, but do you recognise the class I mean, or has the current of the argument carried you along to agree so readily from force of habit?

THEAET. How? What are you referring to?

E. STR. The truth is, my friend, that we are faced with an extremely difficult question. This 'appearing' or 'seeming' without really 'being', and the saying of something which yet is not true—all these expressions have always been and still are deeply involved in perplexity. It is extremely hard, Theaetetus, to find correct terms in which one may say or think that falsehoods have a real existence, without being caught in a contradiction by the mere utterance of such words.[1]

237. THEAET. Why?

STR. The audacity of the statement lies in its implication that 'what is not' has being; for in no other way could a falsehood come to have being. But, my young friend, when we were of your age the great Parmenides from beginning to end testified against this, constantly telling us what he also says in his poem:

'Never shall this be proved—that things that are not are; but do thou, in thy inquiry, hold back thy thought from this way.'[2]

B. So we have the great man's testimony, and the best way to obtain a confession of the truth may be to put the statement itself to a mild degree of torture.[3] So, if it makes no difference to you, let us begin by studying it on its own merits.

THEAET. I am at your disposal. As for the argument, you must consider the way that will best lead to a conclusion, and take me with you along it.

STR. It shall be done.

---

[1] Falsehoods being 'things which are not', as the Stranger next remarks. A common equivalent of 'speaking falsely' is 'saying the thing that is not', see *Theaet.* 188D ff. (p. 114). Campbell correctly interprets the construction. ψευδῆ is placed where it stands for emphasis.

[2] *Parmenides*, frag. 7. I have discussed the nature of the 'ways of inquiry' in *Parmenides' Two Ways* (*Class. Quarterly*, xxvii (1933), p. 97).

[3] The statement itself (that falsehood, or what is not, really exists) is compared to a slave belonging to the *other* party in the suit, against whom Parmenides has borne witness. The immediate sequel submits this statement (not Parmenides) to examination. Parmenides' own statement will be put to the question later (τὸν τοῦ πατρὸς Παρμενίδου ἀναγκαῖον . . . βασανίζειν, 241D).

It is thus agreed to take, if necessary, the ' way of inquiry ' forbidden by Parmenides, and to consider whether and in what sense ' that which is not '—the unreal or the not wholly real or the false—can have any sort of being or existence. The vague formula is wide enough to cover three problems, all of which had their origin in the challenge thrown down to common sense by Parmenides.

(1) ' This appearing or seeming without really being ' covers the metaphysical problem : If there is a world of real being (Parmenides' One Being or Plato's world of real Forms), how can there also be a world of Seeming, which is neither wholly real nor utterly non-existent ? Parmenides had said, there cannot be such a world of Seeming. A thing must either be or not be : if it is, then it is absolutely and completely ; if it is not, then it is not absolutely and completely. In the first part of his poem he had dèduced the nature of the One Reality and found that it excludes plurality, motion, change, and the qualities which our senses seem to reveal. Faithful to his logic, he had dismissed all these appearances of Nature as unreal and false, and left them unaccounted for. But Plato has argued [1] that between knowledge of the perfectly real and the blank absence of any consciousness of the totally unreal, we find in ourselves a faculty of Opinion or belief (*doxa*, in the widest sense), which produces in us states of mind distinct from knowledge in the full sense and must therefore have a different set of objects. Of these objects he has said that ' they partake both of being and of not-being '. There are, for instance, the ' many beautiful things ' which are unlike Beauty itself in that they come into existence and perish, undergo change, and can appear ugly no less than beautiful. In the imagery of the Line and the Cave these objects were called ' likenesses ' (εἰκόνες) or ' images ' (εἴδωλα) of the real Forms.

The first problem here suggested is : how can there be such things as these visible images of unseen realities ? How can anything ' partake both of being and of not-being ' or yield appearances without being real ? The *Theaetetus* has given some account of the physical process by which appearances are given to the senses. Our perceptions of them, as distinct from judgments we make about them, have been admitted to be infallible. But the external objects were declared to have no stable or real being, but only becoming. So there remains the present problem : what sort of existence, short of real being, can such objects have ?

(2) The second problem is the possibility of ' saying or thinking something which yet is not true '. This is the psychological aspect

[1] *Rep.* v, 476E ff.

of the same question. Parmenides had said : ' It is the same thing that can be *thought* and that can be ' ; ' You cannot *know* what is not, nor *utter* it '. Thought must have an object, and that object must be real. Speech must express something, and that something must be real. This had given rise to the question we have already encountered in the *Theaetetus* (188D ff.) : How is it possible to say or think what is *false* ? If I think or speak, I must be thinking of something and meaning something. But what is this something, if what I say or think is false ? There is no such thing as a false fact. How can I state something as a fact when there is no fact to state ?

(3) Finally, there was the problem of negative judgments and statements (whether true or false). It was supposed that the words ' is not ', occurring in a negative statement, must mean that the thing about which the statement was made did not exist. But if it does not exist, I am speaking of nothing ; the sounds I utter have no meaning. There is nothing for a negative statement to mean or refer to.

Some accounts of the *Sophist* represent the whole of what now follows as a solution of the last problem only.[1] But in fact it covers the whole range of questions just mentioned. They are not kept rigidly distinct ; but the discussion falls into sections which, in their main bearings, are concerned with the three sets of problems :

I. 237B–251A. *The Worlds of Reality and Appearance.*

II. 251A–259D. *Affirmative and Negative Statements :* the various meanings of ' is ' and ' is not ', and the corresponding relations among the terms the statements refer to.

III. 259D–264B. *False Speech and Judgment*—the question directly involved in the analysis of Sophistry as the creation of false belief.

I. THE WORLDS OF REALITY AND APPEARANCE

The long section which begins at the point we have now reached and goes on to 251A, deals mainly with the metaphysical contrast of Reality and Appearance. It falls into three subdivisions corresponding to the three categories of Plato's analysis in *Republic* v :

---

[1] Burnet (*Greek Phil.* I, 278) : ' The modern reader would feel no difficulty if Plato had announced a discussion of the possibility of significant negative judgments, and that, as a matter of fact, is the subject of the dialogue.' But the reader would feel a difficulty. He would wonder why it was necessary to hold a review of all the schools of philosophy and what they had said about reality. Why should not Plato say at once that the words ' is ' and ' is not ' are ambiguous, and point out (as he does later) some of their different meanings ?

(a) THE TOTALLY UNREAL

(a) *The totally unreal* (τὸ μηδαμῶς ὄν). This is dismissed from the discussion.

(b) The intermediate region of ' *images* ' (*eidola*), things which have some sort of existence but are not wholly real. The term *eidolon* is defined, and the problems of false judgment and false speech are stated. They cannot be further discussed without considering the meaning of ' real '.

(c) *The perfectly real* (τὸ παντελῶς ὄν). A review is held of earlier and contemporary theories of the nature of the real, and a compromise is suggested between the extreme views of the materialist and the idealist.

This whole section is mainly tentative and inconclusive. It develops the difficulties connected with ' not-being ' in all its senses —the unreal, the negative, the false. At the end (250E) the Stranger says, ' Let us take it, then, that our difficulty is now completely stated. But since Being and Not-being are equally puzzling, there is henceforward some hope that any light, whether dim or bright, thrown upon the one will illuminate the other to an equal degree.' As we proceed, certain difficulties are settled and cleared out of the way ; others are left either unsolved or to await their solution in later sections of the dialogue.

237B–239C. (a) *The totally unreal*

We start, then, with the notion of the totally unreal (τὸ μηδαμῶς ὄν), or ' that which just simply is not ' (τὸ μὴ ὂν αὐτὸ καθ' αὑτό, 238c). Sheer unreality had been the only alternative recognised by Parmenides to perfect reality ; and he had declared that the totally unreal was not to be thought or even spoken of. The ' way ' that starts from it was ' utterly undiscernible ' (frag. 4) and must be left on one side as ' unthinkable and unnameable ' (frag. 8, 15). No being can ever be derived from the sheer non-existence of anything.

In the following section Plato is not criticising, but confirming, this doctrine. The Stranger will not break with Parmenides until sheer nonentity has been disposed of and he enters on the region of unreal appearances and false statement, where it will become necessary to maintain what Parmenides refused to admit—things that have some sort of existence without being wholly real.

237B. STR. (*continues*). Now tell me : we do not hesitate to utter the phrase ' that which has no sort of being ' ? [1]
THEAET. Surely not.

---

[1] τὸ μηδαμῶς ὄν, the ' totally unreal ' or ' absolute nonentity '. We can ' utter this phrase ' (φθέγγεσθαι), but it will be shown to have no meaning.

237B. STR. Then setting aside disputation for its own sake [1]
and playing with words, suppose one of this company were
C. seriously required to concentrate his mind and tell us to
what this name can be applied—'that which is not'. Of
what thing or of what sort of thing should we expect him
to use it himself, and what would he indicate by it to the
inquirer ?

THEAET. That is a hard question. It is scarcely for a
person like me to find an answer at all.

STR. Well, this much is clear at any rate : that the term
'what is not' must not be applied to anything that exists.

THEAET. Certainly not.

STR. And since it cannot be applied to what exists, neither
can it properly be applied to 'something'.

THEAET. How so ?

D. STR. Surely we can see that this expression 'something'
is always used of a thing that exists. We cannot use it
just by itself in naked isolation from everything that exists,
can we ?

THEAET. No.

STR. Is your assent due to the reflection that to speak
of 'something' is to speak of 'some *one* thing' ? [2]

THEAET. Yes.

STR. Because you will admit that 'something' stands
for one thing, as 'some things' stands for two or more.

THEAET. Certainly.

E. STR. So it seems to follow necessarily that to speak of
what is not 'something' is to speak of no thing at
all.

THEAET. Necessarily.

STR. Must we not even refuse to allow that in such a case
a person is *saying something*, though he may be speaking
of nothing ? Must we not assert that he is not even saying
anything when he sets about uttering the sounds 'a thing
that is not' ?

---

[1] The problems to be stated had figured in Eristic debate, but our purpose
is to face the real difficulties seriously.

[2] Compare the argument at *Theaetetus* 188D ff. (p. 114). The accident that
English confines 'some *one*' and 'no *one*' to persons, 'some*thing*', 'no*thing*'
to things, makes translation awkward. Greek has (1) τις, 'some' (masc.
someone, neut. something) with (in poetry) its contradictory οὔτις, 'not-some'
(masc. no-one, neut. nothing) ; and (2) οὐδείς 'not even one' (masc. no-one,
neut. no-thing) with its regular contradictory εἴς γέ τις, 'at least *some* one'
(masc. *some*one, neut. *some*thing), which is used here, and has to be rendered
'some *one* thing', in order to introduce the word 'one'.

204

(a) THE TOTALLY UNREAL

237E.   THEAET.   That would certainly bring the argument to the last pitch of perplexity.

It is hard to translate the above argument because the phrase λέγειν τι is used in two ways, (1) to ' speak of something ' that your words refer to ; and (2) ' to express a meaning ' or say something significant as opposed to ' saying nothing ' or ' talking nonsense ' (οὐδὲν λέγειν). But the ambiguity does not vitiate the argument. We are here taking ' what is not ' as equivalent to ' the totally unreal ', ' absolute nonentity ' and to that only. The suggestion is that, when I utter the sounds ' what is not ', those sounds are meaningless noises : there is nothing whatever for them to refer to, and I have no meaning before my mind which I can hope to convey. How can I talk significantly or think of what has no sort of being at all ? The inference will be that in the expression ' to say the thing that is not ' in the sense of ' to say what is *false* ' (but has some meaning), ' the thing that is not ' cannot be not absolute nonentity. We must find some other interpretation of the words. A false statement conveys meaning to another person and refers to something. How this can be, must be considered later ; all that is established here is that any statement (true or false) which conveys meaning cannot refer to ' absolute nonentity '.

The Stranger's next argument is again based on Parmenides, who had said :

' Thou canst not *know* that which is not (for that is impossible), nor *utter* it.'

If (as Parmenides held and as we are here assuming) the words ' that which is not ' stand for the totally unreal or absolute nonentity, that cannot be the object of any kind of knowledge or consciousness ; and you cannot even find any words to describe it correctly. The Stranger argues, in particular, that we cannot speak of the non-existent at all without using words that are either singular or plural. But how can the totally non-existent have any number —be either one or many ?

238.   STR.   ' No time for boasting yet.' There is more to come, in fact the chief of all the difficulties and the first, for it goes to the very root of the matter.
THEAET.   How do you mean ?   Do not hesitate to state it.
STR.   When a thing exists, I suppose something else that exists may be attributed to it.
THEAET.   Certainly.
STR.   But can we say it is possible for something that exists to be attributed to what has no existence ?

238.   THEAET.   How could it be ?

STR.   Well, among things that exist we include number in general.

B.   THEAET.   Yes, number must exist, if anything does.

STR.   We must not, then, so much as attempt to attach either plurality or unity in number to the non-existent.

THEAET.   That would certainly seem to be wrong, according to our argument.

STR.   How then can anyone utter the words ' things which are not ', or ' that which is not ', or even conceive such things in his mind at all, apart from number ?

THEAET.   How do you mean ?

STR.   When we speak of ' *things* that are not ', are we

C.   not undertaking to attribute plurality to them ?

THEAET.   Yes.

STR.   And unity, when we speak of ' *that* which is not ' ?

THEAET.   Clearly.

STR.   And yet we admit that it is not justifiable or correct to set about attaching something that exists to the non-existent.

THEAET.   Quite true.

STR.   You see the inference then : one cannot legitimately utter the words, or speak or think of that which just simply is not ; it is unthinkable, not to be spoken of or uttered or expressed.[1]

THEAET.   Quite true.

D.   STR.   Perhaps then I was mistaken in saying just now that I was going to state the greatest difficulty it presents ; whereas there is a worse one still that we can formulate.

THEAET.   What is that ?

STR.   I am surprised you do not see from the very phrases I have just used that the non-existent reduces even one who is refuting its claims [2] to such straits that, as soon as he sets about doing so, he is forced to contradict himself.

THEAET.   How ? Explain more clearly.

STR.   You must not look to me for illumination. I who

E.   laid it down that the non-existent could have neither unity nor plurality, have not only just now but at this very

---

[1] ἄλογον, not ' irrational ', but ' incapable of being expressed in discourse ' (λόγος). There is no *meaning* conveyed (cf. *Parm.* 142A). ἄρρητον means that there is nothing for the words to *refer to*. Plato is echoing Parmenides' warning against the ' Way of Not-Being ', ' to leave that way as unthinkable, unnameable ; for it is no true way ' (frag. 8, 15).

[2] Refuting any claim it might make to ' being '. I cannot even deny its existence without contradicting myself by speaking of it at all.

238E. moment spoken of it as one thing : for I am saying ' *the* non-existent '. You see what I mean ?

THEAET. Yes.

STR. And again a little while ago I was speaking of its *being* a thing not to be uttered or spoken of or expressed. Do you follow ?

THEAET. Yes, of course.

STR. Well, then, in trying to apply that term ' being '
239.   to it, was I not contradicting what I said before ? [1]

THEAET. Evidently.

STR. And again in applying the term ' the ', was I not addressing it as singular ? [2]

THEAET. Yes.

STR. And again in speaking of it as ' a thing not to be expressed or spoken of or uttered ', I was using language as if referring to a single thing.

THEAET. Certainly.

STR. Whereas we are admitting that, if we are to speak strictly, we ought not to specify it as either one thing or many or even to call it ' it ' at all ; for even that appellation means ascribing to it the character of singleness.

THEAET. Quite so.

B. STR. In that case there is nothing to be said for me. I shall be found to have had the worst of it, now and all along, in my criticism of the non-existent. Accordingly, as I said, we must not look to anything I have to say for the correct way of describing the non-existent ; we must turn to you for that. Come along now.

THEAET. What do you mean ?

STR. Come, you are young ; show your spirit and make

---

[1] The reference is to 238A : nothing that has existence must be attributed to the non-existent. ' Being ' ($\tau\grave{o}$ $\epsilon\hat{\iota}\nu\alpha\iota$) is something that exists, in the same sense that number exists.

[2] Read $\tau\grave{o}$ ' $\tau\grave{o}$ ' for $\tau o\hat{\upsilon}\tau o$. If $\tau o\hat{\upsilon}\tau o$ is retained, the meaning can only be : I not only used the verb ' to be ', but I used it in the singular number ($\check{\epsilon}\sigma\tau\iota\nu$) in the phrase referred to ($\check{\epsilon}\sigma\tau\iota\nu$ $\dot{\alpha}\delta\iota\alpha\nu\acute{o}\eta\tau o\nu$ $\kappa\tau\lambda$, 238C, 10). But if Plato meant this, why did he not make it clear by writing $\acute{o}\tau\iota$ $\dot{\epsilon}\sigma\tau\acute{\iota}\nu$ for $\epsilon\hat{\iota}\nu\alpha\iota$ at E6 and $\tau\acute{o}$ $\gamma\epsilon$ $\check{\epsilon}\sigma\tau\iota\nu$ for $\tau\acute{o}$ $\gamma\epsilon$ $\epsilon\hat{\iota}\nu\alpha\iota$ at E8 ? For $\tau o\hat{\upsilon}\tau o$ I conjecture $\tau\grave{o}$ ' $\tau\grave{o}$ ', ' in applying the word *the* (singular) to it, was I not addressing it as singular ? ' By using $\epsilon\hat{\iota}\nu\alpha\iota$ we have contradicted the words ' $\mu\grave{\eta}$ $\check{o}\nu$ ' in the phrase ' $\tau\grave{o}$ $\mu\grave{\eta}$ $\check{o}\nu$ ' ; the ' $\tau\grave{o}$ ' is equally objectionable. Cf. *Theaet.* 202A, $o\dot{\upsilon}\delta\grave{\epsilon}$ $\tau\grave{o}$ ' $\alpha\dot{\upsilon}\tau\grave{o}$ ' $o\dot{\upsilon}\delta\grave{\epsilon}$ $\tau\grave{o}$ ' $\dot{\epsilon}\kappa\epsilon\hat{\iota}\nu o$ ' $o\dot{\upsilon}\delta\grave{\epsilon}$ $\tau\grave{o}$ ' $\check{\epsilon}\kappa\alpha\sigma\tau o\nu$ ' $o\dot{\upsilon}\delta\grave{\epsilon}$ $\tau\grave{o}$ ' $\mu\acute{o}\nu o\nu$ ' $o\dot{\upsilon}\delta\grave{\epsilon}$ ' $\tau o\hat{\upsilon}\tau o$ ' ($\tau\grave{o}$ $\tau o\hat{\upsilon}\tau o$, Heind ; $\tau\grave{o}$ $\tau\acute{o}$, Buttmann) $\pi\rho o$-$\sigma o\iota\sigma\tau\acute{\epsilon}o\nu$. Cf. also *Theaet.* 205C, $o\dot{\upsilon}\delta\grave{\epsilon}$ ' $\tau o\hat{\upsilon}\tau o$ ' ($\tau\grave{o}$ $\tau o\hat{\upsilon}\tau o$, Heind ; $\tau\grave{o}$ $\tau\acute{o}$, Buttmann). In our passage ' $\tau\grave{o}$ $\tau o\hat{\upsilon}\tau o$ ' will not do, for $\tau o\hat{\upsilon}\tau o$ has not been used ; and to read $\tau\grave{o}$ ' $\alpha\dot{\upsilon}\tau\grave{o}$ ' would wrongly anticipate $\mu\eta\delta\grave{\epsilon}$ $\tau\grave{o}$ $\pi\alpha\rho\acute{\alpha}\pi\alpha\nu$ ' $\alpha\dot{\upsilon}\tau\grave{o}$ ' $\kappa\alpha\lambda\epsilon\hat{\iota}\nu$ below (239A, 9).

239B.   the best effort you can. Try, without attributing being
        or unity or plurality to the non-existent, to find some form
        of words describing it correctly.

  C.   THEAET. I should need an extraordinary zeal for such
        an enterprise in face of what has happened to you.

This paragraph only reinforces the previous one by emphasising
that the very words 'the non-existent' (absolute nonentity)
cannot be uttered at all without self-contradiction. This point
is not urged against Parmenides, and could not be urged without
descending to captiousness. In all this section on 'the totally
non-existent' Plato is rather confirming Parmenides and accepting
his warning : 'Hold back thy thought from this way of inquiry.'
Plato does not afterwards go back upon the results here reached.
The only later reference to this discussion of nonentity is at 258E
after the other sense of 'that which is not' (*viz.* 'that which is
other than') has been brought to light. The Stranger there says :
'So let no one say that it is *the contrary of the existent* (*i.e.* the
simply non-existent) that we mean when we make bold to say
that 'what is not' exists. So far as any *contrary of the existent* is
concerned, we have long ago said good-bye to the question whether
there is such a thing or not, and whether any account can be given
of it or none whatsoever.' Plato here, as in *Republic* v, accepts
Parmenides' doctrine that the totally non-existent cannot be
thought or spoken of.

This is all he has to say about a problem that has troubled modern
logicians who have discussed the thesis that 'whatever is thought
of must in some sense be '—Parmenides' thesis. Mr. Russell at
one time, by distinguishing 'being' from 'existence', endowed
non-existent things, like Chimaeras, with a sort of 'being ', 'for
if they were not entities we could make no propositions about
them '. But this provision for non-existent entities seems now to
be abandoned in favour of the view that there are descriptions,
e.g. 'round square ', which describe nothing.[1] So logic returns to
the position of common sense, that there is nothing to prevent
us from putting together verbal symbols such as 'round ' and
'square ' in phrases which refer to nothing whatever, because
there is nothing for them to refer to. Plato's view seems to be
that the phrase 'the totally non-existent' is a description, or, as
he would say, a 'name ', that is a name of nothing at all. What
corresponds to it psychologically is the blank absence of any kind
of cognition (ἀγνωσία, *Rep.* v, 477A). He adds that the name does
not even succeed in describing nothing correctly.

[1] See L. S. Stebbing, *Modern Introduction to Logic*, chap. ix, § 5. Happily
we need not discuss other varieties of nonentity discovered by Meinong.

(b) EIDOLON DEFINED

The upshot is that we have no further use for ' nonentity ' and can rule it out of the discussion. It cannot be invoked to account for the existence either of false statement and false belief or of a world of ' appearances ' containing things not wholly real. So far as nonentity is concerned, Parmenides is justified, except that strictly he had no more right than we have to make even negative statements about it or to utter the ' unutterable '.

239C–242B. *(b) Definition of* eidolon *and the problem of false statement and belief*

Having said good-bye to ' nonentity ', we now pass to the region intermediate between sheer non-existence and full reality—the world of *eidola*. Two sets of problems await us here. (1) How is it possible that anything should exist and yet not be wholly real ? What sort of existence can belong to that world of ' appearances ', denied by Parmenides, but recognised by Plato as the object of ' opinion ', distinct from the object of knowledge ? (2) How can false statement and false belief be explained ? If I say something that is significant (not a meaningless noise), my statement must refer to something. But what can it refer to, if it is false ? Having accused the Sophist of being a creator of *eidola*, of false statements and false beliefs, we must meet his objections that there can be no such thing as an *eidolon*, neither wholly real nor wholly unreal, and no such thing as a false statement or belief.

We have glimpses of the sort of arguments used in Plato's time and earlier. In a tract written probably about 400 B.C.,[1] the author, presumably a Sophist, uses a Protagorean argument against those who attacked medicine as ' not a real art ' (οὐκ ἐοῦσα τέχνη) :

' It seems to me in general that there is no art that is not (real), for it is irrational to think that something which is, is not. For what ' being ' (οὐσία) have things that are not, which one could look at and say of it that ' it is ' ? For if it is possible to see things that are not, as you can see things that are, I do not understand how one can regard them as not being, when you can see them with your eyes and think of them in your mind that they are. It is not so. Things that are, are always seen and known ; things that are not, are not seen and known.'

The two problems are now raised successively. (1) The term *eidolon* is defined as meaning a thing that is not wholly real but yet has some sort of existence. If there is such a thing as an *eidolon*, then something that has not ' being ' in the full sense,

---

[1] [Hippocr.] περὶ τέχνης, 2, cited by Apelt (trans., p. 138). In his interesting edition (*Die Apologie der Heilkunst*, Leipzig, 1910) Th. Gomperz argues that the author may be Protagoras himself.

must have some sort of being. (2) Thinking or stating what is false means asserting that what is not the fact is a fact, or that what is the fact is not a fact. We are asserting something ; our words have meaning. So ' what is not the fact ' must have some sort of being ; it is not sheer nonentity. The conclusion will be that we must escape from the Parmenidean dilemma : ' A thing must be either perfectly real or totally unreal ', and recognise a third intermediate region of things that are neither wholly real nor utterly non-existent. There must be some sense in which what is not (wholly real or true) has some sort of existence or meaning.

239C. STR. Well, if you agree, we will leave ourselves out of account ; and until we meet with someone who can perform this feat, let us say that the Sophist with extreme cunning has found an impenetrable lurking-place.[1]

THEAET. It certainly seems so.

STR. Accordingly, if we are going to say he possesses an art of creating ' semblances ', he will readily take advantage

D. of our handling our arguments in this way to grapple with us and turn them against ourselves. When we call him a maker of images, he will ask what on earth we mean in speaking of an ' image ' at all. So we must consider, Theaetetus, how this truculent person's question is to be answered.

THEAET. Clearly we shall say we mean images in water or in mirrors, and again images made by the draughtsman or the sculptor, and any other things of that sort.

E. STR. It is plain, Theaetetus, that you have never seen a Sophist.

THEAET. Why ?

STR. He will make as though his eyes were shut or he had no eyes at all.

THEAET. How so ?

STR. When you offer him your answer in such terms, if you speak of something to be found in mirrors or in sculpture, he will laugh at your words, as implying that he can see.

240. He will profess to know nothing about mirrors or water or even eyesight, and will confine his question to what can be gathered from discourse.

THEAET. Namely ?

STR. The common character in all these things you men-

---

[1] It must be remembered that the various senses of ' that which is not ' are only gradually being disclosed. The Sophist does not lurk in the region of nonentity, above dealt with, but in the field of the not wholly real and the false which we are now entering.

240.   tioned and thought fit to call by a single name when you
         used the expression ' image ' as one term covering them all.
         State it, then, and hold your ground against the man without
         yielding an inch.

         THEAET.   Well, sir, what could we say an image was, if
         not another thing of the same sort, copied from the real
         thing ?

         STR.   ' Of the same sort ' ?   Do you mean another real
B.   thing, or what does ' of the same sort ' signify ?

         THEAET.   Certainly not real, but like it.

         STR.   Meaning by ' real ' a thing that really exists.

         THEAET.   Yes.

         STR.   And by ' not real ' the opposite of real ?

         THEAET.   Of course.

         STR.   Then by what is ' like ' you mean what has not real
         existence,[1] if you are going to call it ' not real '.

         THEAET.   But it has some sort of existence.

         STR.   Only not real existence, according to you.

         THEAET.   No ;   except that it is really a likeness.

         STR.   So, not having real existence, it really is what we call
         a likeness ? [2]

---

[1] Reading οὐκ ὄντος [οὐκ] ὄν with Burnet and others.   The only possible
way (if it be possible) to retain οὐκ before ὄν is to suppose (with Ritter,
N. Unters. 14) that the first οὐκ = *nonne* with λέγεις, the whole sentence
being a negative question.   But it is hard to believe that Plato would
gratuitously make the sentence obscure in this way.   Diès (here and at B12)
and Friedlander (*Plat. Schr.* 521) would understand οὐκ ὄντως οὐκ ὄν and οὐκ
ὄν οὐκ ὄντως (B12) as a ' complete negation ' of ὄντως ὄν : ' *un irréel non-être* '.
This is impossible Greek and also the wrong sense.   An *eidolon* is not the
complete negation of ὄντως ὄν (which is τὸ μηδαμῶς ὄν), but is an ὄν, only not
ὄντως but πώς.

[2] Reading οὐκ ὄν ἄρα [οὐκ] ὄντως.   The subject ' it ' is, as in the previous
sentences, τὸ ἐοικός, *i.e.* εἴδωλον, the term we are defining.   The paradox
lies in saying that an εἴδωλον, which *is not real*, *really is* a likeness.
Another possibility (which would cover all the previous statements) is to
read : οὐκ ὄν ἄρα ὄντως, ⟨ὄν πώς⟩ ἐστιν ὄντως, ἣν λέγομεν εἰκόνα, taking ἣν
λέγομεν εἰκόνα in apposition to ὄν πως and explaining it : ' It (τὸ ἐοικός), without
having real being, really is a thing with some sort of being—a likeness, as
we call it.'   Theaetetus has just said that it *really is* a likeness (εἰκὼν ὄντως)
and that *it has some sort of existence* (ἔστι πως).   The result is a still more
' perplexing combination ' of being and not-being.   Or, taking ἣν λέγομεν
εἰκόνα as subject and εἰκών as loosely used for τὸ ἐοικός = εἴδωλον, we might
read οὐκ ὄν ἄρα οὐσ' ὄντως, ⟨ὄν πώς⟩ ἐστιν ὄντως ἣν λέγομεν εἰκόνα, 'What we call
a likeness, not being really a real thing, really is a thing having a sort of being.'
The insertion of ⟨ὄν πώς⟩ is favoured by the conclusion stated below : ' the
Sophist has forced us to admit that what is not *has some sort of being* (εἶναί
πως).'
   Cf. *Timaeus* 52C, the εἰκών (contrasted with τὸ ὄντως ὄν), is described as
' clinging to existence somehow or other, on pain of being nothing at all '.

240c. THEAET. Real and unreal do seem to be combined in that perplexing way; and very queer it is.

STR. Queer indeed. You see that now again by dovetailing them together in this way our hydra-headed Sophist has forced us against our will to admit that 'what is not' has some sort of being.

THEAET. Yes, I do.

This passage gives no more than a definition of the term 'image' (*eidolon*). It is something that has some sort of existence without being wholly real. This brings out the point made earlier, where the 'semblance' was distinguished from the exact 'likeness' or replica. The sort of 'image' we are concerned with is not only a likeness, but has a less degree of reality, as the reflections and pictures instanced by Theaetetus are thought to be less real than the actual things they image. When we accuse the Sophist of 'practising the art of semblance-making' (φανταστική 239c, 9), we accuse him of creating such unreal images which yet somehow exist. We have still to justify ourselves against his objection that unreal things cannot exist in any way.

The Stranger next points out that the same objection will be raised against the possibility of thinking or saying 'what is not', *i.e.* what is *false*. False beliefs (in his own wisdom) are the particular kind of 'images' or 'semblances' that we have accused the Sophist of creating.

240c. STR. And what now? How can we define his art without contradicting ourselves?

THEAET. How do you mean? What sort of contradiction do you fear?

D. STR. When we say that he deceives with that semblance we spoke of and that his art is a practice of deception, shall we be saying that, as the effect of his art, our mind thinks what is false, or what shall we mean?

THEAET. Just that. What else could we mean?

STR. And false thinking, again, will be thinking things contrary to the things that are [1]?

The context seems to imply that an image has to borrow such existence as it has from its medium. The mirror-image owes its existence to the mirror; so sensible things, as images of the eternal Forms, owe their existence to Space, the everlasting medium in which they appear.

[1] 'The things that are.' 'The facts' would be a more natural translation, but at this stage it seems better to keep the vaguer expression. 'Things that are not' (falsehoods) are things which are contrary to the facts and yet must have some sort of being, for we have already said that we cannot think sheer nonentity (τοὐναντίον τοῦ ὄντος, 258E, which Campbell here wrongly confuses with the plural τἀναντία τοῖς οὖσι, of which we *are* speaking).

240D. THEAET. Yes.

STR. You mean, then, by false thinking, thinking things that are not ?

THEAET. Necessarily.

E. STR. Does that mean thinking that things that are not, are not, or that things that are not in any way, in some way are ?

THEAET. It must at least mean thinking that things that are not,[1] are in some way, if anyone is ever to be in error even to the smallest extent.

STR. And also surely thinking that things which certainly [2] are, are not in any way at all ?

THEAET. Yes.

STR. That also is error ?

THEAET. Yes, that also.

STR. And a false statement,[3] I suppose, is to be regarded
241. in the same light, as stating that things that are, are not, and that things that are not, are.

THEAET. Yes. How else could it be false ?

STR. Hardly in any other way. But the Sophist will deny that. How could a sensible man agree, when the admissions we made earlier are set beside this one ? [4] We understand, Theaetetus, what he is referring to ?

THEAET. Of course we understand. He will say that we are contradicting what was said just now, when we have the
B. face to say that falsehoods exist in thoughts and in statements ; for we are constantly being obliged to attribute

---

[1] Theaetetus does not repeat the Stranger's suggestion τὰ μηδαμῶς ὄντα, but correctly substitutes τὰ μὴ ὄντα, things which are *not the fact*, but are not (as μηδαμῶς might suggest) sheer nonentities.

[2] πάντως, ' in any case ' : ' things which *certainly* have being ' (not παντελῶς, ' things which have the *fullest* sort of being or reality '). The whole means ' denying any existence to facts which certainly do exist '. Cf. 247A, πάντως εἶναί τι, ' is certainly a real thing '.

[3] ' Statement ' is the best rendering for λόγος, not ' proposition ', because of its modern uses. For Plato a ' statement ' is simply the utterance in speech of a judgment made by the mind in its silent dialogue with itself (263E, and *Theaet*. 189E, 206D, 208C).

[4] Omitting ἄφθεγκτα . . . ἀδιανόητα, with Madvig, who pointed out that the words could only mean that our previous admissions were ' unutterable ', etc. (*Advers*. i, 381). Against Diès' excision of τὰ πρὸ τούτων ὁμολογηθέντα as a gloss on προδιωμολογημένα (T) (which he reads with ταῦτα understood as subject) is that a reference to the unthinkableness, etc. of absolute nonentity is not relevant. Theaetetus' next speech states what the ' earlier admissions ' are : namely, that we must not ' attach what has being to what is not '. Nonentity has been ruled out of the discussion once for all.

241B.   what has being to what is not, after agreeing just now that
        this was altogether impossible.[1]

Like the previous paragraph on the meaning of ' image ', this
passage only tells us what false thinking and false statement *mean*,
namely attributing not-being to what is (the fact) or being to what
is not (the fact).   We have still to show that such things as images
can exist and that false judgments can have anything to refer to.
That is to say, we must explain how what is not wholly real and what
is not true can have a sort of existence.   Here is the point at which
we must part company with Parmenides, who would allow no such
thing ; and the Stranger now asks leave to do so.

241B.   STR.   Your recollection is correct.   But you must now
        consider what we are to do about the Sophist ; for if
        we pursue our search for him by ranking him under the art
        of the illusionists and creators of error, you see what an easy
        opening we offer to many perplexities and counter-attacks.
        THEAET.   I do.
        STR.   They are almost without number and we have stated
   c.   only a small fraction of them.
        THEAET.   If that is so, it looks as if it were impossible to
        catch the Sophist.
        STR.   What then ?   Are we to lose heart and give up now ?
        THEAET.   I don't think we ought to, if we have the least
        chance of being able to lay hands on him somehow.
        STR.   Then I may count on your indulgence, and, as you
        now say, you will be content if we can by some twist free
        ourselves, even to the least extent, from the grip of so
        powerful an argument ?
        THEAET.   By all means.
   D.   STR.   Then I have another still more pressing request.
        THEAET.   What is that ?
        STR.   That you will not think I am turning into a sort of
        parricide.
        THEAET.   In what way ?
        STR.   We shall find it necessary in self-defence to put to the
        question that pronouncement of father Parmenides, and
        establish by main force [2] that what is not, in some respect
        has being, and conversely that what is, in a way is not.

[1] This is the ' earlier admission ' referred to : ' Nothing that exists (such as
' Being ') must be attributed to the non-existent ' (238A), an admission
already recalled at 238B.
[2] βιάζεσθαι may allude to Parmenides' own word δαμῇ (δαμάζω) in the lines
quoted above.

(b) FALSEHOOD AS 'SAYING WHAT IS NOT'

241D. THEAET. It is plain that the course of the argument requires us to maintain that at all costs.

STR. Plain enough for the blind to see, as they say. Unless
E. these propositions are either refuted or accepted, anyone who talks of false statements or false judgment as being images or likenesses or copies or semblances, or of any of the arts concerned with such things, can hardly escape becoming a laughing-stock by being forced to contradict himself.

THEAET. Quite true.

242. STR. That is why we must now dare to lay unfilial hands on that pronouncement, or else, if some scruple holds us back, drop the matter entirely.

THEAET. As for that, we must let no scruple hinder us.

STR. In that case, for the third time, I have a small favour to ask.

THEAET. You have only to mention it.

STR. I believe I confessed just now that on this point the task of refutation has always proved too much for my powers, and still does so.

THEAET. You did say that.

STR. Well, that confession, I am afraid, may make you think me scatter-brained when at every turn I shift my posi-
B. tion to and fro. It is for your satisfaction that we shall attempt to refute the pronouncement, if we can refute it.

THEAET. Then you may take it that I shall never think you are overstepping the limits by entering on your refutation and proof. So far as that goes, you may proceed with an easy mind.

This interlude closes the second of the three sections, concerned with (a) the totally non-existent, (b) images and false judgment, (c) the perfectly real. We have now raised the problems confronting anyone who would justify the existence of things not wholly real or not true. Theaetetus has asked the Stranger to proceed with his refutation of Parmenides' prohibition, and with his ' proof '. We are thus led to expect a demonstration (1) that things that are not wholly real (*eidola*) can have some sort of existence, and (2) that it is possible to think and say what is false. In the sequel, this second point is established. But it cannot be said that the possibility of a world of *eidola*, imaging the real world of Forms, is ever demonstrated in this dialogue. That metaphysical problem remains in the background. Perhaps it was held in reserve for the *Philosopher*.

242B–244B.   (c) *The perfectly Real. What does 'real' mean?*

We cannot proceed further to discuss how what is not wholly real can exist at all, without first considering what 'real' means.[1] All philosophers, like common men, make a distinction between things they call 'real' and other things which are not fully 'real'. The next section opens by reviewing the philosophers of the archaic period before Socrates, and the things they had called real.   They are divided into two groups : (1) the physical philosophers, who had recognised the existence of the natural world of material things and are here represented as having believed in more than one 'real thing', and (2) Parmenides, who stands alone in denying the phenomenal world and acknowledging only one Real Thing.   This classification is designed to isolate from all the rest Parmenides, who alone is criticised at length.

242B. STR. Come then, where is one to make a start on so hazardous a theme ?   I think I see the path we must inevitably follow.

THEAET. And that is——?

STR. To take first things that are now supposed to be quite
C. clear [2] and see whether we are not in some confusion about them and too easily reaching conclusions on the assumption that we understand them well enough.

THEAET. Tell me more plainly what you mean.

STR. It strikes me that Parmenides and everyone else who has set out to determine how many real things there are and what they are like, have discoursed to us in rather an off-hand fashion.

THEAET. How so ?

STR. They each and all seem to treat us as children to whom they are telling a story.   According to one there are three real things, some of which now carry on a sort of
D. warfare with one another, and then make friends and set about marrying and begetting and bringing up their children. Another tells us that there are two—Moist and Dry, or Hot and Cold—whom he marries off, and makes them set up house together.[3]   In our part of the world the Eleatic set,

---

[1] In the coming section τὸ ὄν will be translated by 'the real' or 'reality'. This sense of the word has emerged from the contrast between the 'sort of existence' belonging to an *eidolon*, and the real existence of the ὄντως ὄν.

[2] Namely, the meaning of 'real', a word we all use and imagine we understand.

[3] Plato recognises in the pre-Socratic systems the presence of mythical images, especially the two most important : the sex-imagery of the cosmic

216

(c) THE PERFECTLY REAL

242D. who hark back to Xenophanes or even earlier, unfold their tale on the assumption that what we call 'all things' are only one thing. Later, certain Muses in Ionia and Sicily

E. perceived that safety lay rather in combining both accounts and saying that the real is both many and one and is held together by enmity and friendship. 'In parting asunder it is always being drawn together' say the stricter [1] of these Muses. The milder [2] relax the rule that this should always be so and tell us of alternate states, in which the universe

243. is now one and at peace through the power of Love, and now many and at war with itself owing to some sort of Strife.

In all this, whether any one of them has told the truth or not is a hard question, and it is in bad taste to find fault so grossly with men of long-established fame. But one observation may be made without offence.

THEAET. And that is——?

STR. That they have shown too little consideration for ordinary people like ourselves in talking over our heads.

B. Each school pursues its own argument to the conclusion without caring whether we follow what they say or get left behind.

THEAET. How do you mean?

STR. When one or another of them in his discourse uses these expressions 'there really are' or 'have come to be' or 'are coming to be' 'many things' or 'one thing' or 'two', or again another speaks [3] of 'Hot being mixed with Cold', assuming 'combinations' and 'separations', do you, Theaetetus, understand a single word they say? Speaking for myself, when I was younger I thought I understood quite clearly when someone spoke of this thing that is now

Eros, and the warfare of opposed 'powers' (such as Hot and Cold). These images of Love and Strife can be traced all through the ancient science of nature, and survive even in Atomism as the Venus and Mars of Lucretius.

[1] The stricter Muses of Ionia represent the philosophy of Heracleitus. It was a main point of his doctrine that the Harmony of Opposites essentially involves a tension or strife that is never resolved. There is no peace without war.

[2] The milder Muses of Sicily (Empedocles) recognised a Reign of Love (without Strife) and, at the opposite pole, a Reign of Strife (without Love). Between these polar states, worlds come into being and pass away. In one half of the cycle a world is formed by Love gaining upon Strife, in the other, by Strife gaining upon Love.

[3] Reading ἄλλος εἴπη (Rademacher, Diès) for ἄλλοθί πη, which is pointless, whether it means 'elsewhere in his discourse' or 'elsewhere in the universe'.

243B. puzzling us—'the unreal'. But now you see how completely perplexed we are about that.

C. THEAET. I do.

STR. Possibly, then, our minds are in the same state of confusion about reality. We profess to be quite at our ease about the real and to understand the word when it is spoken, though we may not understand the unreal, when perhaps we are equally in the dark about both.

THEAET. Perhaps.

STR. And we may take it that the same is true of the other expressions I have just mentioned.

THEAET. Certainly.

The early philosophers are here all introduced as asking and deciding 'how many' real things there are—one or several. Such a classification may strike us as superficial and as misrepresenting the facts. The Eleatics, for instance, are regarded as the only monists, whereas the Milesians, who said that all things were really water or air, are usually called monists. Aristotle, however, makes out that all who made the 'simple bodies' into principles—whether one or two or three or all four—really regarded Hot and Cold (Fire and Earth) as the fundamental factors.[1] In the argument which follows the philosophers are divided into pluralists 'with more than one real being' and the monist, Parmenides, whom Plato wishes to single out for examination. Plato knew that the real contrast was not between many real beings and one, but between the physical philosophers, who derived a manifold world of Nature from one or more material principles, and Parmenides, whose One Being was not material[2] and could not generate a natural world. Seen in this light, the two groups appear as the ancestors of the two parties in the Battle of Gods and Giants that is to follow—materialists and idealists.

The question now to be put to both groups is : What do you mean by 'real' or 'the real'? The physicists are taken first. They regard (say) two things, Hot and Cold, as somehow primary. From these are derived other things by processes they can only describe in mythical terms, such as 'marriage' and 'warfare'. Whatever this unintelligible account of becoming may mean, what is meant by calling the two principles 'real' in a sense that does not apply to the derived things ?

243C. STR. The general run of these expressions we will consider

[1] *De Gen. et Corr.* B3.

[2] 'Not material', in the sense that, though extended in space, it was not perceptible 'body'.

243D. later, if we so decide. We must begin now with the chief and most important of them all.

THEAET. Which is that? Of course you mean we ought to begin by studying 'reality' and finding out what those who use the word think it stands for.

STR. You have hit my meaning precisely, Theaetetus; I do mean that we must take this line. Imagine them here before us, and let us put this question: 'You who say that Hot and Cold or some such pair *really are* all things,

E. what exactly does this expression convey that you apply to both when you say that they both are "real" or each of them is "real"? How are we to understand this "reality" you speak of? Are we to suppose it is a third thing alongside the other two and that the All is no longer, as you say, two things, but three? For surely you do not give the name "reality" to one of the two and then say that both alike are real; for then there will be only one thing, whichever of the two it may be, and not two.'

THEAET. True.

STR. 'Well then, do you intend to give the name "reality" to the pair of them?'

THEAET. Perhaps.

244. STR. 'But that again', we shall object, 'will clearly be speaking of your two things as one.'

THEAET. You are quite right.

STR. 'We are completely puzzled, then, and you must clear up the question for us, what you do intend to signify when you use the word "real". Obviously you must be quite familiar with what you mean, whereas we, who formerly imagined we knew, are now at a loss. First, then, enlighten us on just this point, so that we may not fancy we understand what you have to tell us, when in fact we

B. are as far as possible from understanding.'

If we put our case in that way to these people and to any others who say that the All is more than one thing, will there be anything unwarrantable in our request?

THEAET. Not at all.

The question here put to the pre-Socratic physical philosophers is : What do you mean by the word 'real', when you assert that there are two *real things* (ὄντα), namely 'the Hot' and 'the Cold' ? Plato's point is that 'real' has a meaning distinct from the meanings of 'hot' and 'cold'. 'Reality' is a third term, not to be identified with hotness or coldness or with the Hot or the Cold.

219

It is, in Plato's view, a Form, of which both the Hot and the Cold
partake and so *have* reality, but which is not identical with either
of them or with both together. If the physicists do not admit
that, they will be in a dilemma. (1) If they identify the meaning
of 'real' with the meaning of (say) 'hot', then the Cold will not
be real, for the Cold is not hot. (2) And if they identify it with
the meaning of 'hot-and-cold', then 'that which is hot-and-cold'
will be the one real thing (composed of two parts), and there will
not be two real things, as they said at first. 'Real', then, must
have a meaning distinct from 'Hot' or 'Cold' or 'Hot-and-cold'.
What is that meaning?

No answer is given by the physicists here. We might reply for
them that by 'the real' they meant material substance—that
underlying something which persists the same through all apparent
change. They belong, in fact, to the materialist party in that
Battle of Gods and Giants which is to be staged later. The Stranger
will then put to the materialist a suggestion as to what 'real'
means for him.

244B–245E. *Criticism of Parmenides' One Real Being*

The Stranger turns next to Parmenides, whom he intends to
criticise in detail, because what is barring the path of discussion
is Parmenides' rigid conception of the One Real Being as alone
having any sort of existence. The arguments are as brief and
abstract as Parmenides' own. He had declared that the whole
of reality is a One Being or Existent Unity, having only such
attributes as can be rigidly deduced from the conceptions of Being
and Unity. Each conception is taken with the utmost strictness.
'Being' implies complete reality ; 'Unity' excludes any plurality.
There is nothing but this One Real Thing ($\check{\epsilon}\nu$ $\check{o}\nu$).

The Stranger's first argument is that, if there is only one real
thing, it is inconsistent to give it *two* names, 'real' and 'one'.
This seems at first sight superficial ; but Plato is once more assuming his own doctrine that 'names', such as 'real' and 'one',
have meanings, and those meanings are Forms of which the thing
bearing the names partakes. If you give your one real thing the
two names 'real' and 'one' (*i.e.* say of it that it is real and that
it is one), then three terms are involved : the meanings of the
two names, which are the Forms 'Reality' and 'Unity', and the
thing which bears those names and partakes of those Forms. In
Plato's view, moreover, the two Forms Reality (Being) and Unity
themselves have the highest degree of reality. Each of them is
quite as much real and one as any one thing that partakes of

them. Accordingly Parmenides' simplest and most fundamental proposition—that there is only one real thing—cannot be stated at all without recognising three real things. The true meaning of the argument is somewhat disguised by the Stranger's avoiding the mention of Forms and speaking only of ‘ names ’ and the thing (πρᾶγμα) which is called by them.

244B. STR. Again, there are those who say that the All is one thing. Must we not do our best to find out what they mean by ‘ reality ’ ?

THEAET. Surely.

STR. Let them answer this question, then : ‘ You say, we understand, that there is only one thing ? ’ ‘ We do ’, they will reply, won't they ?

THEAET. Yes.

STR. ‘ And there is something to which you give the name real ? ’

THEAET. Yes.

C. STR. ‘ Is it the same thing as that to which you give the name one ? Are you applying two names to the same thing, or what do you mean ? ’

THEAET. What will their next answer be ?

STR. Obviously, Theaetetus, it is not so very easy for one who has laid down their fundamental assertion to answer this question or any other.

THEAET. How so ?

STR. In the first place, it is surely absurd for him to admit the existence of two names, when he has laid down that there is no more than one thing.

THEAET. Of course.

STR. And further, it is equally absurd to allow anyone to
D. assert that a name can have any existence, when that would be inexplicable.

THEAET. How is it inexplicable ?

STR. If, on the one hand, he assumes that the name is different from the thing, he is surely speaking of two things.

THEAET. Yes.

STR. Whereas, if he assumes that the name is the same as the thing, either he will have to say it is not the name of anything, or if he says it is the name of something, it will follow that the name is merely a name of a name and of nothing else whatsoever.

THEAET. That is so.

244D. STR. . . .[1]

THEAET. Necessarily.

The question, what Parmenides meant by 'real', is here dropped. His one reality was, at any rate, not material substance underlying and persisting through change; and in the Battle of Gods and Giants he will appear on the side of the gods (the idealists). The argument seems verbal because Plato speaks of 'names', not of the Forms which in his view the names stand for, and it seems strange to us to speak of names as 'real things' (ὄντα) alongside the thing which bears the names. What is meant is that Parmenides, like the physicists, has failed to distinguish between his One Real thing and the two Forms, Reality and Unity, of which it partakes, and to see that he cannot assert his One Real thing without also recognising the reality of those two Forms. In the First Hypothesis of the *Parmenides* (141E) it is shown that if you assume (as Parmenides did) a One which excludes any plurality, you cannot even assert that it exists (has being, is real) or apply any name to it.

The next criticism of Parmenides turns on his description of the One Real thing as ' the whole '. ' Whole ' is the correlative of ' part '; nothing is a whole unless it has parts.[2] Parmenides had called his One Real thing ' the All ' (τὸ πᾶν) and declared it to be a finite sphere, with centre and circumference—language which implies, as the Stranger says, that it has distinguishable parts. The argument that follows is complex and extremely concise. The plan of it is given in the following summary:

PREMISS : If the Real is a whole (one thing with many parts), then the Real is not identical with Unity Itself (which has no parts).

[1] The dilemma stated in the Stranger's last two speeches is complete. It has been shown that the very existence of a name is inexplicable, whether it be distinct from the thing or identical with it. This argument applies equally to the name ' real ' and to the name ' one ', and there is no need for any special application of it to the name ' one '. The speech here omitted is corrupt. It looks as if it might be intended to make that special application ; but since that is not wanted, it is impossible to restore the sense with any probability. The oldest evidence for the text is Simplicius, *Phys.* 89 : καὶ τὸ ἕν γε ἑνὸς ἓν (ἓν om. D) ὂν μόνον καὶ τοῦ ὀνόματος αὐτὸ ἓν ὄν. This (including ἓν) agrees with the Bodleian (B) of Plato. The view that ἑνὸς ἓν can mean ' unity of a unity ' is rightly rejected by Ritter (*N. Unters.* 15), who adopts the reading of T : καὶ τὸ ἓν γε ἑνὸς ὂν μόνον (SC. ὄνομα συμβήσεται), καὶ τοῦτο ὀνόματος, αὐτὸ ⟨τὸ ?⟩ ἓν ὄν, ' And it will result too that the One (they talk of) will be the name of itself only, and *that* the name (not of a different objective reality, but) of a name (the name " one "), while yet it is the One itself.' The last words here are barely intelligible, and the whole statement seems to have no point. If the speech, together with Theaetetus' previous reply οὕτως, were simply omitted, it would not be missed.

[2] Cf. *Theaet.* 204A, ff. (p. 149).

DILEMMA : Either (A) *The Real is a whole of parts* : Then the
Real is not Unity Itself, and there will
be a plurality (*viz.* the Real and Unity
Itself),

or   (B) *The Real is not a whole of parts* : Then
either (a) *Wholeness exists* ; but then

       (1) The Real will not be a thing
that is (οὐκ ὂν ἔσται τὸ ὄν) ;

       (2) There will be plurality (*viz.*
the Real and Wholeness
Itself) ;

or   (b) *Wholeness does not exist* ; but then

       (1) The Real will not be a thing
that is (οὐκ ὂν ἔσται τὸ ὄν) ;

       (2) There will be plurality ; and
also

       (3) There will be no coming-into-
being of a thing that is ;

       (4) There will be no finite number
(only indefinite plurality).

The Stranger begins by establishing a premiss that is used in
the subsequent dilemma. The premiss is : If the Real is a whole
of parts, it has the property of unity (for it is one whole), but it
cannot be identical with Unity Itself ; for Unity Itself (αὐτὸ τὸ ἕν)
is defined precisely as ' that which has no parts ', ' the indivisible '.
This is the mathematical definition of Unity or the unit, as given
by Aristotle : ' Everywhere the one is indivisible either in quantity
or in kind. That which is indivisible in quantity and *qua* quantity
is called a unit if it is not divisible in any dimension and is without position ; a point, if it is not divisible in any dimension and
has position ', etc. (*Met.* 1016 *b*, 23). It follows that if Parmenides'
One real thing is a whole of parts, it is not identical with Unity
Itself.

244D. STR. And what of ' the whole ' ? Will they say that this
is other than their ' one real thing ' or the same ?

E.   THEAET. Certainly that it is the same. In fact they do
say so.

STR. Then if it is a whole—as indeed Parmenides says [1] :
' Every way like the mass of a well-rounded sphere,
evenly balanced from the midst in every direction ; for
there must not be something more nor something less
here than there '——

[1] Frag. 8, 43.

223

244E.   if the real is like that, it has a middle and extremities, and
consequently it must have parts, must it not ?

THEAET. It must.

245.   STR. Well, if a thing is divided into parts, there is nothing
against its having the property of unity as applied to the
aggregate of all the parts and being in that way one, as
being a sum or whole.

THEAET. Of course.

STR. On the other hand, the thing which has these properties cannot be just Unity itself, can it ?

THEAET. Why not ?

STR. Surely Unity in the true sense and rightly defined
must be altogether without parts.

THEAET. Yes, it must.

B.   STR. Whereas a thing such as we described, consisting of
several parts, will not answer to that definition.

THEAET. I see.

The above argument probably implies a criticism of Parmenides,
who had declared that the real was ‘ indivisible ’ (not διαιρετόν,
frag. 8, 22). This meant primarily that the One Being was continuous, not an assemblage of discrete particles separated by empty
space. But he also meant that it had absolute unity, such as
excludes any kind of plurality. The Stranger may imply that, if
Parmenides did identify his One being with absolute Unity, he
was inconsistent in speaking of reality as a sphere with distinguishable parts.

The premiss just established is now used in the dilemma : either
(A) the real has such unity as a whole or sum may have and is
one whole ; or (B) the real is not to be called a ‘ whole ’ at all.
Either possibility leads to a contradiction of Eleatic doctrine.

245B.   STR. Then, (A) is the Real one and a whole in the sense
that it has the property of unity, or (B) are we to say that
the Real is not a whole at all ?

THEAET. That is a hard choice.

STR. Quite true. For if (A) the real has the property of
being in a sense one, it will evidently not be the same thing
as Unity, and so all things will be more than one.

THEAET. Yes.

The other possibility (B) is that the real has not such unity as
belongs to a whole—is not one whole. The consequences of this
supposition are put in a subordinate dilemma. If the real is not
one whole, then either (a) there is such a thing as ‘ Wholeness ’

($a\dot{v}\tau\dot{o}$ $\tau\dot{o}$ $\ddot{o}\lambda ov$)—a real Form which exists, though ' the one real thing ' does not partake of it ; or (b) there is no such thing as ' Wholeness ' at all. The next three speeches of the Stranger deal with alternative (a).

245C.　STR.　And again (B) if the Real is not a whole by virtue of having this property of unity, while (a) at the same time Wholeness itself is real, it follows that the Real falls short of itself.

THEAET.　Certainly.

STR.　So, on this line of argument too, the Real will be deprived of reality and will not be a thing that is.

THEAET.　Yes.

STR.　And further, once more all things will be more than one, since Reality on the one side and Wholeness on the other have now each a distinct nature.

THEAET.　Yes.

The first of the two consequences here is that ' the Real will fall short of itself and will not be a thing that is '. This seems to mean that the Real, since it does not even partake of Wholeness, will ' fall short of itself ' in the sense that it does not include Wholeness, which nevertheless is real.[1] The words $o\dot{v}x$ $\ddot{o}v$ $\ddot{\epsilon}\sigma\tau\alpha\iota$ $\tau\dot{o}$ $\ddot{o}v$ are ambiguous. They may mean ' the Real will be a thing that is not ', *i.e.* a thing of which the negative statement is true, that it ' is not ' the same as Wholeness. Or they can be rendered as above : ' the Real will not be a thing that is ' (for it is not the same as Wholeness, and Wholeness is a thing that is). Both renderings amount to the same thing. In favour of the second are the words ' so on this line of argument also ', which imply that this conclusion is parallel to the one reached above under alternative (A) : ' the Real will evidently not be identical with Unity '. Here we conclude that the Real will not be identical with Wholeness (a thing that is).

The second consequence above is that the Real and Wholeness will be two real things ; so ' all things will be more than one '.

There now remains alternative (b) : that there is no such thing as Wholeness at all.

245C.　STR.　But if, (b) on the other hand, there is no such thing as Wholeness at all, not only are the same things true of the Real, but also that, besides not being a thing that really is, it could never even become such.[2]

---

[1] Parmenides had said : ' Nor may Being be imperfect ; for it lacks nothing, and if it were imperfect it would lack everything ' (Frag. 8, 32).

[2] The word $\ddot{o}v$ goes with $\pi\rho\dot{o}s$ $\tau\hat{\omega}$ $\mu\dot{\eta}$ $\epsilon\dot{l}v\alpha\iota$ as well as with $\mu\eta\delta$' $\ddot{a}v$ $\gamma\epsilon v\acute{\epsilon}\sigma\theta\alpha\iota$ $\pi o\tau\dot{\epsilon}$.

The statement that 'the same things will be true of the Real' on this supposition is at first sight obscure. For the consequences referred to, namely (1) that the Real will not be a thing that is, and (2) that all things will be a plurality, followed from the supposition that there were two real things: the Real (which has not the unity belonging to a whole) and Wholeness. How can the same consequences follow from the present supposition that there is no such thing as Wholeness?

The answer is suggested by arguments in the *Parmenides*, which Plato assumes to be familiar and does not care to repeat. The present supposition is: that (B) the Real has not the unity belonging to a whole, and (*b*) there is no such thing as Wholeness. It follows that the Real, having no unity or wholeness (for there is no such thing), must be a plurality without any unity. This gives the second consequence 'all things will be more than one'—not two this time, but an unlimited plurality (ἄπειρα). The first consequence 'the Real will not be a thing that is (ὄν)' is actually repeated here in the words 'besides not being a thing that is' (πρὸς τῷ μὴ εἶναι . . . ὄν). This cannot now mean that the Real is not the same as Wholeness (a thing that is); for we are now supposing that Wholeness is *not* 'a thing that is'. But there is a sense in which the words (οὐκ ὂν ἔσται τὸ ὄν) will be true. The Real will not be *a* thing that is (ὄν in the singular), because the Real is now an indefinite plurality without any unity.

This explanation may seem far-fetched, but Plato assumes that we have read and understood the *Parmenides*, where similar arguments are set out at length, and he leaves us to think out his meaning for ourselves.[1] He is more interested in stating two supplementary consequences of denying that the Real is a whole, and that there is any such thing as Wholeness. These are (1) that the Real, in that case, cannot even come into being, and (2) that it cannot have number. Theaetetus asks now for an explanation of the first, which has just been stated.

245D. THEAET. Why not?

STR. Whenever a thing comes into being, at that moment it has come to be as a whole; accordingly, if you do not

---

[1] M. Diès (*Autour de Platon*, ii, 480) remarks that, if any positive conclusion can be drawn from the discussions of the existence or non-existence of the One in the *Parmenides*, it would be twofold: ' *on ne peut nier absolument l'unité sans aboutir à une pluralité inconsistante, pure poussière d'être, inconnaissable et impensable ; on ne peut nier absolument la pluralité sans être obligé de refuser, à l'unité qu'on pose ainsi indivisible et solitaire, toute détermination, y compris celle de l'existence et celle même de l'unité.*'

245D. reckon unity or wholeness [1] among real things, you have
no right to speak of either being [2] or coming-into-being as
having any existence.

THEAET. That seems perfectly true.

STR. And further, what is not a whole cannot have any
definite number either ; for if a thing has a definite number,
it must amount to that number, whatever it may be, as a
whole.[3]

THEAET. Assuredly.

STR. And countless other difficulties, each involved in
E. measureless perplexity, will arise, if you say that the real
is either two things or only one.

THEAET. That is plain enough from those we have had a
glimpse of now. One leads to another, and each carries
us further into a wilderness of doubt about every theory
as it is mentioned.

From the second alternative (that the real has not the unity
belonging to a whole, and that there is no such thing as wholeness)
the Stranger has drawn two supplementary conclusions : that
without wholeness you cannot have (1) coming-into-being (*genesis*)
or (2) definite number. These conclusions do not convict
Parmenides of inconsistency, since he denied the possibility of
coming-into-being and of plurality. They seem to be noted as the
two most glaring deficiencies of his system. (1) His deduction of
the nature of the One real being excluded from reality the whole
world of becoming and change. In the next section Parmenides
will be ranked with the Idealists because he recognised an unchanging reality. Here it is noted that he differs from the other idealists
(the ' Friends of Forms ') in not recognising also a world of becoming. (2) Without wholeness and that unity which belongs to a
whole of parts and does not exclude plurality, there can be no
definite number, no sum or total number, only indefinite plurality.
The other defect in Parmenides' conception of the One Being was
that it was intended to exclude plurality. This again is a funda-

---

[1] τὸ ἓν ἦ τὸ ὅλον, MSS. ' Unity ' here seems to mean that unity which is
the property of a whole of parts, and to be used synonymously with ' wholeness '. Cf. 245B 4, ἕν τε καὶ ὅλον.

[2] ' Being ' (οὐσία) here must mean the existence that results from a process
of coming-into-being (γένεσις εἰς οὐσίαν). Campbell cites *Parm.* 153C, where
the coming-into-being of a whole of parts is described. The parts come
into being successively ' from beginning to end ' ; ' the unity or whole itself '
(τὸ ὅλον τε καὶ ἕν) has come into being ' at the same moment as the end '
(ἅμα τῇ τελευτῇ).

[3] Compare the identification of the Whole with the Sum, *Theaet.* 204A ff.
(p. 149).

mental point of difference from the Friends of Forms, who recognise
a world of reality which is one (a whole of parts) and embraces
a definite plurality (πολλά) of real beings, the many Forms, whose
structure the Dialectician is to trace out in his divisions. Further,
each of these Forms is a ' one being ', and yet, if it is definable, it
must be complex, a whole of those parts which will appear in its
definition. Whatever is real, accordingly, partakes both of Unity
and of Plurality.

Plato may have chosen to mark these points of difference here
because he did not want to stress differences among idealists where
they are confronted with materialists in the next section.

245E–246E. *The Battle of Gods and Giants : Idealists and Materialists*

The Stranger now passes from his review of the archaic period
to a picture of the battle that is always being waged by philosophers
upon the fundamental issue between materialism and idealism.

245E. STR. So much, then, for those who give an exact account
of what is real or unreal. We have not gone through them
all, but let this suffice. Now we must turn to look at those
who put the matter in a different way, so that, from a complete
review of all, we may see that reality is just as hard to
define as unreality.

THEAET. We had better go on, then, to their position.

Campbell remarks that ' those who give an exact account ' of the
real obviously include all the pre-Socratic philosophers who have
been mentioned, and that the phrase probably means ' those who
have defined precisely the number and the kinds of being ' (242D).
He adds that the meaning of ' those who put the matter *in a different
way* ' is best inferred from the phrase with which it is contrasted :
it means ' those who speak with less exactness '. There is no reason
to reject this natural interpretation.[1] The Stranger's words do not
imply that he is finally dismissing all the pre-Socratic philosophers
at this point, and passing on to a different set of Schools. He

---

[1] Attempts to interpret the phrases otherwise have been made in the
interests of some theory as to the identity of the ' Friends of Forms ', who
are among οἱ ἄλλως λέγοντες. The word διακριβολογεῖσθαι is rare (Stephanus
quotes only two other occurrences), but transparent ; διακριβοῦμαι is used by
Socrates at *Theaet.* 184D in an apology for ' using language so precisely '.
If the second sense of λόγος, ' reckoning ', is contained in διακριβολογεῖσθαι—
' to give a minute reckoning '—it fits Campbell's interpretation exactly.
Οἱ ἄλλως λέγοντες cannot mean ' the other side '. There is no sense of
antagonism in ἄλλως, and the parties to the Battle (who are both included in
οἱ ἄλλως λέγοντες) are not ranged in opposition to all the pre-Socratics.

means : So far we have considered the earlier philosophers as stating, with precision, exactly how many real things there are —one, or two, or three. We have not examined them all with the same thoroughness as Parmenides ; but that will do. We will now bring into our survey as well ' those who put the matter in a different way ', and so see the difficulty of defining reality *from a complete review* (ἐκ πάντων) of all philosophers, including these pre-Socratics and their successors, the contemporaries of Plato, and perhaps Plato himself.

The earlier division of the pre-Socratics into pluralists and the monist Parmenides suited Plato's purpose of isolating the advocate of a One real thing. Plato was specially concerned to show the defects of Parmenides' position from his own standpoint. He now wishes to survey the whole field of philosophy from a different angle and to group all the philosophers with reference to what he takes to be, at all times, the fundamental issue of the philosophic debate—materialism or idealism. The pre-Socratics had seen that issue as the question between one real thing or many, and argued on those lines with what may seem an archaic and pedantic precision. ' Those who put the matter differently ' have now formulated the issue in its genuine significance. They are carrying on the battle in these new terms, but behind these modern protagonists the pre-Socratics are still ranged in the rear. The conflict of materialism and idealism was not an entirely fresh issue that had arisen for the first time among the contemporaries of Plato. Ever since the sixth century the schools had been divided into two traditions : on the one side the Ionian science of the Milesians and their successors, on the other the Italian tradition of the Pythagoreans and Parmenides. The Ionians, all through, had been seeking the real nature of things in some ultimate kind of matter or body, such as water or air or all the four elements. The Italians had sought reality, not in tangible body, but in supersensible things. The Pythagoreans (who have not been mentioned) made numbers the real nature of things ; and Parmenides' One Being was not tangible body but an object of thought, possessing none of the opposite qualities which our senses delusively profess to reveal. Accordingly, the Ionians had been essentially materialists, not merely pluralists, the Italians essentially idealists, not merely monists. Plato's peculiar veneration for Parmenides shows that he regarded him as the precursor of his own philosophy.

At this point, then, the superficial way of contrasting the physicists with Parmenides according to the ' precise ' number of real things they recognised, is merged in the really significant contrast between materialist and idealist. This is a battle of Gods and Giants which

is declared to be ' *always* ' going on.   On the side of the Gods are
all who at any time believe that unseen things are the true realities ;
on the side of the Giants all who at any time believe that the real
is nothing but body which they can touch and handle.   The two
groups had been represented in earlier days by the Italians and
the Ionians ; but from now onwards no individual schools will be
named.   Here, as always, Plato is philosophising, not writing the
history of philosophy.   When he criticises individual schools, it is
only to determine what he can take from them and what he must
reject.   Both Gods and Giants are now to be asked what, from
their points of view, they mean by ' real '.

246A. STR.   What we shall see [1] is something like a Battle of Gods
and Giants going on between them over their quarrel about
reality.

THEAET.   How so ?

STR.   One party is trying to drag everything down to earth
out of heaven and the unseen, literally grasping rocks and
trees in their hands ; for they lay hold upon every stock and
stone and strenuously affirm that real existence belongs only
to that which can be handled and offers resistance to the
B. touch.   They define reality as the same thing as body, and
as soon as one of the opposite party asserts that anything
without a body is real, they are utterly contemptuous and
will not listen to another word.

THEAET.   The people you describe are certainly a formidable crew.   I have met quite a number of them before now.

STR.   Yes, and accordingly their adversaries are very wary
in defending their position somewhere in the heights of the
unseen, maintaining with all their force that true reality
consists in certain intelligible and bodiless Forms.   In the
clash of argument they shatter and pulverise those bodies
C. which their opponents wield, and what those others allege
to be true reality they call, not real being, but a sort of
moving process of becoming.   On this issue an interminable
battle is always going on between the two camps.

THEAET.   True.

STR.   Suppose, then, we challenge each party in turn to
render an account of the reality they assert.

THEAET.   How shall we do so ?

STR.   It will be easier to obtain from those who place reality
in Forms, because they are more civilised ; harder, from

---

[1] καὶ μήν, as in tragedy, where a person on the stage calls attention to the
entry of a fresh character.

246D those whose violence would drag everything down to the level of body—perhaps, all but impossible. However, I think I see the right way to deal with them.

THEAET. What is that ?

STR. Best of all, if it were anyhow possible, would be to bring about a real change of heart [1] ; but if that is beyond our power, to imagine them reformed and assume them willing to moderate their present lawlessness in answering our questions. The better a man's character is, the more force there will be in any agreement you make with him. However, we are not concerned with them so much as with our search for the truth.

E. THEAET. You are quite right.

Who are the materialists ? There is no need to criticise all the many attempts to identify them with some particular school.[2] As we observed earlier, the question put to the Ionian physicists, ' What do you mean by real ? ' was left unanswered. Now that they are merged in the new grouping of Gods and Giants, the beginnings of an answer come to light : ' the real is tangible body, and nothing else.' This answer had, in fact, emerged in the Atomism of Leucippus and Democritus—the last word of Ionian science. In their system the real is nothing but the atoms, which are essentially bodily substance, impenetrable, offering invincible resistance to touch. This is the materialist's account of the nature of the real. It held the field later in Epicureanism, and right on into modern times as the physicist's answer. Plato never mentions Leucippus and Democritus by name or describes their doctrine in precise terms ; but the inference that he had never heard of Atomism is entirely incredible. The *Sophist* was written some sixty years after the probable *floruits* of Leucippus (about 430) and Democritus (about 420), and Plato had been for perhaps twenty years head of the Academy, to which students (including Aristotle) had come from all quarters of Greece. There is nothing against including the

---

[1] ' To make them better men in actual fact.' ' Better ' has a moral colouring. Materialism, as described in *Laws* x, 889 ff., leads in Plato's view to atheism and ' lawlessness '. The Giants are really making war on Heaven. The parallel with *Laws* 663c : τὴν δὲ ἀλήθειαν τῆς κρίσεως (the decision between the more righteous or the pleasanter life) ποτέραν κυριωτέραν εἶναι φῶμεν— πότερα τὴν τῆς χείρονος ψυχῆς ἢ τὴν τῆς βελτίονος ; is closer than Campbell thinks, though the context is different.

[2] Antisthenes (Dummler, Natorp, Zeller, Maier, etc.) ; Antisthenes and the Atomists, merged in a general polemic on materialism (Campbell) ; the Atomists and Aristippus (Schleiermacher, etc.) ; the Atomists only (Gomperz) ; Melissus (Burnet).

Atomists in the materialist camp.[1]   But Theaetetus' remark that
he has met many of these materialists points rather to ' the crass
unthinking corporealism of the average man '[2]—a type of materialist
who must, no doubt, be included.   On the other hand, this battle
of Gods and Giants is a philosophic battle, not a battle of one school
of idealists against the unthinking average man.   The Giants include all—philosophers or average men—who believe that tangible
body is the sole reality.   That is precisely how they are defined,
and there is no need to look for one set of persons who held that
belief, to the exclusion of others.   In all cases like this, it is better
to suppose that Plato is discussing exactly what he says he is
discussing—the tendency of thought that he defines, not one or
another set of individuals who, more or less, exhibited that tendency.

246E–248A. *A mark of the real is offered for the materialists'
    acceptance*

The Stranger now begins his argument with the materialists.
They identify the real with visible and tangible body, but we do
not yet know what they mean by calling this ' real '.   The argument
leads up to a definition—or rather a mark—of the ' real ', offered
for their acceptance.   The Stranger opens by inducing the ' reformed ' or more reasonable materialist to admit that there are
things, such as moral qualities, which are not visible or tangible
bodies, and yet must exist, since we can be aware of their presence
or absence in people's souls.

246E.   STR.   Well then, call upon these reformed characters to
        oblige you with an answer, and you shall act as their spokes-
        man.
        THEAET.   I will.
        STR.   Let them tell us, then, whether they admit that there
        is such a thing as a mortal living creature.
        THEAET.   Of course they do.
        STR.   And they will agree that it is a body animated by
        a soul ?
        THEAET.   Certainly.
        STR.   Taking a soul to be something real ?
247.   THEAET.   Yes.

[1] Burnet (*Gk. Phil*. i, 279) objects that Democritus could not be meant
because he ' asserted the reality of the void and could not be spoken of as
making impact and contact the test of being '.   But the Atomists ·xpressly
identified the Void with ' not-being ' or ' nothing ' and atoms with ' being '.
You do not refuse to call a man a materialist because he recognises the
existence of empty space, which he calls ' nothing '.
[2] Taylor, *Plato* (1926), 384.

247. STR. Again, they allow that one soul may be just, another unjust, or one wise, another foolish ?

THEAET. Naturally.

STR. And that any soul comes to be just or the reverse by possessing justice or the reverse, which is present in it ? [1]

THEAET. Yes, they agree to that too.

STR. But surely they will admit that whatever can come to be present in a thing or absent from it is certainly a real thing.

THEAET. Yes.

B. STR. Granted, then, that justice or wisdom or any other sort of goodness or badness is real, and moreover that a soul in which they come to exist is real, do they maintain that any one of these things is visible and tangible, or are they all invisible ?

THEAET. They can hardly say that any one of them is visible.

STR. And do they really assert that something that is not visible has a body ?

THEAET. That question they do not answer as a whole without a distinction. The soul itself, they think, does possess a sort of body [2] ; but when it comes to wisdom or any of the other things you asked about, they have not the

C. face either to accept the inference that they have no place among real things or to persist in maintaining that they are all bodies.

STR. That shows, Theaetetus, that they are genuinely re-formed characters. The Giants among them, of the true earth-born breed, would not stick at any point ; they would hold out to the end, that whatever they cannot squeeze between their hands is just nothing at all.

THEAET. I dare say that describes their state of mind.

STR. Let us question them further, then ; for it is quite

---

[1] If this sentence (with the plural ἐναντίων) is to be regularised, it is simplest to read δικαιοσύνης ⟨ἢ φρονήσεως⟩ ἕξει. Παρουσίᾳ (guaranteed by παραγίγνεσθαι following) should not be changed as Campbell suggested. It is the ordinary non-technical word for the presence of a quality in a thing. Cf. *Lysis.* 217D : Hair, turning white with age, comes to be white ' by the presence of whiteness ' in it, as contrasted with the superficial whiteness of a face painted with white lead. *Gorg.* 497, The good are good ' by the presence of goodness ' in them. *Charm.* 159A.

[2] The soul had been regarded both popularly and by philosophers before Plato as consisting of a subtle and invisible kind of matter. The Atomists continued to maintain that it was composed of atoms, like everything else ; only its atoms were round and so specially mobile.

247C. enough for our purpose if they consent to admit that even
D. a small part of reality is bodiless. They must now tell us
this : when they say that these bodiless things and the other
things which have body are alike ' real ', what common
character that emerges as covering both sets of things have
they in view ? It is possible they may be at a loss for an
answer. If that is their state of mind, you must consider
whether they would accept at our suggestion a description
of the real and agree to it.

THEAET. What description ? Perhaps we can tell, if you
will state it.

STR. I suggest that anything has real being, that is so
E. constituted as to possess any sort of power either to affect
anything else or to be affected, in however small a degree,
by the most insignificant agent, though it be only once. I
am proposing as a mark to distinguish real things, that
they are nothing but power.[1]

THEAET. Well, they accept that, having for the moment
no better suggestion of their own to offer.

STR. That will do ; for later on both they and we perhaps
248. may change our minds. For the present, then, let us take
it that this agreement stands between us and the one party.

THEAET. It does.

The meaning of ' power '. Before considering the general significance of this argument with the materialists, something must be said
about the previous history of the word translated ' power '.
' *Dynamis* ' is the substantive answering to the common verb ' to
be able ' *(δύνασθαι)*, and it covers the ability to be acted upon as
well as the ability to act on something else, whereas most of the
corresponding English words—power, force, potency, etc.—suggest
active, as opposed to passive, ability. *Dynamis* includes passive
capacity, receptivity, susceptibility, as well.

The notion of body or matter as endowed with properties both
active and passive, capacities of both causing and suffering modifications, is deeply rooted in primitive common sense. The warmth in
my hand is capable of acting on a stone and making it warm ; it
is also capable of being acted on by ice and reduced to, or replaced

[1] Τίθεμαι γὰρ ὅρον ὁρίζειν τὰ ὄντα ὡς ἔστιν οὐκ ἄλλο τι πλὴν δύναμις. The
construction is difficult. I think the sentence ought to mean that the
mark of real things (not the real things themselves) is nothing but power.
This sense could be obtained if we could translate : ' I am pro~osing a mark
to distinguish real things—that there is nothing else but power (to serve as
such a mark) ' *or* 'that *it* (the mark) is nothing but power.' But neither
rendering seems defensible.

234

by, coldness. The notion had acquired a technical significance in medicine, for obvious reasons. A doctor's business is to find substances that will modify our physical states, things that have healing powers or virtues. Regarding from this standpoint all substances that serve as food or drugs, he studies their properties to find those that will have the right action. He thinks of ' the salt ', ' the bitter ', ' the sweet ', ' the astringent ', etc., not simply as permanent states of a substance, but as ' powers ' or ' virtues ', and of the similar properties of the ' patient's ' body (ὁ πάσχων) as capable of being modified by the action of a corrective drug or diet. Reviewing the use of the word *dynamis* in the medical writers, Dr. Souilhé [1] points out that it tended more and more to take on a special meaning, best illustrated by the Hippocratic tract *On Ancient Medicine*. He concludes [2] that the term comprises two mutually complementary ideas. (1) Substances manifest themselves by their qualities. Things are made sensible by these properties, such as ' the cold ', ' the hot ', ' the bitter ', ' the salt ', which allow them to enter into relation with other bodies. These are so many δυνάμεις, distinct entities which constitute, so to say, the ' exteriorisation ' of the substance. But (2) these entities themselves can only be known in action ; their action is their *raison d'être* ; action characterises and individualises them. ' The cold ' differs from ' the hot ' or from ' the bitter ' or from ' the salt ' because it produces a certain determinate effect. It can be combined with the other qualities, but will never be confounded with them, because its action is not identical with theirs. This action of qualities, again, is their *dynamis*. The term designates at once their essence and their proper manner of manifesting themselves.

Later, Dr. Souilhé observes that in those Hippocratic treatises which show the influence of early cosmological ideas, the term *dynamis* stands for the characteristic property of bodies, their exterior and sensible aspect, which makes it possible to determine and specify them. Thanks to the *dynamis*, the mysterious ' nature ' (*physis*), the substantial ' form ' (*eidos*) or primordial element, makes itself known, and does so by its action. This explains why it was possible, especially at a later date, to pass from the known to the unknown, from the appearance to the reality, and how easy it was to identify the ' nature ' (*physis*) with the *dynamis*.[3]

[1] J. Souilhé, *Étude sur le terme Δύναμις dans les dialogues de Platon* (Paris, 1919), p. 55. [2] *Op. cit.*, p. 36.

[3] For instance, *Protag.* 349B : Are wisdom, temperance, courage, justice, piety, five names for one thing, or is there, underlying each of these names, a peculiar being (οὐσία) or thing having its own proper *dynamis* (πρᾶγμα ἔχον ἑαυτοῦ δύναμιν ἕκαστον), no one of them being like (οἷον) another ? Compare with this Hippocrates, *De natura hominis* 5 (Littré vi, 40) : The four humours

To state the nature of a thing is the same as to state its property, since the nature is made evident only by the property, the two are inseparable, and a genuine causal link unites them. Sometimes the two are almost synonymous ; but usually a distinction is perceptible, which is illustrated by the following passage from Menon's *Iatrica* : ' Philistion holds that we are composed of four forms (ἰδέαι), that is to say, of four elements : fire, air, water, earth. Each of these has its *dynamis* : fire has the hot, air the cold, water the moist, earth the dry '. Dr. Souilhé then shows how the Sophists adapted and transposed this terminology and finally facilitated the introduction of it into philosophy.

In Plato's earlier writings there is hardly any occasion for the term in its medical sense, though *dynamis* meaning the ' virtue ' of a drug occurs in the *Charmides* (156B). But in the *Philebus* (29A), he says that the small portion contained in our bodies of each of the four elements is weak and impure, and ' the *dynamis* it possesses is not worthy of its nature (*physis*) '. And again, the *dynamis* of ' the moist ' is to replenish that which is dried up (31E). The word naturally occurs most frequently in the physical and physiological discussions of the *Timaeus*. It is there used of the active properties of the four elements (32C) ; the pungent properties of substances like soda (66A) ; acrid and saline *dynameis*, coupled with a variety of colours and bitternesses, characteristic of the blood in decomposing blood-vessels (82E) ; the congealing power of fibrine acting on the blood (85D).

The passive *dynamis*, the capacity for receiving ' affections ' of which the nature or constitution is susceptible, is less often mentioned. But in the *Republic* (507C) the most precious work of the creator of the senses is said to be ' the power of seeing and being seen '. The power of seeing is the faculty of vision in the eye ; the power of being seen belongs to colour residing in visible things. It is given to them by the sunlight (509B). Summing up the philosophic use of the word in Plato, Dr. Souilhé says [1] that the Platonic *dynamis* can be defined as the property or quality which reveals the nature of a thing. It may be manifested under one or other of two aspects : as an activity or principle of action,

---

are distinguished by ' convention ' (κατὰ νόμον, *i.e.* the recognised usage of language) by four names ; and equally by nature (κατὰ φύσιν) their forms (ἰδέαι) are distinct : phlegm is not like (ἐοικέναι) blood, or blood like bile ; they differ in colour, and tactile qualities, warmth, cold, dryness, moisture. Things so different in form and *dynamis* cannot be one thing ; eacʰ has its own *dynamis* and *nature* (ἕκαστον αὐτῶν ἔχει δύναμίν τε καὶ φύσιν τὴν ἑωυτοῦ). If you give a man a drug which draws the phlegm, he will vomit phlegm ; if you give him one that draws bile, he will vomit bile.

[1] *Op. cit.*, p. 149.

of movement, or as a state or principle of passivity, of resistance.
By either aspect, or sometimes by both, it unveils the inmost and
hidden nature of things ; still more, it distinguishes their essences.
The *dynamis* makes it possible to give each thing a name conform-
ing to its peculiar constitution, and places things in separate
groups. In a word, it is at once a principle of knowledge and a
principle of diversity.

There are two places in particular where ' the power of acting
and being acted upon '—the phrase we have in the *Sophist*—occurs.
In the first (*Phaedrus*, 270B ff.) the medical associations are recalled.
The art of Rhetoric, instead of being concerned with pedantic
questions of style, the divisions of a speech, and so forth, ought
to study the soul, which oratory is to influence. Rhetoric should
analyse the nature of the soul as medicine analyses the body, and
administer arguments as the doctor administers drugs and diet
with a knowledge of their proper effect. Hippocrates said that
the nature of the body could not be known apart from the nature
of the whole world. This is still more true of the soul ; and if we
would study the nature of anything whatever, we must first analyse
the complex into its simple constituents, and then, when we have
reached the simple, study ' what power it has by nature either to
act upon something or to be affected in some way '. The implication seems to be that the simple and unanalysable nature can only
be manifested and known by the effects it can produce and suffer.

The other passage is the analysis of sensation in the *Theaetetus*
(156A ff.). Here the sentient organ and the external object are
regarded as slow processes of change, having the power respectively
to be acted upon and to act. But where the actual process of
sense-perception is described, it is treated as symmetrical : eye
and object alike are both active and passive. The swift motion
of the visual current comes from the eye to encounter a swift
motion from the object ; both are thus active. These motions
coalesce and generate a pair of offspring : sensation and colour.
The eye then ' becomes full of vision '—a seeing eye ; the object
is saturated with whiteness and becomes a white thing. This is
the passive aspect for both : the organ has its ' affection ', the
object acquires its quality.

Finally, the conception of the active and passive *dynamis* may
be illustrated from Aristotle.[1] Inquiring what qualities must be
present in the simple bodies (earth, water, air, fire), Aristotle considers what are the fundamental qualities that must be common
to all perceptible bodies. He decides on Hot and Cold, Dry
and Moist, qualities of touch which are the essential mark of per-

[1] *De gen et corr.* B, ii.

ceptible bodies as such. These, like all perceptible qualities, are
' powers of acting and being acted upon '; they are the ' affective
qualities' of *Categories* 8. Their power is shown in the action and
reaction of all bodies, animate or not, when they come into contact. In the special case of sensation, if one of the two bodies
is animate, the physical change due to the action of the external
object will be accompanied by an activity of the soul, sensation,
the awareness of physical change.[1]

These developments serve to connect the Stranger's suggestion
to the materialists with the question put earlier to the archaic
physicists : '' When you say Hot and Cold, or some such pair,
really are all things, what do you mean by calling both ' real ' ? ''
The Hot and the Cold are typical ' powers ' in the early cosmolo-
gists,[2] the medical writers, and Aristotle. Now that these physicists
are merged in the materialist party, the suggestion supplies the
answer that was not given earlier. The general mark of what they
call ' real ' is ' the power of acting and being acted upon '. The
' real things ' they recognised are essentially *dynameis*.

We can now consider the drift of the whole argument. The
materialist's warrant for believing in the reality of tangible body
is simply that it has the power of affecting his sense of touch.
But this power of making a difference that he can be aware of is,
we have argued, not confined to visible and tangible things. He
can know that justice is present in or absent from a soul. So
justice has the same right to be called real. The reasonable
materialist must then surrender tangibility as the mark of the
real, and substitute ' the power of acting and being acted upon ',
which belongs to ' the just ' equally with ' the hot ' or ' the cold '.
He is thus ousted from his original position that only bodies are
real and brought some of the way towards the full admission that
not merely the justice residing in an individual soul, but Justice
itself, is real—a unique object of thought that can be known without any use of the bodily senses. No attempt, however, is made
to extract this further concession.

Is Plato himself committed to this ' mark ' of reality—for it is
offered only as a mark, not as a definition ?[3] Theaetetus accepts

[1] *Physics* vii, 2, 244*b*, 10.

[2] *Parmenides* (frag. 9), for instance, uses δυνάμεις for the contrary perceptible
qualities ranged in pairs under the two main ' Forms ', Light (Fire) and
Darkness (Night).

[3] The word ὅρος is used at 247E and again at 248C, not λόγος. It is a mark,
not a definition, of man that he is capable of laughter. ὅρον ὁρίζειν (*Gorg.*
470B) is to draw a boundary-line marking off something from other things;
hence ὅρος comes to mean a ' definition '. λόγος is the definition giving
the explicit statement of a complex content or meaning.

it provisionally, and the Stranger remarks that we may change our minds later. The general impression left is that Plato regarded the argument as one that a reasonable materialist would accept. He himself might hold that nothing is real that cannot be in some way known, and yet not hold that ' to be real ' *means* to possess whatever power of acting or being acted on is thereby implied. That he does not in fact regard this as the definition of ' real ', is clear ; for in a later section (249D ff.) the question, What does reality (Being, Existence) mean ? is put by the Stranger to himself and Theaetetus as still unanswered.

248A–249D. *The Idealists must concede that reality includes some changing things*

The Stranger now turns to the idealists. Will the ' Friends of Forms ' accept the ' power of acting and being acted upon ' as the mark of the realities they believe in ?

248A.   STR. Let us turn, then, to the opposite party, the friends of Forms. Once more you shall act as their spokesman.
THEAET. I will.
STR. We understand that you make a distinction between ' Becoming ' and ' Real being ' and speak of them as separate. Is that so ?
THEAET. Yes.
STR. And you say that we have intercourse with [1] Becoming by means of the body through sense, whereas we have intercourse with Real being by means of the soul through reflection. And Real being, you say, is always in the same unchanging state, whereas Becoming is variable.
B.   THEAET. We do.
STR. Admirable. But now what are we to take you as meaning by this expression ' intercourse ' which you apply to both ? Don't you mean what we described a moment ago ?
THEAET. What was that ?
STR. The experiencing an effect or the production of one,

---

[1] κοινωνεῖν (' are in touch with ', Taylor) is chosen as a neutral word covering all forms of cognition, the usual words (εἰδέναι, γιγνώσκειν, ἐπίστασθαι, αἰσθάνεσθαι, etc.) being too much specialised and associated either with knowledge to the exclusion of sensation and perception or *vice versa*. κοινωνεῖν is ' to enter into relations with '. It is used of social and business intercourse, and also of sexual intercourse, a metaphor already used in the analysis of sensation in the *Theaetetus* (see p. 47). κοινωνεῖν here is a psychological term for cognition, and this use has no connection (such as Campbell imagines) with its use later to describe the ' combination ' of Forms (κοινωνία εἰδῶν).

248B. arising, as the result of some power, from things that encounter one another. Perhaps, Theaetetus, you may not
be able to catch their answer to this, but I, who am familiar
with them, may be more successful.

THEAET. What have they to say, then ?

c. STR. They do not agree to the proposition we put just
now to the earth-born Giants about reality.

THEAET. You mean—— ?

STR. We proposed as a sufficient mark of real things the
presence in a thing of the power of being acted upon or
of acting in relation to however insignificant a thing.[1]

THEAET. Yes.

STR. Well, to that they reply that a power of acting and
being acted upon belongs to Becoming, but neither of
these powers is compatible with Real being.

THEAET. And there is something in that answer ?

STR. Something to which we must reply by a request for
D. more enlightenment. Do they acknowledge further that
the soul knows and Real being is known ?

THEAET. Certainly they agree to that.

STR. Well, do you agree that knowing or being known is
an action, or is it experiencing an effect, or both ? Or is
one of them experiencing an effect, the other an action ?
Or does neither of them come under either of these heads
at all ? [2]

THEAET. Evidently neither ; otherwise our friends would
be contradicting what they said earlier.

STR. I see what you mean. They would have to say this : [3]
E. If knowing is to be acting on something, it follows that
what is known must be acted upon [4] by it ; and so, on this
showing, Reality when it is being known by the act of
knowledge must, in so far as it is known, be changed owing

---

[1] πρὸς τὸ σμικρότατον δρᾶν, cf. 247E, ὑπὸ τοῦ φαυλοτάτου (παθεῖν) and *Phaedrus*
270D, τὴν δύναμιν αὐτοῦ τίνα πρὸς τί πέφυκεν εἰς τὸ δρᾶν ἔχον ἢ τίνα εἰς τὸ παθεῖν
ὑπὸ τοῦ.

[2] The Stranger puts all the possible ways of regarding knowing. He does
not suggest that it must be an action, not a being-acted-upon, but that it
may be either, or both, or neither. The Idealists in their next reply take up
only one of these suggestions—that knowing is an action—and object to that.

[3] *ΞΕ. μανθάνω· τόδε γε* (SC. *λέγοιεν ἄν*). What follows is put into the mouths
of the Idealists, who state their objection to regarding knowing as an action.
They ignore the possibility that knowing is an affection of the soul, acted
upon by the object. M. Diès prints τόδε γε, but translates τὸ δὲ or τὸ δέ γε :
' *mais, ceci, au moins, ils l'avoueront* '—a rendering which makes the Stranger
force on the Idealists the alternative that knowing is an action.

[4] Or ' affected '—a rendering that more clearly implies suffering some change.

248E. to being so acted upon ; and that, we say, cannot happen to the changeless.

THEAET. Exactly.

STR. But tell me, in heaven's name : are we really to be so easily convinced that change, life, soul, understanding have no place in that which is perfectly real—that it has
249. neither life nor thought, but stands immutable in solemn aloofness, devoid of intelligence ?

THEAET. That, sir, would be a strange doctrine to accept.

STR. But can we say it has intelligence without having life ?

THEAET. Surely not.

STR. But if we say it contains both, can we deny that it has soul in which they reside ?

THEAET. How else could it possess them ?

STR. But then, if it has intelligence, life, and soul, can we say that a living thing remains at rest in complete changelessness ?

B. THEAET. All that seems to me unreasonable.

STR. In that case we must admit that what changes and change itself are real things.

THEAET. Certainly.

The Stranger now draws conclusions. (1) As just agreed, if Reality consists solely of unchangeable things, intelligence will have no real existence anywhere. But (2) if Reality consists *solely* of things that are perpetually changing (as the Heracleiteans said), there can be no intelligence or knowledge. (3) Therefore ' Reality or the sum of things ' must contain both changing and unchanging things.

249B. STR. From this, however, it follows, Theaetetus, first, that, if all things are unchangeable [1] no intelligence can really exist anywhere in anything with regard to any object.

THEAET. Quite so.

STR. And, on the other hand, if we allow that all things are moving and changing, on that view equally we shall be excluding intelligence from the class of real things.

THEAET. How so ?

---

[1] ἀκινήτων τε ὄντων <πάντων>, Badham. This gives the conclusion required, and πάντων is supported by πάντα in the next speech. Without πάντων, ἀκινήτων ὄντων must be governed by μηδενί to make sense, and the statement that ' nothing unchangeable has intelligence ' is not a fresh conclusion, having already been stated, nor is it the conclusion demanded by the following context. The point is that, if the *whole* of Reality excludes change, intelligence (which involves life and therefore change) will have no real existence *anywhere*.

249B.   STR.   Do you think that, without rest, there could ever
  C.   be anything that abides constant in the same condition
       and in the same respects ?
       THEAET.   Certainly not.
       STR.   And without such objects can you make out that
       intelligence exists or could ever exist anywhere ?
       THEAET.   It would be quite impossible.
       STR.   Well then, all the force of reasoning must be enlisted
       to oppose anyone who tries to maintain any assertion
       about anything at the same time that he suppresses know-
       ledge or understanding or intelligence.
       THEAET.   Most certainly.
       STR.   On these grounds, then, it seems that only one
       course is open to the philosopher who values knowledge
       and the rest above all else.   He must refuse to accept
  D.   from the champions either of the One or of the many
       Forms the doctrine that all Reality is changeless ;   and
       he must turn a deaf ear to the other party who represent
       Reality as everywhere changing.   Like a child begging for
       ' both ',[1] he must declare that Reality or the sum of things
       is both at once—all that is unchangeable and all that is in
       change.
       THEAET.   Perfectly true.

In the concluding passage the idealists who believe in ' many
Forms ' are grouped with, but distinguished from, the Eleatics,
the champions of the One Being.   What they have in common is
their insistence upon the changelessness of the real :   they both
maintain that the whole of reality, ' the All ', excludes all change
and motion.   It is put to them that this means excluding all life,
soul, intelligence from the real—a position as fatal to the reality
of knowledge as the opposite Heracleitean thesis (already dismissed
in the *Theaetetus*, p. 98), that the whole of the real is in perpetual
change.
    Who are these Friends of Forms ?   The plain fact is that every
feature of their doctrine, which is described in some detail, can be
illustrated from Plato's own earlier works, and that we know of
no other school that held a theory of reality even resembling it.[2]

---

[1] For the benefit of scholars (see Campbell's note) who have never asked
a child, ' Which hand will you have ? ' I quote a letter from Mary Lamb
(Aug. 20, 1815) on a visit to Cambridge :   " We were walking the whole time—
out of one College into another.   If you ask me which I like best, I must
make the children's traditionary unoffending reply—' Both '."

[2] As Ritter (*Platon* ii, 132) remarks, no one could ever have doubted that
the Friends of Forms include the Platonic Socrates of the *Phaedo* and *Republic*,

The Gods, in this battle with the Giants, include all idealists, all believers in unseen intelligible realities. Parmenides is expressly referred to, and the Pythagoreans (though not mentioned) belonged to that western tradition which had always stood in contrast with the materialistic science of Ionia. The battle is one that is always going on between the two camps, on a fundamental issue of philosophy. It is ridiculous to conceive it as a quarrel between (say) Antisthenes or Melissus on the one side and the Megarians or a misguided section of the Academy on the other. Plato knew well enough that his own theory of Forms was by far the most important product of the idealist tradition. He could not leave himself out of the picture. The theory of Forms has already been submitted to the criticism of Parmenides. Why should it not be criticised here by one of Parmenides' disciples ? As we have remarked, it is Plato's purpose in this dialogue to set his own doctrine beside the Eleatic and to mark exactly the points in which he must differ from Parmenides. The gist of the Stranger's criticism is that the Friends of Forms have stated their view of reality in terms that are too Eleatic. They have taken changelessness as the mark of Real being, and relegated all change to the world of Becoming.

The theory of the Friends of Forms is the theory stated in the *Phaedo* and criticised in the *Parmenides*. (1) They ' make a distinction between Becoming and Being and speak of them as separate '. Socrates had used the same words in the *Parmenides* : ' If one distinguishes the Forms by themselves as separate ' ; and Parmenides had repeated it : ' Have you yourself made this distinction you speak of—certain Forms and on the other hand the things that partake of them, each separate from the other ? ' [1] The emphasis in both dialogues falls upon the separation (χωρισμός) of the Ideal world from the many changing things of sense.

(2) The Friends of Forms speak of two contrasted kinds of cognition : intercourse with Becoming by means of the body through sense ; and with Being by means of the soul through reflection. This suggests a complete distinction between two fields of objects, the unseen and intelligible Forms and the visible objects of the bodily senses. All this is in the *Phaedo* (79A) :

if the temporal sequence of the dialogues had been correctly determined earlier than it was. Ritter himself identifies the Friends of Forms with members of the Academy who took the doctrines of personal immortality and of bodiless Forms, as set forth in the *Phaedo*, more seriously and literally than Plato himself intended.

[1] *Soph.* 248A, γένεσιν, τὴν δ' οὐσίαν χωρίς που διελόμενοι λέγετε ; *Parm.* 129D, ἐάν τις διαιρῆται χωρὶς αὐτὰ καθ' αὐτὰ τὰ εἴδη. 130B, αὐτὸς σὺ οὕτω διῄρησαι ὡς λέγεις, χωρὶς μὲν εἴδη αὐτὰ ἄττα, χωρὶς δὲ τὰ τούτων αὖ μετέχοντα ; see Introd., p. 7.

there are two orders of things, the unseen and unchanging, and
the visible that is always changing. We ourselves consist of soul
and body. The soul as unseen is akin to the unseen objects ; the
body, as a visible thing, to the visible. When the soul studies
things ' through the senses ', she is dragged down by the body and
confused ; when she is ' by herself ', reflecting on changeless objects
without the senses, she has wisdom. So again in the *Republic*
(544A) the lower kind of cognition is ' concerned with Becoming '
(περὶ γένεσιν), the higher kind with ' Being ' (περὶ οὐσίαν).

(3) The Friends of Forms take unchangeableness as the mark
of real Being, variability as the mark of Becoming. This had been
asserted in the *Phaedo* with all possible emphasis.[1] The Forms
admit no sort of change, whereas the many sensible things never
remain the same. In the *Phaedo* and *Republic* the ideal world is
constantly spoken of as excluding any change, and this was always
treated as the necessary condition for the existence of knowledge.

Now in the *Parmenides* the last criticism brought against the
theory of Forms was that, if the Forms exist in a separate world
' by themselves ', there is danger that they may be beyond the
reach of the knowledge which exists in our souls here ' in our
world ' (παρ' ἡμῖν). A god might possess perfect knowledge, but
can our imperfect knowledge ever reach the Forms ? Yet Parmenides admits that without the Forms there cannot be any discourse at all. The Forms must exist and be knowable. The
whole drift of the criticism is that the ' separation ' of Forms from
things in our world has been too sharply drawn and over-emphasised.
The same impression is conveyed here by the Stranger. The
Friends of Forms are extremists who, like the Eleatics, want to
make the whole of reality changeless. Although they speak of
knowledge as an intercourse of the soul with reality by reflection,
they will not admit that this is analogous to the intercourse with
Becoming through the senses, for fear that some ' affection ' of
the real should be implied, inconsistent with its unchanging character. The Stranger demands from them, as earlier from the
materialists, a concession. But what exactly is this concession ?

When the Stranger protests that intelligence, life, and therefore
change must have a place in ' that which is perfectly real ', he
cannot mean that everything which is perfectly real must be alive

---

[1] *Soph.* 248A, τὴν ὄντως οὐσίαν ἣν ἀεὶ κατὰ ταὐτὰ ὡσαύτως ἔχειν φατέ, γένεσιν
δὲ ἄλλοτε ἄλλως. *Phaedo*, 78C, ἅπερ ἀεὶ κατὰ ταὐτὰ καὶ ὡσαύτως ἔχει are most likely
to be incomposite, τὰ δὲ ἄλλοτε ἄλλως καὶ μηδέποτε κατὰ ταὐτὰ to be composite.
Αὐτὴ ἡ οὐσία never admits any change : ἀεὶ αὐτῶν ἕκαστον ὃ ἔστι, μονοειδὲς ὂν
αὐτὸ καθ' αὑτό, ὡσαύτως κατὰ ταὐτὰ ἔχει καὶ οὐδέποτε οὐδαμῇ οὐδαμῶς ἀλλοίωσιν
οὐδέμιαν ἐνδέχεται.

and therefore changing. The Forms, considered as objects of knowledge, must be unchangeable. This is asserted in later dialogues,[1] and in the conclusion here : there can be no intelligence without unchanging objects. The Forms are never represented as living and thinking beings. As the conclusion shows, the Stranger means by ' that which is perfectly real ' the *whole* world of real being. ' The real or the sum of things '. (τὸ ὄν τε καὶ τὸ πᾶν 249D) must include ' both all that is unchangeable and all that is in change '. The world of real being, in fact, does not consist solely of the unchanging Forms (as the earlier dialogues had frequently suggested), but must contain as well life, soul, intelligence, and such change as they imply.

What may easily mislead the reader is this : the Stranger's protest follows immediately upon the idealists' objection that, if knowing is an action, reality, in being known, must be acted upon and so changed. It appears at first sight as if the Stranger himself must think that what is known is changed by being known. The conclusion, as we have seen, excludes the idea that the nature or content of a Form could possibly be altered by the act of knowledge. But it may be well to review here the whole argument with regard to knowledge.

In the first place, we may note that the idealists' conception of the intercourse between Becoming and the bodily senses exactly agrees with the analysis of sensation in the *Theaetetus*—a further proof that that analysis is Plato's own. They have reduced the alleged hard and changeless ' being ' of physical bodies to ' a sort of moving process of becoming '.[2] Our intercourse with this process is ' an affection or action arising, as the result of some power, from things that encounter one another ', *viz.* sense-organs and external objects. The conception of the active and passive *dynamis* is the same as that offered to the Giants, and the idealists accept it as belonging to Becoming. All this fits exactly the account given in the *Theaetetus*. The Stranger has, in fact, offered to the materialist Plato's own account of the nature of those perceptible bodies which the materialist regards as real, and of the intercourse we have with them in perception. So far as this sort of cognition is concerned, the reformed materialist who accepts the offer is at one with the Friends of Forms, who already hold that theory.

On the other hand, the materialist was induced to accept the *dynamis* theory, because we proved to him that his original identification of the real with the tangible was not wide enough to include

---

[1] *E.g. Timaeus* 28A, 52A, etc. ; *Philebus* 59A, C.
[2] 246C, γένεσιν φερομένην τινά. Cf. *Theaet.* 156A ff. (p. 46).

certain bodiless things, such as justice, whose reality has as good
a warrant. But what will the Friends of Forms say to making
the power of acting and being acted upon the mark of reality ?
What they do say (248C) is that the *dynamis* theory applies to Becoming only, not to Being or Reality (οὐσία). The point put to
them by the Stranger may be stated thus : ' You conceive our
intercourse with physical objects in this way. Must you not
recognise an analogous intercourse between the soul which knows
by reflection and the reality known ? ' It is a fact that the same
metaphor of sexual intercourse that runs through the analysis of
sense-perception in the *Theaetetus* had been used by Plato for the
intercourse of the highest part of the soul with truth or reality.
Socrates in the *Republic* (490A) says that the true lover of knowledge strives towards reality and cannot rest among appearances.
His passion (ἔρως) will not be blunted nor cease until he lays hold
upon true being with the kindred part of his soul, whereby he
approaches and is married (πλησιάσας καὶ μιγείς) with reality,
begets (γεννήσας) intelligence and truth, and gains knowledge,
true life and nourishment. So only will he cease from travail
(ὠδῖνος). So again in the *Symposium* (212A) the ascent to the
vision of the Beautiful ends in a marriage of the soul with truth
and the begetting of true virtue. The question now put to the
idealists may be interpreted as meaning : Is this marriage of the
soul with reality mere metaphor ? Is not something analogous
to the marriage of sense with its objects involved in the conception
of knowledge ? How else can we overcome that sharp separation
of the thinking soul in our world from the unchanging world of
Forms, which Parmenides had pointed out as threatening Socrates'
presentation of his theory of Forms ?

The subsequent argument may be understood as showing that
Plato, though he still held that the Forms must be changeless, has
become aware that he ought not any longer to speak as if the Forms
were the whole of reality. Life, soul, and intelligence do not exist
only in our world of Becoming ; they too must be real. The sort
of change that they imply must have a real existence. Again,
our own souls, if they are immortal and akin to the Forms, must
be real, though they animate bodies in time and space. Life is
not motion in space or the modification of physical qualities. It is
spiritual movement. In the *Phaedrus* Plato has defined the soul
as that which moves itself and is the source of all other motion ;
and he will repeat this in the *Laws*. Spiritual motions—thoughts,
desires, feelings, etc.—are prior to all physical motions, and they
reside in the soul of the universe and in our own souls. This is
the motion which the idealists are required to admit into ' that

which is perfectly real '. Just as the reformed materialist was induced to surrender the mark of tangibility and enlarge his conception of the real to include some bodiless things, so the reformed idealist must surrender the mark of changelessness and allow that the real includes spiritual motion, as well as the unchanging Forms.

The question whether knowing and being known do not involve something analogous to the physical intercourse of perception seems to be left unanswered. The Stranger neither asserts this nor denies it. In this Battle of the Gods and Giants Plato stands between the two camps. Looking down upon the material world as conceived by the Atomists, he sees a disorderly chaos of atomic bodies, each with its shape filled with that impenetrable solid stuff which the Atomist called ' being ' or substance. In his own theory of matter as stated in the *Timaeus* he pulverises this alleged being and reduces it to a moving process, the restless change of qualitative ' powers '. Thus he describes the contents of space, ' the nurse of becoming ', before the creator imposes form and number in the distinct geometrical figures of the primary bodies.[1] Looking in the other direction at the heaven of bodiless intelligible Forms which he had himself created, again he sees a pattern of Forms, each with its peculiar character, fixed in the immobility of Eleatic ' being '. But is this pattern, as his earlier language had constantly implied, the whole of the real ? In the *Republic* itself knowledge is compared to vision, and without light the eye has not ' the power of seeing ' nor its object ' the power of being seen '. The light comes from a source that is ' beyond being '. Perhaps what is here in his mind may be illustrated by Shelley's image of the dome of many-coloured glass that stains the white radiance of eternity. The Forms are like the pattern of colours on the dome, but reality

[1] *Timaeus* 52D. Space contains the μορφαί (characters or qualities, not shapes ') of the four elements, and is filled with their unbalanced ' powers ' (δυνάμεις), before the creator διεσχηματίσατο εἴδεσι καὶ ἀριθμοῖς. I believe that a careful study of Plato's account of matter in the *Timaeus* 47E ff. leads to the conclusion that he does not reduce matter simply to space, figured by the geometrical shapes characteristic of the four primary bodies. These shapes are not empty, but filled with ' motions ' or changes, which are δυνάμεις (52E), having the power of acting on one another and on the organs of sentient creatures. Such, in the living world, is the irrational element which never exists without the other element of divine order, though it is mythically pictured as a pre-existing chaos (30A, 52D). The changes must be attributed to the irrational element in the world's soul ' before ' it is reduced to order by Reason. They replace the alleged solid impenetrable and unchanging stuff of the Democritean atom, which involves the reduction of all change to locomotion of unchanging bodies and excludes all life from what is declared to be the sole reality (τὸ ὄν, for space, though it exists, is ' not-being '). If this interpretation is correct, the agreement of the *Timaeus* with the *Theaetetus* and *Sophist* is complete.

must include the radiance that shines through them.   The word
'intercourse' suggests the type of relation that subsists in social
fellowship—not action on a purely passive object, but action that
meets with a response.   There is an intelligence in the world, which
answers to our intelligence, and of which, the *Philebus* declares, our
intelligence is a part.   How exactly that intelligence or life or soul
is related to the Forms is a question that can only be answered in
the figurative language of the *Timaeus*.

Here the review of all the philosophers' conceptions of the real
comes to an end.   We set out upon this survey in order to seek a
justification for speaking of *eidola*—things that are not wholly real
and yet have some sort of existence—and also of falsity in thought
and speech.   The reader might now expect that the discussion of
reality as conceived by the materialist and the idealist should lead
on to an explanation of *eidola*, how they are related to ' the perfectly
real '.   But this hope is disappointed.   The next division of the
dialogue has little or no bearing on that metaphysical problem.
What Plato intended we can only guess ; but this looks like another
loose thread, dropped here to be taken up in the projected *Philosopher*.   The reader must turn for further enlightenment to the
Timaeus.   The idealist who has learnt that reality is not only an
unchanging pattern of Forms but contains also a divine intelligence
with the living power of a moving cause, will there find the world
of nature represented as fashioned by that power on the model of
the Forms, and discover what elements of reality may belong to
the moving images of time, in what sense they can partake of being
and of not-being.   But the discussion in the *Sophist* is diverted
here to the other problem of falsity in thought and speech, which
is to be solved at the close (259E ff.).

249D–251A.   *Transition.   What does the idealist mean by ' real ' ?*

This diversion is effected in the next, transitional, section.   Here
the term ' Reality ' or ' Being ' (τὸ ὄν) shifts its meaning.   Like
' reality ' or ' existence ' in English, this term can mean either what
it meant in the last section, ' that which is real ', ' that which exists ',
or what it will mean in the next section, the ' realness ' or ' existence '
which real things or existents have.   Using the same term without
pointing out that its meaning shifts, the Stranger develops an argument which leads apparently to a contradiction of the results we
have just reached, namely, that Reality must include all that is
unchanging and all that is in change, ' both at once '.   We shall now
be led to the admission that ' Reality is not motion and rest both
at once ' ; ' the real is by virtue of its own nature neither at rest
nor in motion '.   The reader who, like Theaetetus, does not see that

' Reality ' has ceased to mean ' the real ' and now means ' realness '
will agree to the Stranger's concluding remark that Reality is as
puzzling as unreality.

The Stranger points out that our conclusion, ' the real consists
of all that is unchangeable and all that is in change ', is parallel to
the early physicist's statement, ' the real consists of the Hot and the
Cold '. Just as we put it to them that the term ' real ' does not mean
' hot ' or ' cold ' or ' hot-and-cold ', but has a distinct sense that
should be defined, so now we put it to the Idealists that ' real '
(realness) does not mean ' moving ' or ' at rest ' but is a third thing
of which Motion and Rest themselves both partake. We have not
yet got a definition of its meaning.

249D. STR. Well then, does it not look now as if we had fairly
caught reality within the compass of our description ?

THEAET. Certainly it does.

STR. And yet [1]—oh dear, Theaetetus, what if I say after
all that I think it is just at this point that we shall come to
see how baffling this question of reality is ?

E. THEAET. How so ? Why do you say that ?

STR. My good friend, don't you see that now we are wholly
in the dark about it, though we fancy we are talking good
sense ?

THEAET. I certainly thought so, and I don't at all understand how we can be deceived about our condition.

STR. Then consider these last conclusions of ours more
carefully, and whether, when we agree to them, we might

250. not fairly be posed with the same question we put earlier to
those who said that the sum of things ' really is ' Hot and
Cold.

THEAET. You must remind me what that question was.

STR. By all means ; and I will try to do it by questioning
you in the same way as I questioned them, so that we may
get a little further at the same time.

THEAET. Very good.

STR. Come along then. When you speak of Movement and
Rest, these are things completely opposed to one another,
aren't they ?

THEAET. Of course.

---

[1] The corrupt βαβαὶ μέντ' ἂν ἄρα has not been convincingly emended. Since
ὡς can hardly be the exclamatory ὥs, Campbell's citation of *Rep.* 361D is
irrelevant. I conjecture : βαβαὶ μέντοι, ‹τί› ἂν ἄρα ‹φ›ῶ, Θεαίτητε, ὡς . . .
βαβαὶ μέντοι is justified by βαβαὶ ἄρα, *Philebus* 23E. Θεαίτητε without the usual
ὦ is used at 218A after a vowel, to avoid hiatus, and here it fills the hiatus
between φῶ (or λέγω) and ὡς (or ὅτι). For τί ἂν φῶ, cf. τί ἂν ἔωμεν, 252D.

250.   STR.   At the same time you say of both and of each sever-
         ally, that they are real ?
  B.   THEAET.   I do.
         STR.   And when you admit that they are real, do you mean
         that either or both are in movement ?
         THEAET.   Certainly not.
         STR.   Then, perhaps, by saying both are real you mean
         they are both at rest ?
         THEAET.   No, how could I ?
         STR.   So, then, you conceive of reality (realness) as a third
         thing over and above these two ; and when you speak of
         both as being real, you mean that you are taking both move-
         ment and rest together as embraced by reality ¹ and fixing
         your attention on their common association with reality ?
  C.   THEAET.   It does seem as if we discerned reality as a third
         thing, when we say that movement and rest are real.
         STR.   So reality is not motion and rest ' both at once ', but
         something distinct from them.
         THEAET.   Apparently.
         STR.   In virtue of its own nature, then, reality is neither at
         rest nor in movement.
         THEAET.   I suppose so.

The phrase ' both at once ' (συναμφότερον) is meant to recall
our previous conclusion, ' Reality or the sum of things is both at
once (συναμφότερα)—all that is unchangeable and all that is in
change '.   Now we say that reality is not motion and change both at
once ; the real, in virtue of its own nature, is neither at rest nor in
motion.   This appears to Theaetetus to be a contradiction ; but
it is not so.   The first conclusion meant that the Real, or the sum
of things that are real, includes both things that are changeless
and things that change.   Our present conclusion means that Reality
(realness),—the Form with which the two other Forms, Motion and
Rest, are associated or combined in the judgments ' Motion is real ',
' Rest is real '—does not include as part of its content or meaning
either ' being in motion ' or ' being at rest ', but is a third distinct
Form.   Hence it is not true to say that the Real ' by virtue of its
own nature '—the real, *qua* real—either is at rest or is in motion.
If ' to be real ' implied either ' being at rest ' or ' being in motion ',
evidently the real could not include both moving and unchanging
things.   This conclusion is in entire harmony with the earlier one.
   The trained Academic reader, accustomed to think of Platonic
Forms, would see that the meaning of ' Reality ' has shifted from

¹ Taking περιεχομένην συλλαβὼν together (Campbell).

' the real ' to ' realness '. But the next sentences describe the natural confusion of mind of the ordinary reader and of Theaetetus himself, who is not alive to the change of meaning.

250C. STR. If so, where is the mind to turn for help if one wants to reach any clear and certain conclusion about reality ?

THEAET. Where indeed ?

STR. It seems hard to find help in any quarter. If a thing
D. is not in movement, how can it not be at rest ? Or how can what is not in any way at rest fail to be in movement ? Yet reality is now revealed to us as outside both alternatives. Is that possible ?

THEAET. As impossible as anything could be.

STR. Then there is one thing that ought to be remembered at this point.

THEAET. And that is——?

STR. That we were completely puzzled when we were asked to what the name ' unreal ' should be applied. You remember ?

THEAET. Of course.

E. STR. And now we are in no less perplexity about reality ?

THEAET. In even greater, I should say, sir, if that be possible.

STR. Let us take it, then, that our difficulty is now completely stated. But since reality and unreality are equally puzzling, there is henceforward some hope that any light, whether dim or bright, thrown upon the one will illuminate
251. the other to an equal degree ; and if, on the other hand, we cannot get sight of either, at any rate we will make the best we can of it under these conditions and force a passage through the argument with both elbows at once.[1]

THEAT. Very good.

---

[1] διωθεῖιͅθαι with an accusative can mean (1) to fend off : *Thuc.* ii. 84, of ships, τοῖς κόντοις διωθοῦντο. *Theaet.* 163C, σκόπει πῇ αὐτὸ διωσόμεθα (' how shall we fend off this argument ? ') ; (2) to force one's way through : διωθεῖσθαι τὸν ὄχλον, Xen. If the word has either of these senses here and ἀμφοῖν is dative, it is hard to see how we can use reality and unreality as instruments when we cannot ' see ' them. Against the interpretation ' force a passage for the argument between both at once ' (ἀμφοῖν gen. governed by διά in διωθεῖσθαι, Campbell, Diès) is the word ἅμα. Otherwise (if the construction could be paralleled) the metaphor of a ship between two invisible rocks is appropriate. Perhaps εὐτρεπέστατα might suit it better than εὐπρεπέστατα. I understand, however, ἀμφοῖν (τοῖν χεροῖν) with no reference to μηδέτερον. Stephanus (Didot, 1831–56, *s.v.* ἄμφω, 282C) : *absolute interdum ponitur* ἀμφοῖν, *subaudita* χεροῖν, *idque more Attico, ut ap. Hom.* ἀμφοτέραις *et* ἀμφοτέρῃσι *sub.* χεροί. He cites *Sophist* 226A, οὐ τῇ ἑτέρᾳ (*sc.* χειρί) ληπτέον. Οὐκοῦν ἀμφοῖν χρή, and instances of the similar omission of ποδοῖν and ὤτα.

The Stranger's words, ' let us take it that our difficulty is now completely stated ', indicate that all that has gone before is a statement of problems, with some hints towards their solution.   Faithful to Socrates' method, Plato has reduced the reader to a state of perplexity that will make him eager for such explanations as are now to come.   At the same time, under the mask of an apparent contradiction, he has changed the subject from a metaphysical consideration of the nature of the real to a different field, which we should call Logic.   Our attention is now fixed on the three Forms, Reality (or Existence [1]), Motion, Rest.   We are to take these Forms in isolation from any existing things that may partake of them and indeed from everything else, and consider in what ways they ' combine ' with one another or refuse to combine.

II. The Combination of Forms and the Problem of Negative Statements

The purpose of the coming section (251A–259D) is to clear up confusions about negative statements containing the words ' is not ' —negative, not false statements.   In particular there was the fallacy that every negative statement denies the existence of something.   It was necessary to show that such a statement as ' Motion is not Rest ' does not deny the existence of either Rest or Motion, but only means that Motion is not the same as Rest, or Motion is *other than* Rest.   Everything in the world that is other than Rest can be negatively described as ' that which *is not* Rest ', but none the less it exists and may be just as real as Rest.   So we succeed in finding a sense in which ' that which is not (so and so) ' exists, or has being.   The conclusion will be the disproof (promised at 241D) of Parmenides' two complementary dogmas : ' That which is, cannot in any sense not be ' and ' That which is not, cannot in any sense be '.

This result is not all that is conveyed in the long discussion of the combination of Forms.   In the middle of it comes a description of Dialectic, the task of the philosopher, who is to trace out the pattern of the world of Forms by his methods of Collection and Division. The whole section is concerned solely with that world and the relations that subsist between the Forms themselves, and are reflected in true statements that we can make about them.   The Stranger is, in fact, fulfilling the wish expressed by Socrates in the *Parmenides*, when he said it would interest him if anyone could show that the problem of one thing having many names and

---

[1] The shift will be marked in the translation by the use of ' existence ' instead of ' reality ' for οὐσία, τὸ ὄν.   ' Exists ' is a more natural word for that meaning of ' is ' which we are going to distinguish from others.

participating in many Forms, which his theory was to solve, has its counterpart within the world of Forms itself.[1]

251A–C. *Exclusion of the trivial question, how one individual thing can have many names*

The opening paragraph makes it clear that we shall be concerned only with the relations of Forms to one another, not with the old question of the participation of an individual concrete thing in many Forms. Once more that question is impatiently dismissed as not meriting further discussion.[2]

The transition here necessarily seems a little abrupt, because the shift to a fresh set of problems has been disguised by the apparent contradiction which has reduced Theaetetus to perplexity. The link of thought is : Being and Not-being have proved to be equally puzzling. Let us now consider statements (λόγοι) in which the words ' is ' and ' is not ' occur, and see if we can discover how Motion and Rest can both *be*, and yet Being itself can *not-be* either moving or at rest. So we pass to statements in which we ' give names to things '.

251A. STR. Let us explain, then, how it is that we call the same thing—whatever is in question at the moment—by several names.

THEAET. For instance ? Give me an example.

STR. Well, when we speak of a man we give him many additional names : we attribute to him colours and shapes and sizes and defects and good qualities ; and in all these and countless other statements we say he is not merely

B. a ' man ' but also ' good ' and any number of other things. And so with everything else : we take any given thing as one and yet speak of it as many and by many names.

THEAET. True.

STR. And thereby, I fancy, we have provided a magnificent entertainment for the young and for some of their elders who have taken to learning late in life. Anyone can take a hand in the game and at once object that many things cannot be one, nor one thing many ; indeed, they delight in forbidding us to speak of a man as ' good ' ; we must

C. only speak of a good as good, and of the man as man. I imagine, Theaetetus, you often meet with these enthusiasts, sometimes elderly men who, being poorly endowed with intelligence, gape with wonder at these discoveries and fancy

[1] See Introd., p. 11.
[2] It was dismissed at *Parm.* 129A ff. as solved by the earlier statement of the Theory of Forms, and will be described as ' childish ' at *Philebus* 14D.

251C. they have lighted here on the very treasure of complete wisdom.[1]

THEAET. I have indeed.

It is widely agreed among scholars who allow Plato to take notice of his contemporaries that the phrase 'old men who have taken to learning late in life' is pointed at Antisthenes. We know so little of Antisthenes that the reference cannot be taken as certain. The words would fit Euthydemus and his brother Dionysodorus, who do put forward the view here mentioned.[2] On the other hand, it was suggested by Schleiermacher that Antisthenes was attacked under the name of these Eristics. He had been a pupil of the rhetorician Gorgias, and had opened a school after Socrates' death, at which date he can hardly have been under fifty. He may have developed an interest in what we call logical questions late in life.

The theory here dismissed as trivial objects to calling one thing by many names, because one thing cannot be many nor many one. We must not say ' this man is good ' but only that ' a good is good ', ' a man is man '—one name for one thing. This is not a ' denial of predication ', but rather a theory of predication (if we are to use that term), and one which is not altogether contemptible.

The theory has been brought into relation with the doctrine ' dreamt ' by Socrates at *Theaetetus* 201E (p. 143) ; but it may be independent. It can be stated as follows. A good white man is a complex thing, with three parts, each of which has its own proper name. ' Good ' is the name of this goodness which exists here, ' man ' is the name of this man, and so on. I may call the complex thing a ' good white man ', or I may call each elementary constituent by its own name ; but I ought not to say ' this man is good ' : the name good belongs, not to him, but to his goodness. Antisthenes, we are told by Aristotle,[3] ' showed his simplicity by his contention that nothing should be spoken of except by its proper verbal expression (*logos*), one expression for one thing '. If *logos* here includes not only many-worded formulas, such as ' good white man ', but also single names, Antisthenes' doctrine may be the same as the theory in the *Sophist*.

Plato would reply that a common name is not simply the name of this individual thing and others like it, but has a universal meaning, which is a unique Form. ' This man is good ' means that this thing partakes of the Form, Good. There is nothing against one thing partaking of any number of Forms. It is mere pedantry to object

---

[1] Cf. *Philebus*, 15E, ἡσθεὶς ὥς τινα σοφίας εὑρηκὼς θησαυρόν.

[2] *Euthyd.* 272B, γέροντε ὄντε ἠρξάσθην ταύτης τῆς σοφίας.

[3] *Metaph.* 1024b, 32.

that ' good ' is strictly the name only of the goodness present in this man. Why should we not use the compendious form of words ' This man is good ' or ' partakes of goodness ' ? This answer has been sufficiently indicated in the *Parmenides*. What here concerns us is not statements about individual things (such as the theory contemplates) but the problems presented by statements about Forms. How and to what extent can Forms partake of one another ?

251C–252E. *Proof that some Forms will combine, others will not*

The Stranger's next words indicate that this question is addressed not only to elderly pedants but to all philosophers.

251C. STR. Well then, we want our argument to be addressed
  D. to all alike who have ever had anything to say about existence ; so let us take it that the questions we shall put now are intended not only for these people but for all those others whom we have been conversing with earlier.
  THEAET. And what are the questions ?
  STR. Are we not to attach Existence to Motion and Rest, nor anything else to anything else, but rather to treat them in our discourse as incapable of any blending or participation in one another ? Or are we to lump them all together as capable of association with one another ? Or shall we say that this is true of some and not of others ? Which of
  E. these possibilities shall we say they prefer, Theaetetus ?
  THEAET. I am not prepared to answer that on their behalf.
  STR. Then why not answer the questions one at a time and see what are the consequences in each case ?
  THEAET. Very good.

The word translated ' combine ' (κοινωνία) happens to be the same that was used in the metaphysical section for our ' intercourse ' with the objects of perception or of thought ; but the two meanings are entirely distinct. The word itself means no more than ' to have relations with ' something, and the relations now to be described between Forms are not psychological. A Form is not imagined as perceiving or thinking of another Form when it ' combines ' with it. The relation is expressed by other metaphors used synonymously. In a positive statement we are said to ' connect ' (προσάπτειν) the two Forms. The Forms themselves are said to ' mix ' or ' blend ' (συμμείγνυσθαι) or to be incapable of blending (ἄμεικτα) ; to ' fit together ' (συναρμόττειν opposed to ἀναρμοστεῖν 253A) ; to be ' consonant ' (συμφωνεῖν 253B) ; to ' accept ' or ' receive ' one another (δέχεσθαι) ; to ' partake ' of one another (μεταλαμβάνειν

255

or μετέχειν). The contrary of this combination is sometimes
called 'division', 'disjunction' (διαίρεσις) or 'separation'
(διακρίνεσθαι).[1] Plato, here as elsewhere, wisely refuses to allow
any one metaphor to harden into a technical term. Nearly all
language is metaphorical, and every metaphor has misleading
associations. By varying the word, Plato helps the reader to free
his conception of the relation intended from such associations and
to escape the illusion that philosophical language can be really
precise and unambiguous. The following definitions, however, may
be useful. Two Forms are said to 'combine' when they stand
(eternally) in such a relation that their names can occur in a *true
affirmative statement* of a certain type. For example, 'Motion exists'
means that the Form Motion blends with the Form Existence.
A *true negative statement* such as 'Motion does not rest' reflects
the fact that the two Forms, Motion and Rest, are (eternally)
incompatible—refuse to blend. There are also true negative statements of the type 'Motion is not Existence' or 'Motion is not Rest'
which express the fact that the Forms in question are *different*,
though they may not be incompatible (for Motion is compatible
with Existence). These definitions are in terms of statements that
we can make about Forms ; hence the proviso that the statements
must be true. We can, indeed, connect two names in a false statement, *e.g.* 'Motion is Rest' ; but the Forms referred to do not
combine. The combinations and disjunctions exist eternally among
the Forms themselves. They are reflected only in true statements.

The relation between Forms that combine is also called 'participation' ; but it must not be assumed that this relation is the same
that subsists between an individual thing (*e.g.* a man) and the Form
(Man) that he 'partakes of'. Plato nowhere implies that the Form
Motion partakes of the Form Existence, or the Form Man partakes
of the Form Animal, in the same way as this man partakes of the
Form Man. He uses the same word with his usual disregard for
precise terminology, and he nowhere gives any explicit account of
either relation. It seems obvious, however, that he cannot have
regarded the two relations as the same. The word κοινωνεῖν,
as well as μετέχειν, is used of individuals which 'share in' a common
Form ; but he would not describe a man as 'blended with' the
Form Man. Further, 'participation' as between Forms is a symmetrical relation. At 255c, D Existents (ὄντα) are divided into two
Forms or Kinds (τὸ καθ' αὐτό and τὸ πρὸς ἄλλο) and then Existence

[1] *Parm.* 129E, συγκεράννυσθαι καὶ διακρίνεσθαι. Aristotle, π. ἑρμ i, uses σύνθεσις
(' putting together ') for the combination of two terms in an affirmative
proposition, and διαίρεσις for the disjoining of the two in a negative proposition.

is described as ' partaking of ' both these subordinate Forms. So
the generic Form partakes of (blends with) the specific Form no
less than the specific partakes of the generic. This consideration
also shows that the relation is not that of subject to predicate ; for
that is not symmetrical. The Aristotelian terms ' subject', ' predicate ' and ' copula ' should not be used at all to describe what is in
Plato's mind. This will become clearer as we proceed.

That the terms whose combination or non-combination is discussed here are Forms is clearly stated by the Stranger where he
refers to the results obtained : ' Since we have agreed that *kinds* [1]
(γένη) are related in the same way (as letters or musical sounds)
as regards blending' (253B). It is true that from the combination or non-combination of Forms among themselves, consequences
follow with regard to the truth and falsity of statements about
individual things. For instance, if the Form Motion did not partake
of Existence, then no statement implying that a moving thing or
a particular motion exists would be true. Some such consequences
are referred to, but we are actually discussing Forms, not individual
things.

The three possible alternatives with regard to the extent of
combination among Forms are now considered in turn. The first
is that no Form combines with any other, which means that no
affirmative statement about a Form is true. This alternative is
analogous to Antisthenes' view that a thing must not be called
by any name but its own. Apply that to Forms, and the result
is that a Form can only be named ; nothing can be said about it.

251E.   STR.   And first, if you like, let us suppose them to say that
           nothing has any capacity for combination with anything
           else for any purpose.   Then Movement and Rest will have
           no part in Existence.
252.   THEAET. No.
           STR.   Well then, will either of them exist, if it has no
           association with Existence ?
           THEAET. No, it will not exist.
           STR.   That admission seems to make short work of all
           theories ; it upsets at one blow those who have a universe
           in motion, and those who make it a motionless unity, and
           all who say their realities exist in Forms that are always
           the same in all respects [2] ; for they all attribute existence

[1] Here, as elsewhere, the term ' kind ' (*genos*) is used indifferently as a
synonym of Form (*eidos*).
[2] The three classes mentioned above (249B) at the end of the argument
with the idealists. The earlier philosophers are recalled in the next speech.

252.   to things, some saying they really *are* in movement, some
        that they really *are* at rest.
        THEAET. Quite so.
B.   STR. And further, those who make all things come together
        at one time and separate at another, whether they bring
        innumerable things into a unity and out of a unity,[1] or divide
        things into and combine them out of a limited set of elements;
        no matter whether they suppose this to happen in alternation
        or to be going on all the time—however it may be, all this
        would be meaningless if there is no blending at all.[2]
        THEAET. True.
        STR. Moreover, the greatest absurdity of all results from
        pursuing the theory of those very people who will not allow
        one thing to share in the quality of another and so be called
        by its name.
C.   THEAET. How so ?
        STR. Why, in referring to anything they cannot help using
        the words ' being ' and ' apart ' and ' from the others ' and
        ' by itself ' and any number more. They cannot refrain
        from these expressions or from connecting them in their
        statements, and so need not wait for others to refute them ;
        the foe is in their own household, as the saying goes, and,
        like that queer fellow Eurycles,[3] they carry about with them
        wherever they go a voice in their own bellies to contradict
        them.
D.   THEAET. True ; your comparison is very much to the pur-
        pose.

According to the theory of Socrates' ' dream ' in the *Theaetetus*
(201D, p. 143), each simple element can only be named ; you cannot
add that it ' is ' or call it ' that ' or ' each ', etc. These terms are
' running round ' and being attached to everything ; whereas the
element can only be called by its proper name. Here the Stranger
remarks that the (perhaps kindred) theory of the elderly pedants,
which as applied to Forms would mean that every Form is by itself
apart from all the rest and refuses to combine, cannot be stated
without self-contradiction.

---

[1] Cf. Ar., *Met.* 984*a*, 10, συγκρινόμενα καὶ διακρινόμενα εἰς ἕν τε καὶ ἐξ ἑνός (of
Empedocles' four elements).
[2] ' No blending ' means no blending of Forms. If no Form partakes of
any other, the statements that ' Motion exists ' and ' Rest exists ' are either
false or meaningless. If that is so, it follows that physical things cannot
partake of Motion or of Rest ; and this is fatal to all cosmologies.
[3] A ventriloquist, mentioned by Aristophanes.

Ritter [1] understands Plato to assert here that there is no thinking except in the form of a judgment connecting a subject and a predicate and no sort of actuality or determination, to be grasped by thought, except in relation to other determinations. This, he says, implies that no word by itself has any meaning, but only when combined with other words in a judgment. Accordingly, ' Being ' has no meaning save in a judgment, either as subject or as predicate, or as determination of subject or predicate, each of which always pre-supposes the other. Burnet [2] echoes this : ' The solution is briefly that *is* and *is not* have no meaning except in judgements or pre-dications (λόγοι).' ' Being, Rest, and Motion . . . have no meaning except in a judgement.'

I cannot see that Plato says, or implies, anything of the sort. The point is difficult to argue, because ' meaning ' is an extremely ambiguous word.[3] But Plato's view of a ' meaning ' is simple. The name ' circle ' which I now utter *means* the Form ' Circle ', an eternal and unchanging object of thought, which we can know and (if it be complex) define. The name is an articulate sound conventionally attached to this Form. Hence, if two people speak the same language, when one utters the sound ' circle ', the other will have the same meaning more or less clearly before his mind and understand the sound. Plato nowhere suggests that the name ' circle ' has no meaning by itself and only acquires a meaning when, and for so long as, someone thinks of the Form and utters its name together with other names in a statement. All that he asserts here is that, unless some Forms at least have to one another the relation he calls ' combining ' or ' blending ', no affirmative statement about any Form can be true. Hence you cannot even say that ' every Form stands apart by itself ', for all these words have meanings, and unless those meanings are combined in a fact corresponding to the statement, the statement must be either false or meaningless.

The misunderstanding may be due to the false notion that Plato here means by ' Being ' the copula, which is supposed to connect subject and predicate and to have no meaning except in a judgment. But Plato does not speak of subjects or predicates or of the copula. ' Being ' in this context clearly means the Form, Existence. And even if ' Being ' meant the copula, it is hard to see why ' Rest ' and ' Motion ' and all other words should be declared to have no meaning save in a judgment. The whole notion seems to be entirely unfounded.

The Stranger next quickly dismisses the second alternative.

[1] *Neue Untersuchen* (1910), p. 55 ; *Platon*, vol. ii, p. 189.
[2] *Gk. Phil.* I, 282 ff.
[3] See Ogden and Richards, *The Meaning of Meaning*.

252D.   STR.   Well, suppose we allow that all are capable of combining with one another.

THEAET.   Even I can dispose of that suggestion.

STR.   How?

THEAET.   Because then Movement itself would come to a complete standstill, and again Rest itself would be in movement, if each were to supervene upon the other.

STR.   And that is to the last degree impossible—that Movement should come to be at rest and Rest be in motion?

THEAET.   Surely.

STR.   Then only the third choice is left.

THEAET.   Yes.

E.   STR.   And observe that one of these alternatives must be true: either all will blend, or none, or some will and some will not.

THEAET.   Certainly.

STR.   And two of the three have been found impossible.

THEAET.   Yes.

STR.   Whoever, then, wishes to give a right answer will assert the remaining one.

THEAET.   Quite so.

252E–253C.   *The texture of philosophic discourse*

Some Forms will blend, some not. This means that some affirmative, and some negative, statements (of the types under consideration) about Forms are true. These true statements will make up the texture of philosophic discourse—that ' dialectical ' argument which is entirely about Forms.[1] The Stranger next compares this texture of discourse with the texture of sounds in speech and music. In both these cases we find elements that will combine and others that will not.

252E.   STR.   Then since some will blend, some not, they might be
253.   said to be in the same case with the letters of the alphabet. Some of these cannot be conjoined, others will fit together.

THEAET.   Of course.

STR.   And the vowels are specially good at combination— a sort of bond pervading them all, so that without a vowel the others cannot be fitted together.

THEAET.   That is so.

STR.   And does everyone [2] know which can combine with which, or does one need an art to do it rightly?

---

[1] *Rep.* vi, 511B. The phrase ' texture of discourse ' is based on Plato's later remark that ' all discourse depends on the weaving together (συμπλοκή) of Forms ' (p. 300).

[2] In Burnet's text (1899) πῶς is misprinted for πᾶς.

253. THEAET. It needs art.

STR. And that art is——?

THEAET. Grammar.

B. STR. Again, is it not the same with sounds of high or low pitch ? To possess the art of recognising the sounds that can or can not be blended is to be a musician ; if one doesn't understand that, one is unmusical.

THEAET. True.

STR. And we shall find differences of the same sort between competence and incompetence in any other art.

THEAET. Of course.

STR. Well, now that we have agreed that the Kinds [1] stand towards one another in the same way as regards blending, is not some science needed as a guide on the voyage of discourse, if one is to succeed in pointing out which Kinds are

C. consonant, and which are incompatible with one another ; also, whether there are certain Kiuds that pervade them all and connect them so that they can blend, and again, where there are divisions (separations), whether there are certain others that traverse wholes and are responsible for the division ?

THEAET. Surely some science is needed—perhaps the most important of all.

The interpretation of the Stranger's last speech is vital, if we would understand the description of the science of Dialectic or Philosophy which is to follow. The Stranger is speaking of the whole texture of philosophical discourse, the actual process of conversation aiming at the discovery of truth. The metaphor of the voyage of discourse (' travelling through arguments ') recalls the terms used in the *Republic* [2] of Dialectic, which is concerned solely with Forms. Here the object is ' to point out which Forms are consonant with which, and which are incompatible '. The whole texture of philosophic discourse will consist of affirmative and negative statements about Forms, which should correctly represent their eternal combination or disjunction in the nature of things.

Specially important is the analogy drawn in the last clauses between the vowels which ' pervade ' (διὰ πάντων κεχώρηκεν) the whole texture of speech and certain Forms which pervade (διὰ πάντων) the texture of discourse and enable Forms to blend. These

---

[1] ' Kinds ' (γένη), synonymous with ' Forms ' (εἴδη), here as elsewhere.

[2] *Soph.* 253B, διὰ τῶν λόγων πορεύεσθαι. *Rep.* 510B, ψυχὴ . . . οὐκ ἐπ' ἀρχὴν πορευομένη ἀλλ' ἐπὶ τελευτήν ; 511B, the metaphor of climbing, ἐπιβάσεις, ἰών, καταβαίνῃ ; 517B, τὴν ἄνω ἀνάβασιν ; 533C, ἡ διαλεκτικὴ μέθοδος μόνη ταύτῃ πορεύεται ; 534C, ἀπτῶτι τῷ λόγῳ διαπορεύηται, etc.

pervasive Forms are obviously the meanings of certain words used in affirmative statements. They are, in fact, the meanings of the word ' is ', which we shall distinguish presently.

There are also certain Forms which ' traverse wholes and are responsible for the division of them ' (διαίρεσις). These disjoining Forms are the meanings of the words ' is not ' in true negative statements. They correspond to the ' divisions of wholes '. The phrase ' traversing wholes ' (δι' ὅλων) must be distinguished from the phrase ' pervading all ' (διὰ πάντων) used of the conjunctive Forms, the meaning of which is determined by the description of the vowels as ' running through all ' the letters (διὰ πάντων κεχώρηκεν 253A). The disjunctive Forms that appear in ' divisions ' for which they are responsible are said to ' traverse wholes '. ' Wholes ' means Forms considered as complexes divisible into parts (or species). The disjunctive Forms correspond to lines of division either passing *between* such complexes and separating them or passing *through* them and separating their parts. These expressions will recur in the coming account of dialectical method.

253C–254B. *Description of the science of Dialectic*

Finally, it has been agreed that, to guide the course of philosophic conversation as here described, a science is needed—a technique and the body of knowledge attained by it. This science is now identified as the philosopher's science of correctly dividing the structure of reality according to those Forms or Kinds which are the meanings referred to in philosophic discourse. This knowledge will guide the progress of actual discourse as the musician's knowledge of harmony guides him in the composition and discourse of actual music.

253C.   STR. And what name shall we give to this science ? Or —good gracious, Theaetetus, have we stumbled unawares upon the free man's knowledge [1] and, in seeking for the Sophist, chanced to find the Philosopher first ?

THEAET. How do you mean ?

D.   STR. Dividing according to Kinds, not taking the same Form for a different one or a different one for the same—is not that the business of the science of Dialectic ?

THEAET. Yes.

STR. And the man who can do that discerns clearly *one* Form everywhere extended throughout many, where each one lies apart, and *many* Forms, different from one another,

---

[1] Cf. the comparison of the philosopher to the free man, *Theaet.* 172D ff. (p. 83).

253D. embraced from without by one Form ; and again *one* Form connected in a unity through many wholes, and *many* Forms, entirely marked off apart. That means knowing how to
E. distinguish,[1] Kind by Kind, in what ways the several Kinds can or can not combine.

THEAET. Most certainly.

STR. And the only person, I imagine, to whom you would allow this mastery of Dialectic is the pure and rightful lover of wisdom.

THEAET. To whom else could it be allowed ?

STR. It is, then, in some such region as this that we shall find the Philosopher now or later, if we should look for him.

254. He too may be difficult to see clearly ; but the difficulty in his case is not the same as in the Sophist's.

THEAET. What is the difference ?

STR. The Sophist takes refuge in the darkness of Not-being, where he is at home and has the knack of feeling his way ; and it is the darkness of the place that makes him so hard to perceive.

THEAET. That may well be.

STR. Whereas the Philosopher, whose thoughts constantly dwell upon the nature of reality, is difficult to see because his region is so bright ; for the eye of the vulgar soul cannot
B. endure to keep its gaze fixed on the divine.

THEAET. That may well be no less true.

STR. Then we will look more closely at the Philosopher presently, if we are still in the mind to do so ; meanwhile clearly we must not loosen our grip on the Sophist until we have studied him thoroughly.

THEAET. I entirely agree.

The imagery of the Cave in the *Republic* is here once more recalled —the dark region of the world of Seeming inside the Cave, and the sunlit region of Reality outside. There seems to be a promise, not fulfilled in the *Sophist* or the *Statesman*, that we shall return to seek the philosopher in his proper home, the world of Forms, with which this account of Dialectic is entirely concerned.

The general sense of that account is clear. The expert in Dialectic will guide and control the course of philosophic discussion by his knowledge of how to ' divide by Kinds ', not confusing one Form with another. He will discern clearly the hierarchy of Forms which

---

[1] Διακρίνειν, an echo of the genus διακριτική, including all the arts described as διαιρετικά , from which we derived earlier the definition of the cathartic *elenchus* of Socrates (226c).

constitutes reality and make out its articulate structure, with which the texture of philosophic discourse must correspond, if it is to express truth. The method is that method of Collection and Division which was announced in the *Phaedrus* and has been illustrated in the *Sophist*. Finally, to discern this structure clearly is the same thing as ' to know how to distinguish in what ways the several Kinds can or can not combine '. In other words, the science will yield the knowledge needed to guide us to true affirmative and negative statements about Forms, of which the whole texture of philosophic discourse should consist.

Before we attempt to interpret in detail the speeches describing Dialectic, it is necessary to clear away certain misconceptions and, above all, to grasp, if we can, how Plato conceived this science and its objects. The whole subsequent discussion of the ' combination ' or ' blending ' of Forms is usually called ' logical ', and with some justification ; but it is very important to make out in what sense Plato can be said to have a Logic, and how his Logic differs from the traditional Logic we have derived from Aristotle.

First, Dialectic is not what is now known as ' Formal Logic '. The identification is suggested by Professor Taylor,[1] who remarks on our passage : ' Logic is here, for the first time in literature, contemplated as an autonomous science with the task of ascertaining the supreme principles of affirmative and negative propositions (the combinations and " separations ").' If ' autonomous ' means that Dialectic is a Formal Logic, concerned with propositions and independent of Ontology (the science concerned with the structure of reality), this statement seems to me misleading. Formal Logic may be described as the study of (1) propositional forms—not actual significant statements, but the patterns or types under which statements can be classified ; (2) the constituents of these propositional forms (subjects, predicates, relations between terms, etc.) ; and (3) formal relations of inference between propositional forms. The beginning of Formal Logic is marked precisely by the introduction of symbols. These were, so far as we know, first used by Aristotle, in such formulas as this :

> If A belongs to all B
> and B belongs to all C
> then A belongs to all C.

The symbols A, B, C are algebraic signs for which you can substitute any one of a whole class of appropriate terms, as any actual numbers can be substituted for the x, y, z of an equation. The introduction of symbols means that attention is now fixed on the form of state-

[1] *Plato* (1926), p. 387.

ments apart from their content. ' A belongs to B ' is not a statement, nor is it either true or false. The blanks must be filled by significant words, to yield a true or false statement. Plato does not use symbols or construct propositional forms. The factors he recognises are these : (1) The immutable structure of Forms or Kinds, eternally combined or disjoined in the system of truth or reality ; these are the meanings, to which common names are conventionally attached. (2) Our thoughts (διάνοια) about these objects, our acquaintance with them, reasonings (λογισμός) about them, judgments (δόξαι) in which such reasonings terminate : all these are mental existents. (3) Statements (λόγοι), the vocal expression of thoughts and judgments, consisting of spoken names and verbs. The meanings of common names and verbs are the Forms. Statements are not propositional forms but actual significant statements, existing only while we utter them. The science of Dialectic does not study formal symbolic patterns to which our statements conform, nor yet these statements themselves. Nor does it study our thoughts or ways of reasoning, apart from the objects we think about. It is not ' Logic ', if Logic means the science either of *logoi* or of *logismoi*. What it does study is the structure of the real world of Forms. Its technique of Collection and Division operates on that structure. It is a method for which some rules are laid down ; but these are rules of correct procedure in making Divisions ; they are not laws of inference or laws of thought. There is no place in this scheme either for ' propositions ' that no one propounds or for the propositional forms of Formal Logic, as distinct from actual significant statements. All the statements analysed in the sequel are actual significant statements about certain ' Kinds '. They are either true or false, and statements such as ' Motion is Rest ' are rejected by simple inspection, not as formally incorrect, but as obviously untrue. All through, Plato is speaking of the real nature of the Kinds mentioned and their actual relations in the structure of reality, not about symbolic patterns under which statements can be classified. There is nothing to show that he had ever conceived of such a science as Formal Logic.

It might be objected that Plato believed in eternal truths, for instance the truths of mathematics. Is not ' The angles of a triangle are equal to two right angles ' a ' proposition ', which, being eternally true, must be independent of my thought of it and of my written or spoken statement ? Plausible as this seems, we must, I think, answer No. If I make the above statement, it must, being true, reflect in some way the fact it refers to. But I may be misled if I start from the verbal statement, analyse its grammatical structure into elements related in certain ways, and then assume that the structure of the fact corresponds, point by point, with the grammatical structure I have analysed. If I finally call the fact so constructed a ' proposition ', I shall be tacitly implying that the structure of the fact answers to the structure of the verbal statement. Suppose, for example, I analyse ' Man is rational ' into a subject ' Man ', a predicate ' rational ', and a link ' is ' coupling the two—the ' copula '. I seem then to have two elements of different kinds (for I shall say that ' subjects ' have certain peculiarities which ' predicates ' have not) and a link tying them together. But it does not follow that the fact my statement reflects consists of two disparate elements and a link between them. That is not how Plato describes the facts he is here concerned with. He says, the Form Man and the Form Rational are combined or blended in reality. When two things—say, two colours—are blended, there is no link coupling them together ; nor is there any suggestion that the two elements are of different sorts, one a ' subject ', the other a ' predicate '. There is nothing but the mixture. The so-called ' copula ' vanishes. It is a trick of grammatical structure, essentially the link between grammatical ' subject ' and ' predicate '. As Plato has nothing to say here of ' subjects ' and ' predicates ', he never mentions the ' copula'. It is, in fact, often dispensed with in Greek. Ὁ ἄνθρωπος λογικός is a complete statement without an ἐστί. This may be the reason why Aristotle says much less about the ' copula ' than English writers, who cannot say ' Man rational ' for ' Man is rational '.

This may not be the end of the matter ; the word ' is ' has several meanings, which we shall presently distinguish. But Plato's language seems to show that he did not imagine eternal truths as existing in the shape of ' propositions ' with a structure answering to the shape of statements. He conceived them as ' mixtures ' in which Forms are blended ; and the word *logos* is reserved for spoken statements. Hence the term ' proposition ' had better be avoided altogether ; and we must realise that Dialectic is not Formal Logic, but the study of the structure of reality—in fact Ontology, for the Forms are the realities (ὄντως ὄντα). In Plato's view the study of patterns of the statements we make would belong to Grammar or to Rhetoric. There is no autonomous science of Logic, distinct on the one hand from Grammar and Rhetoric and on the other from Ontology.

Let us now consider the first part of the sentence describing Dialectic : [1]

[1] The interpretation here offered owes something to Stenzel, *Studien z. Entw. d. plat. Dial.* 62 ff., and to M. Diès' introduction to the dialogue.

' The man who can do that (divide according to Kinds, without confusing one Form with another) discerns clearly *one* Form everywhere extended throughout many, where each one lies apart, and *many* Forms, different from one another, embraced from without by one Form.'

The structure of Forms is conceived as a hierarchy of genera and species, amenable to the methods of Collection and Division. This first half of the sentence refers specially to the preliminary process of Collection, described in the *Phaedrus* as ' taking a synoptic survey of widely scattered Forms (species) and bringing them into a single (generic) Form '.[1] So here there are at first a definite number of Forms [2] (πολλά), ' each one lying apart '. These are the scattered species to be collected, including the specific Form (or Forms) that we wish ultimately to define. The dialectician surveys the collection and ' clearly discerns ' by intuition the common (generic) character ' extended throughout ' them all. So he divines the generic Form that he will take for division. This generic Form he now sees as a unity which is complex, ' embracing ' a number of different Forms, which will figure in the subsequent Division as specific differences or as specific Forms characterised by their differences.

The second half of the sentence is less easy to interpret :

' and again *one* Form connected in a unity through many wholes, and *many* Forms entirely marked off apart '.

As the first half described the results of Collection, this second half appears to describe the results of the subsequent Division. The many Forms, which after Collection were seen to be embraced by a single generic Form, are now seen ' entirely marked off apart '. Division has brought to light all the differences that distinguish them. The indivisible species in which Division terminates are ' entirely separated ' in the sense that they are mutually exclusive and incompatible : Man cannot blend with Ox as both blend with Animal or as Man blends with Biped, Ox with Quadruped. With these many Forms is contrasted the ' one Form connected in a unity through many wholes ' (δι' ὅλων πολλῶν). The term ' wholes ' is applied to the many (specific) Forms because, now that they have been completely defined, they are seen as complexes : each is a whole whose parts are enumerated in the defining formula, such as ' Man is the rational biped Animal '. Finally, through all

---

[1] *Phaedrus* 265D, εἰς μίαν τε ἰδέαν συνορῶντα ἄγειν τὰ πολλαχῇ διεσπαρμένα.
[2] Not ' individuals ', as Campbell imagines. The whole procedure deals with Forms only.

these subordinate wholes—Man, Ox, Horse, etc.—the single generic Form Animal is, as it were, dispersed. It blends with each specific Form, and yet in virtue of its own nature it is ' connected in a unity ' traversing them all.

The Structure of the World of Forms

The extreme compression and consequent obscurity of this account of the field of Dialectic may be explained if we suppose that Plato, as the Stranger's subsequent speeches suggest, intended to analyse the relations of Forms in more detail in the *Philosopher*. Where it stands in the *Sophist*, the account is almost a digression, and Plato may have wished to restrict it to the smallest possible space. It will, however, be convenient to attempt here a picture of the structure of Forms, based on such indications as he gives. This question has a bearing on the problem left over from the *Parmenides* : How and in what sense is a Form both one and many ?

Here it must once more be stated that no satisfactory account of the relations of Platonic Forms can be given in terms of Aristotelian logic. We have seen that Plato was not concerned with proposi- tional forms ; his Dialectic studies realities, and his conception of these realities was radically different from Aristotle's. When Aristotle comes to consider the constituents of propositions—sub- jects and predicates—metaphysical assumptions are involved. There are things—substances—whose nature is such that their names can only stand as subjects ; other things—attributes—whose names can stand as predicates. The most real things in the world are concrete individual substances, having a core of essential being together with that material substrate which prevents them from being anything but subject, and a fringe of inherent and dependent attributes. Specific and generic concepts are not primary sub- stances with an independent existence, not full-blooded realities, but abstractions. As a consequence, the higher we ascend in the hierarchy of genera and species, the further we are from full reality. The higher the term, the poorer in content and the more abstract it becomes. Every proposition, we are told, has a subject and a predicate. The subject proper is the real, independently existing, substance. Predicates are all the things asserted to ' belong to ' a substance, including its species and genus, its qualities, quantity, etc. Finally, these predicates are classed in categories—a set of pigeon-holes to one of which (and only one) any given predicate can be assigned.

Now, all this cannot be foisted upon Plato. His ontology, as Aristotle was not slow to point out, was fundamentally different. The individual members of a class of things existing in time and

268

space are not ' real ' things (ὄντως ὄντα). They become and perish and change ; they are indefinite in number and unknowable. They cannot enter into truths that can be known ; they are not the subjects of the universal truths of science. The goal of Dialectic is not to establish propositions ascribing a predicate to all the individuals in a class. The objective is the definition of an indivisible species—a Form—by genus and specific differences. What we define is not ' all men ' but the unique Form ' Man '. A definition is not a subject-predicate proposition. The many-worded formula ' three-sided plane figure ' is the explicit statement of the complex contents of the Form ' Triangle '. The two expressions are equivalent ; neither is a ' predicate ' of the other. The Platonic statement ' Man (the Form) is Animal (partakes of, blends with the Form Animal) ' is not the same as the statements, ' All men are animals ' or ' Animal (the predicate) belongs to all men (as subjects) '. The Platonic science has nothing to say about ' all men ' or ' some men ' or ' this man '. The only terms it contemplates are Forms.

The question how Plato conceived the relations of Forms to one another presents a peculiar difficulty. His metaphysics are far removed from the unconscious ontology of common sense, embedded in the structure of the Greek language, which fits the Aristotelian view. Yet Plato insists on using ordinary language, and we are reduced to inferring his conception partly from what we know of his metaphysics, partly from the metaphors he employs.

At the head of a Table of Division stands a generic Form, say ' Animal '. We divide that Form, down through the subordinate differences to the indivisible species, Man, Ox, Lion, etc. Below that are only the indefinite number of individual men, oxen, lions, of which we take no account. Now, when we divide ' Animal ', what are we dividing ? Not the class of all individual animals, but a single complex Form or nature, of which the subordinate Forms are called ' parts ' (μόρια, μέρη). The generic Form is said to ' embrace ' them, as a whole embraces its parts, and also to ' pervade ' them as a single character ' extended throughout them all '. It is this whole that we divide, as the *Phaedrus* says, ' according to its natural articulations ' (κατ' ἄρθρα ᾗ πέφυκεν, *Phaedr.* 265E).

That being so, Plato cannot hold that the higher we ascend in the hierarchy of genus and species, the poorer the terms become in content.[1] Were that true, the highest of all would be the poorest. The upward movement of thought would lead to the most shadowy of abstractions, not (as we learnt in the *Republic*) to the fullest and richest of realities, the source of all other reality and truth. One of the important Kinds presently to be mentioned is Being (Exist-

---

[1] On this point, see Stenzel, *Zahl und Gestalt*, 115 ff.

ence, Reality). Suppose that Form to stand at the head of the whole hierarchy. If it were the barest of all abstractions, nothing could be got out of it by an attempt to divide it into parts. It would have no parts, but be as simple and indivisible as the One Being of Parmenides. In Plato's view the highest Form, whether it be called ' Being ' or ' the One ' or ' the Good ', must be not the poorest, but the richest, a universe of real being, a whole containing all that is real in a single order, a One Being that is also many. Such a Form is as far as possible from resembling an Aristotelian category ; for the categories are precisely the barest of abstractions, at the furthest remove from substantial reality.

Now consider the lowest Forms in the hierarchy, the *infimae species*. Each of these is called indivisible (ἄτομον εἶδος) because the process of Division can be carried no further. Below the *infima species*, such as ' Man ', there is nothing but the individual men which partake directly of that Form and of which we take no account. But the species is not simple and unanalysable ; if it were, it could not be defined, and the object of the whole procedure is to define it in terms of the generic Form and all the differences that occur in its ancestry. The names Animal, Biped, Rational, are the names of parts or constituents of the complex specific Form, Man. This Form too is a One that is also many. So both the generic Form and the specific are complex. The generic Form contains all the species and its nature pervades them all. The lowest species contains the nature of the genus and all the relevant differences.

Here a diagram may help us. In the traditional Logic of modern times, circles are used to symbolise genus and species as classes. The large circle is a pen in which all animals are herded ; the smaller

pens contain all lions, all men, etc. These are sets of individuals identical with ' some animals '. But Plato is not concerned with individuals.[1] A different diagram is needed to symbolise the

[1] Proclus in *Parm*. i, p. 42 (Cousin), interpreting *Soph*. 253D, correctly observes, moreover, that the genus (μία ἰδέα διὰ πολλῶν τεταμένη) is not an aggregate (ἄθροισμα) of the species, but present in each of the species, being prior to them, and partaken of by each of them.

relations of Forms. We may obtain it, if we keep faithfully to Plato's metaphor of 'blending'.

Take a circle to represent the generic Form 'Animal', and suppose its area to be coloured blue. The blueness stands for the character or nature 'Animality'. Now divide the circle into two semicircles, and let one be coloured red, symbolising the nature of the difference 'Biped' (the other will stand for 'Many-footed'). The

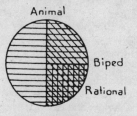

Animal
Biped
Rational

two colours will now be blended in the semicircle. Next add the further difference 'Rational', a third colour blending with the other two. The blend of these three colours will stand for the complex content of the specific Form 'Man', if we assume that to be definable as 'rational biped animal'.

If we now imagine boundary lines and colours representing all the other differences to have been filled in, the total result will be a picture of the complex generic Form, Animal. The circumference of the circle will symbolise that the genus is 'a single Form embracing the many different Forms' which are its parts. The original colour, blue, symbolises that the nature, animality, 'pervades' all parts of the area. The species are 'many Forms, different from one another and embraced from without by a single Form'. They are complex and definable 'wholes'. The generic Form that is divided is not the abstraction, animality. The differences are not parts of the meaning of animality; if 'biped' were part of the meaning of 'animality', all animals would be biped. What is divided is the total complex Form, Animal, pictured by the complete pattern of colours.

This representation is supported by the description of the Form, Animal, in the *Timaeus* (30A). God created the visible universe as a living creature, with body, soul, and intelligence. After what pattern? Not after the pattern of any 'part' (τῶν ἐν μέρους εἴδει, i.e. species of animal); for then it would be imperfect; but after the pattern of 'that of which all living creatures other than itself, severally and in their kinds, are parts (μόρια); for that embraces and contains within itself all the intelligible animals (specific Forms of species of animal), as this (visible) cosmos contains ourselves and all other visible creatures that exist (classes of individual animals) '. Again at 39E the Creator, designing to fashion all living creatures within the cosmos after the pattern of his model, ' purposed that this world also should receive such and so many Forms as intelligence discerns contained in the Living Creature that truly is (ἐνούσας ἰδέας τῷ ὃ ἔστι ζῷον) '.

Only by picturing the complex Form, Animal, in this way can we satisfy the conditions : (1) that the generic Form must be a whole of which the specific Forms are parts, (2) that the highest Form in a Table of Division must be the richest, not the poorest, in content ; (3) that every specific Form must be likewise a whole of parts, complex and definable.

Let us now take the completed diagram, with all its blended colours, to represent the Real, the complete pattern of Forms which the dialectician has to divide, and can divide because it is complex. This is what was called ' the perfectly real ' (τὸ παντελῶς ὄν) or ' the All ' (τὸ ὄν τε καὶ τὸ πᾶν) in the argument with the Friends of Forms, in so far as the Real consists of a pattern of unchanging Forms. This complex of Forms was what the Friends of Forms originally recognised—a unity that was also a many, as contrasted with the Parmenidean Unity, which excluded plurality. We agreed that this changeless pattern must be recognised as a necessity of thought and discourse. We added, it is true, that it is not the whole of reality ; the real must include such change as is involved in life and intelligence. But we are not now concerned with that addition, but only with the unchanging pattern of Forms, as the object of knowledge.

As soon, however, as we had reached the conclusion that the Real must contain ' all that is unchanging and all that is in change ', we argued that the Real cannot be the same thing as realness. If we take any two Forms, Motion and Rest, realness is a ' third thing ' that must belong to and ' embrace ' both, just as we put it to the physicists that realness cannot be the same thing as ' Hot ' or ' Cold ', or as ' the-Hot-and-the-Cold ', which in their view constituted the Real. It is this realness (Existence) that will presently be described as one of the most important Kinds. It is a single Form or character extended everywhere throughout the many diverse Forms that blend with it. In the diagram it will appear as the single colour diffused over the whole area, before the other colours are added. It is simply the meaning of the word ' Existence ', when we say that Motion or any other Form ' has existence ', ' exists '. The other Forms, such as Motion and Rest, are parts of the Real ; they are not parts of realness. If ' realness ' has any definition, neither

Motion nor Rest nor any other subordinate Form can appear in its
definition, any more than ' biped ' can appear in the definition of
' animality '.

254B–D. *Three of the most important Forms, selected for purposes*
of illustration : Existence, Motion, Rest

The Stranger now returns from his digression on Dialectic to the
next stage of his argument. The purpose of the coming section,
on the blending of Forms, is to bring to light those meanings of ' is '
and ' is not ' which are relevant to the proof that ' what is not '
(in certain senses) may nevertheless exist. The discussion is simpli-
fied by taking three Forms—Existence, Motion, Rest—in isolation
from all others, and considering what true statements, affirmative
or negative, can be made about them, and what these statements
mean.

254B. STR.   Now that we are agreed, then, that some of the Kinds
will combine with one another and some will not, and that
some combine to a small extent, others with a large number,
while some pervade all and there is nothing against their
   C. being combined with everything, let us next follow up
the argument in this way. We will not take all the Forms,
for fear of getting confused in such a multitude, but choose
out some of those that are recognised as most (*or* very)
important, and consider first their several natures and then
how they stand in respect of being capable of combination
with one another. In this way, though we may not be able
to conceive Being and Not-being with perfect clearness, we
may at least give as satisfactory an account of them as
we can under the conditions of our present inquiry,[1] and see
   D. if there is any opening allowing us to assert that what is
not, *really is* what is not, and to escape unscathed.
THEAET.   Yes, we had better do that.
STR.   Now, among the Kinds, those we were just now
discussing—Existence itself and Rest and Motion—*are* very
important.[2]

---

[1] Possibly a hint that in what follows we shall not draw all the distinctions
that a complete account would require, or at least not emphasise those which
do not directly bear on the conclusion desired.

[2] This sentence is usually mistranslated, μέγιστα being rendered as if it were
τὰ μέγιστα and taken as subject : (1) Apelt : ' *Die wichtigsten Gattungsbegriffe,*
die wir vorher durchgingen, waren doch das Seiende selbst, sowie Stillstand und
Bewegung.' (γενῶν is, of course, not the antecedent of ἄ : the relative would
be ὦν). (2) Campbell : ' *The most important kinds are those which we have*
just been considering.' (3) Diès : ' *Or les plus grandes des genres sont ceux*
précisément que nous venons de passer en revue : l'être lui-même, le repos et le

254D. THEAET. Quite so.

STR. And observe, we say that two of the three will not blend with one another.[1]

THEAET. Certainly.

STR. Whereas Existence can be blended with both ; for surely they both exist.

THEAET. Of course.

STR. So they make three in all.

It has become the established practice to call these very important Kinds, together with Sameness and Difference, the Platonic ' Categories '. The use of this term is based partly on the mistranslation above noted, which makes Existence, Motion and Rest ' *the* most important Kinds ', partly on a passage in the *Enneads* where Plotinus, after demolishing the Aristotelian categories, deduces these five Kinds as ' *the* Kinds or principles of Being ' (γένη or ἀρχαὶ τοῦ ὄντος). Plotinus was probably thinking not only of our passage but of the appearance of Being, Sameness, and Difference in the highly figurative description of the composition of the world-soul in the *Timaeus*.[2] That passage, however, which says nothing about Motion and Rest, lends no support to a list of five Kinds or principles ; and the argument here in the *Sophist* gives no ground whatever for imagining that these five Kinds hold the place afterwards occupied by Aristotle's categories, or for calling them ' categories ' at all. There may be some sense of that vague and ambiguous word as used by modern philosophers, that might be considered appropriate. But we are concerned with the use of it in the fourth century

mouvement.' The point is important because all these renderings mean that Existence, Motion, and Rest are *the* most important kinds. Plato does not assert this. The previous speech said that we would select ' *some* of those that are recognised as most (or very) important '. The present speech tells us which these ' some ' are ; but they are only *some* of the most important, not *the* most important. The subject is ἃ νυνδὴ διῆμεν : μέγιστα is predicate, standing first for emphasis and because it provides the link with the former speech. We might translate : " Now this description ' most important ' (or ' very important ') among the Kinds does apply to those we have been discussing, namely Existence, Rest, Motion." Accordingly, we take those as the ' *some* ' we said we would take. But there are others of the highest importance, as the earlier speech implied. Sameness and Difference, presently added, are equally important, and actually ' wider ' than Motion and Rest, being ' all-pervading ' like Existence. These speeches leave open the possibility that there may be any number of other μέγιστα γένη, which we do not require to mention for our purpose. The consequences of mistranslation will be noted presently.

[1] That Motion will not blend with Rest was remarked at 252D. The point of these sentences is that Existence, Motion, Rest, are three distinct Forms, no one of them identical with any other.

[2] 35A, 37A.

B.C., and to introduce it into Plato in any other sense than Aristotle's is to court confusion.

Plato never uses the word 'category'. There is no evidence that κατηγορία ever meant anything but 'accusation' until Aristotle gave it a technical use in Logic. The verb κατηγορεῖν was used in ordinary speech to mean 'to declare', 'to assert'. Aristotle, needing a special word for what is asserted about a subject, adopted κατηγόρημα for 'predicate', and κατηγορία for 'predicate' or 'predication'. 'Category' finally was used as a short expression for the 'modes' or 'fashions of predication' (σχήματα τῆς κατηγορίας) arrived at by taking a subject—say 'Socrates'—and tabulating all the kinds of assertion you can make about it. 'Socrates is a man, an animal': these predicates are essential and belong to the category of Substance. 'Socrates is white': this is Quality. Socrates is five feet tall: this is Quantity. 'Socrates is in the Lyceum': this is Place; and so on. The *Categories* gives a list of ten such modes of predication; elsewhere it is doubtful whether a smaller number may not suffice.

Further, these predicates appear to be entities of different kinds and related to the subject in different ways. Hence the categories also provide a classification of all the things there are according to their mode of existence. They are then ultimate and irreducible classes, reached by pushing the question 'What is this?' to the furthest point. 'What is Socrates? A man. What is a man? An animal. What is Animal? A Substance.' Here we reach an ultimate class of entity. 'What is this? Red. What is red? A colour. What is colour? A Quality.' Once more we have reached an ultimate class; and so with the rest.

No one of these classes can be reduced or subordinated to any other. They are the *summa genera* of things, to one, and only one, of which any thing that exists can be assigned. If we now think of genera as classes, a *summum genus* is one of the widest classes, with the greatest extension. It is easy to see why Plato's phrase μέγιστον γένος, which could be (wrongly) translated 'very wide' or 'widest genus', should be confused with Aristotle's categories.

The confusion is entirely unwarranted. No one of Plato's five Kinds (Forms, not classes) is, in Aristotle's opinion, a category. Take 'Being' or 'Existence'. In several places Aristotle says that Being (Existence) and Unity are not categories, precisely because they can be predicated of everything; they do not fall into any one of his ten pigeon-holes. The same is true of Sameness and Difference. As Plato goes on to remark, you can say of any thing that it is the same as itself, and different from everything else.

For that very reason Aristotle denies that they are categories. That Motion and Rest should be categories could never occur to Aristotle's mind ; nor do modern critics explain how Motion and Rest can be *summa genera* either of entities or of predicates. The upshot is that Plato never uses the word, and Aristotle, who does use it, considers it inapplicable to any of the five Kinds.

The confusion that results from introducing the word may be illustrated from Campbell's Introduction to the *Sophist*. On one page (xvii) he says : ' These predicates of sameness and difference are found to be no less universally applicable than the form of Being. Thus Being, Sameness, or Difference, to use Aristotelian language, are universal predicaments or categories. Everything, of which we can speak, exists, is the same in one relation, different in others, and is either at rest or in motion or both in different ways.' Campbell's reason for calling the Kinds ' categories ' is precisely the reason why Aristotle refuses them that name. On the next page the reader is startled by the statement : ' But the categories of Plato are not connected with the theory of Predication, towards which, as appears even from *Soph.* 261C, Plato had made but little progress. Even those of the *Sophist* are rather ontological than logical, and are more nearly analogous to the ' four causes ' of the *Metaphysics* : denoting, to use a convenient distinction of Plotinus, rather the elements than the kinds of Being '. To this it may be replied that Aristotle's categories *are* connected with the theory of Predication ; that he never calls his four causes categories ; that categories are kinds, not elements, of Being. In fact, the Aristotelian use of ' category ' is totally misleading and irrelevant ; and the word had no other technical use in the fourth century.

Such are the confusions that result from interpreting Plato in terms of Aristotelian Logic. Plotinus and modern critics have been misled by the phrase ' very important (or very wide) Kinds '. The word ' *genus* ' later came to be used in opposition to *eidos*, ' species '. But Plato in the *Parmenides* and throughout the *Sophist* uses ' Kind ' (γένος) and ' Form ' (εἶδος) indifferently.[1] Both mean, not ' genus ' or ' species ' or ' class ', but ' Form ' or ' Nature ' (φύσις and ἰδέα are used synonymously). No one of the Kinds is thought of as a class, either of entities or of predicates. The epithet μέγιστον may mean no more than ' very important '.[2] But the

---

[1] In the passage before us the Stranger says, ' let us choose some of the most important Forms (εἴδη) ', and then ' among the Kinds (γενῶν) those we have been discussing are very important '.

[2] ' The highest Kinds ', ' the most important Kinds ' (Campbell) ; ' *die wichtigsten* ' (Apelt) ; ' *les plus grandes* ' (Diès). ' Highest ' should be avoided as suggesting *summum genus*.

meaning ' wide ' may be included in the same sense that is applicable
to the generic or specific Forms (not classes) pictured as areas in
our diagram. In making his tables of Division earlier, Plato has
spoken of dividing a complex generic Form into parts that are
μέγιστα.[1] This probably means ' wide ' as well as ' important ',
for in a table of Division the differences should be taken in an order
of descending wideness ; the field of the generic Form is narrowed
at each step. Existence, Sameness, Difference are ' very wide '
in that they pervade and blend with every other Form and with
one another. But Plato does not say that these very wide or very
important Forms are *the* widest in the sense that there are no others
of equal extent. Unity has just as good a claim as Being ; for it
is true of everything that it is one. The *Parmenides* shows clearly
enough that Plato was aware of this, and Plotinus is hard put to
it to explain why Unity is not included.[2] Further, Motion and
Rest are not so wide as the others ; being contraries, they divide
the field of existents between them, and exclude one another. This
in itself is enough to show that ' *the* widest Forms ' would be a
mistranslation.

The really serious consequence of the confusion with categories
is that some modern critics, misled by Plotinus, read a metaphysical
significance into the passage that follows, and in particular suppose
that Motion and Rest are here treated with reference to the part
they play in the economy of the universe.[3] There is, however, no
suggestion in the text that any one of these five Kinds is to be
deduced or evolved out of any other. They are simply posited
from the outset as some (but not all) of the very important Forms.
The whole purpose of what follows is to elucidate the nature of
Existence, Sameness, Difference (not of Motion and Rest). The
analysis of these three will yield all the senses of the words ' is '
and ' is not ' that we are seeking. For this purpose Plato requires
two other terms which are contraries having the relation of Incompatibility (ἀμείκτω πρὸς ἀλλήλω, 254D) as well as that of Difference. He chooses Motion and Rest because (as the Stranger says)
we have been discussing them, and for no ulterior reason. They
come from the list of contrary terms that had figured in Zeno's
dilemmas, mentioned at *Parm.* 129D : ' Likeness and Unlikeness,

---

[1] 229B, ' Is there only one kind (γένος) of Instruction, or several, and two of
them μεγίστω ? ' Dividing Ignorance ' through the middle ' (κατὰ μέσον),
we find one Form (εἶδος) that is μέγα and counterbalances all the rest. At
220B Fishing is divided κατὰ μέγιστα μέρη.

[2] *Enn.* VII, ii, 9.

[3] A theory of this kind, due to Professor Joachim, is summarised by Mr.
Mure (*Aristotle*, 1932, pp. 55 ff.).

Plurality and Unity, Rest and Motion, and all such things '.[1] Any other pair of incompatible Forms would do as well. Had Plato used symbols, he might have written, not Motion and Rest, but A and Not-A, standing for any pair of contraries. If the reader will substitute these symbols for Rest and Motion in the following argument, he will find that its meaning and conclusions are in no way affected by the change. What is discussed is solely the nature and meanings of Existence, Sameness, and Difference. The nature of Motion (as such) and Rest (as such) is not in question at all.[2] The only fact about them that is relevant is that they are contrary and incompatible.

A diagram representing the three chosen Forms in isolation from all others will suffice to symbolise all the relations that will be distinguished in the coming analysis. The line dividing Motion from

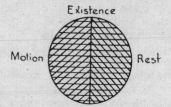

Rest stands for their incompatibility. Three different colours symbolise the different natures of the three Forms. Motion and Rest blend with Existence, but not with one another.

Before we go on to the introduction of the two other all-pervading Forms considered—Sameness and Difference—we may take note of the statements already made about Existence, Motion, and Rest :

Motion (or Rest) blends with Existence (and with other Forms, including Sameness and Difference).

Motion does not blend with Rest.

These are statements of Compatibility and Incompatibility. Plato does not emphasise negative statements of this type, denying that one Form blends or combines with or partakes of another. As already remarked, the relation intended is not the meaning of the ' copula ', linking subject to predicate in traditional Logic ; for we can equally say ' Existence blends with Motion '. Hence, though the word ' partaking ' is used, the relation is not the same as that which connects an individual man to his specific Form,

---

[1] Again, *Phaedrus* 261D refers to the Eleatic Palamedes' (Zeno's) proofs that things are ' like and unlike, one and many, at rest and moving '. Cf. Introd., pp. 7, 8.

[2] Save in so far as certain consequences about (*e.g.*) actual motion would follow if ' Motion exists ' were not true.

Man, in ' Socrates is human '. All statements assigning ' names '
to individual things have been ruled out at the beginning of this
whole discussion (251A, p. 253). The ' copula ' has no place anywhere in Plato's scheme of the relations of Forms. The above
two statements are taken as equivalent to

> Motion (or Rest) exists.
> Motion does not rest.

' To exist ' and ' to rest ' are verbs, and verbs are later defined
as names for ' actions ', though, as we shall see, this definition is
not to be taken as strictly adequate.[1] Actions, the meanings of
verbs, are treated as Forms. Plato does not go into the question
whether such Forms differ in any important way from Forms
which are the meanings of nouns or adjectives. These types of
statement, expressing Compatibility or Incompatibility, are not
further analysed in the sequel. One particular set of statements
of such a type will specially concern us, namely :

> Motion (or any other Form) exists.

Every such statement, whatever Form may stand as subject, is
true. If we substitute :

> Motion *is* an existent
> Motion *is not* a thing at rest,

the word ' is ' will mean ' is the same as '—the other sense of ' is ',
presently to be considered.

254D–255E. *Two further Forms, Sameness and Difference, distinct from these three and all-pervading*

The Stranger next introduces two fresh Forms, Sameness and
Difference, and shows in detail that neither of these can be identified
with any of the three, Existence, Motion, Rest. We shall thus
have five distinct irreducible Forms in all, whose combinations
we can study.

254D.　STR. And each one of them (Existence, Motion, Rest) is
different from the other two,[2] and the *same* as itself.

E.　THEAET. That is so.

　　STR. But what do we mean by these words we have just
used—' same ' and ' different ' ? Are they a pair of Kinds
distinct from those three, though always necessarily blending
with them, so that we must consider the Forms as five in
all, not three ? Or, when we say ' same ' or ' different ',

255.　are we unconsciously using a name that belongs to one or
another of those three Kinds ?

[1] See p. 308.
[2] This statement at once notes that Difference is distinct from Incompatibility ; for Motion and Rest are not incompatible with Existence.

255.   THEAET.   Possibly.

STR.   Well, Motion and Rest at any rate cannot be (identical with) Difference or Sameness.

THEAET.   Why not ?

STR.   Neither Motion nor Rest can be (identical with) anything that we say of both of them in common.

THEAET.   Why ?

STR.   Because Motion would then be at rest, and Rest in motion ; for whichever of the two (Motion or Rest) becomes applicable to both (by being identified with either Sameness or Difference, which *are* applicable to both) will force the other (Rest or Motion) to change to the contrary of its

B.   own nature, as thus coming to partake of its contrary.

THEAET.   Quite so.

STR.   But both do partake of Sameness and Difference.

THEAET.   Yes.

STR.   Then we must not say that Sameness or Difference is (identical with) Motion, nor yet with Rest.[1]

THEAET.   No.

STR.   Are we, however, to think of Existence and Sameness as a single thing ?

THEAET.   Perhaps.

STR.   But if ' Existence ' and ' Sameness ' have no difference in meaning, once more, when we say that Motion and Rest

C.   both ' exist ', we shall thereby be speaking of them as being ' the same '.

THEAET.   But that is impossible.

STR.   Then Sameness and Existence cannot be one thing.

THEAET.   Hardly.

[1] This argument is highly compressed and somewhat obscure even with the additions I have interpolated in the translation. We want to prove that neither the word ' Motion ' (or ' being in motion ') nor the word ' Rest ' (or ' being at rest ') can mean the same thing as either the word ' Sameness ' (or ' being the same ') or the word ' Different ' (or ' being different '). The proof is : (1) We know that

Motion	blends with	Sameness
Rest	,, ,,	Sameness
Motion	,, ,,	Difference
Rest	,, ,,	Difference.

(2) We now say : Anything that can be asserted of (blends with) both Motion and Rest—and Sameness and Difference do blend with both—cannot be identical with either. (3) For suppose (for example) that Motion is identical with Sameness. Then ' Motion ' can be substituted for ' Sameness ' in any statement. So the second statement above (' Rest blends with Sameness ') becomes ' Rest blends with Motion '. But this is false. Therefore Motion is not identical with Sameness. The same proof holds of all the other identifications of Motion with Difference, Rest with Difference, Rest with Sameness.

255C. STR. We may, then, set down Sameness as a fourth Form,
additional to our three.
THEAET. Certainly.

The nature of Sameness is somewhat neglected in the sequel,
though Campbell's remark that ' the distinction between Being
and Sameness is hardly maintained in what follows ' is not justified.
The distinction is clear, but not dwelt upon, because our main
concern is with Difference : we are trying to clear up confusions
about the meanings of ' is not ' rather than the meanings of ' is '.
Every Form, we have seen, is ' the same as itself ' (254D). That
is, every Form is what it is, has a nature which is peculiar to it
and constant, so that it is ' always the same ' (ἀεὶ ὡσαύτως ἔχει),
or keeps its identity. This identity appears in the diagram as the
peculiar colour standing for the nature or essence (οὐσία) of the
Form. This essence is, of course, distinct from its existence.
Sameness itself is considered as a single Form of which all these
samenesses are instances, as Colour might be called the one Form
of which all the diverse colours in our diagram are instances. Thus
Sameness is all-pervading, like Existence, and is distinct from
Existence. We have thus two meanings of ' is ' : ' exists ' and
' is the same as '.

255C. STR. And are we to call Difference a fifth ? Or must we
think of Difference and Existence as two names for a single
Kind ?
THEAET. Perhaps.
STR. But I suppose you admit that, among things that
exist, some are always spoken of as being what they are [1]
just in themselves, others as being what they are with
reference to other things.
THEAET. Of course.
D. STR. And what is different is always so called with reference to another thing, isn't it ?
THEAET. That is so.
STR. It would not be so, if Existence and Difference were
not very different things. If Difference partook of both
characters [2] as Existence does, there would sometimes be,

[1] The addition of the words ' being what they are ' is justified by the
statement below (D7) that what is different is *what it is* (τοῦθ᾽ ὅπερ ἐστὶν) with
reference to another thing. Cf. also *Parm.* 133C, ὅσαι τῶν ἰδεῶν πρὸς ἀλλήλας
εἰσὶν αἵ εἰσιν, for instance, αὐτὴ δεσποτεία αὐτῆς δουλείας ἐστὶν ὅ ἐστι.

[2] I.e. τὸ καθ᾽ αὑτό and τὸ πρὸς ἄλλο. Note that Existence, which *includes*
both these Forms, is said to *partake of* both. This is one of the places which
show that ' partaking ' is symmetrical in the case of Forms.

255D. within the class of different things, something that was different not with reference to another thing. But in fact we undoubtedly find that whatever is different, as a necessary consequence, is what it is with reference to another.

THEAET. It is as you say.

STR. Then we must call the nature of Difference a fifth
E. among the Forms we are singling out.

THEAET. Yes.

STR. And moreover we shall say that this nature pervades all the Forms ; for each one is different from the rest, not by virtue of its own nature, but because it partakes of the character of Difference.

THEAET. Quite so.

Difference is here distinguished from Existence by the fact that Existence blends with (' partakes of ') both the characters belonging respectively to things which ' are what they are just in themselves ' (καθ' αὐτά) and things which ' are what they are with reference to other things ' (πρὸς ἄλλα). I have avoided the words ' absolute ' and ' relative ' because some of their associations are misleading.[1] The term ' relative ' may, however, be used, provided that we understand how Plato and Aristotle conceived of relative terms, as distinct from ' relations '.

In Aristotle relative terms figure as one of the categories, because he supposed that every proposition has a subject and a predicate, and relative terms must consequently be a special class of predicates. Plato before him had observed that some ' names ' (as he would say) had the peculiarity that a thing only has such a name ' towards ' or ' in comparison with ' or ' with reference to ' something else (πρὸς ἄλλο). Thus at *Rep.* 438A, Plato speaks of ' things which are such as to be *of* something ' or ' *than* something '. ' The greater ' is such as to be greater *than* something ; and so with ' more ' and

[1] Mr. Mure, *Aristotle*, p. 57, writes : ' Though he does identify otherness with not-being, he then introduces a distinction between self-subsistent and dependent (relative, adjectival) being, and identifies otherness with dependent being—a proceeding dubious enough in itself, and one which increases a certain confusion present throughout the discussion between being in the sense of the abstract, minimal, characterisation of all that is, and being in the sense of Reality as a complete whole.' Again at p. 180, ' Plato's distinction of self-subsistent from dependent being is possibly the source of Aristotle's conception of substance and accident '. Plato is not guilty of this ' dubious proceeding '. He is not speaking of self-subsistent and dependent or adjectival being. Both in Plato and in Aristotle τὸ πρός τι means ' *relative* ', not ' dependent ' or ' adjectival ' or ' accidental '. This misunderstanding is connected with attempts to find in this part of the *Sophist* an evolution of reality on the lines suggested by Plotinus.

'less', 'heavier' and 'lighter' (comparatives), 'doubles' and 'halves', hot things *as compared with* (πρός) cold things. So too knowledge is knowledge *of* something; thirst is thirst *for* something.[1] These names which things have 'towards' or 'with reference to' something else were called 'relative' (τὰ πρός τι).

Chapter 7 of the *Categories* follows Plato closely: "All those (things? predicates?) are said to be 'with reference to something' (πρός τι), which are what they are *of* (or '*than*', etc.—any genitive) other things or are in any other way (*e.g.*, the dative case) 'towards something'." Examples are: 'The greater is what it is (greater) *than another thing* (ἑτέρου)'. 'A habit is a habit *of something*, knowledge is knowledge *of something*, attitude is the attitude *of something*.' 'A mountain is high *in comparison with* (πρός) something.' 'What is similar is similar *to something else* (dative).' All relatives have correlatives (ἀντιστρέφοντα): a slave is said to be the slave *of a master*, the master to be master *of a slave*. 'Correlatives,' we are told, 'are thought to come into existence simultaneously'; the existence of a master implies the existence of a slave; but this is not true of all; the objects of knowledge or of perception (the knowable, perceptible) can and do exist before the knowledge or perception of them exists; whereas knowledge and perception cannot exist without their objects. Specially illuminating is the discussion whether any substances are relative. Primary substances and their species are not. 'Wood' is relative only in so far as it is someone's property, not *qua* wood. But are 'head' and 'hand' relative or not? A head or hand must be the head or hand *of somebody*. The writer is inclined to think that 'head' and 'hand' are not relative, because, although we know that a head must be somebody's head, we can know the essential nature of 'head' without knowing whose head it is. But, he adds, it is hard to say that no substance is relative without an exhaustive examination, which he does not attempt.

It would not occur to a modern writer on Logic to wonder whether 'head' or 'hand' must be a relative term because such a thing must belong to somebody. Obviously, the author of the *Categories* did not conceive of relations as subsisting *between* two things, as they are now symbolised by R standing between a and b in aRb. He thinks of 'relative things' or 'relative names'; some are substantives, some adjectives, all are predicates. Perception and its object are correlative things; yet you can destroy perception without destroying its correlative. Perception and knowledge are not conceived as relations subsisting *between* the subject and the

---

[1] πώματος. It so happens that 'of', 'for', and 'than' are all expressed in Greek by the genitive case.

object, and necessarily disappearing with the suppression of either.
The examples given are nouns and adjectives, not verbs, which fall
under other categories : ' action and passion ', ' state ', ' position '.
Space and Time relations again belong to other categories. ' In
the Lyceum ' is a predicate in the category of Place ; ' yesterday ',
a predicate in the category of Time. Prepositions, not being ' predicates ', have no place in any category, and it does not occur to the
writer that a preposition in itself means a relation.[1] ' Relations ',
in fact, are not recognised as a class of entity distinct from predicates. The author considers only nouns and adjectives signifying
properties with the peculiarity that a subject has these properties
' with reference to something else '. A man has the property
' fatherhood ' towards his son. It was reserved for still living logicians to discover that a proposition like ' Socrates is shorter than
Phaedo ' has two subjects with a relation between them, and no
predicate at all.

   That Plato conceived relative terms in the same way is clear
from the *Phaedo*, where he speaks of a man partaking of tallness
in the same sense that he partakes of beauty. Socrates has *in him*
a tallness towards (as compared with, πρός) a shortness that is *in*
Simmias. These characters (ἰδέαι) residing in the two men are
distinguished from the unique Forms (Tallness itself, Shortness
itself), of which we might call them instances. These individual
properties cannot change into their contraries (any more than the
Forms can do so). If Simmias grows to be taller than Socrates,
the tallness in Socrates either ' perishes ' or ' gives way to the
approach ' of its contrary. Thus the *Phaedo* clearly treated relations
as properties, and whatever inferences may be based on the passage
about size and number in the *Theaetetus* (p. 45), he has not abandoned Forms of relative terms.

   This reduction of relations to ' relative things ' or ' names '
explains the passage before us. ' Different ' is a relative name which
things have towards other things. Difference is not a relation
subsisting between the two things. Two different Forms are said
to ' partake of the character of Difference ' (μετέχειν τῆς ἰδέας τῆς
θατέρου) in addition to having their own nature, though it must
be remembered that ' partake ' should mean no more than ' blend
with '. ' Difference ' is a Form which ' pervades ' all the Forms
(διὰ πάντων διεληλυθυῖα), just as Existence pervades them all.
In this way Difference can be said to be a character (ἰδέα) or nature
(φύσις) ' dispersed ' over the whole field of Reality (260B).
Every Form has its own peculiar nature, essence, constant identity,

---

[1] The word ' preposition ' is introduced into some translations of the
Categories, but it is not in the text.

'sameness'; it always is what it is. But just because this nature is peculiar and unique, every Form has its 'difference' distinguishing it from any other. Its name blends with Difference in the negative statement that it *is not* any other.

The class of relative things is introduced in connection with Difference, not with Sameness; but Plato seems to regard Sameness as a relative thing. Thus he says, Motion is the same as itself 'because of its participation in Sameness *towards itself*' (διὰ τὴν μέθεξιν ταὐτοῦ πρὸς ἑαυτήν, 256B). It is equally true of Sameness that it pervades all the Forms.

255E–257A. A review of true statements involving the five Forms shows that there are any number of true statements asserting that 'what is' in a sense 'is not'

It is now established that all the five Forms are distinct. No one can be reduced to, or identified with, any other (nor, we may add, evolved or deduced from any other). The Stranger now proceeds to formulate statements in which the names of these Forms appear. The statements are taken as obviously true. The purpose is to see in what ways one of these Forms (Motion is taken as the example) blends with others in true affirmative statements or is disjoined from them in true negative statements. The statements are grouped in pairs, affirmative and negative, such as

> {Motion is not (Rest)
> {Motion is (*i.e.* exists).
> {Motion is the same (as itself)
> {Motion is not the Same (Sameness).

Such statements had been represented as contradictory by Eristics, imitating Zeno's disproof of the existence of a Many by dilemmas leading to such alleged contradictions. That Plato had these dilemmas in mind is clear from his reference to them below (259D). Here he is content to show that all these statements are true and consistent, when the ambiguities of 'is' and 'is not' are recognised.

255E. STR. Now, then, taking our five Kinds one by one, let us make some statements about them.

THEAET. What statements?

STR. First about Motion: let us say that Motion is altogether different from Rest. Or is that not so?

THEAET. It is so.

STR. So Motion is not Rest.

THEAET. Not in any sense.[1]

---

[1] Possibly '*altogether* different' and 'not *in any sense*' mean that Motion and Rest are not only different but also incompatible.

256.   STR. But Motion *is* (exists), by virtue of partaking of Existence.

THEAET. Yes.

STR. And once more Motion is different from the Same (Sameness).[1]

THEAET. No doubt.

STR. So Motion is not the Same (Sameness).

THEAET. No.

STR. But on the other hand, Motion, we said, is the same as itself, because everything partakes of the Same (Sameness).[2]

THEAET. Certainly.

STR. Motion, then, is both the same and not the Same : we must admit that without boggling at it. For when we say it is ' the same ' and ' not the Same ' we are not using

B.   the expression in the same sense : we call it ' the same ' on account of its participation in the Same with reference to itself ; but we call it ' not the Same ' because of its combination with Difference, a combination that separates it off from the Same (Sameness) and makes it not the Same but different, so that we have the right to say this time that it is ' not the Same '.

THEAET. Certainly.

STR. So too, supposing Motion itself did in any way participate in Rest, there would be nothing outrageous in speaking of it as stationary. ⟨But it does not in fact participate in Rest at all.

THEAET. No, it does not.

STR. Whereas it does participate both in Sameness and in Difference, so that it is correct to speak of it as both the same and not the Same.⟩

THEAET. Perfectly correct, provided that we are to agree that some of the Kinds will blend with one another, some will not.

C.   STR. Well, that is a conclusion we proved at an earlier stage, when we showed that such was indeed their nature.

THEAET. Of course.[3]

---

[1] In Greek the appearance of contradiction is increased by ταὐτὸν meaning both ' Sameness ' and ' the same '.

[2] Reading αὐτῇ . . . πᾶν ταὐτοῦ with Madvig. This reading better expresses the meaning (which is the same, anyhow) than the αὐτη . . . πάντ' αὐτοῦ of the manuscripts.

[3] I understand the argument here as follows. We have just said that Motion is the same and not the same (as partaking of Difference). This sounds like a contradiction : how can what is the same partake of Differ-

256C. STR. To go back to our statements, then : is Motion different from Different (Difference), just as it was other than
the Same (Sameness) and other than Rest ?

THEAET. Necessarily.

STR. Motion, then, in a sense is not Different, and also is
different, in accordance with the argument we stated just
now.

THEAET. True.

We have now collected the following pairs of statements, which
an Eristic would regard as contradictory but which are in fact all
true and consistent :

{ Motion is not (Rest)
{ Motion is (*i.e.* exists).
{ Motion is not the Same (Sameness)
{ Motion is the same (as itself).
{ Motion is not Different (Difference)
{ Motion is different (from Difference).

The same procedure is now used to refute the fundamental Eleatic
doctrine that there is no sense in which that-which-is (τὸ ὄν) can
not-be.   There is a sense in which the Real (everything that is real,
including Realness or Existence itself) ' is not '.   Anything real is
the subject of innumerable true statements, asserting that it is not

---

ence ? ' Same ' and ' Different ' sound as if they were contraries and so incompatible, like Motion and Rest, which are contraries and incompatible.   But
suppose Motion and Rest were merely different, not incompatible : then
Motion could partake of Rest and be called stationary.   That is impossible
because Motion and Rest are in fact incompatible.   But the sameness which
Motion has towards itself and the difference it has towards other things are
not incompatible.   So there is no contradiction in saying Motion is the same
and not the same.   (Cf. Brochard, *Études*, 143.)

If this is the meaning, the text is intolerably elliptical and obscure.   Hein-
dorf suspected a lacuna, which he filled thus : 256B, 7, προσαγορεύειν; < νῦν δὲ
οὐ μεταλαμβάνει. ΘΕ. οὐ γὰρ οὖν. ΞΕ. ἄτοπον ἄρα στάσιμον αὐτὴν προσαγορεύειν.>
ΘΕ. ὀρθότατά γε . . .   This makes Theaetetus' reply somewhat more intelligible, but still leaves the argument obscure.   I propose < νῦν δὲ οὐδαμῶς
μεταλαμβάνει. ΘΕ. οὐ γὰρ οὖν. ΞΕ. ταὐτοῦ δέ γ' ἅμα καὶ θατέρου μετέχουσαν
ὀρθῶς ἔχει καὶ ταὐτὸν αὐτὴν καὶ οὐ ταὐτὸν προσαγορεύειν> as above translated.
Theaetetus' reply will then mean : ' Perfectly correct, provided that we are
to admit that some Kinds (such as Motion, Sameness, Difference) will combine,
others (Motion and Rest) will not.'

Other critics suppose that Plato is suggesting that there is, after all, a
sense in which Motion does partake of Rest, *e.g.* the uniform motion of a
sphere in the same place (Diès), or because Motion partakes of stability in
that it can be measured and described (Ritter, *N. Unt.* 61).   But I agree
with Brochard that the reference to earlier statements asserting that Motion
and Rest are incompatible excludes such interpretations.

(is different from) anything else that is real. We take first Motion as an instance of a real thing, and point out that

> ⎧ Motion is a thing that is not (Existence)
> ⎨ Motion is a thing that is (*i.e.* exists).

256C. STR. What, then, of the next point? Are we to say that Motion is different from three of the four, but not from the
D. fourth, when we have agreed that there were five Kinds in the field we set before us for examination?

THEAET. How can we? We cannot allow that their number is less than it was shown to be.

STR. So we may fearlessly contend that Motion is different from Existence.

THEAET. Without the smallest fear.

STR. In fact, it is clear that Motion really is a thing that is not (Existence) and a thing that is, since it partakes of Existence.

THEAET. Perfectly clear.

This conclusion is now generalised: it applies to all the Forms. Of any Form it can be said that it is a thing that is not (any other Form) and also a thing that is (*i.e.* exists). Finally, it is pointed out that this is as true of Existence itself as of any other Form.

256D. STR. It must, then, be possible for 'that which is not' (*i.e.* is different from Existence) to be (to exist), not only in the case of Motion but of all the other Kinds. For in
E. the case of them all the nature of Difference makes each one of them different from Existence and so makes it a thing that 'is not'; and hence we shall be right to speak of them all on the same principle as things that in this sense '*are not*', and again, because they partake of Existence, to say that they '*are*' (exist) and call them things that have being (existence).

THEAET. No doubt.

STR. So, in the case of every one of the Forms there is much that it *is* and an indefinite number of things that it *is not*.[1]

THEAET. So it appears.

257. STR. And, moreover, Existence itself must be called different from the rest.

THEAET. Necessarily.

[1] This means that many affirmative statements are true of any Form, and also any number of negative statements, expressing its difference from other Forms. This conclusion is next applied to Existence itself.

257. STR. We find, then, that Existence likewise 'is not' in as many respects as there are other things ; for, not being those others, while it *is* its single self, it *is not* all that indefinite number of other things.

THEAET. That is so.

STR. Then we must not boggle even at that conclusion, granted that Kinds are of a nature to admit combination with one another. If anyone denies that, he must win over our earlier arguments to his side before he tries to win over their consequences.

THEAET. That is a fair demand.

In this passage τὸ ὄν primarily means the single Form, Existence itself, one of the five Forms we selected. We have seen that

> {Existence is (exists [1]).
> {Existence is not (any other Form).

But the conclusion applies equally to what Parmenides meant by τὸ ὄν, 'that which exists', the Real, if we understand this as a collective name for all the existing Forms which make up reality. It is true of anything that is real, that it exists and is not anything else, and of the Real as a whole that it is not any one of its parts. In fact, τὸ ὄν here, like τὸ ἕτερον earlier, is verbally ambiguous. The ambiguity enables the statement to cover two conclusions, which are both true. The second is

> {Any existent is (exists)
> {Any existent is not (any other existent).

We have thus established the first point against Parmenides' dogma that there is no way in which 'that which is' can 'not-be'. We have shown that an unlimited number of negative statements are true of any existent or of Existence itself.

257B–258C. *There are also any number of true statements asserting that 'what is not' in a sense 'is'*

The next section refutes Parmenides' complementary dogma : 'There is no sense in which that-which-is-not can be.' This section is concerned with 'that which is not' (τὸ μὴ ὄν) in the sense explained, namely 'the different', *i.e.* any existent defined as different from some other existent ; for example, 'the not-tall', 'the not-beautiful'. It is first pointed out that 'that which is not' in this sense is distinct from 'Non-existence' and from 'the non-existent', both of which are covered by the phrase 'the contrary of what exists (*or* of Existence)', τοὐναντίον τοῦ ὄντος.

---

[1] Or perhaps 'is the same as itself'—has a being or identity of its own.

257B.   STR.   Now let us mark this.

THEAET.   Yes ?

STR.   When we speak of ' that which is not ', it seems that
we do not mean something contrary to what exists but only
something that is different.

THEAET.   How ?

STR.   In the same way that when, for example, we speak of
something as ' not tall ', we may just as well mean by that
phrase ' what is equal ' as ' what is short ', mayn't we ? [1]

THEAET.   Certainly.

STR.   So, when it is asserted that a negative signifies a contrary, we shall not agree, but admit no more than this :

c.   that the prefix ' not ' indicates something different from the
words that follow—or rather from the things designated by
the words pronounced after the negative.

THEAET.   Exactly.

' The different ' is ' the not so-and-so '.   Remembering that the
discussion is confined to the world of Forms and their relations,
we can now see that the whole field of reality, divided up into all
the subordinate Forms, can be regarded as covered by Forms,
every one of which can be negatively described as ' that which is
not so-and-so '.   So ' the nature of the Different ' is distributed
over the whole field, just as much as the nature of Existence.   ' The
not-beautiful ' is the collective name for all the Forms there are,
other than the single Form, ' Beautiful '.   ' The not-beautiful ' is
a special name for this ' part ' of the Different, just as the various
species (' parts ') of knowledge have special names.

257C.   STR.   And here, if you agree, is a point for us to consider.

THEAET.   Namely ?

STR.   The nature of the Different (Difference) [2] appears to
be parcelled out, in the same way as knowledge.

THEAET.   How so ?

STR.   Knowledge also is surely one, but each part of it that
commands a certain field is marked off and given a special

D.   name proper to itself.   Hence language recognises many
arts and forms of knowledge.[3]

[1] ' Short ' is the contrary of ' tall ' ; but ' equal ' is not ; so the equal is
different from the tall, not contrary.   Similarly ' the not-beautiful ' is not
necessarily ' the ugly '.

[2] The ambiguity of θάτερον in all this section—' the different ' (that which is
different) and ' Difference itself '—will be discussed below.

[3] Knowledge and its species are a mere illustration.   There is no suggestion
that the species of knowledge correspond to ' parts of the Different '.   Every
Form is a part of the Different, but there is not a species of knowledge for
every Form.

257D. THEAET. Certainly.

STR. And the same thing is true of the parts of the single nature of the Different.

THEAET. Perhaps; but shall we explain how?

STR. There exists a part of the Different that is set in contrast to the Beautiful?

THEAET. Yes.

STR. Are we to say it is nameless, or has it a special name?

THEAET. It has. Whenever we use the expression 'not Beautiful', the thing we mean is precisely that which is different from the nature of the Beautiful.

STR. Then tell me this.

E. THEAET. What?

STR. May we not say that the *existence* of the not-Beautiful is constituted by its being marked off from a single definite Kind [1] among existing things and again set in contrast with something that exists?

THEAET. Yes.

STR. So it appears that the not-Beautiful is an instance of something that exists being set in contrast to something that exists.

THEAET. Perfectly.

STR. What then? On this showing has the not-Beautiful any less claim than the Beautiful to be a thing that exists?

THEAET. None whatever.

258. STR. And so the not-Tall must be said to exist just as much as the Tall itself.

THEAET. Just as much.

STR. And we must also put the not-Just [2] on the same footing as the Just with respect to the fact that the one exists no less than the other.

THEAET. Certainly.

STR. And we shall say the same of all the rest, since we have seen that the nature of the Different is to be ranked among things that exist, and, once it exists, its parts also must be considered as existing just as much as anything else.

THEAET. Of course.

STR. So, it seems, when a part of the nature of the Different

---

[1] τινὸς ἑνὸς γένους, *viz.* the Beautiful; not '*any* single kind', or '*some* kind' (ἑνός γέ τινος γένους).

[2] The 'not-Just' is not 'the unjust', but any Form that is different from 'the Just'. For πρὸς, cf. *Theaet.* 180A, πρὸς τὸ μηδὲ σμικρὸν ἐνεῖναι. Note that the moral Forms (Beautiful, Just) once more appear alongside the rest.

258.   and a part of the nature of the Existent (Existence) [1] are
B.   set in contrast to one another, the contrast is, if it be per-
missible to say so, as much a reality as Existence itself ;
it does not mean what is contrary to ' existent ', but only
what is different from that Existent.

THEAET.   That is quite clear.

STR.   What name are we to give it, then ?

THEAET.   Obviously this is just that ' what-is-not ' which
we were seeking for the sake of the Sophist.

STR.   Has it then, as you say, an existence inferior to none of
the rest in reality ?   May we now be bold to say that ' that
which is not ' unquestionably *is* a thing that has a nature of
C.   its own—just as the Tall was tall and the Beautiful was
beautiful, so too with the not-Tall and the not-Beautiful [2]—
and in that sense ' that which is not ' also, on the same
principle, both was and *is* what-is-not, a single Form to be
reckoned among the many realities ?   Or have we any
further doubts with regard to it, Theaetetus ?

THEAET.   None at all.

The Stranger has now completed his promised refutation of
' Father Parmenides' pronouncement ' by showing ' that in a certain
respect what is not, exists, and again what exists, in a sense is
not ' (241D).

Translation of the foregoing argument into another language
reveals that the terms τὸ ὄν, ταὐτόν, θάτερον are used ambiguously.
Τὸ ὄν means sometimes ' Existence itself ', sometimes ' the existent ' or ' that which is so-and-so ' ; ταὐτόν sometimes ' Sameness ',
sometimes ' that which is the same ' ; θάτερον sometimes ' Difference ',
sometimes ' that which is different '.   But it is clear that Plato
was not blind to these ambiguities.   He has indicated the two
senses of τὸ ὄν quite clearly in the passage at 249D ff. where the
Stranger passed from the discussion of the Real (that which is real)
as containing both things that move and things that are at rest to

---

[1] Understanding ἡ μορίου τῆς θατέρου φύσεως καὶ (μορίου) τῆς τοῦ ὄντος
(φύσεως) ἀντίθεσις.   ' A part of the nature of the Existent ', *i.e.* ' that which
is so-and-so ' (*e.g.* Beautiful).

[2] Keeping the manuscript reading, without inserting $\langle μὴ\ μέγα \rangle$ and $\langle μὴ$
καλόν $\rangle$.   It is unlikely that both these phrases would be accidentally omitted.
ὥσπερ is answered, not by οὕτω δέ, but by καί (before τὸ μὴ μέγα).   Τὸ μὴ
μέγα καὶ τὸ μὴ καλόν are particular examples of ' the different ', or ' the not-so-
and-so ' (τὸ μὴ ὄν) which ' has a nature of its own '.   Grammatically τὸ μὴ μέγα
καὶ τὸ μὴ καλόν is in apposition to the preceding τὸ μὴ ὄν and shares its predicate
βεβαίως ἐστὶ τὴν αὑτοῦ φύσιν ἔχον.   Then οὕτω δὲ καί, κτλ. gives the general
conclusion applying to τὸ μὴ ὄν = τὸ ἕτερον, the ' single Form ' of which
' the not-Tall ', ' the not-Beautiful ', etc., have been called ' parts '.

Realness or Existence as a Form of which everything that is real partakes. Further, no writer who was unaware of the ambiguities could have constructed an argument which is perfectly lucid when the various meanings are kept distinct.

What is really puzzling to us is the description of 'the not-Tall', 'the not-Beautiful', etc., as 'parts of the nature of the Different (or Difference)'. At the outset where the five selected Forms are proved to be distinct, θάτερον clearly means the single Form, Difference. At 255D it is called 'the nature of Difference' (ἡ θατέρου φύσις), and this is said to 'pervade' all the Forms, each of which 'partakes of its character'. But what is meant by calling 'the not-Beautiful', etc., 'parts of this single nature' (257D)?

Clearly 'the not-Beautiful', etc., are not parts of the single Form, Difference itself, the meaning of the word 'different'. A Form can have parts in two senses. (1) If it is complex, the simpler Forms by which it is defined can be called parts, in that their names stand for parts of the meaning of its name. 'Figure' is part of the meaning of 'Triangle'. This sense does not apply. 'Not-Beautiful' is not a part of the meaning of 'Difference'. (2) 'Parts' may also mean 'species'—a meaning actually suggested by the analogy with knowledge and its species at 257C. But, once more, 'the not-Beautiful' is not a species of Difference, as numerical and conceptual difference might be said to be. 'The not-Beautiful' evidently means 'that which is different from the Beautiful'—a collective name for all the Forms there are, other than the Beautiful itself. These other Forms, whether singly or as a group, are not species of a generic Form 'Difference'. What is 'the not-Beautiful' a 'part' of?

It is a part of the whole field of Forms which make up the Real. It is, in fact, the whole group of Forms that is separated off from and contrasted with the single Form, the Beautiful itself. In the *Statesman* (262B ff.) it is pointed out that such a part (μέρος) is not a Form (εἶδος). The Stranger there objects to the division of animals into men and beasts, *i.e.* human and not-human. Negative terms like 'Barbarian' (non-Greek), though they have a name, have no Form that could be subdivided. 'Not every part is a Form, though every Form is a part.' So 'the not-Beautiful' is not a Form, but a group of Forms, negatively described, which is a part of the Real.[1]

When it is said to be 'a part of the Different' or 'of the nature of the Different', the Different must mean 'that which is different'. Since every part of the field of Forms is different from every other

---

[1] Such a group of Forms is a whole (ὅλον) or complex of diverse parts, in the sense in which 'whole' is used in the description of Dialectic at 253D.

part, the whole field can be called 'the Different'; it will bear the collective name 'that which is not', just as well as the name 'that which is'; and any Form or group of Forms can be called both existent and 'a part of the Different'. In a Table of Division of genus into species, every positive determination we reach as we descend is called a 'difference'. This technical term may be derived from Plato's analysis here. It signifies that each positive element of content we discover in dividing the generic Form is a 'difference', marked off by a line of division from something else. Positively, it is an element in the identity (sameness) of the species we shall define by it; negatively, it differentiates that species from others. Thus 'the not-Beautiful' is 'a part of the Different', though not of Difference itself; and the nature of Difference can be described as diffused over the whole field of Forms, no less than is Existence. The thought is clear; but the language is certainly confusing, partly thanks to Plato's way of thinking of Difference, not as a relation between things, but as a property of which things that are different 'partake'.

258c–259d. *Conclusion : We have refuted Parmenides' dogma that 'what is' cannot in any sense not-be, and that 'what is not' cannot in any sense be*

The Stranger now formulates the conclusions. Parmenides forbade us to assert 'that things that are not, are'. That is to say, he recognised only one sense of 'is not', namely 'is totally non-existent'. We have ruled out that sense long ago; and now we have brought to light another sense, which allows us to assert that things which are not (are different from other things) nevertheless are (exist).

258c. STR. You see, then, that in our disobedience to Parmenides we have trespassed far beyond the limits of his prohibition.
THEAET. In what way?
STR. In pushing forward on our quest, we have shown him results in a field which he forbade us even to explore.
THEAET. How?
D. STR. He says, you remember,
'Never shall this be proved, that things that are not, are;
but keep back thy thought from this way of inquiry'.
THEAET. Yes, he does say that.
STR. Whereas we have not merely shown that things that are not, are, but we have brought to light the real character of 'not-being'. We have shown that the nature of the
E. Different has existence and is parcelled out over the whole field of existent things with reference to one another; and

258E.   of every part of it that is set in contrast to 'that which is' we have dared to say that precisely that *is really* 'that which is not'.

THEAET. Yes, sir, and I think what we have said is perfectly true.

For the purposes of the formal conclusion now to be stated—that things that are not (are different) exist—the relevant senses of 'is' and 'is not' are Existence and Difference. The third all-pervading Form, Sameness ('is the same as'), is left in the background without explicit mention. The next speech (1) rules out non-existence (the only sense of 'not-being' that Parmenides would recognise) as a sense of '*is not*' that has no application to Forms, and (2) describes how Existence and Difference are two Forms, both extending over the whole field of reality and everywhere blending.

258E.   STR. Then let no one say that it is the contrary of the existent that we mean by 'what is not', when we make bold to say that 'what is not.' exists. So far as any contrary of the existent is concerned, we have long ago[1] said good-bye

259.   to the question whether there is such a thing or not and whether any account can be given of it or none whatsoever.

But with respect to the 'what-is-not' that we have now asserted to exist, an opponent must either convince us that our account is wrong by refuting it, or, so long as he proves unable to do that, he must accept our statements:

that the Kinds blend with one another;

that Existence and Difference pervade them all, and pervade one another;

that Difference (*or* the Different),[2] by partaking of Existence, *is* by virtue of that participation, but on the other hand *is not* that Existence of which it partakes, but is different; and since it is different from Existence (*or* an existent), quite clearly it must be possible[3] that it should *be* a thing that *is not*[4];

---

[1] At 238c, where τὸ μηδαμῶς ὄν, 'the simply non-existent', was dismissed as not to be spoken or thought of. There are no true statements saying that any Form does not exist. But it is true of every Form other than Existence itself that it is not (identical with) Existence.

[2] As before, θάτερον is verbally ambiguous and the formula covers the two statements: (1) that the Form Difference *is not* (the same as) Existence, but *is* (exists); (2) that the different (that which is not so-and-so) *is not* (the same as) a thing that is (*viz.* a certain existent, the so-and-so it differs from), but *is* a thing that is (an existent).

[3] ἔστιν ἐξ ἀνάγκης εἶναι, 'It is possible, necessarily, for it to be'. Cf. 256D, ἔστιν ἐξ ἀνάγκης . . . εἶναι in the same sense.

[4] *I.e.* (1) Difference is not Existence; and (2) the different is not some other definite existent with which it contrasted.

259B.   and again, Existence, having a part in Difference, will be
        different from all the rest of the Kinds ; and, because it is
        different from them all, it *is not* any one of them nor yet
        all the others put together, but is only itself [1] ; with the
        consequence, again indisputable, that Existence *is not*
        myriads upon myriads of things, and that all the other
        Kinds in the same way, whether taken severally or all
        together, in many respects *are* and in many respects *are
        not*.

        THEAET. True.

We may here collect the meanings of ' is ' and ' is not ' that have
been brought to light.

(1) ' Is ' means ' *exists* '. Every Form exists ; consequently ' the
non-existent ' has no place in the scheme, and we have ruled out
that sense of ' is not '.

(2) ' Is ' means ' *is the same as* '. Every Form is (the same as)
itself. The contradictory ' is not ' means ' *is different from* '.

It will be noticed that neither of these two senses of ' is ' has
anything to do with ' the copula ', the supposed link between
subject and predicate in Aristotelian logic. The statement that
Plato ' has discovered the ambiguity of the copula ' is far removed
from the facts.

There remain statements expressing the relation of two Forms
that are neither wholly different nor wholly the same, but related
as generic to specific Form or as specific to generic Form. The
diagram given earlier shows the specific and generic Forms over-
lapping and ' blending ' ; but they do not coincide. A definition
is a statement of complete identity : ' Man is (the same as) rational
biped Animal '. But genus and species are related as whole to
part. At *Parm.* 146B it is said that ' everything stands to everything in this way : either it is the same or different, or, if it is
neither the same nor different, then one thing is a part, the other
a whole '. Hence ' part ' is the regular Platonic term for ' species '.
Plato has not occasion to analyse statements of the type : ' Man
is Animal '. Perhaps he regarded them as statements of partial
identity : ' the Form Man is (the same as) a part of the Form
Animal '. The appropriate word would be ' partake of ' (μετέχειν),
indicating that genus and species are blended, but do not coincide.
But he does not use ' partake of ' with any precision or distinguish

----

[1] Here the distinction between the Form Existence as discussed in all this
section and the Existent (the Real, the whole world of real Forms) is clearly
recognised. The corresponding statements are : (1) Existence *is not* (the
same as any other Form), but *is* (the same as) itself ; (2) the Existent (any
Form or group of Forms) *is not* (the same as) any other existent, but *is* (exists).

' partaking' from the mutual relation called ' blending' or ' combining' (σύμμειξις, κοινωνία). The reason for supposing that this use of ' is ' would fall under ' is the same as ' is that the whole discussion recognises only three all-pervading Forms—Existence, Sameness, Difference—which are already accounted for.

It may be added that this whole account of the blending or mutual participation of Forms cannot be directly applied to the old problem, raised in the *Parmenides*, of the participation of individual things in Forms. M. Brochard [1] writes : ' The relations of things to Forms are no doubt the same as the relations of Forms among themselves.' But this is not so. In the *Parmenides* and again at *Soph.* 251A and in the *Philebus*, the old question how one thing can have many names is distinguished from the problem of the interrelations of Forms and dismissed as already solved by the theory of Forms, though the precise nature of this participation may remain obscure. Also, as we have seen, in speaking of Forms ' participation' is synonymous with ' blending' or ' combination' and is a symmetrical relation, whereas the participation of things in Forms traverses the boundary between things and Forms and is not a symmetrical relation : Forms do not partake of things. This problem, therefore, remains where it was.

Next follows a short interlude, pointing out the bearing of the conclusions just reached upon eristic controversy of the type started by Zeno.

259B.   STR.   And if anyone mistrusts these apparent contradictions,
he should study the question and produce some better
c.   explanation than we have now given ; whereas if he imagines
he has discovered an embarrassing puzzle and takes delight
in reducing argument to a tug of war, he is wasting his pains
on a triviality, as our present argument declares. There
is nothing clever in such a discovery, nor is it hard to make ;
what is hard and at the same time worth the pains is something different.

THEAET.   And that is——?

STR.   What I said before : leaving such quibbling alone as
leading nowhere, [2] to be able to follow our statements step
by step and, in criticising the assertion that a different thing
D.   is the same or the same thing is different in a certain sense,
to take account of the precise sense and the precise respect
in which they are said to be one or the other. Merely to

---

[1] *Études*, 148.
[2] ἀνήνυτα (Badham) seems to be the most probable correction of δυνατά yet proposed.

259D. show that in some unspecified way the same is different
or the different is the same, the tall short, the like unlike,
and to take pleasure in perpetually parading such contradictions in argument—that is not genuine criticism, but may
be recognised as the callow offspring of a too recent contact
with reality.[1]

THEAET. I quite agree.

III. FALSE SPEAKING AND THINKING

The last main division of the argument opens here (259D) and
continues to 264B, where the final definition of the Sophist is resumed
and completed. It explains how there can be Falsity in speech and
thought. In the *Theaetetus* all attempts to explain this failed
because the discussion was deliberately confined to an apparatus
which excluded the Forms. These have now been brought into
account, and we shall find that, when Forms are recognised as the
meanings of common names and therefore as entering into the meaning of all statements, it will be possible to give false statements a
meaning without invoking non-existent things or facts for them
to refer to.

259D–261C. *Introductory statement of the problem*

The introductory section states the problem in terms which are,
at first sight, puzzling in that they seem to ignore the distinctions
that have just been drawn. Some critics here accuse Plato of gross
confusion and fallacy.[2] Such accusations are groundless. The subsequent analysis of falsity is as lucid as the previous account of the
blending of Forms. Such obscurity as there is occurs only in this
introductory passage, which is ' dialectical ' and dramatic. The
purpose is to make the reader feel that there is a difficulty to be
cleared up, and to represent the perplexity of the respondent, who
does not yet see just what the difficulty is, still less how to solve
it. In such passages Plato does not use terms with precision or
observe all the distinctions of which a very clear-headed reader would
be conscious.

The difficulty which every reader is meant to feel lies in seeing
how the preceding demonstration that ' is not ' has two senses

---

[1] The phrase recalls 234B where young men were said to be imposed on
by the Sophist's wizardry until they were undeceived by ' contact with reality '
(ἐφάπτεσθαι τῶν ὄντων). The Stranger here indicates that the dilemmas of
Zeno and his later imitators turned on ambiguities of the kind he has just
cleared up.

[2] Apelt (note on 260C) declares that there is no possible transition from the
μὴ ὄν which has been shown to exist to τὸ μὴ ὄν in the sense of ' the false ', and
that the confusion of these two is rampant throughout the rest of the dialogue.

—'does not exist' and 'is different from'—bears on the question whether false statements can have any meaning. The connection is as follows. It was common ground that 'to say what is false' is, in some sense, 'to say things that are not' (τὸ τὰ μὴ ὄντα λέγειν), as the Stranger will observe presently. The question is, what sense can 'things that are not' bear in this phrase? The Sophist's argument was : 'To say the thing that is not' can only mean 'to say nothing' or 'to speak of nothing' (οὐδὲν λέγειν), that is, to 'talk nonsense'.[1] You cannot speak of what does not exist ; there are no non-existing things or facts to speak of. Therefore all false speech must be meaningless. This is a quite serious difficulty, not easily disposed of. What are we talking about when we make a false statement ?

Plato has now shown that 'the thing that is not' does not (as the Sophist assumed) always mean 'the non-existent' ; it can also mean something which is different from something else. Both these 'somethings' are something (ὄν), not nothing. He intends to interpret the phrase 'to say, or speak of, that which is not' by means of this second sense, as equivalent to 'to say, or speak of, something different from the actual facts, but not simply non-existent'. The question is, what sort of existence that 'something different' can have. If we can discover that, we can assert that a false statement has meaning.

But this explanation is still to come. At present all we know is that 'that which is not' is ambiguous. The Stranger is thinking of the sense he will use in his explanation ; the Sophist, who is represented as defending his position, still feels that 'saying what is not' involves somewhere an element of unreality or non-existence, which he will challenge as illegitimate. Theaetetus, like the ordinary reader, may well be excused for not having taken in the full sense of the foregoing analysis. Once we realise the dialectical character of the passage, we shall see that Plato himself is not guilty of confusion.

The phrase just used by the Stranger, 'the offspring of a too recent contact with reality', recalled the earlier reference to young men deluded by the Sophist's wizardries. It also recalls the 'old men who have taken to learning late in life' (251B), who were coupled with the young as delighting in the sophism : One thing cannot have many names. The position of these men who would 'separate everything from everything else' is now mentioned again. Their difficulties arose from not recognising the existence of Forms as the meanings of common names, or seeing that one thing can

[1] Cf. 240D (p. 212) and the full statement of this argument at *Theaetetus* 188D ff. (p. 114).

partake of many Forms.   The Stranger begins by pointing out that
' all discourse depends on the weaving together of Forms '.

259D.   STR.   Yes, my friend, and the attempt to separate every-
E.   thing from every other thing not only strikes a discordant
note but amounts to a crude defiance of the philosophic
Muse.[1]
THEAET.   Why ?
STR.   This isolation of everything from everything else
means a complete abolition of all discourse ; for any dis-
course we can have owes its existence to the weaving together
of Forms.
THEAET.   True.

260.   STR.   Observe, then, how opportune was our struggle with
those separatists, when we forced them to allow one Form
to blend with another.
THEAET.   In what respect ?
STR.   In respect of securing the position of discourse as
one of the kinds of things that exist.   To rob us of discourse
would be to rob us of philosophy.   That would be the most
serious consequence ; but, besides that, we need at the present
moment to come to an agreement about the nature of discourse, and if its very existence had been taken from us,
B.   we should naturally not be able to discourse any further.
And that would have happened, if we had yielded the point
that there is no blending of any one Form with another.

All discourse depends on the ' weaving together (συμπλοκή) of
Forms '.   ' Weaving together ' is not a synonym of ' combining ' or
' blending ' ;   it includes all statements, affirmative or negative.[2]
It is not meant that Forms are the only elements in the meaning of
all discourse.   We can also make statements about individual
things.   But it is true that every such statement must contain at
least one Form—one of those ' common terms ' (Theaet. 185) which
are necessary to all thought or judgment about the objects of direct
perception.   So (at 252C) it was objected against the separatists
that they could not express their theory at all without ' connecting
in their statements ' (συνάπτειν ἐν τοῖς λόγοις) terms like ' is ',
' apart from ', ' the rest ', etc., which are common terms.   The

---

[1] ἄμουσος is almost a synonym of ἀφιλόσοφος.   Crat. 406A derives Μοῦσα and
μουσική from μῶσθαι = ζήτησίς τε καὶ φιλοσοφία.   Phaedo 61A quotes the
Pythagorean saying that Philosophy is the highest form of ' Music '.

[2] In Aristotle, de interpr. init. συμπλοκή is used for the contextus verborum in
a sentence, as distinct from isolated words.   So below at 262C, ἡ πρώτη συμπλοκή,
and 262D, πλέγμα.

point here made, that every statement or judgment involves the use of at least one Form, is important because the recognition of Forms as entering into the meaning of all statements will solve the problem of false speech and thinking.

260B. THEAET. That is certainly true. But I do not understand why we need an agreement about discourse at the present moment.

STR. I may be able to suggest a line of thought that will help you to understand.

THEAET. What is that ? *Form*

STR. We saw that 'not being' is a single kind among the rest, dispersed over the whole field of realities.

THEAET. Yes.

STR. We have next to consider whether it blends with thinking and discourse. *Forms*

THEAET. Why that ?

c. STR. If it does not blend with them, everything must be true ; but if it does, we shall have false thinking and discourse ; for thinking or saying 'what is not' comes, I suppose, to the same thing as falsity in thought and speech.

THEAET. Yes.

STR. And if falsity exists, deception is possible.

THEAET. Yes.

STR. And once deception exists, images and likenesses and appearance will be everywhere rampant.

THEAET. Of course.

STR. And the Sophist, we said, had taken refuge some-
D. where in that region, but then he had denied the very existence of falsity : no one could either think or say 'what is not', because what is not never has any sort of being.

THEAET. So he said.

STR. But now that 'what is not' has been found to have its share in existence, perhaps he will not fight with us further on that point.

The 'not-being' which we found to be a single Form distributed over the whole field of reality was 'Difference'. When the Stranger asks whether 'not-being' blends with speaking and thinking, the real question is whether there is any sense of 'what is not' that will justify our combining that phrase with speaking and thinking in the expression 'to speak of, or think, what is not'. The Sophist originally maintained that there can be no justification, because 'what is not' always means 'the non-existent'. We have ousted him from that position by showing that it sometimes has another meaning, ' the different ', which is compatible with existence.

But a second line of defence remains, as the Stranger goes on to suggest. The Sophist may accept the ambiguity of ' what is not ', and still deny our right to assert the possibility of saying and thinking what is not. The meaning of ' what is not ' here has still to be defined and justified. ' What is not ' may not always mean ' the non-existent '; but in this particular phrase it suggests some element of unreality (which, as we have argued, is not the same thing as ' difference '). So the Sophist is represented as raising a further objection.

260D. STR. (continues). On the other hand, he may perhaps say that some things partake of not-being, some do not, and that speech and thinking are among those that do not; and so once more he might contend that the art of creating
E. images and semblances, where we say he is to be found, has no existence at all, since thought and speech have no share in not-being, and without that combination there is no such thing as falsity.

That is why we must begin by investigating the nature of discourse and thinking and appearance, in order that we
261. may then make out their combination with not-being and so prove that falsity exists, and by that proof pin down the Sophist there, if he is amenable to capture, or else let him go and pursue our search in some other Kind.

The Sophist's second line of defence is here stated as the Sophist himself would state it, not as it would be put by anyone who was confining himself to the precise use of the terms defined in the last section. ' Some things ', he suggests, ' partake of not-being, some do not.' If ' things ' (εἰδῶν) meant Platonic Forms, we have just shown that no Forms partake of ' not-being ' in the sense of non-existence, and that all Forms partake of it in the sense of Difference. But eidos is a vague word, sometimes meaning no more than ' entity ', ' thing '; and by ' not-being ' the Sophist clearly means falsity. We have still to discover how ' the false ' (a term strictly applicable only to thought and speech) is related to ' the non-existent ' and ' the different '. The last section dealt solely with the world of Forms where non-existence and falsity have no place. The thought and speech which can partake of falsity are not Platonic Forms but the thoughts which exist in our minds and the speeches we utter.[1] No result reached so far has shown how they can ever be false.

[1] At 263D the thinking, judgment, and ' appearing ', which ' occur in our minds' are called γένη (' things ' or ' kinds of thing '), if we read τὰ γένη with B (γένη T : γε Stobaeus).

Theaetetus' next speech expresses the perplexity to which he and the reader are reduced by the ambiguities of ' not-being '. That Plato himself was misled by them is entirely incredible ; for as soon as the argument begins again the thought once more runs perfectly clear.

261A. THEAET. Certainly, sir, what we said at the outset about the Sophist seems true : that he is a hard sort of beast to hunt down. Evidently he possesses a whole armoury of problems, and every time that he puts one forward to shield him, we have to fight our way through it before we can get at him. So now, hardly have we got the better of his defence that ' what is not ' cannot exist, when another

B. obstacle is raised in our path : we must, it seems, prove that falsity exists both in speech and thought, and after that perhaps something else, and so on. It looks as if the end would never be in sight.

STR. A man should be of good courage, Theaetetus, if he can make only a little headway at each step. If he loses heart then, what will he do in another case where he cannot advance at all or even perhaps loses ground ? No city, as

c. they say, will surrender to so faint a summons. And now that we have surmounted the barrier you speak of, we may have already taken the highest wall and the rest may be easier to capture.

THEAET. That is encouraging.

261C–262E. *Every statement is a complex of heterogeneous elements (name and verb)*

The Stranger opens the discussion by pointing out that every statement is complex. The simplest statement must contain at least one ' name ' and one verb. The terms ' name ' and ' verb ' are defined.

261C. STR. Then, as I said, let us take first statement [1] and judgment, so as to establish clearly whether not-being has any point of contact with them, or both are altogether true and there is never falsity in either.

THEAET. Very good.

[1] 'Statement.' So far λόγος has been translated ' discourse '; but the following analysis is concerned with what Aristotle calls the ἀποφαντικὸς λόγος, a statement which can and must be either true or false, as distinct from questions, prayers, etc. A ' judgment ' (as explained later) is here equivalent to an unspoken statement made by the mind in its internal dialogue with itself.

261D. STR. Now, remembering what we said about Forms and letters,[1] let us consider words in the same way. The solution of our present problem promises to lie in that quarter.

THEAET. What are you going to ask me about words ?

STR. Whether they all fit together, or none of them, or some will and some will not.

THEAET. That is plain enough : some will, some will not.

STR. You mean perhaps something like this : words which,

E. when spoken in succession, signify something, do fit together, while those which mean nothing when they are strung together, do not.

THEAET. What do you mean ?

STR. What I supposed you had in your mind when you gave your assent.[2] The signs we use in speech to signify being are surely of two kinds.

THEAET. How ?

262. STR. One kind called ' names ', the other ' verbs '.

THEAET. Give me a description of each.

STR. By ' verb ' we mean an expression which is applied to actions.

THEAET. Yes.

STR. And by a ' name ' the spoken sign applied to what performs these actions.

THEAET. Quite so.

STR. Now a statement never consists solely of names spoken in succession, nor yet of verbs apart from names.

THEAET. I don't follow that.

B. STR. Evidently you had something else in mind when you agreed with me just now ; because what I meant was just this : that these words spoken in a string in this way do not make a statement.

THEAET. In what way ?

STR. For example, ' walks runs sleeps ',[3] and so on with all the other verbs signifying actions—you may utter them all one after another, but that does not make a statement.

---

[1] At 253A (p. 260).

[2] Probably what Theaetetus had in mind was the combination of Forms in affirmative statements and the incompatibility of Forms expressed by negative statements, which was illustrated by the fitting-together (συναρμόττειν) or not fitting of vowels and consonants at 253A. But the Stranger is referring only to the illustration and is thinking of the fact that a statement cannot consist of a combination of two nouns only or of two verbs only, any m're than a word can consist of two consonants without a vowel.

[3] The inverted commas in Burnet's text between βαδίζει and καθεύδει (and below, between λέων and ἵπποι) should be omitted.

262B. THEAET. Naturally.

STR. And again, if you say 'lion stag horse' and any other names given to things that perform actions, such a string
C. never makes up a statement. Neither in this example nor in the other do the sounds uttered signify any action performed or not performed or nature of anything that exists or does not exist,[1] until you combine verbs with names. The moment you do that, they fit together and the simplest combination becomes a statement of what might be called the simplest and briefest kind.

THEAET. Then how do you make a statement of that kind ?

STR. When one says 'A man understands', do you agree that this is a statement of the simplest and shortest possible kind ?

D. THEAET. Yes.

STR. Because now it gives information about facts or events in the present or past or future : it does not merely name something but gets you somewhere [2] by weaving together verbs with names. Hence we say it 'states' something, not merely 'names' something, and in fact it is this complex that we mean by the word 'statement'.

THEAET. True.

STR. And so, just as some things fit together, some do not,
E. so with the signs of speech : some do not fit, but those that do fit make a statement.

THEAET. Quite so.

The definition of 'word'. Aristotle defines spoken words as tokens (σύμβολα) or signs (σημεῖα) of mental affections ; and the written word as a token of the spoken word. He remarks that, although languages have different spoken and written signs, the mental affections are the same in all men and so are the things (πράγματα) of which the mental affections are likenesses (*De interpr.* I).

---

[1] πρᾶξιν οὐδ' ἀπραξίαν refers to the former example (ἐκείνως) of the string of verbs, which does not state that any action is actually performed, or not performed, by any agent. οὐδὲ οὐσίαν ὄντος οὐδὲ μὴ ὄντος refers to the latter example (οὕτως) of the string of names, which does not state that there actually exists (ὄντος), or does not exist, anything with the nature (οὐσία) expressed by any of the names. This does not mean that the words themselves have no meaning, and are senseless noises ; but that such concatenations are not statements of fact, do not refer (or profess to refer) to any actual fact or event.

[2] περαίνειν τι, the opposite of οὐδὲν περαίνειν, ' to get nowhere '. Cf. *Theaet.* 180A.

Plato defines a word, not as the token of a mental affection, but as a vocal sign (σημεῖον τῆς φωνῆς 262A) used to signify *being* (περὶ τὴν οὐσίαν δήλωμα [1]). This at once implies that every word stands for something or means something ; it is not a meaningless noise. It follows that no element in a false statement can be simply meaningless. But ' being ' is an ambiguous expression.

(1) ' Being ' may mean the nature of a thing. At *Laws* 895D, Plato says that in the case of everything there are always three factors : the ' *being* ' or nature (οὐσία), the *definition* or account (λόγος) of the nature, and the *name* (ὄνομα). The nature is a counterpart of the definition. So at *Phaedrus* 245E the ' essential being or definition of soul ' (ψυχῆς οὐσίαν καὶ λόγον) is ' that which moves itself '. At *Cratylus* 393D, where significant or descriptive proper names are in question, it is said that Astyanax (Lord of the city) and Hector (Warden) have the same ' force ' (δύναμις) : one meaning can be expressed in different syllables or letters, so long as the *being of the thing* (οὐσία τοῦ πράγματος) as expressed in the name (δηλουμένη ἐν τῷ ὀνόματι) prevails. *Cratylus* 383E : Things (πράγματα) have a constant being (βέβαιος οὐσία) of their own, which we cannot alter ; so have actions (πράξεις). The example at *Laws* 895D is the *name* ' even ' as applied to numbers. This has the *definition* ' divisible into two equal parts ', and the corresponding *being* (οὐσία) is this property of numbers. Every such nature is, in Platonic terms, a Form (*eidos*)—the meaning of a common name, which, if complex, is definable.

(2) In the case of Forms the *nature* and the *thing* are one and the same. So at *Protagoras* 349B it is asked whether the five names of the cardinal virtues all apply to one thing (ἐπὶ ἑνὶ πράγματι), or is each name applied severally to ' a peculiar nature or thing ' (ἴδιος οὐσία καὶ πρᾶγμα) having a property of its own. But there are also proper names attached by convention to individual things. In the statement we shall presently take as typical, ' Theaetetus sits ', ' Theaetetus ' stands for an individual thing, and (as the *Cratylus* showed) does not necessarily express its nature. The name may have no ' meaning ' in itself ; it merely stands for the thing we choose to attach that sound to. The definition of ' word ' must cover such names as these ; ' sign signifying being ' includes this second sense : ' standing for something that exists '. At *Cratylus* 388C a name is said to have two functions : it is a tool (1) to convey information (διδασκαλικόν) and (2) to distinguish things (τὰ πράγματα διακρίνειν, διακριτικὸν τῆς οὐσίας). ' Thing ' or ' being ' here has the wider sense, covering any object distinguished

---

[1] δήλωμα, cf. *Laws* 792A : Crying is to infants a *means of signifying* their desires (δήλωμα ὧν ἐρᾷ)—not a happy kind of sign (σημεῖον) !

by a name, whether that object be a Form (the nature which is the *meaning expressed* by common name) or an individual thing which may be indicated conventionally by a proper name *standing for* it.

Plato's definition of 'word' thus covers two senses. (1) A common name *signifies* or '*means*' a 'nature' which is a Form, as well as '*standing for*' or *indicating* existing things. (2) A proper name *stands for* or *indicates* an existing thing only. With his usual disregard for precision, Plato uses all the common words for 'signify', 'mean', 'indicate', indiscriminately. But in order to understand the analysis of the statement, 'Theaetetus sits', we shall find it necessary to distinguish between a proper name like 'Theaetetus' and a 'common term' like 'sits'.

Names and Verbs.—At *Cratylus* 425A the notion that speech or statement (λόγος) consists of names and verbs is taken as familiar, without explanation. It was probably due to grammarians, for the previous context refers to their classification of letters into vowels, sonants, and mutes. A statement is 'a combination of names and verbs' (431B). Aristotle repeats this.[1] Other parts of speech are ignored. Aristotle is understood as meaning that a noun and a verb are, as Plato here remarks, necessary and sufficient for the minimum statement that can be true or false. Later grammarians seem to have taken the same view. Ammonius observes that other parts of speech (conjunctions, prepositions, articles, etc.) cannot, when put together, make up a statement (λόγος) : they are accordingly 'parts of speech' (λέξις), not 'parts of statement' (λόγος). Plutarch (*Plat. Qu.* x) says that Plato speaks only of names and verbs because a statement really does consist of these parts. A name ('Socrates') or a verb ('is beaten') calls up the idea of a person or a thing ; but words like μέν, γάρ, περί, do not. Apart from the mention of a person or thing they are empty noises, not significant either (as names and verbs are) by themselves, nor yet when strung together. He compares them to salt in a dish of meat or the water in a cake, which is not properly 'part' of the cake, but serves to hold it together. Only names and verbs are 'parts of statement' (λόγος). This neglect of the minor parts of speech led to serious consequences in Logic. It facilitated the theory that every proposition has a subject (noun) and a predicate (normally adjective or verb) ; and the nature of relations was obscured by the

---

[1] *De Interpr.* i. Cf. *Rhet.* 1404*b*, 26, ὄντων δὲ ὀνομάτων καὶ ῥημάτων ἐξ ὧν ὁ λόγος συνέστηκεν. Stenzel (*Studien z. Entwicklung d. plat. Dialektik*, 88) thinks that ῥῆμα includes any predicate (*Aussage*), *e.g.* καλός in ὁ παῖς καλός (cf. art. *Logik* in P.W. *Encycl*. Halbband XXV, 1011).

failure to recognise the claim of prepositions to have meanings of their own.

It will be noticed that Plato takes as the typical minimum statement the combination of a name (noun) and a verb expressing an action, not such a sentence as ' Socrates is wise '.   But he is not writing a treatise on logic.   If he were, his definition of ' verb ' as ' an expression applied to actions ' would be obviously defective, as ignoring verbs expressing states ; and to define ' name ', as he does, in terms of the verb—' the spoken sign applied to what performs these actions '—would be odd.   The definitions are not meant to be precise.

The upshot of this section is that every statement is complex, consisting of heterogeneous elements (name and verb) which severally have meanings and, when put together, form a whole having significance as a whole.   The fact or event which the statement corresponds to and professes to represent as a whole, is also complex, consisting of heterogeneous elements (agent and action), which fit together in a coherent structure.

262E.   *Every statement is about something and is either true or false*

Two more points are now added.   (1) One element in the complex statement is the name of the agent, about which the statement is made.   (2) Every statement as a whole is either true or false.

262E.   STR.   Now another small point.
   THEAET.   Yes ?
   STR.   Whenever there is a statement, it must be about something [1] ; it cannot be about nothing.
   THEAET.   That is so.
   STR.   And must it not have a certain character ? [2]
   THEAET.   Of course.

The assertion that ' every statement is about something ' indicates that one element in the complex statement is the name of the agent or (to use the later term) subject, and the agent itself is one element in the existing fact.   In the examples we shall take, Theaetetus himself is the subject both in the true statement ' Theaetetus sits ' and in the false ' Theaetetus flies '.   Probably the Stranger means here to emphasise that the subject of both state-

---

[1] The simple genitive τινός ' of something ' is used ; and at 263A Theaetetus speaks of the statement about him as ' mine ' (ἐμός), as if this genitive were possessive.   But in the same breath he speaks of it as ' about me ' (περὶ ἐμοῦ) ; and that is evidently what both expressions mean.

[2] That ' character ' or ' quality ' means truth or falsity, here as at *Philebus* 37B, is obvious from what follows (263A, B).

ments is the actually existing Theaetetus. Whatever element of unreality we may look to find in the false statement, at any rate the subject is not unreal or non-existent. A false statement is not a statement about a non-existent subject, nor does it deny the existence of its subject. To ' speak of or say what is is not ' does not mean ' to make a statement about nothing '.

The importance of this point may explain why Plato selects as examples true and false statements about an individual thing, Theaetetus, not about a Form, such as we had in the previous section. That Theaetetus exists here and now is common ground with his opponents ; but they would have denied the existence of Forms like Motion and Rest, and Plato does not want to lay himself open to that objection here. Granted that Forms do exist, the objection is invalid, and the analysis now offered of the meaning of true and false statements would apply also to statements about Forms.

262E–263B. *The definition of true statement*

The Stranger next takes two statements about the same subject, one obviously true, the other inconsistent with it and obviously false. He then proceeds to give, with surprising brevity, his definitions of true and false statement.

262E. STR. Now let us fix our attention on ourselves.
   THEAET. We will.
   STR. I will make a statement to you, then, putting together a thing with an action by means of a name and a verb. You are to tell me what the statement is about.
263. THEAET. I will do my best.
   STR. ' Theaetetus sits '—not a lengthy statement, is it ?
   THEAET. No, of very modest length.
   STR. Now it is for you to say what it is about—to whom it belongs.
   THEAET. Clearly about me : it belongs to me.
   STR. Now take another.
   THEAET. Namely——?
   STR. ' Theaetetus (whom I am talking to at this moment) [1] flies.'
   THEAET. That too can only be described as belonging to me and about me.
   STR. And moreover we agree that any statement must have a certain character.
B. THEAET. Yes.

[1] Not an imaginary Theaetetus or Theaetetus at some other moment, but the real Theaetetus here and now.

263B.   STR.   Then what sort of character can we assign to each
of these ?
THEAET.   One is false, the other true.
STR.   And the true one states about you the things that
are (or the facts) as they are.
THEAET.   Certainly.

This brief definition of true statement occurs in earlier dialogues.
(1) At *Euthydemus* 283E, Euthydemus maintains that it is impossible to speak falsely. For if you speak of the thing that the
statement is about, that thing must be one among the things that
are (τῶν ὄντων). So you are speaking of the thing that is (τὸ ὄν).
But to speak of the thing that is or the facts (τὸ ὄν λέγειν καὶ τὰ
ὄντα), is to speak the truth. Ctesippus objects that one who speaks
falsely ' does in a way speak of things that are, but not *as* they are '
(τὰ ὄντα μὲν τρόπον τινὰ λέγει, οὐ μέντοι ὥς γε ἔχει, 284C).
Ctesippus is evidently quoting a popular definition : ' The true statement speaks of things that are, or states facts, *as they are* '. (2)
Again at *Cratylus* 385B Socrates remarks to Hermogenes that the
true statement ' speaks of the things that are, as they are ' or ' states
that the things that are, are ' (ὃς ἂν τὰ ὄντα λέγῃ ὡς ἔστιν). Here
the phrase is ambiguous in form, but the difference is rather grammatical than substantial. The definition is given as current and
accepted without discussion. Both here and in the *Euthydemus*
(where ὡς ἔχει must mean ' *as* they are ') the notion is that
truth consists in the *correspondence* of the statement with the
' things that are ' or ' the facts '. How they correspond is not
explained.

But for our present purpose of discovering what a *false* statement
can mean or correspond with, it is important to be clear about the
meaning of ' things that are ' or ' facts '. We have seen that all
facts represented by statements are complex. In the case of the
true statement ' Theaetetus sits ', there are (1) the thing about which
the statement is made—an existing thing, Theaetetus ; (2) the
' action ' referred to by the verb ' sits '—another existing thing ; and
(3) the whole complex existing fact—Theaetetus-sitting—composed
of those two elements. Let us take this complex existing fact and
suppose that it is, or contains, all the ' things that are ', which the
statement is to correspond with.

This existing fact—Theaetetus-sitting—is a complex object of
perception ; and, if we may assume that my judgment ' Theaetetus
sits ' simply represents what I actually see with no element of
inference, my statement will be true. We shall then get the following scheme :

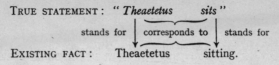

TRUE STATEMENT : " *Theaetetus   sits* "

stands for | corresponds to | stands for

EXISTING FACT : Theaetetus   sitting.

Here each of the two words *stands for* one element in the complex fact. The statement as a whole is complex and its structure *corresponds to* the structure of the fact. Truth means this correspondence.

Common sense might accept this account of true statement ; and this, no doubt, was the popular meaning of ' speaking of things that are ', or ' stating facts, *as they are* '. If all statements were true and were of the type here exemplified, the account might be taken as complete. But here the difficulty begins. How are we to define false statement on these lines ? If we define true statement by the correspondence of its structure with the structure of an existing fact which it refers to, the Sophist will object that a false statement cannot be defined as corresponding with anything, because there are no non-existent facts for it to correspond with or mean or refer to. A false statement, therefore, means nothing. This involves a problem which modern logicians are still discussing. ' Charles I died on the scaffold ' corresponds to a fact ; ' Charles I died in bed ' and ' Charles I did not die on the scaffold ' do not. If I judge or believe either of these statements, how can there be an ' objective falsehood ' or ' negative fact ' to provide an object for my belief ? [1]

263B–D. *The definition of false statement*

The language in which Plato now states his solution is extremely simple, and consequently vague and ambiguous. The meaning of the literal translation here given will be discussed later.[2]

---

[1] See, for instance, Russell, *Philosophical Essays* (1910), On the Nature of Truth and Falsehood.

[2] The text is as follows :

ΞΕ.   Ὁ δὲ δὴ ψευδὴς ἕτερα τῶν ὄντων (sc. λέγει περὶ σοῦ).

ΘΕ.   Ναί.

ΞΕ.   Τὰ μὴ ὄντα ἄρα ὡς ὄντα λέγει.

ΘΕ.   Σχεδόν.

ΞΕ.   Ὄντων (Cornarius : ὄντως ΒΤ) δέ γε ὄντα ἕτερα περὶ σοῦ.   πολλὰ μὲν γὰρ ἔφαμεν ὄντα περὶ ἕκαστον εἶναί που, πολλὰ δὲ οὐκ ὄντα.

I cannot follow M. Diès' explanation : *Ainsi la proposition est fausse quand elle affirme d'un sujet ce qui n'est point de lui.   C'est bien toujours de l'être qu'elle exprime. Elle exprime ce qui est, mais autrement qu'il n'est pour le sujet donné : elle dit être, de lui, ce qui n'est pas, et, ne pas être, ce qui est* (*Sophiste*, p. 283).

263B. STR. Whereas the false statement states about you things *different* from the things that are.

THEAET. Yes.

STR. And accordingly states *things that are-not* as being.

THEAET. No doubt.

STR. Yes, but things that *exist*, different from things that *exist* in your case. For we said that in the case of everything there are many things that are and also many that are not.

THEAET. Quite so.

C. STR. So the second statement I made about you, in the first place, according to our definition of the nature of a statement, must itself necessarily be one of the shortest possible.

THEAET. So we agreed just now.

STR. And secondly it must be about something.

THEAET. Yes.

STR. And if it is not about you, it is not about anything else

THEAET. Certainly.

STR. And if it were about nothing, it would not be a statement at all ; for we pointed out that there could not be a statement that was a statement about nothing.

THEAET. Quite true.

D. STR. So what is stated about you, but so that what is different is stated as the same or what is not as what is— a combination of verbs and names answering to that description finally seems to be really and truly a false statement.

THEAET. Perfectly true.

In his later speeches here the Stranger emphasises the points (1) that this false statement has a subject, (2) that this subject is Theaetetus, not anyone else, and (3) that the subject cannot be nothing at all.

(2) ' Theaetetus, not anyone else '. This refers to the wrong view that a false statement, if it means anything, must be a true statement about *something else*. This is asserted by Euthydemus [1] in defence of the thesis : ' It is impossible to contradict '. The argument is : Every thing or fact (ὄν, πρᾶγμα) has its verbal expression describing how it is (*or* that it is, λόγος ὡς ἔστιν). When you and I are said to contradict one another, I am uttering the verbal expression of one thing, you that of another. We must be speaking of two different things. Socrates remarks that this means that every statement must be true (as Antisthenes said: πᾶς λόγος ἀληθεύει). Thus a false statement had been given a meaning at the cost of making it a true statement about something else.

[1] *Euthydemus* 285D.

(3) ' The subject cannot be nothing at all '. This dismisses the alternative wrong view that the false statement can have no meaning because it is about nothing that exists. (It may be added that the Theory of Forms provides a meaning even for false statements which seem to have no existing subject, such as ' The present King of France favours Free Trade '. The description has a meaning, though it stands for no existing person. But Plato does not consider such statements.)

To return now to the first three speeches. I have tried to give a literal translation ; but what does it mean ? The ordinary reader might naturally suppose that the thing described as ' different from the things that are in your case ' or ' different from the facts about you ' must be a non-existent fact, other than the existing fact. And he might take the third speech as meaning that this non-existent fact *is* a fact, though other than the existing fact.[1] He would then conclude that Plato intended to define false statement by correspondence with a non-existent fact on the same lines as the diagram of true statement above :

FALSE STATEMENT : " *Theaetetus   flies* "

stands for | corresponds to | stands for

NON-EXISTENT FACT :   Theaetetus   flying.

But that is precisely the explanation we must exclude. The Sophist will rightly repeat his objection : " There is no such thing as the non-existent fact, Theaetetus flying. Your statement is not false, but meaningless—not a statement at all, for there is nothing for it to mean or refer to. A false statement is not a true statement about a ' different fact ', which is not a fact at all, because it does not exist."

We must not, then, attribute this explanation to Plato. His purpose is to meet this very objection, and he has deliberately chosen a statement which is not only false now but could not be true at any time, since Theaetetus can never fly. Let us restore the existing fact and set the false statement beside it. All we now have is :

FALSE STATEMENT : " *Theaetetus flies* "

stands for |

EXISTING FACT :   Theaetetus sitting.

[1] Cf. H. Jackson on *The Sophist* (*Journ. Philol.* xiv, 223) : 'ψευδὴς λόγος may be defined as λόγος ὁ τάτε ὄντα λέγων μὴ εἶναι καὶ τὰ μὴ ὄντα εἶναι . . . provided that by τὰ ὄντα are meant the facts which the proposition, thought or spoken, purports to represent, and by μὴ ὄντα *facts other than these* ' (my italics).

The name *Theaetetus*, as before, stands for the thing, Theaetetus:
as the Stranger has emphasised, the false statement is about an
existing subject. ' *Flies* ' does not stand for the other element in
the fact, ' sitting '. The Sophist will now say : ' *flies* ' has no
meaning ; there exists nothing for it to refer to. Therefore the
statement as a whole has no meaning. It is not a statement at
all.

We can get no further, so long as we confine ourselves to what
we have called the existing fact, such as common sense recognises
and such as seemed sufficient to provide a satisfactory account of
true statement. We must fill out Plato's scheme with elements
he has furnished elsewhere and here takes for granted. There are
other ' things that are ' to be brought in, namely the Forms, which
we have so far ignored. Plato evidently means the Forms to come
in. The whole section on combination of Forms was avowedly to
furnish the key to false statement. He has said that ' all discourse
depends on the weaving together of Forms ' (259E), *i.e.* at least one
Form enters into the meaning of any statement.[1] In the passage
before us he refers to statements made earlier about Forms : ' in
the case of everything there are many things that are, and also
many that are not '. This was said of Forms in a context where
individual things were not in question at all. . Finally, we have
seen that the failure of the *Theaetetus* to explain false statement
was due to the deliberate exclusion of Forms.

All this shows that our diagram of the true statement and its
meaning is not yet complete. There is another ' thing that is '
to be added, namely a Form. In the true statement one term is
a proper name " *Theaetetus* ", standing for the existing subject.
There is no Form, Theaetetus. But the other term ' *sits* ' is a
common term ; and in the theory of Forms common terms have
meaning in two ways. (1) Like the proper name, they *stand for*
or *indicate* particular existents : ' *sits* ' stands for ' sitting ', the
second component of the existing fact. (2) They also have *meanings*
of their own, as significant articulate sounds. The word ' sitting ',
spoken by itself, conveys a meaning to the hearer's mind ; it is not
a senseless noise. If I say, ' Sitting is always more comfortable than
standing ', he understands what I am talking about. This meaning
is not the particular attitude of a particular person here and now,
but is what Plato calls a Form, which is a real thing, whether
Theaetetus is actually sitting or not, and whether or not anyone
says he is sitting. This Form, Sitting, is part of the meaning of
the true statement, and must be added to the scheme :

[1] Compare also the passage on ' common ' terms in the *Theaetetus*, 185 ff.
(p. 104).

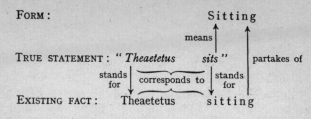

FORM :   Sitting

TRUE STATEMENT : "*Theaetetus   sits*"   partakes of

stands for | corresponds to | stands for

EXISTING FACT :   Theaetetus   sitting

The word ' *sits* ' has now a double significance : it *stands for* a part of the existing fact, and it *means* the Form. To put it differently, the phrase ' thing that is in your case ' (ὅν περὶ σοῦ) has two senses : (1) an existing element in the fact in which you are the other element, (2) the Form of which this existing element ' partakes '. This Form is an object of knowledge, not of perception, and is permanently real, independently of any existing facts ; whereas the particular ' sitting ' which is part of the existing fact, occurs at some time and place and ceases to be. Complicated as the diagram now is, the briefest true statement involves, on Plato's principles, all these ' things that are ' and their relations.

Now the introduction of Forms provides a meaning for the false statement, "*Theaetetus flies*", without our having to invoke a non-existent fact or objective falsehood. The diagram for the false statement will be :

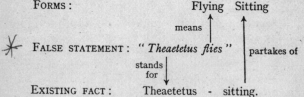

FORMS :   Flying Sitting

means

FALSE STATEMENT : "*Theaetetus flies*" partakes of

stands for

EXISTING FACT :   Theaetetus - sitting.

Each element in the statement has now a meaning ; and so the statement as a whole has meaning. What is missing in the case of the false statement is : (1) the relation ' partaking ' between the actual ' sitting ' and the *different* Form Flying ; (2) "*flies*" does not stand for this ' sitting ', though it has a meaning of its own, which the word calls up to the hearer's mind ; (3) the statement as a whole does not correspond with the fact as a whole or with any fact. Only by thus using the theory of Forms can Plato meet the Sophist's objection that false statement cannot exist because there is nothing for it to mean.

315

We can now interpret the literal translation above given of the Stranger's first three speeches :

(1) Ὁ δὲ δὴ ψευδὴς ἕτερα τῶν ὄντων (λέγει περὶ σοῦ).
' Whereas the false statement states about you things different from the things that are '.

In the illustration the ' different thing ' is the meaning of the word ' *flies* ', viz. the Form, Flying, which is different from the Form Sitting. Sitting is a ' thing that is ' and can be truly stated about Theaetetus, because the existing fact contains an element which ' partakes ' of it—what we might call an ' instance ' of Sitting.

(2) Τὰ μὴ ὄντ' ἄρα ὡς ὄντα λέγει.
' And accordingly states *things that are-not* as being.'

Here a result established in the section on the combination of Forms is invoked : it was shown that every Form ' is not ' in the sense that it is not (is different from) any other Form.[1] So we can substitute ' things that are not ' (τὰ μὴ ὄντα) for the phrase in the previous speech ' things different from the things that are ' (ἕτερα τῶν ὄντων). Flying is a thing that is not (is different from) Sitting, but is none the less real. Thus we have found a satisfactory meaning for ' that which is not ' in the expression ' speaking that which is not ', used as the equivalent of ' saying what is false '. And we have found this meaning by invoking the Forms and using the results of the section on combination.

(3) Ὄντων δέ γε ὄντα ἕτερα περὶ σοῦ. πολλὰ μὲν γὰρ ἔφαμεν ὄντα περὶ ἕκαστον εἶναί που, πολλὰ δὲ οὐκ ὄντα.
' Yes, but things that *exist*, different from things that *exist* in your case. For we said that in the case of everything there are many things that are, and also many that are not.'

The first sentence points out that the phrase just used, ' things that are not ', does not mean ' things that do not exist ' (but only ' different things '). Flying is a thing that *really is*, and is different from another thing that *really is*, viz. Sitting.[2] Both Forms are real. That Plato is thinking of Forms here is evident from the second sentence. This refers to two earlier statements about Forms : (1)

---

[1] This particular result was expressly recalled by the Stranger at the beginning of the present discussion : ' We saw that " not-being " (*i.e.* Difference) is a single Form among the rest, dispersed over the whole field of realities ' (' things that are ', ὄντα), 260B.

[2] In this sentence both ὄντων and ὄντα are emphatic.

256E, ' In the case of every *Form* there is much that it is, and an indefinite number of things that it is not ' ; (2) 259B, ' Existence is not myriads upon myriads of things, and all the other *Kinds* in the same way, whether taken severally or all together, in many respects are and in many respects are not.' So when we speak now of Flying as that which is not Sitting (or any other Form), we can use this negative description without implying non-existence.

In his concluding speeches the Stranger emphasises once more that the false statement, *Theaetetus flies*, is a statement, not ' about nothing ' but about the Theaetetus who exists here and now, and who is equally the subject of the true statement, *Theaetetus sits*. The name *Theaetetus* stands for a ' thing that is ' in the sense of an element of existing fact, no less than *flies* means a ' thing that is ' in the other sense—a Form. Finally, the false statement is defined as a combination of verbs and names stating about its subject ' what is different as the same or what is not as what is '. This rather obscure expression seems meant to recall the conception of false judgment in the *Theaetetus* as some kind of ' misjudgment '—mistaking one thing for another. In the attempt to imagine how this could happen, the empiricist apparatus was enlarged until we reached the notion of ' interchanging pieces of knowledge '. [1] But this theory broke down, because, on the empiricist assumptions we were then working with, a ' piece of knowledge ' could be nothing but an old record stored in the memory.[2] Now that the *Sophist* has brought the Forms into the account, a ' piece of knowledge ' can mean a Form which we know. Hence the notion of ' thinking that one thing is another ' or ' mistaking one thing for another ' can be revived with a new meaning. The ' things ' we interchange are not old memory images, but eternally real objects of thought. So at 253D it belongs to dialectic ' not to take the same *Form* for another or another for the same '. With this correction, the description of the hunt for birds in the aviary is, perhaps, meant to be accepted as a rough mechanical image of what happens in our minds when we mistake objects of knowledge.

It is certainly surprising that Plato should be content with a statement of his solution so brief and ambiguous. Presumably the fact that Forms are involved and the relevance of all the earlier discussion of their combination was so clear to his mind that he took the reader's understanding of these points for granted.

---

[1] *Theaet.* 199C (p. 136).
[2] It will be remembered that our knowledge of numbers was so described at *Theaet.* 196A (p. 128).

263D–264B. *Judgment being simply unspoken statement, false judg-*
ment and false ' appearing ' are possible

The final step in the argument is now taken by identifying judgment (δόξα) with unspoken statement.   From this it follows that
false judgment must be just as possible as false statement.   The
meaning of δόξα, ' judgment ', as here defined must not be confused
with Plato's use of the word elsewhere for ' Opinion ' considered as
having a different class of objects (δοξαστά) from those of knowledge
(γνωστά).   Judgment differs from knowledge in that it can be true
or false, but its objects may be entirely Forms and their relations,
which the *Republic* classed as objects of knowledge, not of opinion.
The final definition of false statements above given covers false
statements about Forms.

263D.   STR.   And next, what of thinking and judgment and appear-
ing ?   Is it not now clear that all these things occur in our
minds both as false and as true ?
THEAET.   How so ?
STR.   You will see more easily if you begin by letting me
give you an account of their nature and how each differs
E.   from the others.
THEAET.   Let me have it.
STR.   Well, thinking and discourse [1] are the same thing,
except that what we call thinking is, precisely, the inward
dialogue carried on by the mind with itself without spoken
sound.
THEAET.   Certainly.
STR.   Whereas the stream which flows from the mind
through the lips with sound is called discourse.
THEAET.   True.
STR.   And further there is a thing [2] which we know occurs
in discourse.
THEAET.   Namely ?
STR.   Assertion and denial. [3]
THEAET.   Yes.

[1] Thinking (διάνοια) and discourse (λόγος) are both used in the wide sense
which includes, not only judgment (δόξα) and statement (λόγος) which must
be true or false, but all forms of thinking and speech, questions, commands,
etc.   The account of thinking as unspoken discourse at *Theaet.* 189E (p. 118)
and 206D (p. 155), is here briefly repeated.

[2] αὐτό, BT should be retained : ' a thing (presently to be mentioned) '.
Cf. αὐτά at *Theaet.* 207D (Campbell).

[3] φάσις and ἀπόφασις cover (1) affirmation and negation, which appear in
the affirmative or negative form of the spoken statement, and (2) the mental

264. STR. Then when this occurs in the mind in the course of silent thinking, can you call it anything but judgment?

THEAET. No.

STR. And suppose judgment occurs, not independently, but by means of perception, the only right name for such a state of mind is 'appearing'.[1]

THEAET. Yes.

STR. Well then, since we have seen that there is true and false statement, and of these mental processes we have found thinking to be a dialogue of the mind with itself, and judg-

B. ment to be the conclusion of thinking, and what we mean by 'it appears' a blend of perception and judgment, it follows that these also, being of the same nature as state-ment, must be, some of them and on some occasions, false.

THEAET. Of course.

STR. You see, then, that we have discovered the nature of false judgment and false statement sooner than we expected just now when we feared there would be no end to the task we were setting ourselves in the search for them.

THEAET. I do.

'Appearing' (φαντασία) is briefly described because the process meant by the term here has been discussed at length in the *Theaetetus*. It is not 'imagination', the faculty which pictures an absent or imaginary object not perceived at the moment. It is that combination of perception and judgment which, as the *Theaetetus* described, occurs when I see an indistinct figure and, rightly or wrongly, judge it to be someone I know.[2] 'It appears to me' to

acts of assent and dissent—saying 'yes' and 'no'—to questions which the mind puts to itself, as described at *Theaet*. 190A, φάσκουσα καὶ οὐ φάσκουσα (p. 118). Judgment was there defined as the mind's final decision when all doubt and debate is over.

[1] Φαντασία here, as at *Theaet*. 152C (p. 32), is simply the substantive equivalent to the verb φαίνεσθαι. In his next speech the Stranger substitutes 'φαίνεται ὃ λέγομεν, 'what we mean by "it appears"'.

[2] *Theaet*. 193B ff. (p. 124) and 195D, σύναψις αἰσθήσεως πρὸς διάνοιαν (p. 128). This description is repeated in the *Philebus* 38 ff. Then in a later passage (39B ff.) imagination is separately described as the work of a sort of painter in the mind who makes pictures (ζωγραφήματα) or likenesses (εἰκόνες) of things. These are called 'pictured semblances' (φαντάσματα ἐζωγραφημένα), but the name φαντασία is not used of the faculty. Where Aristotle describes the imaging faculty which he calls φαντασία, 'Imagination', he points out that it is not 'judgment together with perception', nor 'by means of perception' (δι' αἰσθήσεως, Plato's phrase here), nor a 'combination of judgment and perception' (συμπλοκὴ δόξης καὶ αἰσθήσεως = Plato's σύμμειξις αἰσθήσεως καὶ δόξης here), *de anim*. 428a, 25. Aristotle means that he is giving φαντασία a new sense, which is not to be confused with Plato's use of the word here.

be so-and-so. This judgment rightly or wrongly interpreting a present perception is all that 'appearing' means here. It is the one kind of judgment that may be false which the psychological apparatus of the *Theaetetus* was adequate to describe. The Stranger here notes that we are now fully justified in asserting that such false judgments (like others) have a meaning and can exist.

264B–D. *Transition, connecting these results with the interrupted Division of Image-making*

Far back (at 236) the art of Image-making, which we had divined to contain the essential characteristic of the Sophist, was divided into the making of likenesses (εἰκαστική) and the making of semblances (or appearances, φανταστική). We were then arrested by the problems of unreal appearance and false statement : how can such things have any sort of existence ? We have since explained how false statement, at any rate, can exist, and the Stranger now points out that we are justified in resuming the interrupted Division.

264B.   STR.   Then let us not lose courage for what remains to be
     C.   done. Now that these matters are cleared up, let us recall our earlier divisions by forms.
           THEAET.   Which do you mean ?
           STR.   We distinguished two forms of Image-making : the making of likenesses and the making of semblances.
           THEAET.   Yes.
           STR.   And we said we were puzzled to tell under which of these two we should place the Sophist.
           THEAET.   We did.
           STR.   And to increase our perplexity we were plunged in a whirl of confusion by the apparition of an argument that called in question all these terms and disputed the very existence of any copy or image or semblance, on the ground
     D.   that falsity never has any sort of existence anywhere.
           THEAET.   True.
           STR.   But now that we have brought to light the existence of false statement and of false judgment, it is possible that there should be imitations of real things and that this condition of mind (false judgment) should account for the existence of an art of deception.
           THEAET.   Yes, it is.
           STR.   And we agreed earlier that the Sophist does come under one or other of the two kinds mentioned.
           THEAET.   Yes.

The connection between 'appearing' (φαντασία), just now described as the blend of perception and judgment, and the art of creating semblances or appearances (φανταστική) under which we shall place the Sophist, is to be found in the earlier description of this art.[1] The sculptor who deliberately distorts the actual proportions of his original in order to make his statue 'appear' correct, produces semblances (φαντάσματα) such as are rife in painting and fine art generally. He imposes on us false judgments by means of our senses (φαντασία). Similarly the Sophist creates in us false beliefs in his wisdom on all subjects.

This, however, is the only sort of 'appearing' explained in this dialogue. It is not what we mean by 'appearance' when we speak of a world of appearance, as opposed to reality. 'Appearance' there suggests some sort of unreality in the object; whereas when 'it appears to me' that a distant figure is a friend, that judgment may be true, and, if it is false, there is nothing wrong with the object: the falsity lies wholly in my judgment. Hence, all that has been said about 'appearing' throws no light on what may be called the problem of the *eidolon*, which the Stranger seemed to raise where the Division was interrupted. He spoke of two problems: (1) 'this appearing or seeming without really being'[2] and (2) 'saying something which yet is not true'. We have solved the second, but what has become of the first? The words naturally mean: How can there be something which seems real without being real? This is the problem of appearances, as opposed to reality. Later, moreover, an *eidolon* was defined as something that is not wholly real (ὄντως ὄν) but yet has some sort of existence (ὄν πως). Then followed the long discussion of theories of the 'perfectly real', after which we expected some account of how a world of imperfectly real things—the objects of sense—could exist. But this hope was disappointed. The whole subsequent discussion of the combination of Forms was confined to the world of perfect reality, and has told us nothing about the status of imperfectly real things. That problem remains where it was.

Burnet,[3] indeed, takes Plato as meaning that the explanation of 'not-being' as 'difference' has solved the *eidolon* problem. 'In the course of the foregoing discussion' [258B], he writes, 'the remark was thrown out that we have found the Not-being which was necessary to justify our account of the Sophist. This is not explained further, but the point is quite simple. We called him an

---

[1] At 235E ff. (p. 197).
[2] 236E, τὸ φαίνεσθαι τοῦτο καὶ τὸ δοκεῖν, εἶναι δὲ μή. Here it is the *object* that appears but is not real.
[3] *Gk. Phil.*, p. 286.

image-maker, and he replied that there was no such thing as an image, since an image is really not real. We now see that there is nothing in this objection ; for the art of image-making, like all other arts, includes a part of Being and a part of Not-being.[1] The image is not the reality, indeed, and the reality is not the image, but that involves no difficulty. We are dealing with a particular art, that of Image-making, and in it " not real " has a perfectly definite and positive signification. The " not real " is not the unreal, but just the image, which *is* quite as much as that of which it is the image.'

It is hard to be satisfied with this, as a solution of the *eidolon* problem. It amounts to saying : ' When I say an image is not perfectly real, and yet has a sort of existence, all I mean is that an image is not the same thing as its original, but is just as real.' Burnet appears to think that this is the solution, for he says later (p. 349) : ' Plato laid the ghost of the two-world theory which had haunted Greek philosophy since the time of Parmenides, and that is what he meant by saying that the sensible world was " the image of the intelligible ". He had shown already in the *Sophist* that to be an image is not to be nothing. An appearance *is* an appearance, and is only unreal if we take it for what it is not.' Burnet seems to mean that Plato, in his maturity, no longer held that the sensible world is partly unreal (as he had said in the *Republic*) or any less real than the intelligible world. The unreality or falsity of ' appearance ' lies wholly in our thoughts about the world, not in the objects themselves. They are only unreal if *we* take them for what they are not.

But if Plato came to hold that objects of perception are merely different from intelligible objects, but just as real, what ground remains for denying that sense-perception is knowledge in the full sense ? The *Theaetetus* admitted that perception was infallible ; it was not knowledge because it lacked the other mark of knowledge : its objects are not real. If we now say that the objects are just as real as Forms, perception has every claim to be knowledge. This cannot be reconciled with the *Timaeus*. Also, it would be strange if a conclusion amounting to a revolution in Platonism should not even be stated explicitly, but left to be inferred from the apparently very different statement that an image is not the same as its original, but none the less exists. The whole question is, what sort of existence the image has, for it has been defined as ' not really real '. A

[1] This obscure statement seems to be based on the use of knowledge and its species as an illustration at 257c (p. 290). But this was a mere illustration, and Plato does not say that any art ' includes a part of Being and a part of Not-being '.

ghost is a ghost, and is not the same thing as the tangible body it resembles : anyone will admit that ; but it does not settle the question what kind or degree of reality a ghost has.

Our conclusion must be that the *eidolon* problem is not yet solved ; nor shall we find a solution later in this dialogue. The reason may be that Plato could not solve it or that the problem was reserved for another occasion (perhaps, for the *Philosopher*). In the *Sophist* he is justified in shelving it because the only *eidola* we are now concerned with are those which the Sophist is accused of creating. The Sophist does not create the world of sensible objects ; these are the work of that divine image-making which will presently be distinguished from the human image-making of fine art and sophistry. The *eidola* created by the Sophist are false beliefs in our minds. Hence it was said at 260c, and is repeated here, that the existence of images and semblances depends on the existence of deception, and deception depends on the existence of false belief. We were only bound to prove that false belief could exist, and that has been done. The metaphysical status of ' appearances ' in any other sense lies beyond our scope. The explanation, if it is to be found anywhere, must be sought in the *Timaeus*. I suspect that, when Plato had finished the *Statesman*, he found himself unable to carry out his intention of continuing the present conversation in the *Philosopher* and there gathering up the loose threads. So he abandoned his scheme and started another trilogy—*Timaeus, Critias, Hermocrates* —in which all that he had to say about the *eidolon* problem could be cast into the form of a myth.

264D–268D. *Division VII. The Sophist as a species of Image-maker*

That Plato was consciously shelving the *eidolon* problem appears in the coming section. If he had thought it was already solved, he would have taken up the Division of Image-making at the point where it was dropped and proceeded to subdivide semblance-making (φανταστική). But we find the Stranger now going back, behind the art of Image-making, to the most general conception, Art, precisely in order that the divine creation of images—the world of appearance—may be set aside as not relevant to the definition of Sophistry. In fact, the shelving of the unsolved problem is openly effected here, in terms evidently meant to recall the contrast of reality and appearance as set forth in the *Republic*. These terms would be extremely misleading, if Plato had really abandoned his old doctrine of the partial unreality of sense objects.

The final Table of Division is as follows:

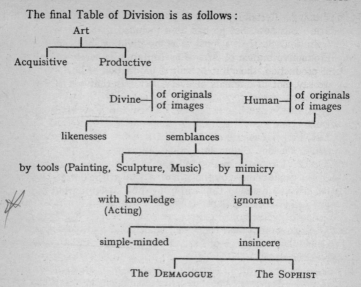

264D. STR. Now, then, let us set to work again and, as we divide
E. the Kind proposed in two, keep to the right-hand section
at each stage. Holding fast to the characters of which the
Sophist partakes until we have stripped off all that he has
in common with others and left only the nature that is
peculiar to him, let us so make that nature plain, in the
265. first place to ourselves, and secondly to others whose
temperament finds a procedure of this sort congenial.

THEAET. Very good.

STR. Well, we began by dividing Art into Productive and
Acquisitive.

THEAET. Yes.

STR. And under the head of the Acquisitive we had glimpses
of the Sophist in the arts of hunting, contention, trafficking,
and other kinds of that sort.[1]

[1] This reference to the five tentative Divisions of the Acquisitive branch
is significant. They only provided ' glimpses ' or indistinct visions of various
types called sophists, not the essential feature. With ἐφαντάζετο compare
φανταζόμενον used of the figure indistinctly seen at a distance, *Philebus* 38c.
The third main branch of Art, the Separative (διακριτική), from which was
derived the Cathartic method of Socrates in Division VI, is here ignored.
It gave us no glimpse of the Sophist.

265.   THEAET. Certainly.

STR. But now that he has been included under an art of Imitation, clearly we must start by dividing into two the

B.   Productive branch of Art. For Imitation is surely a kind of production, though it be only a production of images, as we say, not of originals of every sort. Is that not so ?

THEAET. Assuredly.

STR. Let us begin, then, by recognising two kinds of Production.

THEAET. What are they ?

STR. The one Divine, the other Human.

THEAET. I don't understand yet.

STR. Production—to recall what we said at the outset—we defined as any power that can bring into existence what did not exist before.[1]

THEAET. I remember.

C.   STR. Now take all mortal animals and also all things that grow [2]—plants that grow above the earth from seeds and roots, and lifeless bodies compacted beneath the earth, whether fusible or not fusible. Must we not attribute the coming into being of these things out of not-being to divine craftsmanship and nothing else ? Or are we to fall in with the belief that is commonly expressed ?

THEAET. What belief do you mean ?

STR. That Nature gives birth to them as a result of some spontaneous cause that generates without intelligence. Or shall we say that they come from a cause which, working with reason and art, is divine and proceeds from divinity ? [3]

---

[1] Production, so defined at 219B, included agriculture, manufacture, and fine art. The definition is not intended to suggest creation *out of nothing*, with no pre-existing material.

[2] φυτά (cf. 233E, ' you and me and all other creatures ', φυτά) covers all things that come to be by a natural process, including metals (fusible) and minerals, the regular nameable compounds of elements. The elements (ἐξ ὧν τὰ πεφυκότα, 266B) are also products of divine workmanship (as in the *Timaeus*) ; but it is not implied that the elements are created *ex nihilo*. The only question here is whether the compound ' creatures ' grow out of the elements spontaneously or by a process directed by divine craftsmanship.

[3] The construction of θείας is ambiguous. (1) If it is taken with ἐπιστήμης, τὴν φύσιν γεννᾶν remains as the main verb ; but the contrast is between Nature which *generates* and the divine Artist who *makes*. And why should ' knowledge ' be said to ' come from divinity ' (ἀπὸ θεοῦ γιγνομένης) ? (2) By taking θείας with ἀπὸ αἰτίας understood, we get a cause or causation which might be said to ' come from divinity ' and is contrasted with causation of spontaneous origin (αὐτομάτη, cf. Ar., *Phys.* 196a, 24), as μετὰ λόγου τε καὶ ἐπιστήμης is contrasted with ἄνευ διανοίας. As verb φήσομεν γίγνεσθαι will then be

265D. THEAET. Perhaps because I am young, I often shift from one belief to the other ; but at this moment, looking at your face and believing you to hold that these things have a divine origin, I too am convinced.

STR. Well said, Theaetetus. If I thought you were the sort of person that might believe otherwise in the future, I should now try by force of persuasion to make you accept that account. But I can see clearly that, without any

E. arguments of mine, your nature will come of itself to the conclusion which you tell me attracts you at this moment. So I will let that pass : I should be wasting time. I will only lay it down that the products of Nature, as they are called, are works of divine art, as things made out of them by man are works of human art. Accordingly there will be two kinds of Production, one human, the other divine.

THEAET. Good.

STR. Once more, then, divide each of these two into two parts.

THEAET. How ?

266. STR. As you have just divided the whole extent of Production horizontally, now divide it vertically.

THEAET. Be it so.

STR. The result is four parts in all : two on our side, human ; two on the side of the gods, divine.

THEAET. Yes.

STR. And taking the divisions made in the first way (horizontally : divine and human), one section of each part will be the production of originals, and the remaining two sections will be best described as production of images. So we have a second division of Production on that principle (originals and images).

B. THEAET. Explain once more how each of the two parts (divine and human) is divided.

STR. Ourselves, I take it, and all other living creatures and the elements of natural things—fire, water, and their kindred—are all originals, the offspring, as we are well assured, of divine workmanship.[1] Is it not so ?

THEAET. Yes.

---

supplied from the previous speech, as by Campbell, whose punctuation may be preferred to Burnet's.

[1] In this phrase the metaphors of generation (γεννήματα) and of the crafts-man's workmanship (ἀπειργασμένα) are combined, as at *Timaeus* 28c, ' the *maker* and *father* of this universe ', and *Symp.* 209A, poets (' *makers* ') and creative artists are *begetters* of spiritual children.

266B.   STR.   And every one of these products is attended by images
which are not the actual thing, and which also owe their
existence to divine contrivance.

THEAET.   You mean——?

STR.   Dream images, and in daylight all those naturally
produced semblances which we call [1] ' shadow ' when dark
C. patches interrupt the light, or a ' reflection ' when the
light belonging to the eye meets and coalesces with light
belonging to something else on a bright and smooth surface
and produces a form yielding a perception that is the reverse
of the ordinary direct view.[2]

---

[1] Taking λέγεται with σκιὰ μὲν . . . διπλοῦν δέ. The Lexica do not seem to
recognise ' reflection ' as a sense of διπλοῦν, but it can hardly agree with φῶς,
leaving the reflection nameless. Are we to understand διπλοῦν φάντασμα, ' a
duplicate image ' ?

[2] In the ' ordinary direct view ' (ἔμπροσθεν = in front, opposite) the two
lights or ' fires ' which coalesce are the visual ray or stream of fire from the
eye and the fire outside, i.e. either sunlight reflected from the body looked at
or, when the body is self-luminous, its own light. In reflection from a mirror,
the ray of light from my eye (οἰκεῖον φῶς = τὸ ἐντὸς ἡμῶν πῦρ, Tim. 45B)
and the light belonging to the object (ἀλλότριον φῶς, e.g. the light which comes
from the real face of another person I see in the mirror, cf. πυρὶ ἔξωθεν ἀλλοτρίῳ,
Tim. 43C, 1) coalesce on the surface of the mirror, and the united ray is then
thrown back from it to my eye. So the reflection seen is explained in the
same way as direct vision, except that in reflection the coalescence occurs
at the mirror's surface, not at the surface of the reflected object (see Taylor
on Timaeus 46A). The reversal of the image is best explained by a diagram :

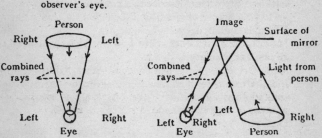

A. DIRECT VISION
of person facing the
observer's eye.

B. REFLECTION
of person facing a mirror.

In (A) Direct Vision the light from the *right* side of the person's face is supposed
to reach the *left* side of my eye.   In (B) Reflection the light from the *left* side
of the person's face is supposed to reach the *left* side of my eye.   (There is
no sign that Plato thought of all the rays from the object as entering the eye
at the centre of the lens and spreading out again on the retina, or knew
anything of lens and retina.)

266C. THEAET. There are, indeed, these two products of divine workmanship : the original and the image that in every case accompanies it.[1]

STR. And what of our human art ? Must we not say that in building it produces an actual house, and in painting a house of a different sort, as it were a man-made dream for waking eyes ?

D. THEAET. Certainly.

STR. And so in all cases, we find once more twin products of our own productive activity in pairs—one an actual thing, the other an image.

THEAET. I understand better now, and I recognise two forms of production, each of them twofold : divine and human according to one division, and according to the other a production of actual things and of some sort of likenesses.

At this point we have got back to the human art of Image-making, now clearly distinguished from divine production of natural objects and from the useful crafts, like building. Image-making includes all the fine arts, with political rhetoric and sophistry. The chief object of the further subdivision is to place the demagogue and the Sophist in the lowest class. First the subdivision already made (εἰκαστική and φανταστική) is declared to be now justified.

266D. STR. Let us remind ourselves, then, that of this production of images there were to be two kinds, one producing like-
E. nesses, the other semblances, provided that falsity should be shown to be a thing that really is false and of such a nature as to have a place among existing things.

THEAET. Yes, it was to be so.

STR. And that has now been shown ; so on that ground shall we now reckon the distinction of these two forms as beyond dispute ?

THEAET. Yes.

267. STR. Once more, then, let us divide in two the kind that produces semblances.

THEAET. How ?

---

[1] These originals and images make up the contents of the visible world (ὁρατά or δοξαστά of Rep. vi, where they are described in similar terms, 510A). They are the work of the divine craftsman of the Timaeus, who fashions the visible world after the pattern of the Forms. The Forms themselves, which are not created, are, of course, not mentioned here. But the Platonist will recall that the actual things here called originals are themselves only copies or images of the Forms. They are those eidola whose ambiguous existence still remains a problem.

267. STR. There is the semblance produced by means of tools, and another sort where the producer of the semblance takes his own person as an instrument.

THEAET. How do you mean ?

STR. When someone uses his own person or voice to counterfeit your traits or speech, the proper name for creating such a semblance is, I take it, Mimicry.[1]

THEAET. Yes.

STR. Let us reserve that section, then, under the name of mimicry, and indulge ourselves so far as to leave all the

B. rest for someone else to collect into a unity and give it an appropriate name.

THEAET. So be it.

STR. But there is still ground for thinking that mimicry is of two sorts. Let me put it before you.

THEAET. Do.

STR. Some mimics know the thing they are impersonating, others do not ; and could we find a more important distinction than that of knowing from not knowing ?

THEAET. No.

STR. And the mimicry we have just mentioned goes with knowledge ; for to impersonate you, one must be acquainted with you and your traits.

C. THEAET. Of course.

STR. And what of the traits of Justice and of virtue generally ? Are there not many who, having no knowledge of virtue but only some sort of opinion about it, zealously set about making it appear that they embody virtue as they conceive it, mimicking it as effectively as they can in their words and actions ?

THEAET. Only too many.

STR. And are they always unsuccessful in appearing to be virtuous when they are not really virtuous at all ? Do they not rather succeed perfectly ?

THEAET. They do.

D. STR. We must, then, distinguish the ignorant mimic from the other, who has knowledge.

THEAET. Yes.

STR. Where, then, must we look for a suitable name for each ? No doubt it is hard to find one, because the ancients,

---

[1] Cf. *Crat.* 423B. Should we read ὅταν τὸ σὸν σχῆμά τις τῷ ἑαυτοῦ (SC. σχήματι) χρώμενος, ⟨σῶμα⟩ σώματι προσομοιῶν ἢ φωνὴν φωνῇ, φαίνεσθαι ποιῇ, ' when a man produces a semblance of your traits by using his own, making his body or his voice like yours ' ?

267D. it would seem, suffered from a certain laziness and lack of discrimination with regard to the division of Kinds by forms, and not one of them even tried to make such divisions, with the result that there is a serious shortage of names. However, though the expression may seem daring, for purposes of distinction let us call mimicry guided by opinion 'conceit-mimicry ',[1] and the sort that is guided by knowledge ' mimicry by acquaintance '.

E.

THEAET. So be it.

STR. It is the former, then, that concerns us ; for the Sophist was not among those who have knowledge, but he has a place among mimics.

THEAET. Certainly.

STR. Then let us take this conceit-mimic and see if his metal rings sound or there is still a crack in it somewhere.

THEAET. Let us do so.

STR. Well, there is a gaping crack. There is the simple-minded type who imagines that what he believes is knowledge, and an opposite type who is versed in discussion, so that his attitude betrays no little misgiving and suspicion that the knowledge he has the air of possessing in the eyes of the world is really ignorance.

268.

THEAET. Certainly both the types you describe exist.

STR. We may, then, set down one of these mimics as sincere, the other as insincere.

THEAET. So it appears.

STR. And the insincere—is he of two kinds or only one ?

THEAET. That is for you to consider.

STR. I will ; and I can clearly make out a pair of them. I see one who can keep up his dissimulation publicly in long speeches to a large assembly. The other uses short arguments in private and forces others to contradict themselves in conversation.[2]

B.

THEAET. Very true.

STR. And with whom shall we identify the more long-winded type—with the Statesman or with the demagogue ?

THEAET. The demagogue.

STR. And what shall we call the other—wise man or Sophist ?

THEAET. We cannot surely call him wise, because we set him down as ignorant ; but as a mimic of the wise man he

C.

---

[1] δοξομιμητική, cf. 223B, δοξοπαιδευτική, education in the conceit of virtue ; *Philebus* 49D, δοξοκαλία, δοξοσοφία, the conceit of beauty and wisdom.

[2] Cf. the subdivision of Disputation at 225B (p. 176).

268c. will clearly assume a title derived from his, and I now see that here at last is the man who must be truly described as the real and genuine Sophist.

STR. Shall we, then, as before collect all the elements of his description, from the end to the beginning,[1] and draw our threads together in a knot ?

THEAET. By all means.

D. STR. The art of contradiction-making, descended from an insincere kind of conceited mimicry, of the semblance-making breed, derived from image-making, distinguished as a portion, not divine but human, of production, that presents a shadow-play of words—such is the blood and lineage which can, with perfect truth, be assigned to the authentic Sophist.

THEAET. I entirely agree.

---

[1] The construction of the final definition is obscured by the effort to frame it so as to mention all the specific differences in order ' from the end to the beginning ' (productive art). At 226A there is another summary in this reverse order (τὸ χρηματιστικὸν γένος, ἐριστικῆς ὂν τέχνης, τῆς ἀντιλογικῆς, τῆς ἀμφισβητητικῆς, κτ) where the genitives are used as in a genealogy : ' A the son of B, the son of C,' etc.

ADDENDUM

SOPH. 263C. ὃν ὕστερον δὴ λόγον εἴρηκα περὶ σοῦ, πρῶτον μέν, ἐξ ὧν ὡρισάμεθα τί ποτ' ἔστι λόγος, ἀναγκαιότατον αὐτὸν ἕνα τῶν βραχυτάτων εἶναι.

The superlative ἀναγκαιότατον throws a quite unnecessary emphasis on the obvious fact that ' Theaetetus flies ' is a statement of the shortest possible type. αὐτόν, moreover, seems superfluous ; most translators ignore it. I suspect that Plato wrote λόγος ἀναγκαιότατος, ' according to our definition of *the minimum statement* ' (cf. *Rep*. 369D, ἡ ἀναγκαιοτάτη πόλις). It was, in fact, τῶν λόγων ὁ πρῶτός τε καὶ σμικρότατος that was defined above (262C), rather than statement in general. αὐτόν must then conceal the main verb, perhaps φατέον, as at 263B, 2.

INDEX

Account (*Logos*) :
 of grounds of knowledge, 141
 added to true belief, 142
 meanings of, 142
 combination of names, 144
 expression in speech, 154
 enumeration of elements, 155
 statement of distinguishing mark,
  158
 definition by genus and difference,
  161, 170
Anamnesis :
 in *Meno*, 2
 and Midwifery, 27 f.
 in *Phaedo*, 5, 108
 not abandoned, 129
Animal, Form of, 271
Antisthenes :
 alleged author of Socrates'
  ' dream ', 144
 on predication, 254, 257
 held ' every statement is true ', 312
Appearing ' (φαντασία) :
 Protagoras' use of, 32, 116
 problem of appearances, 200 ff.
 as blend of perception and judgment, 319
Aristotle :
 account of Platonism, 9
 logic, contrasted with Plato's, 268
 on relative terms, 282
 definition of ' word ', 305
Atomism, 231, 247

Battle of Gods and Giants, 228 ff.
Belief, see Judgment

' Categories ' :
 falsely so called, 106, 274 ff.
 Aristotle's, 275
Cathartic Method, 177 ff.
Change, two kinds of, 95

Charmides, on recognition of knowledge, 140
Classification, by Division, 171
Collection :
 preceding Division, 170
 Divisions of *Sophist* as substitute
  for, 187
Collection and Division :
 Division illustrated, 170 ff.
 Seven Divisions of Sophist, 172 ff.
 methods of, 184 ff.
 as Dialectic, 262 ff.
Combination :
 of Forms, 252 ff.
 meaning of, 255
 of letters compared to Forms, 260
 of words in statement, 304
Common terms :
 in *Theaetetus*, 105
 in every statement, 300
Compatibility, statements of, 278
Cratylus, doctrine of, 99
Cyrenaics, 48

Definition (*Logos*) :
 of individual thing, impossible, 162
 as object of Collection and Division, 184
 Socratic, 185
Democritus, 231
Dialectic :
 procedure, 30
 analogy with weaving, 183
 science of, described, 262 ff.
 not Formal Logic, 264
Dialexeis, 191
Difference :
 distinct from Incompatibility, 279
 as all-pervading Form, 279 ff.
 distributed over all reality, 290
 verbal ambiguity of θάτερον, 292
Division, see Collection and Division
Dynamis, see Power

333

INDEX

The Library of Liberal Arts

SCHILLER, J., Wilhelm Tell

SCHLEGEL, J., On Imitation and Other Essays

SCHNEIDER, H., Sources of Contemporary Philosophical Realism in America

SCHOPENHAUER, A., On the Basis of Morality
Freedom of the Will

SELBY-BIGGE, L., British Moralists

SENECA, Medea
Oedipus
Thyestes

SHAFTESBURY, A., Characteristics

SHELLEY, P., A Defence of Poetry

SMITH, A., The Wealth of Nations (Selections)

Song of Roland, Terry, trans.

SOPHOCLES, Electra

SPIEGELBERG, H., The Socratic Enigma

SPINOZA, B., Earlier Philosophical Writings
On the Improvement of the Understanding

TERENCE, The Brothers
The Eunuch
The Mother-in-Law
Phormio
The Self-Tormentor
The Woman of Andros

Three Greek Romances, Hadas, trans.

TOLSTOY, L., What is Art?

VERGIL, Aeneid

VICO, G. B., On the Study Methods Our Time

VOLTAIRE, Philosophical Letters

WHITEHEAD, A., Interpretation of Science

WOLFF, C., Preliminary Discourse on Philosophy in General

XENOPHON, Recollections of Socrates and Socrates' Defense Before the Jury